"*Jim Rayburn was one of the greatest Christians I ever knew. Jim had a profound influence on my life when I was a student at Wheaton and later when I was a pastor and leader for Youth for Christ. It is up to us to carry the torch that he so courageously carried for so many years.*"

—Billy Graham

THE DIARIES OF JIM RAYBURN

THE DIARIES OF

Jim Rayburn

selected and edited by
KIT SUBLETT

Morningstar Press
Colorado

Whitecaps Media
Houston

The Diaries of Jim Rayburn
© 2008 by The Estate of James Chalmers Rayburn, Jr., and Kit Sublett
All rights reserved

ISBN-13: 978-0-9758577-7-9

Unless otherwise noted, Scripture quotations are from The Holy Bible,
English Standard Version, copyright © 2001 by Crossway Bibles, a division of
Good News Publishers. Used by permission. All rights reserved.

Scripture quotations marked KJV are taken from the King James Version of
the Bible

The Bible verse marked NIV is taken by permission from The Holy Bible, New
International Version, copyright © 1973, 1978, 1984 International Bible
Society, Colorado Springs, Colorado

Epigraph used by permission of Billy Graham

Jim Rayburn's prayer "Give us the Teen-agers" first appeared in the book
Young Life © 1963 by Emile Cailliet

This publication is a joint project of
Morningstar Press and Whitecaps Media

Contents

To the Reader

My Dad was amazing. Young people, high school kids particularly, adored him. He gave his whole life to communicating to those kids how wonderful God is, and how very much each one, individually, is loved by God as well. He got through to kids in a way no one else was doing, or had ever done before. When his club got so big there was no place to hold it, he moved it to the local funeral home so almost five hundred kids could squeeze into the parlor room to hear him. Watching and listening to Jim interact with high school kids was a treat, an unforgettable experience.

In writing his biography, *From Bondage To Liberty: Dance, Children, Dance*, I included many of his diary entries throughout the book. Most readers were moved and inspired and wanted more.

Someone from outside the family was needed to tie these journals together and give them additional context. Kit Sublett seemed uniquely qualified for that task. Not only is he a gifted writer, he has a historian's gene in his DNA and he also spent twenty years on the staff of Young Life, the work my father birthed. Kit did an outstanding job of shedding light on the people, the places, and the times, reducing what would have been a 1,500-page book down to its current size. Thank you, Kit, for all the hard work that only fellow writers fully understand.

Several other people who knew Dad personally provided the inspiration and the means to see this project realized. They have requested to remain anonymous but without their vision and assistance this book would not have been possible. The Rayburn family is deeply grateful to this small but special group. May these diaries be the inspiration to readers that we have all dreamed about.

Readers should know that my father wrote these journals entirely for his own use, not to be read by others. One could argue that God has

Jim Rayburn III and his father at the Chalet, Frontier Ranch, 1963.

preserved them for a broader audience though, for during the writing
of Dad's biography these diaries were miraculously spared in a fire that
consumed almost everything around them. In the cleanup they were re-
trieved intact from a wet, and badly charred, cardboard box.

As you read the words my father wrote at the close of each day it will
soon become apparent that his life was not an easy one. He battled de-
bilitating migraine headaches, his wife of thirty-nine years was chroni-
cally ill for thirty-five of them, his work seemed always on the edge of financial disaster, and challenges faced him continuously. His astounding
commitment to prayer saw him through. These diary entries will clearly
show that great men of faith who achieve grandiose things still put their
pants on one leg at a time.

Not only was Dad humble, adventurous, passionate, winsome, and
Godly, he was exceptionally funny and his sense of humor worked over-
time. I have a treasure chest full of funny, wonderful memories with
him that I love to share with individuals and audiences alike. Although
funny enough to entertain others with humor alone, the breadth and
depth of my father's influence on the broader Christian Church is simply astounding. In the area of effective young people's ministry he simply
changed the thinking and "rewrote the books." His followers, and their

followers in turn, are now dispersed throughout the nation and around the world, involved in hundreds of life-giving and lifesaving works too numerous to mention. Truly, the impact this man had upon Christendom, and society as well, is beyond measure.

I've been told these diaries are a virtual treasure of insight and inspiration for all who take Jesus Christ seriously. With that thought in mind it is the hope and prayer of the Rayburn family that as you read you will be blessed beyond measure and drawn closer to God than ever before. We know that's what Dad would have wanted.

May God our Father, and Jim, our earthly father, richly bless you and speak to you as you read these accounts of a life well lived, the life of Jim Rayburn Jr.

—JIM RAYBURN III
on behalf of the Rayburn Family

For more information about Jim Rayburn, Jim Rayburn Jr., Jim Rayburn III, and the broader family, including books and audio CDs, visit www. jimrayburn.com.

Preface

Pioneer. Visionary. Rebel. Leader. Churchman. Jim Rayburn was all of those things. He was also a mountain climber, daredevil, world traveller, raconteur, and considered by many to be the best communicator of the gospel of the twentieth century. Sought out by governors, industrialists, and academics alike, he also counted the leading Christians of his day as his friends. But Jim Rayburn's favorite people to spend time with were high school students. "By far and away the greatest job in the world today," he said, "is just to thumb the pages of this New Testament, which was written to make Jesus Christ known, and to do it in the presence of a group of people who are listening, who know you care about them, and no beans about it; people that you've taken the time and the trouble to prove to that you really care." Fitting for the man who founded and led Young Life for the first twenty-four years of its existence.

The liberals called him too fundamental; meanwhile the fundamentalists found him entirely too liberal and conservatives found him too radical. In response, Rayburn himself quipped, "Fundamentally, I am a liberal conservative."

He was born on July 21, 1909, in Marshalltown, Iowa. His father, James Chalmers Rayburn, Sr., was a travelling evangelist for the Presbyterian church. His mother, Elna Beck Rayburn, was a strict disciplinarian who held down the fort in Newton, Kansas, where the family moved when Jim was eight. Jim was the oldest of four boys, all of whom became successful in their chosen careers. Growing up in a family of all boys no doubt fueled Jim's zest for adventure and fun.

Certainly, growing up with an evangelist father impacted Jim's understanding of and appreciation for the gospel. The senior Rayburn was a gifted communicator in his own right, and passed those gifts on to his oldest son.

But as much as the Rayburn parents talked about God's grace, the theology they lived by was very much a legalistic affair. It was only when Jim was on his own that he discovered in a deep way the boundless freedom God offers through Christ (as is discussed in his 1935 journal).

By the time Jim graduated from Kansas State College (now Kansas State University) in 1932, he had fallen in love with Helen Maxine Stanley, two-and-a-half years his junior. After graduation Jim began graduate studies at the University of Colorado in Boulder, but quit after only a few courses in order to join his father's ministry. In September of that year, Jim and Maxine ran off and got married by a justice of the peace. Jim was twenty-three years old, and Maxine, twenty. When his parents found out, they were apoplectic, insisting on a second, "official," wedding, which was held in their home a few months later.

Maxine was quiet, sweet, and new to the Christian faith. Her parents had divorced when she was young, and her mother abandoned her when she was fourteen years old. She would deal with issues of abandonment and a lack of self-worth for many years to come. The fact that Maxine came from a broken home was a strike against her in Jim's parents' eyes.

Roy Riviere, who served at Jim's side for many years in Young Life, was asked to describe his old boss. Rayburn was of "comparatively small stature," Riviere observed, "but you would not look at him and think there was anything wrong—he just wasn't tall, he wasn't heavy. You couldn't possibly be around him long without finding out that what he *was* physically was really wound up tight. He was a formidable outdoorsman in the sense of hiking and mountain climbing and snow skiing, some of that sort of thing."

The two first met when Riviere was a high school student in Tyler, Texas, in the earliest days of Young Life. "He had a good speaking voice," Roy continued. "He had a western twang, but not any noticeable bad accent of any sort. I used to get a kick out of the fact that Jim really wanted to be a Texan, and I happened to know he came from Kansas. But he managed to sound like the rest of us from Texas because he liked being a Texan, and of course that was a point in his favor, in my opinion."

Jim was a dashing figure. He was a snappy dresser, but never in the over-the-top sort of way favored by many evangelical preachers of the time. Though only of average height, he managed to dominate any room that he entered, even when it included men who were older or more prominent than he. He prided himself in being comfortable with all types of people—from the most influential to the lowliest—and in his ability to put them at ease with his good nature and humor.

His prayer life was legendary. As you will see on these pages, it was not uncommon for Jim to spend hours on his knees. That intimacy with his Savior paid off—Jim had an uncommon ability to discern and communicate spiritual truth. He also had an uncanny ability, no doubt borne out of his hundreds of hours in God's Word and in prayer, to "dream big dreams" for God—and see them come to fruition against all odds.

In 1934, Jim was hired by the Presbyterian Board of Missions to work in the small communities of Arizona and New Mexico. He became, he joked later, "the bishop of all out-of-doors," filling in as pastor to places like Chama, New Mexico, and Douglas, Arizona.

While pastoring people of all ages, Jim realized that his real calling was with high school-aged people. The principles and approach that would later become Young Life began to formulate in his mind in these desolate little towns. Near the end of his life, he reflected, "I woke up with my bride one day in a town where there was a school full of people who didn't have the foggiest chance to know the truth about Jesus Christ. They didn't have a chance; there wasn't anybody there that knew enough about Him to tell them. And, furthermore, they weren't interested in listening to anyone who sounded like someone who might be going to get around to talking about Jesus Christ."

Over the years the Lord brought many insights to Jim's mind. Ideas like the fact that the key to effective evangelism was "gaining a sympathetic hearing" for the gospel: it wasn't enough to proclaim the message of Christ—the audience needed to be open to hearing it, and specifically to hearing it from the person delivering the message. Rayburn, and in turn, the entire Young Life staff, learned to do that by "earning the right to be heard."

In Jim's words, "Christ is the strongest, grandest, most attractive personality ever to grace the earth. But a careless messenger with the wrong method can reduce all this magnificence to the level of boredom ... it is a sin to bore anyone with the gospel."

One of his favorite verses to explain Young Life's approach was Colossians 4:5: "Walk in wisdom toward them that are without, redeeming the time" (KJV). Jim loved to explain how important it was to "walk in wisdom" toward non-Christians and all that doing so entailed.

The most essential part of walking in wisdom was the simple but too often overlooked act of caring and showing an interest. Jim once commented, "Our young people today, six- or eight-million in the high school age alone, are waiting, waiting for somebody to care about them like [Christ did.] I mean there are six- or eight-million in our nation that nobody has ever talked to about Jesus Christ, that nobody has ever said a prayer for, that nobody has ever cared about. There are millions of them in our own nation, and they are waiting for somebody to care about them enough to take the time and trouble to pour out compassion on them, to prove their friendship, to bridge this tragic and terrible gap that exists in our culture between teenagers and adults—to emulate the example of Jesus Christ."

While Jim fervently believed that "everyone has a right to know Jesus Christ, to know the facts concerning Him," he also knew that Young Life's resources were limited. As a result, Jim sought to reach the "up and outers" or "key kids" in hopes that they, in turn, would open the doors to the greater majority.

An illustration from the world of architecture may help explain Jim's importance. Believed by many to be one of the most beautiful buildings in the world, St. Paul's Cathedral in London was the crowning masterpiece of famed architect Sir Christopher Wren. Fittingly, he is buried in the cathedral's crypt. His grave, however, is not marked by an ornate monument, as was the style in that day. Instead, a simple black marble floor slab reads, *Lector, si monumentum requiris, circumpice.* "Reader, if you seek his monument, look all around you."

In much the same way, you will not find an ornate tomb or stone monument for Jim Rayburn (or even a simple gravesite, as Jim willed his body to science). If you seek his monument, simply look all around Young Life: every aspect of its ministry—and its flavor—stems from Jim Rayburn's personality. Its use of and appreciation for humor, its sense of adventure, and the speaking style employed in club messages, all began with Jim more than sixty years ago. The fact that Young Life has a vital camping program has its roots in Jim's own childhood vacations to Colorado. When Jim first suggested that Young Life own its own resorts for the high school crowd, most of those around him thought the idea was impracticable; now most cannot envision Young Life without them. The fact that since 1946 Young Life has been headquartered in Colorado Springs (and the subsequent migration there of other ministries, beginning with The Navigators in 1953) comes from Jim's personal love of the Rockies. Young Life's tradition of seeking excellence in all things comes directly from Jim, as does its emphasis on communicating the gospel clearly to its intended audience. And most importantly, the passion that Young Life has for Jesus Christ, and the emphasis it places on having a personal relationship with Him, comes directly from Rayburn.

But Jim's impact reaches far beyond the ministry he started. The thousands of churches who practice "seeker friendly" evangelism, and all who practice "friendship evangelism" can trace their legacy to the events recorded in these journals.

There was something different about Jim Rayburn and, in turn, Young Life. Unlike so many of his contemporaries, and many evangelical leaders who have followed since, Jim's motivation for telling others about Christ was never about reaching a certain goal. It was because, as

2 Corinthians 5:14 says, "Christ's love compels us" (NIV)—put another way, Jim and his friends were so excited about life in Christ that they just had to share Him with others. As one of the early Young Life staff observed, Young Life was different because "we befriended the non-Christian." And not just for a single meeting—Jim prayed that God would give Young Life "the teenagers, each one at least long enough for a meaningful confrontation with Thee."

Though he believed in keeping statistics, Jim warned against putting much emphasis on their use. He sagely noted that "we're never going to justify Young Life with numbers because our count may not match heaven's." That being said, it is still helpful as a measure of Jim's impact to note that by 2007 the ministry that he founded had grown to a full-time staff of over 3,000 ministering in over 4,500 locations in 58 countries. More significantly, those staff were joined by 16,000 volunteer leaders and 11,000 committee members. Every year, over 60,000 young poeple visit Young Life's twenty-one properties.

The figures stated above are merely the current figures. They do not count the tens of thousands of former Young Life staff and volunteer leaders who have gone on to impact the world through other ministries after having learned the relational style of ministry during their time in Young Life. And the statistics do not show the untold number of young people who first encountered Jesus Christ in a high school Young Life club. Over the years, literally millions of lives have been impacted by Young Life in one way or the other. Bill Starr, who followed Jim as the head of Young Life, said, "To me he was the greatest guy in my life. And as a Christian he's had more influence than anybody else in the world."

———

Jim Rayburn began keeping a daily journal when he was a young man, the first known diary being the one for 1935. He kept them through 1969, a year before his death. Not every one of those thirty-five years has a diary, although twenty-eight of them do.

They tell the tale of Jim's triumphs, his heartaches, his self-perceived failings, and his passion for his Savior. Jim's story—and his journals— are marked by breathtaking highs and soul-crushing lows.

Rayburn's son, Jim Rayburn III, became the custodian of the journals, keeping them safe and in good condition as the years after his father's death turned into decades. In 2005 Jim III asked me to undertake the project of putting the journals into a form that would make them accessible to the general public.

What follows is a distillation of the diaries. My role has been to provide needed context, and to stay out of the way as much as possible. It is my hope that by reading this book you will get to know Jim Rayburn— in his own voice, and in his own words. Jim's is an amazing story, and an even more amazing life. May you be encouraged and challenged by what you encounter in the pages that follow.

As Jim's longtime friend Ted Benson once said, "Praise God for the small-town Kansas boy who moved mountains and slew giants to make a path for the Gospel."

—KIT SUBLETT
Houston, 2007

Some Explanatory Notes

Jim Rayburn wrote something in his journal almost every day his entire adult life. There are periods, most often during the summer months, and sometimes for weeks at a time, when he is silent. But most years, day in and day out, he recorded something each day. The resulting transcript runs to over 1,300 typewritten pages.

What you have in your hands is a greatly condensed version of those thousands of daily entries. I have tried to pick the entries that most exemplified Jim's ministry, life, and thoughts.

For many years Jim's journal entries tended to have three or sometimes four parts each day: a headache entry; a numeric notation of some sort, perhaps referring to his daily time in prayer and Scripture; the attendance at the meetings he spoke to that day; and the main journal entry itself. Through the years he stopped recording attendance and the numerical entries, replacing them at times with mileage records and some sort of code made up of dots.

I have chosen to include many but not all of the headache entries in order to convey what a tremendous problem these were for Jim. They seem to be one of his main reasons for keeping the journals in the first place and there are many days when there is no entry other than the headache portion. In keeping with the way they were recorded in his journals, I have put them at the first part of the entry and in smaller print.

I have not included the spiritual notations or the coded portions since their meaning is not entirely clear. I have also not always included the attendance figures. He kept these figures religiously during his early ministry, but ceased to be as consistent with them once Young Life began to really take off.

Unless otherwise noted (by bracketed ellipsis points), the main jour-

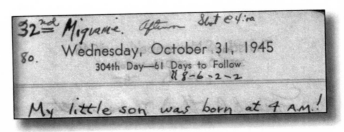

JIM'S NOTATIONS
Before its main entry begins ("My little son was born at 4 A.M!"), Rayburn's diary
for this day has a headache entry, an attendance entry ("80."), and an
example of the coded notations Rayburn made almost every day.

nal entries are presented in their entirety. Often they mix the mundane
with the profound; rather than editing out the mundane I have usually
kept it in since by doing so the entries present a more accurate picture
of Jim's day-to-day life. Occasionally Jim would use ellipsis points of his
own. Those appear as he wrote them; mine appear with brackets [...]

I have sought to be faithful to Rayburn's words, including his spelling, capitalization, and punctuation, even when incorrect. Rather than
"pretty it up," I have maintained its integrity in order to give the reader a
feel for the way Rayburn wrote. To the best of my ability, what you have
before you is what Jim wrote. The exceptions to this are when he forgot
to add a period at the end of a sentence or use an apostrophe where needed (or put it in the wrong place). In those cases, for the sake of readabil-
ity, I have sometimes taken the liberty of correcting Jim's punctuation.
Fortunately, Rayburn had nice handwriting, but there were certainly
times when he was writing in a hurry or on a moving train or a bumpy
airplane. When a word is unclear in the original, it is indicated by a
double asterisk (**).

Jim spelled well. In those rare instances where he made a mistake, I
have noted it with the traditional "[*sic*]" notation.

Being a personal journal, Jim abbreviated quite a bit. Sometimes
I have expanded those abbreviations using brackets (for example,

"me[aning]" in the January 29, 1947, entry).

There are certain abbreviations that Jim used often. Due to their frequency I have chosen not to spell them out each time. Some of them are:

aft for afternoon
comm for committee
CS for Colorado Springs
DL for Dallas
d.t.b. for down to business
DV for Denver
IQ for Colorado Springs
L for left-side (headache description)
M.B.C. for Miracle Book Club
Mig for migraine
mtg for meeting
R for right-side (headache description)
SS for Sunday School
thot for thought
Y.L. for Young Life
y.p. for young people

In a rather old-fashioned manner, Jim consistently hyphenated words beginning with "to" (to-day, to-night, to-morrow). I have maintained his spelling in order to preserve the feel of the journals as much as possible.

The same is true with Jim's use of an ampersand for the word "and"—rather than spell it out, I have used an ampersand.

For emphasis, or occasionally for a little artistic flair, Jim underlined words or put them in capital letters. I have tried to recreate that here (but you really have to see the journals themselves for the full effect).

For the most part, I have kept donors' names anonymous.

Jim travelled a large amount of the time. Location entries on the

date line are mine, not Jim's, and are based on my research (if he recorded his location it will be found in the main journal entry as well as
on the date line). I have added them in order to provide context—they
represent where he spent the most significant portion of the day. If there
isn't a location in the date line that means he was at home.

There is an inherent problem with presenting a journal as a narrative:
the author did not write it that way! Most people write journals only for
their own personal use and therefore don't provide context—their own
memory provides the needed context. To help the reader better understand Jim's journals, I have used two main devices to give that context.

The first device is the use of explanatory notes, set in italics. Anything that I felt was important for the "flow" of the story of Jim's journals, I have included in these notes.

The other device is footnotes. I have used them for information that
is not central to the story, but that gives added detail. You don't need to
read them, but you'll be rewarded if you do.

When there is a break in the action of more than a week it is indicated by a separator.

1935

EARLY DAYS
*A formal portrait of Jim from
around the time he finished
Dallas Theological Seminary
(right). Several years earlier, in
March 1934, Jim and Maxine
left his parents' home in
Newton, Kansas, to begin life on
their own in New Mexico and
Arizona (below).*

As 1935 began, Jim was twenty-five years old. Maxine would turn twenty-three on January 29. They had been married for just over two years and had been living in Chama, New Mexico, for about ten months. It was their first place to live by themselves, after living the first year of their marriage with Jim's parents in Newton, Kansas.

In January the Presbyterian Board of National Missions moved them from Chama to Douglas, Arizona, on the Mexican border. Jim spent his days trying to get Sunday School classes started in the small towns around Douglas.[1]

Jim tackled his job with great enthusiasm, travelling all over the countryside, stirring up interest, recruiting, and training teachers for the Sunday School classes. Maxine would often accompany him, and they would camp out under the stars at night. In later years she would recall these as some of her happiest times with Jim, recalling, "Life was very full, very happy, and very busy—and we were very poor."

Tuesday, January 29

Maxine's birthday—got her a little perfume. She and I spent the whole day traveling over field. Visited McNeal, where I spoke in school, also went to schools at Whitewater, Webb, Ash Creek, and Sunglow. All worth investigating. McNeal and Sunglow seem best prospects. No work at either of these. Feeling rather low to-night.[2] Contacts to-day not as enthusiastic as I had hoped.

Thursday, January 31

Had a fine day. Went 30 miles east to McDonald school. Had a good

---

[1] The 1935 journal was the only one not actually available for this book. These entries come from a transcription of the actual diary.

[2] Though he had written in his journal every day of 1935 to this point, this is the first entry in Jim's journals where he records not feeling well. There will literally be thousands more over the years.

time with the 3 boys that make up the student body. Drove across country to Bernardino. Rough trip but interesting. Went to Pleasant View school. Fine contact. Lively, intelligent, interested youngsters. Want Sunday School and are going to get it if I know anything. I thank God for these fine experiences.

Tuesday, February 5 (Portal, Arizona)

Started on trip. Stopped first at Apache [Arizona] school.[3] Teachers both very friendly. Spoke in both rooms. All pupils and teachers seem anxious for Sunday School. Played with boys at recess. Gave away Valentines and Sunday School papers (300). Drove on to Portal. Met teacher—very anxious for Sunday School and willing to help. Drove up in Cave Creek Canyon. Beautiful place. Picked camp spot and cooked supper. Went to bed outside but started to rain so we spent the night in the car.

Wednesday, February 6 (Portal, Arizona)

Got up early and went to the school at Portal and talked to the children. Had a wonderful time. Gave out lots of papers. Children very interested and wide awake. All want Sunday School badly apparently. Went through Paradise and on up to Hilltop. Had the same fine experience there. Enjoyed both places and was heartily renewed. Should develop splendidly. We had a wonderful trip over the mountains from Paradise to Chiricahua National Monument. The Monument is indescribable. Wonderful. Pitched camp and had fine meal. Wags[4] "went crazy" twice and it was stormy so we drove home. Arrived 9:00 p.m.

Saturday, February 16

Made fifteen calls at Double Adobe to-day and didn't have much luck

---

[3] Apache is about forty miles from Douglas; Portal is another ten miles north.

[4] Wags was the Rayburns' dog.

getting teachers. Got back in mid-afternoon and met Ralph[5] downtown. Talked to him all p.m. He and Sidebotham[6] were here for dinner this evening. Do not feel well. Hope and pray for a great day to-morrow. Maxine read the ten verses of Bible to-night. We are fifteen chapters ahead of schedule.

Wednesday, February 20
We went over to Aqua Prieta [Mexico] this a.m. and got fine veal for twenty cents a kilo and pork for thirty cents a kilo.

Went to Pleasant View District to-day and spent all afternoon calling. Called on almost everyone. All friendly. Had supper with the Blevins. Awfully nice people. Organized Sunday School to-night. Have a good set-up, I believe. Seems to be considerable interest.

Jim was a perpetual optimist as well as a hard worker, as these next entries show.

Sunday, February 24
Left for Apache about 9:00 this a.m. Only two families out there but they seem interested and I believe we can get something going out there. Spent some time in Cave Creek this afternoon then drove on over to Hilltop and had dinner with Reiders. Fifteen at church, snowing. A fine service and much interest shown. Want Sunday School. Drove home through snow. Arrived about 10:15 and went right to bed.

Sunday, March 3
Got up early—Left for Apache at 9:00. No one came to the service but

---

[5] Ralph Hall. Known as "the missionary cowboy," Hall had hired Jim for this position. He and his wife lived in Albuquerque. His ministry to ranches and other outposts had begun years earlier on horseback in what was then the "New Mexico Territory."

[6] Rev. Bryce Sidebotham. He was the pastor of the Presbyterian church in Douglas when Jim and Maxine arrived.

the Knowlands. Drove over to Portal. Rained hard before service time. No one came except two little girls. Sure was disappointed in those two places. Felt pretty bum when we got home. Went to Double Adobe to-night and had a fine service—attendance 42—so feel better.

Tuesday, March 5
Around home all day. Wrote lots of letters and attended to all my business at bank, etc. Very busy day. Feel bum but got some Adrephine[7] to-night and it sure does relieve. Went to picture show to-night. Enjoyed it.[8]

Thursday, March 7 (Hilltop, Arizona)
Left this a.m. for Hilltop. Arrived there in time to call on whole community and announce at school before 4:00 p.m. Had Sunday School for kids. All very interested. Had a nice time. Church Service at 7:30 p.m. 26 present, which means practically the whole community. Went home with Calverts to-night. Had dinner at Reiders. Old man Reider "warming-up."

> *Even though Young Life would not begin for another five years, the Lord used Jim's years in Arizona and New Mexico to shape his future ministry. Jim's decision to focus on high school students came as a result of working with people of all ages during this time. He observed that the older members of the communities he was reaching out to were set in their ways and not receptive to the gospel. Children, on the other hand, were too receptive: the same ones would respond to every invitation to receive Christ that Jim gave.*

---

[7] Adrephine is a combination of adrenaline and Ephedrine and is used as an astringent for the nose, throat, and larynx. In addition to the migraines he suffered from, Jim also had breathing trouble for many years.

[8] Moviegoing was frowned upon by Jim's parents, as well as other conservative Christians of the day. But at this time in his life, Jim went to "the pictures" often.

He became increasingly aware that the high school years were the time when individuals were both open to the gospel and able to make a responsible decision for Christ. As he wrote many years later about that age, "God ordained into the seasons of maturity a springtime where faith flowers best, a time when the nerve ends of personality are especially tuned to respond to the magnificence of the Gospel."

These next entries, about a series of meetings in Payson, Arizona, are an example of the work Jim was doing.

Monday, March 18 (Payson, Arizona)

Went to high school at 11:30 a.m. Had a good contact there. […] Went to 5, 6 and 3, 4 and 1, 2 schools [grades] right after noon. Got home and ran off copies of Booster Choir Songs then had the children at 4:00 p.m. A very fine meeting—good singing. Just had time to grab a bite to eat before service this a.m. 99 present to-night. Children sang and all seemed to have a good time. […]

Tuesday, March 19 (Payson, Arizona)

This has been a fine day, in spite of the fact that we have had snow and quite cold. 25 young people at young people's meeting to-night and 80 at church though it was stormy. All in all it was a fine service. The children's choir grew to 27 to-day, and the children did a fine job of singing.

Wednesday, March 20 (Payson, Arizona)

Another fine day. Ralph arrived this a.m. and we had church together out in the woods. Had 30 for Junior Choir in the afternoon and had a splendid time. About 110 or 112 at church to-night and we had a fine service. Ralph preached a great sermon—the response was fine.

Thursday, March 21 (Payson, Arizona)

We went to the Tonto Natural Bridge this morning and enjoyed the trip very much. Had a good camp lunch and a fine Junior Choir this p.m. I was very sick with a headache. We had another fine crowd—over 100 to-night—and Ralph preached a splendid sermon. Two young women came forward.

Friday, March 22 (Payson, Arizona)
Another busy day—had lunch in the woods then—children's meeting—talked about "tree"—gave invitation—15 children 10 years old or older came forward. About that many younger ones raised their hand. Another fine evening crowd and sermon. 24 people came forward and stayed for after meeting which I conducted.

Saturday, March 23 (Payson, Arizona)
Spent a.m. looking over the Payson "manse" and talking about building—good children's meeting in the afternoon. Spent most all the rest of day with Ralph in camp. Got home at 10:00 p.m. and hit the hay.

Sunday, March 24 (Payson, Arizona)
We had 45 at Sunday School and 50 at church. Ralph presented the Petition for church in a very fine way. Most all signed—we ate dinner and spent the afternoon in the woods. Only about 12 for young peoples meeting—75 for church. Ralph didn't have people come forward, but over a dozen raised their hands on his invitation—61 signed church petition.

Jim had little patience for the trappings of "religion" and "religious" people.

Thursday, April 11 (Miami, Arizona)
Presbytery a perfect bore and farce. Sat through the whole thing and shall regret it the rest of my life.
[...]

Sunday, April 14 [Payson, Arizona]
Fifty-two at Sunday School this a.m. I never have seen such a hopeless bunch. [...]

Monday, May 20

[...]

Came home and went to visit Bradfords—they are swell—real con-
secrated people—Lester (Baptist Minister) seems to be a sap.

———

*Even though Jim had no patience for religious "saps," he still had
some of his parents' legalistic tendencies.*

Wednesday, June 26 (Montlure Presbyterian Camp, Greer, Arizona)
Talked in Bryce Sidebotham's class this a.m. on "Dancing." Pretty hard
for some of the class to take but I firmly believe that real progress was
made.

Had session with Janet Enyeart over dance—cooled her off.

———

Wednesday, August 28 (Rustler's Park, Arizona)[9]
Dad came to-day—Talked to my older class in a.m. Preached at night.
Sidebotham and his young people up to-day. Good service to-night.
Fine interest.

Thursday, August 29 (Rustler's Park, Arizona)
Dad spoke to young people on subject of "Punishment of Wicked," and
"Virgin Birth" to-day—then the folks left about 3:30 p.m.

[...]

———

Thursday, September 12
Spent all morning working on yard—had another talk with Woolsley.

This is our third anniversary[10]—got Maxine a little electric mixer

---

[9] Frustrated with denomination-run camps like Montlure, Jim and Maxine put on
their own camp in August 1935 at Rustler's Park in the Chiricahua Wilderness.

[10] The third anniversary of their first wedding, not the "official" one Jim's parents

and an electric sandwich toaster. She used them for supper.

Friday, September 13

This was a fine day that I spent studying and reading my Bible and praying—accomplished a lot and feel better fit for starting out to-morrow
because of this day.[11]

——◦◦◦——

Sunday, September 22

23 at Sunday School [in] Double Adobe this morning—all children, but
we had a good time—28 at Rucker, a good Sunday School, preached,
we were well received. Back to Double Adobe via Douglas—16 out to
church—again mostly children—just Mr. Shaw, Richard** and Marge**.
Home about 10:30 very tired.

——◦◦◦——

*Jim used lots of different ways to get "in" with kids, including coach-
ing football, leading Boy Scout troops, and taking boys camping.*

Friday, October 11

Had a fine scout meeting to-night with the four boys at Silver Creek—
Scouting will be the smallest thing that we accomplish with these boys.

Wednesday, October 16 (Tucson)

At Synod all day—nothing much of interest. Met lots of old friends etc.
Sessions mostly lousy. Talked to Dr. Fendrick about seminary.[12]

——◦◦◦——

The Rayburns moved to Dos Cabezas, Arizona, on October 24.

---

insisted upon (see Preface).

[11] The next several days he ran "young people's meetings" in Clifton, Arizona.

[12] Dr. Fendrick was the keynote speaker at the Synod meetings. This is the first
mention of seminary in Jim's journals. The longer he served in full-time ministry, the
more pressing he felt the need to get proper theological training. It would be another
year before he would actually enroll, and then at Dallas Theological Seminary.

They were only there for a day or two before Jim had a series of
meetings to speak at in Payson, 200 miles away.

Tuesday, October 29 (Payson, Arizona)

Spent the morning out in the woods at our old camp spot—for study and prayer. Afternoon called on Wilsons** and had a Junior Choir meeting.[13] Had Junior prayer meeting at 7:00—10 present—good response. 50 at church to-night. I preached on 1 Timothy 1:12.[14]

Wednesday, October 30 (Payson, Arizona)

Out in the woods again this a.m. for 3 hours. Am enjoying these times alone this week.

Had 16 children and 3 young people at Prayer meeting to-night. About 8 adults at their meeting.

47 at church. [Jimmy] Glenn preached. Nose bad!!!

Thursday, October 31 (Payson, Arizona)

A Wonderful Day!! Trip to top of Tonto Rim this afternoon. Beautiful. Campfire, steak and marshmallows, cold night, new moon, drive home—all helped make it an ideal outing. No services to-day on account of High School play.

Sunday, November 3

The greatest service of my ministry to-night—Preached—"Denying Christ" and added an anti-dance sermon for final service of Payson meetings. Mr. and Mrs. Bob Stewart, Mr. and Mrs. Hancock, and a dozen others accepted Christ on the invitation—much conviction. God certainly spoke to hearts to-night and answered prayers marvelously. Spent the afternoon in prayer. Wonderful Day!!!

---

[13] Though not known as a musician or singer (as Maxine put it, he did not have a soloist's voice), Jim had helped lead the music in his father's tent campaigns.

[14] "I thank him who has given me strength, Christ Jesus our Lord, because he judged me faithful, appointing me to his service."

The houses the Rayburns lived in during their time with the Presbyterian Board of Missions were simple, to say the least (primitive and rundown may be more accurate). While in one—either in Dos Cabezos or Clifton, the various accounts conflict—Jim discovered a book that would forever change his life and play a significant part in the founding of Young Life. He That is Spiritual by Lewis Sperry Chafer had been published in 1918. Jim found a copy one day and once he began reading it, could not put it down. The book introduced Jim to Dr. Chafer, and indirectly led him to go to Dallas Theological Seminary, which Chafer had founded in 1924.

The following excerpts are from their time in Dos Cabezos. Jim had trouble breathing through his nose, requiring surgery over the years. Like he did with all his medical problems, he used his journal to keep track of this problem each day.

Tuesday, November 5

Nose good.

Worked at getting straightened around all day. This evening I had a miraculous escape from a bad explosion or burn when the gasoline lamp blew gasoline all over me and a lighted candle in the kitchen. Got a few burns on my right hand.

Thursday, November 7

Nose good.

Got my books and papers straightened out this a.m. and have my room in pretty good shape. Severe headache this afternoon which got better after supper and I had a good evening.

Friday, November 8

Nose good.

Spent the day around home. Got quite a bit done—particularly some interesting reading on "Spirituality." To bed about 11:00. Beautiful evening.[15]

Sunday, November 17 (Clifton, Arizona)

Nose Terrible.

Clifton—78 at Sunday School this a.m.—35 at church, 7 of whom were young people and 7 children. A good service—people most cordial. Dinner at Andersons'—Bible games for children at church in p.m.—Supper at Sidebothams[16]—C.E. [Christian Education] about 20 present. The usual meeting—nothing Christian about it. No interest—no value, wish I could do something about it.

———

Jim and Maxine were anxious to start a family. Sadly, they would suffer two miscarriages before their daughter Ann was born in 1937. One of those miscarriages occurred in late 1935.

Saturday, November 30

Nose good.

Maxine had a hemorrhage this a.m. and we were very worried about miscarriage. I went to Willcox [Arizona] for Doctor but failed to locate one. She got better through the day and is getting along fine to-night. I cooked the meals etc., and tried to get a little preparation for to-morrow.

Sunday, December 1

Nose good.

Attendance Sunday School at Dos Cabezas this a.m. Only 9 present.

---

[15] It is not known if Jim's reading on "Spirituality" was from Chafer's book. If it was (which seems probable since Chafer uses the term frequently in *He That is Spiritual*) it means Jim found the book in Dos Cabezos. However, in retelling the story years later Maxine recalled that Jim found the book when they were living in Clifton, where they moved four months later (February 1936). Unfortunately, there is no journal for 1936 that could shed light on where Jim found the book.

[16] By this time Rev. Sidebotham and his wife had moved from Douglas to Clifton. From 1936–1943 he served as the pastor of Sausalito Presbyterian Church near San Francisco, where the Rayburns visited them in 1941.

Maxine in bed all day. I got meals and did fairly well. Left for White-water at 1:30 with 5 young people. Arrived at 3:00—Just 50 miles. Went to Double Adobe and got just Marjorie. Young People's meeting a huge success with 40 present and about every community represented. Home by 10:00 p.m. Great day!!

Monday, December 2

Nose fine.

Cleaned the house and took care of Maxine all day. Had a scout meeting to-night. Good meeting—18 boys present. Stayed up late reading.[17]

Wednesday, December 4

Nose good.

Went out with Mr. Thompson this a.m. and got wood. Home at 11:00 with a terrible headache. Got over it with aspirin. Met with my scouts this afternoon and evening preparatory to to-morrow night's installation service.

Maxine not so good to-night—Kirbys up for awhile after supper.

Thursday, December 5

Nose fine.

Troop Installation—Dos Cabezas—Ed Saxton

Ed and I went to dinner at Kirbys' before the installation and Edith brought Maxine's dinner to her. Maxine had a miscarriage at 10:00 p.m. Ed and I didn't get to bed until 2:00 a.m.

Friday, December 6

Nose fine.

Maxine felt fine this a.m. but worse again to-night so decided to take her to Douglas. Left 8:00—arrived 10:00. Went to Palomar Hotel and Dr. Duncan came and examined her and thought everything was o.k.

---

[17] Since he only rarely mentions reading in the 1935 journal it is very possible that he has indeed discovered *He That is Spiritual* and this is what he is referring to here.

Saturday, December 7

Nose fine.

Left Douglas about 2:00 p.m. Home around 5:00. To bed early very tired.

Sunday, December 8

Nose fine.

Spent the day at home caring for Maxine and resting and reading—First Sunday I've laid off in almost a year.

Wednesday, December 18 (camping)

Left for Eagle at 11:00 a.m. Met Ralph at Clifton about 3:00. Had supper on Grays Peak. Arrived in Eagle about 6:30. Good crowd of 56 present for meeting: very well received. Ralph and I made camp up the creek. Very cold.

Thursday, December 19 (Clifton, Arizona)

Got up about 9:00 a.m. Enjoyed the cold night in my bed-roll. Left Eagle about 11:00—dinner on top again—very cold. Into Clifton and got a cabin at Awalts. Good crowd of 55 to-night. Good interest. Raining to-night.

1940

JIM'S JOURNAL FOR THE WEEK OF FEBRUARY 25, 1940
Most of the diaries Rayburn used devoted a full page to each day; the 1940 journal, however, had an entire week on each two-page spread.

The longest period of silence in Jim's journals is the four-year gap between the 1935 and 1940 journals. Much happened during that time period.

Jim and Maxine moved from Arizona to Dallas in the fall of 1936 so that Jim could receive the seminary training he longed for. In the summer of 1937 Jim almost died after his appendix ruptured. His recovery was complete and miraculous. On October 17 of that year, the Rayburns had their first child, Elna Ann. Following Ann's birth, Maxine began a battle with depression which would last for decades.

Jim began taking ergotamine tartrate (brand name Gynergen), a common prescription to relieve the symptoms of migraine headaches. His entries often have phrases like "took shot—complete relief." These are referring to shots of Gynergen.

By the beginning of 1940, Jim and Maxine had been married for seven years and Maxine was pregnant with their second child. Jim was thirty years old and had completed his first three-and-a-half years of the four-year seminary program at Dallas Theological Seminary (DTS).

Jim thrived under the tutelage of Dr. Chafer. "This wonderful man of God," Jim recalled years later, "this great teacher of grace would just romp down our young necks every day about the fact that the gospel of the Lord Jesus Christ was what Jesus Christ had done for man plus nothing else in the whole world. There wasn't anything you could add to it, there wasn't anything else you could do about it. It was all completely done and wrapped up and ready to deliver to anybody who'd take it."

Jim and his seminary friends were so inspired by Dr. Chafer's teaching of God's grace that they were determined to take action. "I used to sit in those classrooms and think 'If I don't do something about this, I'm going to burst!'" Jim explained.

Jim and his peers began various attempts to reach high school

*students in the Dallas area. One of the men heard about a na-
tional organization called Miracle Book Club, begun by a woman
named Evelyn McFarlane McClusky,[1] and soon the men aligned
their efforts under the Miracle Book Club umbrella. Around the
spring of 1939 Jim began a chapter of the Miracle Book Club in
Gainesville, Texas, about seventy miles from Dallas.*

*At the insistence of its young pastor, Clyde Kennedy, Jim was
also hired by the First Presbyterian Church in Gainesville as the
director of Christian Education and choir director on a part-time
basis.*

*By the spring of 1940, thanks to concerted prayer by Gaines-
ville High School students and Dallas seminarians alike, Jim's
MBC chapter was beginning to take off. It also helped that they
began meeting at members' homes on weeknights rather than at
the school in the afternoon as had been the practice. Jim's journal
for that spring faithfully records the progress.*

Monday, January 22 (Gainesville)
Our last M.B.C. meeting at Clarks. 20 present. Fine meeting!

Monday, January 29 (Gainesville)
32 at M.B.C. for our first meeting at Brodheads'.[2] That is our biggest
crowd to date. The Lord certainly blessed. I got home about 10:30. Got
Maxine some candy for her birthday.

Monday, February 5 (Gainesville)
51 at M.B.C! On a rainy night! This has been a truly wonderful day—

---

[1] Leah Evelyn McFarlane McClusky (1889–1994). McClusky had started Miracle
Book Club in 1933 in Portland, Oregon. By 1940 there were hundreds of chapters
around the nation, and the ministry was based out of Richmond, California. The
name derived from a book Mrs. McClusky had read that called the Bible "the miracle
book."

[2] Howard Brodhead, Jr., was a high school student in Gainesville. The Brodhead
family lived very close to First Presbyterian Church.

The Lord has put it into our hearts to pray then wonderfully answered the prayers. I arrived home about 11:00. Elna Ann has temp.

Saturday, February 10 (Gainesville)

Went to Gainesville on the bus. Had a good choir rehearsal to-night.

Sunday, February 11 (Gainesville)

Clyde[3] was sick so I had both sermons to preach to-day on top of every-thing else. The Lord really blessed and gave me a particularly fine message this morning.

Monday, February 12 (Gainesville)

The M.B.C. Banquet went off with a bang! About 80 present and a truly wonderful response to the fine program. We had 9 in my car coming home and really had a grand time.[4] Harold Longstreth,[5] Addie Sewell,[6] & Tim Hatch!

Monday, February 19 (Gainesville)

Worked hard all day. Had 60 at M.B.C. to-night and one girl—Wanda—gloriously saved & testified to her Salvation. I was poor to-night. Do pray that the Lord will overrule and bring the kids back! [...]

---

[3] Clyde Johnson Kennedy (1907–1962). Kennedy was the new pastor at First Presbyterian Church in Gainesville. He was a tremendous encouragement to Jim and his work with high school kids, encouraging him to do whatever it took to reach them.

[4] Dallas Seminary did not have classes on Mondays so that students could have time to return to the campus after weekend ministry opportunities. In Jim's case, he typically stayed in Gainesville overnight on Sunday nights so he could have his Miracle Book Club the next night. He would return to the seminary late on Mondays or early Tuesday morning.

[5] Longstreth was two years behind Jim at DTS. The only other time he is mentioned in the journals is in March of the next year when he appears to be displeased with the break between Young Life Campaign and Miracle Book Club: "Had lunch with Harold Longstreth and we got this business of the 'split' straightened out and good fellowship restored."

[6] This is the first time Add Sewell appears in Jim's journals. He would play a role in Jim's life for the next two decades, and will be mentioned often in these pages.

Monday, February 26 (Gainesville)

This is a real stand-out day of my life. 10 y.p. accepted Christ this p.m. at M.B.C. A truly wonderful demonstration of the Power of God. I got frightfully sick with a migraine in P.M. & had a hard time getting home but came Praising the Lord for the Salvation of these dear kids and all the other wonderful blessings that he gave this week-end.[7] 52 [at MBC]

Wednesday, February 28

Pounding the Thesis again to-day.[8]

Thursday, February 29

Still at the Thesis hot & heavy.

Sunday, March 3 (Gainesville)

Had a wonderful meeting of the MBC officers this afternoon at Brodheads'. Fine prayer by all and intense interest.

   [...]

Monday, March 4 (Gainesville)

I had a terrible migraine from noon on. Mrs. Moore[9] gave me some of her codeine and it got me through the meeting & home in good shape— then I really hurt for a couple hours. Had our largest M.B.C. crowd to-night 65! Lots of fine boys. Mother here at home—since Sat. night.[10]

---

[7] Jim had spent much of the weekend tending to three members of his Miracle Book Club who had been involved in a near-fatal car accident on February 21 (Howard Brodhead, Jr., Loveta Murphy, and Felix Parsons). He had also taken part in the funeral of 58-year-old Gainesville resident Carl Moore on Sunday (Moore was not involved in the accident).

[8] Jim's 11,000 word thesis was called "An Investigation of the Dispensational Method of Biblical Interpretation." He received a grade of 98 from Dr. Chafer on it.

[9] Catherine Greenwood Moore. Mrs. Moore's husband Carl is the man whose funeral Jim had recently taken part in.

[10] Mrs. Rayburn had come to help with the soon-to-be-delivered new baby the Rayburns were expecting.

Monday, March 11 (Gainesville)

Heard the Trinity U Choir at high school and had lunch with them.[11] 55 at MBC at Brodheads' to-night—a truly wonderful meeting. <u>7 made a public confession of Christ</u> as Savior—"Burr" Nichols, football captain,[12] "Bud" Teage & "Tippy" Marshall, Ann Culp, Carrie Lou Lindell, _____, _____[.][13] —That makes Nineteen who have testified to Salvation in the past 4 weeks! 102 on the M.B.C. roll.

Tuesday, March 12 (Gainesville)

Worked hard on my Heb. to-night and am still at it at 12:30 a.m.

Wednesday, March 13

Our little "Mary Margaret" was born at 7:15 P.M. I took Maxine to the hospital about 3:30—she had considerable pain by that time but this was nothing compared to last time. Praise the Lord for this wonderful gift of His love & the high privilege of being entrusted with another little life.[14]

Saturday, March 16 (Gainesville)

Mother, Elna Ann, Tim [Hatch] & I left for Gainesville at 2:00 P.M. after visiting the hospital. Had a fine dinner party at Mrs. Scott's.[15] [...]

---

[11] Trinity University, then located in the town of Waxahachie, was the leading Presbyterian college in Texas. It later moved to San Antonio.

[12] William Thomas "Burr" Nichols was a standout football player at Gainesville High School. Tragically, he died in a car accident on November 1, 1941. His parents wanted Jim to preach the funeral, but Jim was in Minnesota at the time and unable to perform the service. They said Jim was the only preacher that Burr ever listened to.

[13] The blank spaces are Jim's.

[14] Mary Margaret would later become known as "Sue" after another child had trouble pronouncing Mary Margaret, calling her "Sue Sue." The nickname stuck.

[15] Mrs. Annie Scott. Jim used to stay at her house when he was in Gainesville overnight. She was a faithful supporter of both Jim and his brother Bob for the rest of her life. She referred to them as "My Boy Jim" and "My Boy Bob."

Sunday, March 17 (Gainesville)

We all had dinner at Kennedys' & Mother & babe[16] & Tim left for Dallas at 2:30. The MBC officers met with me until 3:30.

We had a wonderful prayer service for M.B.C. after church. 12 y.p. present and real prayers offered up. Great day! The Lord has blessed.

Monday, March 18 (Gainesville)

No migraine To-day.

90[17] at M.B.C. to-night. The greatest attendance ever and a wonderful meeting. Truly the Lord is answering our prayers in a wonderful way. He is the Faithful One! Home with Clyde K. by 11:00.[18]

Monday, March 25 (Gainesville)

A very busy day with lots of running around to do. A wonderful M.B.C. meeting. 74 present in spite of Spring Vacation. 3 accepted Christ & I called on all who have been saved in the club & there were 17 who stood—others were not present. The best spirit we have had in any meeting & the Lord gave me real liberty in the Word for which I praise Him.

Friday, March 29

This is truly a red letter day in my life. Maxie came this p.m. and told me very sweetly of how the Lord has been dealing with her & has led her to the place of loving surrender to His Will. It is a real rebuke to my own heart that I have not oftener talked to her of the Lord's precious deal-

---

[16] Ann Rayburn.

[17] The number was originally written as 82. Jim, or someone else, has changed it to 90.

[18] As to Clyde Kennedy's influence on Rayburn, Jim's own words, cited in his son's biography of him, *From Bondage to Liberty: Dance, Children, Dance*, put it this way: "We decided we'd have a prayer meeting, those two kids and me. In the pastor's study that Sunday night, we started to pray for the club. The pastor met with us. He was pushing on me all the time. He didn't care if I did any work around the church. He just wanted to see those kids reached for Christ. He said, 'Don't monkey around with the people who come to church. I'll take care of them. You go on down to that high school.'" (The prayer meeting referenced by Jim in this quote most likely occurred earlier than the one referenced in the previous day's journal entry.)

ings in my own life. May the Lord become daily more precious to her in a life of complete yieldedness to his perfect will, is my prayer for her & for myself.

Monday, April 1 (Gainesville)

100 at MBC To-night—What a club—what a victory the Lord has wrought—most amazing to see all the worldly & otherwise indifferent-to-the[-]Gospel youngsters that come. 20 at J-High club & 27 at Myra.[19] Howard B[rodhead] drove home with Tim [Hatch] and I to-night. Arrived 11:30.

Sunday, April 7 (Gainesville)

A marvelous Day. 180 at church in a.m. and 135 in p.m. to hear Paul Moore who brought great missionary messages. Felix [Parsons] and Loveta Murphy gave their lives to the Lord in complete surrender—an amazing & beautiful demonstration of the Grace of God.[20]

Monday, April 8 (Gainesville)

123 at M.B.C. Talk about thrills!! This ministry is the most precious that has ever come to me. One girl gloriously saved & real liberty in the Word on J[ohn] 8 & 9. Good testimonies & prayer. In every way the Power of God was manifested. 24 at Myra, 15 at J.H.S.

Friday, April 19

M.B.C. Convention started to-night with over 300 registered delegates. The Banquet was fine but the program afterward dragged. Mrs. McC[lusky] talked with me for a long time about taking the State work.

---

[19] Myra, Texas, is a small community about fifteen miles from Gainesville where Jim and Tim Hatch had recently started a Miracle Book Club chapter.

[20] Felix Parsons, Jr., and Loveta Murphy were two of the students in the car accident on February 21.

Lewis Sperry Chafer at a DTS picnic.

Also Al Brown.[21] My only prayer is that God will give definite leading and I know He will.[22]

Saturday, April 27

Had meeting with Mrs. McC[lusky] & the M.B.C. teachers and officers this a.m.—Told them of my plans for M.B.C. Much genuine interest. Received $21 to-day. $5 from Nachadoches [*sic*, Nacogdoches], $1 from Dallas, $15 from Dad. Seems like the Lord's indication that He will provide. Oh, to FULLY TRUST HIM.

---

[21] Allan Howard Brown. Originally from California, Brown was a year behind Jim at Dallas Seminary. He is the one who had originally brought Miracle Book Club to the attention of his fellow DTS men.

[22] In an interview many years later, Wally Howard recalled that this conference was held at Dallas Seminary. According to Howard, Mrs. McClusky announced Jim's new position as state director for Texas before he had actually agreed to take it.

Monday, April 29

170 at M.B.C. to-night. It was wonderful. 6 kids [—] 3 boys & 3 girls accepted Christ as their Savior. Some of these said they had in the meeting last week but did not acknowledge it until this week. 20 at Jr. High M.B.C. 1 girl saved. 27 at Myra.

The success of the Gainesville Miracle Book Club chapter was tremendously significant to Jim and his friends, many of whom were leading MBC chapters of their own—they knew Jim was on to something. The success eventually led directly to the founding of Young Life. To his final days, Jim could recite with accuracy the attendance of the Gainesville club during the spring of 1940.

Jim graduated from DTS that May as the president of his thirty-seven member class. That summer, he and several seminary friends put on the "Young Life Campaign" in Gainesville, Houston, and Dallas. The campaign was a version of his father's tent meetings, geared toward young people, featuring Jim as the speaker. Gainesville's campaign was first, at the Cooke County Fairgrounds.

His primary co-workers were Add Sewell and Tim Hatch. Add was a year behind Jim at DTS, and Hatch was two years behind. Hatch's association with Young Life would be short-lived. Sewell, on the other hand, helped Jim begin Young Life and stayed with the ministry for the next twenty-two years.

A few other key players are introduced in the next several entries, including fellow DTS students Ted Benson, George Cowan, and Wally Howard. Benson would serve on Young Life staff on and off over the next several years in various administrative capacities, and would remain close to Rayburn until Jim's death in 1970. Cowan and Howard, along with Jim, Add Sewell, and Gordon Whitelock, would be the first five people on the Young Life payroll. Cowan left Young Life shortly after its founding to work with Wycliffe Bible Translators, of which he eventually became presi-

dent. Wally Howard served in many important capacities during his twenty years on the Young Life staff.

The other key player introduced in these entries is Herbert J. Taylor of Chicago. Ted Benson worked for Taylor's Christian Workers Foundation during the summers and Mr. Taylor and his wife Gloria agreed to underwrite the 1940 Young Life Campaign. He went on to serve for many years on the board of trustees of Young Life and was a tremendous guiding light to the ministry for decades.

Tuesday, May 7

Praise The Lord. I got thru the final all right I think so school is over—except for part of my Greek Commentary.

Thursday, May 9

Finished my Greek Commentary to-day. It is wonderful to know that I am all done with school work.

Saturday, May 11 (Gainesville)

M.B.C. picnic & talk about the Y.L.C. this summer.[23] The Lord blessed & afterward Glenn,[24] Ad[d], Ted [Benson], George Cowan, Wally [Howard] and I got together for a wonderful time of prayer about this work.

—∿∿—

[23] This is the first time "Young Life" or "Young Life Campaign" appears in Jim's journals. Here, Jim is referring to that summer's tent campaign—at this point the men were not thinking of breaking with Miracle Book Club. They had gotten the name from a British evangelistic group called National Young Life Campaign. Jim had met its head, Frederick P. Wood, when Wood spoke at DTS in 1937.

[24] Probably DTS student Glenn Wagner. Wagner was a former All-American football player who Jim used to draw a crowd to meetings. He would often pray with Jim and his other fellow DTS students for their clubs. He went on to have a long ministry with the Pocket Testament League.

Tuesday, May 21

Sick with migraine this a.m. Got full relief by noon with "shot."
Rested this afternoon. Very weary. Good day. Ad[d] was over for prayer
to-night. Word from Ted Benson this a.m. that Taylor of Chi[cago] will
contribute $100.00 per month for travel exp.[25] The Lord is Good!

Sunday, July 7 (Gainesville)

Had a fine time at communion & study this A.M. The First Service—
about 300 present—Spoke on "Life's Greatest Opportunity." The Lord
greatly blessed. At our 9:15 meeting a much larger crowd and the Spirit
really worked. Very weary but a great day.

Monday, July 8 (Gainesville)

Start of children's meetings 30 present. Morning Bible study only 7
adults. I got a severe migraine headache and had to take a shot—Got
complete relief. Preached to-night on The Gospel of John "The Greatest
Story In the World"—Not much liberty & punch but a good hearing.[26]

Tuesday, July 9 (Gainesville)

A truly wonderful meeting to-night. The Lord richly led & blessed as I
spoke on "Healing the Paralytic" Mk 2:1–12. Bible Study 19 present—
Children 53. Ad[d], Tim & I had a wonderful time of Prayer after the
meeting. I spoke at Kiwanis Club. Good Reception!

Wednesday, July 10 (Gainesville)

I spoke at Rotary this noon. Excellent write-up in paper of both that &

---

[25] This is the first mention of H. J. Taylor in Jim's journals. The two men had almost
certainly not met at this point.

[26] For many years the degree of "liberty" Jim felt in speaking was one of his main
criteria in judging his success. Less subjective and ultimately more significant to
the development of Young Life was the other idea in this sentence: gaining a good
"hearing" from his audience. This eventually became the major goal of all of Young
Life's activities with high school students—"gaining a sympathetic hearing for the
gospel." The third criteria that Jim often mentioned was a "fine spirit" at the meeting.

Kiwanis yesterday. The Lord gave another wonderful blessing to-night as I spoke on "I am ready"—Luke 22:31–34,[27] Luke 21: 10–13.[28] Clyde, Ad[d], Tim & I had fine prayer aft. Much fine response.

Thursday, July 11 (Gainesville)

Our Best crowd to-night—nearly 500! I spoke on "The Sin of Being Satisfied." Pharisee & Publican.

Friday, July 12 (Gainesville)

Rain to-day & much smaller crowd. Spoke on Zacchaeus.

Saturday, July 13 (Gainesville)

Terrible migraine.

Children's choir—Poor Crowd. Spoke on II K[ings] 5: 1–19 Naaman. Dad came in after the evening service.

Sunday, July 14 (Gainesville)

A very disappointing afternoon crowd—I spoke on—"Prodigal Son" for Christians. A fine crowd of about 500 at 9:15. "Neglect"—The Lord greatly blessed! A fine young fellow SAVED! Louise Shurig's brother. Offering was $50.00.

Monday, July 15 (Gainesville)

Dad left this A.M. He seemed to really enjoy himself. This afternoon I had one of the greatest experiences of my life. 25 young people out for Prayer. The Spirit was present in great Power bringing confession of sin,

---

[27] "'Simon, Simon, behold, Satan demanded to have you, that he might sift you like wheat, but I have prayed for you that your faith may not fail. And when you have turned again, strengthen your brothers.' Peter said to him, 'Lord, I am ready to go with you both to prison and to death.' Jesus said, 'I tell you, Peter, the rooster will not crow this day, until you deny three times that you know me.'"

[28] "Then he said to them, 'Nation will rise against nation, and kingdom against kingdom. There will be great earthquakes, and in various places famines and pestilences. And there will be terrors and great signs from heaven. But before all this they will lay their hands on you and persecute you, delivering you up to the synagogues and prisons, and you will be brought before kings and governors for my name's sake. This will be your opportunity to bear witness.'"

Loveta Murphy (front row, right) and other members of
the choir at the Gainesville Young Life Campaign.

burden for the lost, & much love for Christ. It is amazing to see what He
can do with <u>kids</u>! […]

Tuesday, July 16 (Gainesville)

Another fine prayer meeting this P.M. 22 kids. Best night crowd on
week-night except last Thur. I spoke on "Why Are Men Lost"—J
3:1–3[29]—Gen[esis]. No visible results. […]

Wednesday, July 17 (Gainesville)

A disappointing crowd of only 250 to-night as I spoke on "How Good

---

[29] "Now there was a man of the Pharisees named Nicodemus, a ruler of the Jews. This
man came to Jesus by night and said to him, 'Rabbi, we know that you are a teacher
come from God, for no one can do these signs that you do unless God is with him.'
Jesus answered him, 'Truly, truly, I say to you, unless one is born again he cannot see
the kingdom of God.'"

... to go to Heaven" Romans 10: 1–3,[30] 3:14ff.[31] No response to the invitation. Very great heartache over this cold situation as Tim, Ad[d] & I met for Prayer to-night. The Young People went to Valley View to-day.

Thursday, July 18 (Gainesville)

A fine y.p. prayer meeting of about 25 or 26 this P.M. The kids are really praying! Another disappointing crowd & no visible results to-night as I spoke on John 9—"Confessing Christ." Am wondering much why the Lord cannot send His blessing. Rec'd $13.00 from Narberth Miss. Soc.[32] to-day!

Friday, July 19 (Gainesville)

A wonderful y.p. prayer meeting 30 present for almost 1½ hrs. of continuous prayer. A fair crowd this eve. Three testimonies by Felix, Loveta, Lew [Allen][33] & then I spoke briefly on "The Love of God" & Rev. 20:11ff.[34] Five young people responded to the invitation & I had a splendid time dealing personally with them.

Saturday, July 20 (Gainesville)

Another fine time of prayer with 25 y.p. & then they went to Marietta, Okla., for a street meeting.[35] Children's Choir was splendid to-night & wonderful testimonies from the y.p. Five y.p. accepted Christ[—]Carrie

---

[30] "Brothers, my heart's desire and prayer to God for them is that they may be saved. I bear them witness that they have a zeal for God, but not according to knowledge. For, being ignorant of the righteousness that comes from God, and seeking to establish their own, they did not submit to God's righteousness."

[31] "Their mouth is full of curses and bitterness ..."

[32] Narberth Presbyterian Church of Narberth, Pennsylvania, was an early supporter of Jim's work.

[33] Lew Allen was a Gainesville student.

[34] "Then I saw a great white throne and him who was seated on it. From his presence earth and sky fled away, and no place was found for them ..."

[35] Marietta, Oklahoma, is about twenty-five miles north of Gainesville.

Lou Lindell & Willie May & Bill H**. A very wonderful blessing. Had prayer with Ad[d] & Tim 'till midnight.

Sunday, July 21[36] (Gainesville)

31 Today.[37] Many nice gifts from Gainesville people.

PRAISE THE LORD. HE USES YLC.

I preached on "God's Secrets" for over an hour this P.M. and the Lord blessed. To-night "What Shall I Do With Jesus"—25 or 30 responded to invitation among them Burr Nichols & Dave Wyatt. Really touched I believe. My offering was $295.00. We accepted invitation to stay over to-morrow.

Monday, July 22 (Gainesville)

One of the greatest days of my ministry. 47 young people met for prayer this afternoon. The deepest most searching & earnest and burdened prayer that I have ever heard. 20 forward to-night. Many adults for re-consecration. Marvelous service. Stayed with Tim & Ad[d] until 2:00 a.m.

Tuesday, July 23 (Gainesville)

[…] We got the budget raised ($375.00). We left for Dallas after supper and got home about 10:15 P.M. Got the car (dents etc.) fixed to-day.

———

The next meetings were held in Houston from July 28–August 11, in a tent set up at the intersection of Waugh and Peden streets.

One of the helpers in the Houston campaign would play a significant role in Young Life's early years. Ollie Dustin lived in Houston and had graduated three years earlier from San Jacinto High School. For the next several months after the campaign, whenever

---

[36] Jim's thirty-first birthday.

[37] This is one of the only times in all of Jim's journals he did not hyphenate the word *today*.

The campaign tent set up in Houston.

Jim travelled to Houston he would put Ollie's secretarial skills to work, dictating letters to her and having her type up reports. In November 1942 Ollie became the first woman on Young Life staff.

Thursday, August 1 (Houston)

(Spoke on J 1:12[38] & Zacchaeus)

60 High School kids out to-night—205—total attendance. Really praise the Lord for this service. Felt fine all day & got in a good bit of prayer & Bible Study. Never like I really should. Oh to be more consumed with my Lord & His Word.

Wednesday, August 7 (Houston)

Tropical storms due to strike to-night so we had to let them take down the tent: Meeting at Berachah Church. Small crowd. Good service. One girl (Martha Goldsmith) forward on invitation. (I preached "Naaman.") Supper at Murrays.

---

[38] "But to all who did receive him, who believed in his name, he gave the right to become children of God."

Thursday, August 8 (Houston)
Storm didn't arrive. Had lunch at Dustins'.[39] Call from Dallas says we must put Campaign up to 18th. Our largest crowd & 82 high school kids + over 30 from a girls school. I spoke from "John 9." Great service.

Rayburn, Sewell, and Hatch next returned to Dallas for the final Young Life Campaign of the summer, held at the corner of Carroll and Capitol in North Dallas from August 18–September 1.

Sunday, August 18
We started Dallas YLC to-day. 220 in aft & over 350 at 9:30 service. Our biggest opening day so far. People very cordial & receptive. I have not been at my best to-day—probably due to physical condition but the Lord has blessed greatly & enabled.

Monday, August 19
260 to-night. I preached on "Consider God's Word." 51 at the children's meeting.

Tuesday, August 20
105 at the children's meeting.

325 at church. I preached "Healing the Paralytic." Excellent service. The Lord seemed to specially bless.

Thursday, August 22
High school night—Spoke on J 1:12[40] and Zacchaeus—119 H.S. students—our biggest crowd to date—about 400. Really Praise the Lord for to-day. Had wonderful time of prayer both before and after the meeting.

---

[39] The Dustins lived about two miles from the Campaign site, and Ollie's mother often provided the men with meals.

[40] "But to all who did receive him, who believed in his name, he gave the right to become children of God."

Saturday, August 24

A fine Sat. night crowd. I had a severe migraine but got complete relief
with a "shot" at about 7:00 p.m. Spoke on II Kings 5:1–19.

Sunday, August 25

A good aft. crowd. I spoke on the "PRODIGAL SON." Full tent to-night
for "Neglect"—over 500. Best crowd of the summer I believe.

———

*After the exhausting summer, Jim, Maxine, and the girls travelled
to Kansas to see Jim's family. While the rest of the family stayed in
Newton, Jim went on to Chicago to report to Herb Taylor on the
summer campaigns. Then Jim and four of his friends went to Arizona for several days of relaxation. All of this travelling was done
in Jim's brand-new red Pontiac.*

Monday, September 9 (Chicago)

Called on Loveless in Wheaton—Went to Chicago. Dinner with Clyde
Dennis[41] & Bob Walker.[42] Spent the aft. talking to Bob Walker. Out to
Wheaton in Eve.

Tuesday, September 10 (Chicago)

[...] Wonderful time with Mr. Taylor this aft. Great fellow. An honor
to have him so interested in our work. Another indication of Lord's
leading. Left for home at 10:30 after Ted [Benson] & I decided to wire
Loveta [Murphy] to get ready to go to Wheaton[.][43]

---

[41] Clyde Dennis was a Chicago printer and publisher. Young Life used him
extensively in the early years to print various materials.

[42] Robert Walker was the Assistant Secretary for the Christian Workers Foundation.
As such, he was often Herb and Gloria Taylor's representative in Young Life matters.
He later became the editor of *Christian Life* magazine and served on Young Life's
board of trustees for several years.

[43] The Christian Workers Foundation had agreed to sponsor part of Loveta's tuition.

Thursday, September 12 (Amarillo, Texas)

Left Newton at 6:00 a.m. Gainesville at 12:30. Saw Loveta—Clyde—
Ate supper at Dr. Locke's. Left with Ad[d], Tim, Herschel Bennet, &
Ed Headington[44] for Grand Canyon at 7:10. We are near Amarillo by
mid-night—enjoying the trip in back seat.

Friday, September 13 (Flagstaff, Arizona)

To the Rim of the Sandia's early this a.m. & into Albu[querque] at 8:30.
[...] Meteor Crater in aft. Sunset Crater at 5:30 P.M. We all cherished it.
Got car stuck in the lava. Got out about 10:30. Camped near Flagstaff.

———

*Jim's understated journal entry, "Got car stuck in the lava," did
not record the laughter of his travelling companions. They got a
kick out of seeing the ever-confidant Jim at a loss when he got his
ten-day-old car stuck in the lava beds while showing off to them.*

*The new school year began with Jim serving as the Texas state
director of the Miracle Book Club (a non-salaried position). The
Rayburns were no longer able to live at the seminary since Jim had
graduated, so they began to look for a house of their own. Jim also
began teaching almost half the student body at DTS on "Young Life
methods."*

*Two additional significant players are introduced in these pas-
sages. John E. Mitchell, Jr., was a leading Dallas businessman,
along with his brother Orville. The Mitchell brothers had become
acquainted with Jim's work during the Dallas Young Life Campaign in August. Both men would serve as longtime Young Life
board members.*

*On Thursdays Jim took the train to Houston and spent the
day there, making contacts and getting office work done with Ol-*

---

[44] Ed Headington was a young geologist from Dallas. He and Rayburn knew each
other from Scofield Memorial Church, where both attended. He and his brother
Clare had an oil and gas exploration outfit, Headington Oil.

lie Dustin's help. Thursday afternoons after class several DTS men would drive Jim's car down to Houston (240 miles to the south), meet Jim for dinner, and spread out around the city to lead the city's Miracle Book Club chapters. After their clubs, Jim and the men would drive back to Dallas together. They would spend the several-hour drive reporting on their club meetings, discussing things they were learning about reaching non-Christian high school students, and praying. They would arrive back at the seminary in the early hours of Friday morning.

Monday, September 23

85 at Gainesville M.B.C.[45] Met Maxine & Babes at train and we came home.[46] Went to Mrs. Elmore's. They were waiting for us.[47]

Saturday, September 28

Attended a wonderful prayer meeting to-night at Torrence Graham's. About 20 present and much burden of prayer for the development of the work.

Tuesday, October 1

A <u>momentous</u> day. I spoke to the chapel on YLC and MBC. Fine response. Tomorrow's attendance at the classes will tell the tale. We moved & sure are in love with our country home.[48]

---

[45] The first club of the new school year.

[46] Maxine and the girls had been in Newton since September 5.

[47] Smith and Mary Elmore of Dallas. She was known as "Aunt Mary" by early Young Life workers. The family was active at Scofield Memorial Church. Jim was able to send anyone to their home to live and she would feed them as well.

[48] This is possibly the house they lived in at 4119 Travis Street, about three miles from the seminary.

Wednesday, October 2

Another momentous day! 65 fellows signed up for the class on "Young Life methods."[49] Praise the Lord! Cincinnati 2–Detroit 5—First game of World Series. Newsom [pitched][50]. Maxine and I shopped. The new house is swell!

Wednesday, October 9

Interviewed John E. Mitchell. He is for us & will serve on the Board—Praise the Lord! Good classes this P.M.[51]

Thursday, October 10 (Houston)

Left early for Houston. Had a fine contact at Addicks High School and the Lord gave blessing! Fine rally to-night and we made the plans for six new clubs—to start Thursday—one week from to-day. Good interview with Mr. Goldsmith.[52]

Monday, October 14 (Gainesville)

Got a contact in Valley View for MBC next week. Good meeting in Gainesville but only 65—about ½ boys. Good meeting with Dr. Locke, Richard Pyle, Dorothy Kinne** about local committee and finances. They want to raise $50.00 per mo. Coleman Luck[53] began at St. Jo—20.

---

[49] Out of the sixty-five men, over forty of them went on to lead Miracle Book Clubs for Jim during that school year.

[50] Detroit Tigers pitcher Bobo Newsom. Newsom's father had passed away the day before.

[51] Mitchell agreed to serve on the temporary board that Jim was putting together for Young Life Campaign which, at that time, was meant for the non-Miracle Book Club events that Jim was putting on, like the summer tent meetings and hotel "rooftop rallies" during the school year. The "good classes" Jim refers to are his "Young Life Methods" classes he was leading at DTS.

[52] O. T. Goldsmith. He was a Houston businessman and served on the original Young Life board of trustees.

[53] Coleman Luck led the Miracle Book Club chapter in Saint Jo, Texas, about twenty-five miles from Gainesville. At the time, he was a student at DTS. He helped Jim in the tent campaigns of the next summer (1941). After receiving his doctorate, he had a successful career teaching at Moody Bible Institute in Chicago.

Harry Jeager [*sic*, Jaeger][54]—Myra—20.

Thursday, October 17 (Houston)
Went to Houston on the a.m. Zephyr.[55] My afternoon Miracle Book Club fell through. Good start at Milby in the evening with 12. Ed[56] had 13 at San Jacinto—Tim [Hatch] 12 at Reagan. Addie 3 at Jeff Davis—Dwight[57] had 0 at Lamar.

Thursday, October 24 (Houston)
To Houston on Rocket.[58] Good trip. Prayer & study on way. Lots of correspondence turned out with "Ollie's" assistance this P.M. 12 at Milby. 18 at San Jacinto 3 at Jeff. Davis. 22 at Reagan. 0 at Lamar. Good time coming home in car.

—⁓—

*Maxine had suffered a devastating nervous breakdown in October
1937. She suffered another breakdown three years later, requiring a
three-week stay in a sanitarium.*

Tuesday, October 29
Maxine bad this a.m. so I called off the contacts of the day & came home early. Made apt with Dr. Schwenkenberg** for to-morrow.

Wednesday, October 30
Took Maxine to Schwenkenberg**. He is fine <u>but</u> very frank to say that there may be no easy or inexpensive way out for us.

---

[54] Harry J. Jaeger, Jr., was a student at DTS.

[55] The *Sam Houston Zephyr* was a train that ran daily between Dallas and Houston.

[56] Probably Ed Wichern or Ed Headington.

[57] Most likely Dwight "Dee" Small.

[58] The *Texas Rocket* was the train Jim most often took between Dallas and Houston.

Thursday, October 31 (Houston)

Picked up a mob of rough-necks to-night out in Harrisburg—some of them promised to come to Miracle Book Club next week. The Lord seemed to lead these guys.

Wednesday, November 6

Dr. Schwenkenberg** definitely decided that Maxine needs to go to the hospital.

Thursday, November 7 (Houston)

Excellent Houston trip. Elna Ann went with me. Three of the guys I picked up last week came to the meeting & seemed to be quite interested. Praise the Lord.

Saturday, November 9

Took Maxine to Hospital this a.m. Hated to leave her out there. Left for Houston at 5:00 P.M. Went out to Dustins' for the night.

Jim's weeks continued to be busy: Monday nights he led the Gainesville Miracle Book Club. He led another club in Dallas on Tuesday night. The Dallas Seminary class on Young Life Methods met on Wednesdays. Thursdays were spent in Houston. Additionally, he was holding other meetings—both for Miracle Book Club and also under the name of Young Life Campaign—in various cities around the state. Entries from the end of the year paint the picture.

Thursday, November 21 (Houston)

Went to Houston in car with fellows. Dictated to Olive all afternoon. 16 at my group to-night. Good time. We got home at 3:00 a.m. Fine trip.

Monday, December 2

Only 40 at Gainesville M.B.C. Very disappointed! Must pray more about this.

Tuesday, December 3

Started the group at Mr. Mitchell's to-night.[59] Fine time. Excellent prospects. 8 fellows and 3 girls present.

Wednesday, December 4

Good classes at Sem[inary] to-day!

Thursday, December 5 (Nacogdoches, Texas)

Swell Chapel program at S.F. Austin Teachers [College] at Nacogdoches. Maxine and E.A. [Elna Ann] went along. Fine college meeting at night.

Friday, December 6 (Ft. Worth)

Wonderful Y.L. Rally to-night at Ft. Worth. 350 present. Great meeting![60]

Saturday, December 7

Good Y.L.F. [Young Life Fellowship] at the "Y" this evening. 31 Present. Fine Spirit.

Sunday, December 8

A bad day. All family feeling bad and Maxine apparently doing no good nervously. But we had a wonderful time of prayer to-gether about it to-night. Believe the Lord, & He <u>alone</u>, can solve our problems.

Monday, December 9

The Best Day for Months. The Lord has answered our prayer & Maxine is a different person. Gainesville M.B.C. 96! Spoke on "The Ark"—The

---

[59] John E. Mitchell and his two brothers owned a twelve-acre block that contained their houses, as well as a small building they had built for Boy Scout meetings, which is where this club, known as "Old Club 37," met. The designation as Club 37 probably came because it was the thirty-seventh Miracle Book Club chapter under Jim's supervision. And after all, who would want to go to Old Club Number One?

[60] Held at the Texas Hotel in Ft. Worth (now the Hilton Fort Worth), this was the first of several "rooftop rallies" that Jim would hold in cities around Texas.

kids really testified & PRAYED! Praise the LORD. It's All of Him. All the fellows had great work.

Tuesday, December 10

Fine day at the office. 15 at Mitchell's for M.B.C. Spoke on "Gravity"— "Circle of earth,"[61] Ecclesiastes 1:7.[62] And briefly on "The Reason for Gospel." Something wrong with us that we can't cure. Bible starts there so does Gospel. Jesus Christ Answer.

Wednesday, December 11

Another good day & very busy at the office.

Thursday, December 12 (Houston)

Rather poor & ineffective day at Houston.

—⁓—

At this point in time, Jim's relationship with the Miracle Book Club was becoming strained. Increasingly, Jim was wanting to branch out on his own. However, when the split did come a few months later, Jim claimed that he had not been thinking of breaking away from the Miracle Book Club.

Nonetheless, he was doing more and more under the name of Young Life Campaign, including holding rallies in cities around Texas. To raise support for those efforts and his MBC activities, Ted Benson encouraged him to form a board of trustees.

The year ended on a positive note.

Tuesday, December 24

A RED LETTER DAY in my life, and SURELY IN THE DEVELOPMENT

---

[61] An allusion to Isaiah 40:22.

[62] "All streams run to the sea,
    but the sea is not full;
to the place where the streams flow,
    there they flow again."

of Young Life Campaign—Organized Board—Mr. John E. Mitchell, Chrmn of Board—Ted Benson, Sec.-Treas., Dr. Chafer. Wonderful spirit. Mr. Mitchell gave check for $200.00 for the work. It is a great— marvelous blessing—the money, Yes—but this man's confidence in the work is the greatest gift of grace in it.

Wednesday, December 25

A delightful day at home. The kiddies were lovely and had a grand Christmas—it will always remain a memorable day. Our blessed Lord has been very good to us. How little of any of these, His blessings, we could ever deserve.

1941

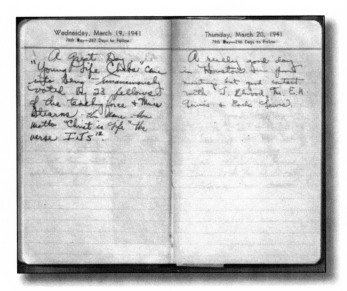

TWO IMPORTANT ENTRIES FROM JIM'S 1941 JOURNAL. *The first, March 19, records the vote by Jim's club leaders at Dallas Theological Seminary to break away from the Miracle Book Club. The second, October 11, reflects the official legal beginning of Young Life. The incorporation papers were filed five days later.*

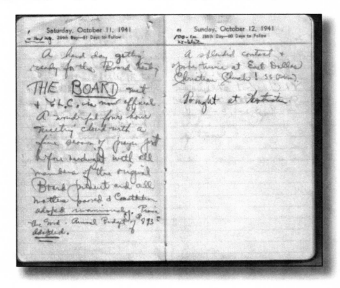

The new year began with Jim conducting a Young Life Campaign in Louisiana. As his work in other areas progressed, Jim had less time to spend on the Gainesville club and it suffered.

Wednesday, January 1 (Winnfield, Louisiana)

Winnfield, LA.

A rowdy New Year's Watch Party at Brother Mac's house—

Then, about 1:30 a.m. I was enabled to begin the day and the New Year with a very precious time of fellowship with the Lord for over an hour, seeking His Will for my life for the year to come. He was very near to-night and it was a rich experience which I know He will use through the year. How I do want this to be the year when He shall have COM-PLETE CHARGE OF ME and mine.

For the third straight night the crowd at YLC was a disappointing one of about 100. Three [came] forward, all said they were Christians.

Saturday, January 4 (Winnfield, Louisiana)

The migraine came on full blast (R) and was very severe all night. Relief by 9:00 a.m. [...]

I was very well satisfied with the response from the message on Propitiation,[1] Reconciliation, Redemption, "The Three Effects of God's Salvation"—The intelligent young people, & Judge Moss spoke very highly of it.

Tuesday, January 7

[...]

Had a wonderful meeting of the Mitchell M.B.C. at Landrums' to-night (Mr. Mitchell was sick). 10 boys & 6 girls. A couple fine new fellows that seemed interested. The Lord led as I spoke to them on "The Three Divisions of the Bible" or "Outline of the Whole Bible"[:] I Para-

---

[1] Propitiation is the biblical concept that God's wrath must be appeased and that Christ's death has provided complete atonement for our sins and fully satisfied God's wrath. It was a favorite theme of Rayburn's over the years.

dise Lost. II Prog. of Redempt. III Paradise Regained.

Thursday, January 9 (Houston)

Left for Houston on the Rocket. Arrived just a little late and went to Dustins' for lunch. This was one of the very best of days. The Chapters —8 in aft. and 13 at night were fine and the Lord really blessed. It looks like we could really "Go"** from here.

Used general presentation of John 1–21 and 20:31.[2] "The Seven Signs."

Beside all this, Ollie got out 8 or 10 very important letters, for which I praise the Lord. We got home at 3:00 a.m. Uneventful trip. The Lord wonderfully enables.

———

Though well-meaning, Evelyn McClusky and her Miracle Book Club methods were at odds with the way Jim and his crew ran their meetings. Characterized by Ted Benson as being all "lilies and lace," the materials and programs suggested by Miracle Book Club were seen by the men as effeminate and ineffective for reaching non-Christian high school students.

Tuesday, January 14

Had lots of time in the office so got lots of letters out and other good done. Wrote a long letter to Mrs. McClusky. The problem of our relationship to MBC is an acute one—I must be more & more in prayer about it. Only the Lord's will matters. We must know & that right soon.

I had a fine meeting at Mitchells' to-night although only 13 present. I spoke on the Threefold outline of the Scriptures and ended with an introduction to the Gospel of John using John 20:31.

---

[2] "But these are written so that you may believe that Jesus is the Christ, the Son of God, and that by believing you may have life in his name."

Frances and Orville Mitchell with their sons Orville, Jr., and Bob, in 1941. Orville and his brother John were longtime board members and Bob went on to become Young Life's Executive Director from 1977–1986.

Wednesday, January 15

A swell day at the office with most of the time for prayer and Bible reading & study and the evening at home. I need more days like this one. How I do praise the Lord for that swell office.[3]

Monday, January 27 (Gainesville)

The Gainesville work was particularly hard. I do not know the answer—but I know the Lord does—to this problem of the coldness and the deadness of the chapter meetings. Oh for a greater burden for these kids and a deeper Spirit of prayer.—

42 present. Ought to be 100. There are lots to blame but I'm the <u>main one</u>!

---

[3] With the help of the Mitchell brothers, Maxine had set up an office for Jim at DTS.

Tuesday, January 28

Just talked a lot at the office to-day and didn't get too much done, but to-night was <u>real</u>! Had 20 y.p. at Mitchells'. 11 boys & 9 girls and a very promising crowd they are. They gave RAPT attention and several <u>fine</u> new kids were MOST complimentary after it was over. The Lord truly blessed me in a marvelous way to-night in giving out His Word. Oh how I long to be able to present it "winsomely,"[+] and in such a way that the Holy Spirit can save souls. There were lost ones there to-night.

John [Mitchell] and I had a precious time of fellowship and prayer after the meeting for an hour. I thank God for this fellow!

―――

By February, the showdown was set between Miracle Book Club and Young Life Campaign. On one side were Mrs. McClusky and her MBC hostesses (the women in whose homes the chapters met), and on the other side were Jim and the DTS men who led the chapters.

At Rayburn's invitation, Mrs. McClusky came to Dallas in late February. He timed her visit to coincide with the next Young Life Campaign "Rooftop Rally" (or "Mass Meeting"), this one to be held in Dallas at the prestigious Baker Hotel. He wanted Mrs. McClusky to see the effectiveness of his new, non-MBC-style ministry. Rayburn no doubt knew the meeting would be a hit, but the record attendance of 2,000 surprised even him and gave him the proof he needed to prove his "Young Life methods" were paying off. Helping in the rally as a pianist was Jim's younger brother, Bob.

[+] This is the only time Jim uses the word "winsomely" or "winsome" in his journals, but the need for Christians to attractively represent the truth of the Christian faith to non-believers was quickly becoming one of his favorite soapboxes. Jim felt strongly that Jesus was winsome, so His followers should be, as well. He told a Christian audience in 1954, "I think all of us agree that the main reason why the Church is here is to represent the Lord Jesus Christ. The big effort with which we need to be concerned today ... is to be sure that young people understand the issues involved in the Christian faith and, especially, that they have an opportunity to become attracted to our winsome and wonderful Savior."

Monday, February 24

[…]

This is the RED LETTER DAY! Attendance at the Young Life MASS MEETING at the Baker Hotel was 2000, & some crowded out. Program SUPERB. BOB, MAURIE D AND REG Gerig really hit! Several y.p. SAVED and many decisions—GREAT SPIRIT—especially among the men of the school.[5]

Tuesday, February 25

All day with Mrs. McClusky. Very uncomfortable deal trying to get out from under the load of this M.B.C. mess. Have apparently had good fellowship with her in this matter.

Bob is enjoying** his stay here. We had Jack & Mary Mitchell[6] for dinner. Very fine fellowship.

Wednesday, February 26

Migraine to-night. Relieved by "shot," at 10:30 P.M.

Really a terrible experience this evening trying to get the hostesses to see the necessity for leaving MBC. Never got in such a hard place. Don't believe we are getting to first base with these women.

Took Bob to the train at 10:00 P.M. and rejoice and praise the Lord for the wonderful way that God touched his heart about the school, Jack, the fellows, etc.[7]

Answered prayer here.

---

[5] Here he is referring to the Dallas Seminary students who were helping out.

[6] Dr. John Greenwood Mitchell (1893–1990). "Dr. Jack" was a visiting professor at DTS and a much-beloved Bible teacher. Jim had him speak several times to early staff conferences. He founded Multnomah School of the Bible in Portland, Oregon.

[7] Jim's younger brother, Robert Gibson Rayburn (1915–1990), was the academician of the Rayburn family, later founding and serving as the first president of both Covenant College and Covenant Seminary. This entry implies that he had problems with DTS, however the journals do not shed light on what they were. Bob Rayburn did eventually receive his Doctorate of Theology from DTS in 1944.

The Miracle Book Club logo, ca. 1941.

Thursday, February 27 (Houston)

Very hard time doing any good with two little handfuls at my Houston Classes this week.[8] Too weary to do well. Feel rather sick.

Slept on floor of car all the way home.

Friday, February 28

Met with "Coc**" this a.m. about the y.p. work. Found out more about Madam McC's treachery in dealing with these women.

Fine meeting with the fellows (teachers) this p.m.

Maxine and I called on Millets to-night and fully explained all this thing. The Lord was very good in leading us to this.[9]

Praise to Him!

The month of March was a time of ups and downs as Jim made the break from Miracle Book Club official and then dealt with both the promise and the fallout of his decision.

Saturday, March 1

A difficult day.

Called on Dr. Chafer—he, in turn, called a meeting of our Board

---

[8] "Classes" here refers to his Miracle Book Club chapters. Leaders were known as "teachers." "Two little handfuls" probably refers to Ann (age 3½) and Sue (11 months). Jim often took one or both of them with him on short trips due to Maxine's health problems.

[9] The Millets were supporting Jim and Maxine financially.

with Jo S——and Paul B——& to-night we met & tried to fix things with them for the hostesses. Very little success.

Fine spirit with Dr. L.S. [Chafer] and John E.M[itchell]. Talked for a long time with Dr. L.S. Chafer about the school. Very precious fellowship. It is the Lord that brings this all to pass.

Thursday, March 6 (Houston)

Definitely "down" this night. Heavy rainstorms washed out my afternoon class & only 11 at the night Milby group. Y.P. seem to be going rapidly nowhere for the Lord. (That is probably because I am not really ministering in the fullness of the Spirit myself lately). Oh that I could just LET God work out His life in me. Problems seem to drive me away from the Lord instead of to-ward Him.

Elna Ann went with me and we got home at 3:00 a.m.

Had some real victory to-day in spite of being sort of "down in the dumps" to-night.

Tuesday, March 11

Great meeting at Mitchells' to-night 40 y.p. More boys than girls! This is the greatest crowd to talk to that I have ever had. Perfect attention! Oh to get out of the way so that the Holy Spirit can <u>do a job</u> on these kids. His <u>own way</u>!

Friday, March 14

About the worst day of my life—since I've been in the Lord's work.

A letter from Maury Jacques[10] just about floored me. All misunderstanding and false accusation. Oh to get away from all this. Came home & the Lord led me straight to II Cor. 4. Wonderful! Oh to get my eyes on Him.

---

[10] Maurice "Maury" Jacques was the national head of the Miracle Book Club. Jacques had written an angry letter to Jim about the split. He later apologized to Rayburn for writing it.

Saturday, March 15

Fine meeting of y.p. fellowship to-night. The Lord gave me liberty in speaking from II Cor. 4. Feel much better than ever before about the mix-up over McCluskyism.

Sunday, March 16

A grand day with some real prayer and a chance to hear R. G. Le-Tourneau[11] to-night at Scofield [Memorial Church].

Have had great blessing from the Lord and His Word in regard to the MBC mess!

Wednesday, March 19

A Great Day. "Young Life Clubs" came into being—unanimously voted by 23 fellows of the teaching force & Miner Stearns[12]—the name—the motto "Christ is Life"[—]the verse 1 J 5:12.[13]

Saturday, March 22

A very full day climaxed by a mess of the meeting with S—— & the hostesses that just left me worn out and sick. There is NO USE ever trying to get along with that outfit. Praise the Lord for at least keeping us sweet!

---

[11] Robert Gilmore LeTourneau (1888–1969). LeTourneau was a Christian industrialist and philanthropist from Longview, Texas. He is considered to be the father of the earthmoving business, and his company produced most of the earthmoving equipment used by the American forces in World War II. LeTourneau and his wife Evelyn were strong Christians, even providing chapel services at their factories.

[12] Miner B. Stearns was not a member of the "teaching force" for Miracle Book Club but was a former DTS student who happened to attend the meeting. Interestingly, the meeting was held in the basement of Stearns Hall, then the Men's dormitory, named in honor of Dr. Stearns.

[13] "He that hath the Son hath life; and he that hath not the Son of God hath not life" (KJV). Young Life's letterhead for the first few years bore the slogan "He that hath the Son hath Life."

Less than a month later the first "Young Life Conference" was held—a weekend trip to Bachman Lake in Dallas (bordering on Love Field). Over two hundred high school students from around the state attended.

Friday, April 18

Young Life Conference!—Bachman Dam.

Conference got off to a fine start to-night with 230 registered delegates and a marvelous time. Largest delegations are from [Murray] Smoot's[14] & Wally's groups in Dallas, Orv's [Orville Shick's][15] in Ft. Worth, Ad[d]'s from Terrell, Dee Small[16] from Addicks, Alf Dodds'[17] from Garland.

I felt bum all day and didn't even go around the camp until 5:00 P.M. but the fellows—specially Grant Whipple[18] & Ralph Hetrick[19] really have worked & everything is ready to go. Invaluable assistance from Mr. and Mrs. E. C. Landrum.

Saturday, April 19

Young Life Conference!!

It would be impossible to really describe this day. My heart com-

---

[14] John Murray Smoot (1917–2006). Smoot graduated from DTS in 1944 and served on the staff of Young Life in the early 1940s before beginning a long and distinguished career as a Presbyterian pastor in his native Baltimore.

[15] Orville Shick helped with the tent campaign of 1941, however his involvement in Young Life was limited to his time at Dallas Seminary.

[16] Dwight "Dee" Small's involvement with Young Life was limited to the early 1940s.

[17] Alfred "Alf" Dodds received his ThM from Dallas in 1943. His involvement with Young Life was limited to his time at the seminary.

[18] Otis Grant Whipple, Jr. (1911–2003). Whipple was in his last semester at DTS. The son of missionaries to China, Whipple moved to Bellingham, Washington, after seminary, where he was on Young Life staff and helped his father run The Firs, a Christian camp. Both father and son served for a time on the Young Life board of trustees.

[19] Ralph Myron Hetrick graduated from DTS in 1942. He then worked with Young Life for a short time in the Pacific Northwest before becoming a pastor.

pletely overflows with gratitude & praise to God for His Faithfulness in the face of my own unbelief & for what HE has wrought in the hearts of these dear young people. The fagot service was unbelievably glorious.[20] Surely well over 100 testimonies without the least bit of persuasion. Many y.p. (perhaps 15 or 20) really professed openly faith in Christ as Savior for the first time. Great spirit among leaders and y.p. as well. The HOLY SPIRIT is here in power! Feel better than for months spiritually, physically and all. II Tim 2:13.[21]

Sunday, April 20
Young Life Conference!!!

The Conference reached a glorious climax and all of our hearts have been stirred to the depths by this new experience of His Grace & Power & Love. Many y.p. really born again, I believe & such real stirring of heart among the young people. Wonderful fellowship & cooperation among the leaders—seminary fellows and all. Dr. EDMUND [sic, Edman] was great![22]

Had a swell time of prayer to-night after everyone was in bed. The Lord has been GOOD ...

—⁓—

Jim had a surgical procedure on a hernia a few days later. While he recovered at home he had a chance to slow down and reflect.

Thursday, April 24
Operated on at 8:00 a.m. Done at 10:00. Watched much of it thru reflector.

[...]

---

[20] "Fagot" services were common in Christian camping circles in those days. Campers threw a stick or bundle of sticks (a fagot) into a fire as they testified about what the Lord had done in their lives.

[21] "If we are faithless, he remains faithful—for he cannot deny himself."

[22] V. Raymond Edman (1900–1967). He was the newly-appointed president of Wheaton College and was the speaker for the Young Life Conference.

Flyer for the 1941 Houston Young Life Campaign. L–R: Jim Rayburn,
Coleman Luck, and Orville Shick.

Thursday, May 1

To-day I got to come home from the hospital and it was a joyous occasion. I am very comfortably situated in the little back room at home.

To-day also marks the beginning of our <u>second</u> year of just looking to the Lord to provide our material needs.[23] It is amazing to find that in the first year of "no salary" living our income <u>by His Faithfulness</u> has been IIIOIIX. III III.[24] I can't believe it—in view of my own failures in

---

[23] Miracle Book Club had not provided Jim with a salary, and Young Life was only just beginning. Since Jim's graduation from seminary, he and Maxine had been living by faith. Jim kept a careful record of cash donations they had received in the back of his journal.

[24] $3,080.33. Jim carefully notated each personal gift he received during the previous twelve months in the backs of the 1940 and 1941 journals. These ranged from collections taken up at Miracle Book Club chapters ("Wally's Chap. 7 38¢") to offerings from the Young Life Campaigns in the summers ("Gainesville offering $285.50"). Most common, though, were the dozens of small gifts from individuals

prayer & service. It is ALL our blessed Lord!

—∾—

Monday, May 12

I rose at 4:50 this a.m. and spent from then until 6:00 a.m. in prayer & the Word. It was a very wonderful experience to me because I had asked the Lord to bring this to pass in my life if He would have me to observe the morning time. Oh how I long to go on with Him—100%— gaining strength, grace, and wisdom for whatever each day may bring in the stillness of His Presence before the day begins. Only by His enabling grace will I ever do it! In myself I am the world's biggest FLOP.

I have been out more to-day—feel much stronger.

I am reveling in "Borden of Yale"—What a life![25]

The babies are SO SWEET.

[...]

—∾—

Thursday, May 22 (Houston)

I arose at 5:15 and had a half hour of prayer. I am very grateful to God for enabling me to begin my day with early morning prayer now for 11 consecutive days. That is the kind of thing I do not do—in myself.

The Rally in Houston to-night was very enthusiastic and encouraging & seemed clearly to indicate that we should go ahead with the Campaign—so, it is dated for June 8–22. I praise the Lord for the enthu-

---

("Mrs. Cox $2.00"). Together, all these gifts equal Jim's income for the last twelve months: $3,080.33. In 1941, this was not a bad income—the average yearly salary in 1940 was around $1,300.

[25] *Borden of Yale '09* was written by Mrs. Howard Taylor. William Whiting Borden (1887–1913) was the heir to the Borden dairy fortune. Rather than pursuing further monetary riches he decided to become a missionary. He died at the age of twenty-five in Egypt, preparing to serve as a missionary to Muslims. In his Bible he had written three phrases which described his uncompromising view of living for Christ: "No reserves. No retreats. No regrets."

siasm of the adults, [O. T.] Goldsmith, [George] Simpson,[26] [Leonard] DeFriend, Fordyce, Evans.

On my Dallas sleeper—ready for a time of prayer & bed at 11:15.

Friday, May 23 (train to Chicago)

A very busy day getting ready to leave. Worked with Wally all aft. on the Y.L.C. folder.

Elna Ann going with me. She went right to sleep as soon as we got in our upper berth. Was too weary to have much prayer to-night. Oh that I might never have days "too busy" to pray.

———

From June 8–22 the second annual Young Life Campaign in Houston was held. Jim's entries give a good idea of the flavor of these meetings as well as his messages. Young Life was very much in an experimental phase at this early stage. Many things were tried under the banner of Young Life—children's meetings, evangelistic campaigns, tract distribution, radio broadcasts, sound trucks, and street meetings. They tried everything and rejected much.

Monday, June 9 (Houston)

136 tonight.

[...]

The evening service was one of unusual blessing—The Lord is certainly blessing these first few services.

I spoke to-night on "A Vital Quality—Missing."[27] Romans 9:3,[28]

---

[26] George E. Simpson was a Houston real estate agent. He served on the original Young Life board of trustees.

[27] He spoke on this topic numerous times over the next several months. Based on the verses cited, it appears that the vital quality that Jim found missing was concern for and identification with the non-believer. It would be a sentiment he sounded for decades.

[28] "For I could wish that I myself were accursed and cut off from Christ for the sake of my brothers, my kinsmen according to the flesh."

10:1,[29] Exodus 32:32.[30]

—⁓—

Wednesday, June 18 (Houston)

175—70 h[igh] s[chool]

Good evening service. I did my best preaching, I believe, on Rom. 4:3.[31]
Intro: Something <u>wrong</u> with us—that we can't DO anything about—
(as we studied last night). God has a treatment for our problem—for
all who "<u>Believe</u>." End: Abraham—Isaac—Gen 22. Example of what it
means to believe God. Just take him at His word—without understanding or knowing "how" & "why"—etc.

[...]

Friday, June 20 (Houston)

Nurses—100.

Evening—150.

Spoke at Memorial Hospital Nurse's home at 6:30 a.m. on II
C[orinthians] 5:9.[32]

Very weary to-day & did not get much done. It was beastly hot but
rained and that helped a lot.

I preached to-night on The Meaning of the Death of Christ—

1. A Penal Death.	Rom 5:12–[33]
2. A Substitutionary [Death].	II Cor 5:——
3. A reconciling [Death].	1 Pet. 2:——

---

[29] "Brothers, my heart's desire and prayer to God for them is that they may be saved."

[30] "But now, if you will forgive their sin—but if not, please blot me out of your book
that you have written."

[31] "For what does the Scripture say? 'Abraham believed God, and it was counted to
him as righteousness.'"

[32] "So whether we are at home or away, we make it our aim to please him."

[33] "Therefore, just as sin came into the world through one man, and death through
sin, and so death spread to all men because all sinned."

I believe this is a very fine message with a world of possibilities, but I really need some attractive illustrations & more vivid & punchy stuff!

Sunday, June 22 (Houston)

120

200

"God's Secrets" was very well received this P.M. and I believe wonderfully effective. I praise God for this.

To-night I spoke to a fine crowd on "Unbelief—The Most Terrible Crime of the Age,"—Using John 3:17, 18, 36[34] and II Cor 5:19[35] ("Not imp[uting] trespasses.") It seems an effective presentation of plain Gospel. Needs more organization and illustration.

[...]

———

The next campaign that summer was in the seaside city of Galveston, Texas. Hitchcock is a town near Galveston where early staff man George Cowan had developed some work.

Sunday, June 29 (Galveston)

Y.P.S.S. [Young People's Sunday School]—35

Aft.—40

EVE—175.

A very good evening crowd—I spoke on "The Sin of Being Satisfied" Luke 18:12ff.[36] Did not have the liberty I should have had. We are bogged

---

[34] "'For God did not send his Son into the world to condemn the world, but in order that the world might be saved through him. Whoever believes in him is not condemned, but whoever does not believe is condemned already, because he has not believed in the name of the only Son of God' ... Whoever believes in the Son has eternal life; whoever does not obey the Son shall not see life, but the wrath of God remains on him.'"

[35] "To wit, that God was in Christ, reconciling the world unto himself, not imputing their trespasses unto them; and hath committed unto us the word of reconciliation" (KJV).

[36] "[The pharisee prayed] 'I fast twice a week; I give tithes of all that I get.' ..."

down here. Should be more zest and punch in anything we do for the Lord Jesus. I pray that He will overrule my own sorry tendencies and do a job in my heart.

Thursday, July 3 (Galveston)

32—Hitch[cock]

115—Eve

Began this day with George [Cowan], Coleman [Luck], Orville [Shick] & I in prayer at tent. Burdened about our own failure & the lack of power in the meeting.

And How God Worked! More professions of faith at Hitchcock this a.m. Then to-night—I spoke on "Justification"—"being justified freely by His Grace." 6 young men–responded to the invitation. One of our greatest services. All big fellows—5 Accepting the Lord—Had wonderful time of prayer with them—Then big "successful" street meeting & prayer meeting at the tent until nearly midnight.

Friday, July 4 (Galveston)

110 EVE   Hitch[cock] 25

Spoke on "Propitiation" to-night. Rom. 3[37] & 1 J 2:1.[38]

A full day. Child. meeting, Hitchcock—then sound truck all aft, tract distr[ibution], evening service, big street meeting & about 35 for a fine prayer meeting until nearly midnight.

Many Dallas y.p. giving their "4th" [of July] vacation to these services.

———

The summer saw additional tent campaigns in Dallas and a few

---

[37] Most likely Romans 3:25: "Whom God put forward as a propitiation by his blood, to be received by faith. This was to show God's righteousness, because in his divine forbearance he had passed over former sins."

[38] "My little children, I am writing these things to you so that you may not sin. But if anyone does sin, we have an advocate with the Father, Jesus Christ the righteous." Verse two continues, "He is the propitiation for our sins, and not for ours only but also for the sins of the whole world."

other Texas cities. Other than a series of meetings in Teague, Texas,
in 1942, these would be the last of the tent meetings. Increasingly,
the idea of week-long "Young Life Conferences" (the forerunners of
Young Life camps) became more of an emphasis.

As the new school year began, Jim continued with the same
schedule he had the year before: the Gainesville club on Monday
night, Old Club 37 at the Mitchells' in Dallas on Tuesday night,
and the Houston clubs on Thursday.

He was also laying the groundwork to lead a new club at the
Masonic Home in Ft. Worth, as well as laying the legal ground-
work for Young Life's incorporation.

Thursday, October 9
Getting ready for the "BOARD" meeting.

Had wonderful day of real prayer & Bible reading. Greatly
refreshed.

Friday, October 10 (Ft. Worth)
A marvelous evening at Ft. Worth with the "Masons." They beat N. Side
26–0 but the marvelous part was the contact the Lord enabled me to
have with those boys. I am going to PRAY now for those kids—that I
may be USED of Him in there![39]

Saturday, October 11
400 This wk.
10 Board Mtg.
A hard day getting ready for the Board meeting.

THE BOARD met & Y.L.C. is now official. A wonderful four hour

---

[39] The Masonic Home's football team was known as the Mighty Mites. Though the
school was tiny and the players were outweighed by their opponents by at least thirty
pounds a man, they had become a force in Texas high school football and had a
statewide and even national following. They would outscore their opponents 244–32
this season (often with Rayburn in attendance), but miss the state playoffs due to a
technicality. Their story is told in the book *Twelve Mighty Orphans* by Jim Dent.

meeting closed with a fine season of prayer just before midnight with all members of the original Board present and all matters passed & Constitution adop[t]ed unanimously. Praise the Lord. Annual [*sic*, Monthly] Budget of $893.00 Adopted.

On October 16, the incorporation papers for The Young Life Campaign were officially filed with the State of Texas. The full-time staff was comprised of Jim (overseeing the work in Dallas and serving as field director), Wally Howard (West Texas), Add Sewell (East Texas), and Gordon Whitelock (South Texas). George Cowan was part-time in the Galveston area. There were thirty-two clubs that fall, all in Texas; most, if not all, former MBC chapters.

On October 24 Jim left for a thirty-nine day trip to Minnesota, Illinois, and Pennsylvania to promote Young Life. He would spend much of the rest of his life on the road continuing that task.

Just before Jim left, he performed the wedding ceremony of Add Sewell and Loveta Murphy, one of the first converts in Jim's Gainesville club.

Monday, October 20 (Gainesville)

G.Y.L.C. [Gainesville Young Life Campaign] 26.
A fine spirit in the meeting & in election of officers. Betty Jean Brooks elected President.

Everything in the Lord's work in Gainesville is very dead. Oh for a real revival!

Married Ad[d] & Loveta.[40]

---

[40] This was added later, as it is written at the bottom of the page and in pencil.

Saturday, November 1 (Hinckley, Minnesota)

Audiences this wk 1360. No. of Mtgs 17[41]

[...]

This has been a fine restful day. I got up early & have read 26 Psalms besides having lots of time for prayer and other things!

Word from Ted indicates that the Campaign made its first month's expenses! The glory & thanks all belongs to the Lord. It seems almost unbelievable, but "he is able to do exceedingly abundantly ABOVE. ..."[42]

Monday, November 17 (Chester, Pennsylvania)

P.M.** [prayer meeting?]—4 Evening—75.

I got wonderful rest this morning—sleeping until 10:30 in real restful sleep for a change. Wrote letters & studied & prayed and visited with Dwight Pentecost.[43]

This evening I spoke with real blessing of God upon myself & manifest among the hearers on "Life's Greatest Opportunity," Luke 18:35–42. Only a small crowd but much good accomplished by the Holy Spirit, I believe.

I have a deep and abiding feeling of His Presence & sense of real yieldedness to Him. This dates from a special experience of surrender & dedication to Him which I experienced Saturday night here in my room.

---

[41] For years Jim kept track of the attendance figures of the meetings he addressed and often summed them up at the end of the week.

[42] Ephesians 3:20: "Now unto him that is able to do exceeding abundantly above all that we ask or think, according to the power that worketh in us" (KJV).

[43] John Dwight Pentecost (1915–). Pentecost had graduated from Dallas a few months earlier and was serving his first pastorate when Jim visited him in Pennsylvania. Pentecost went on to a distinguished teaching and writing career at DTS. He and his wife were some of the first homeowners at Young Life's Trail West Village.

Thursday, November 20 (Chester, Pennsylvania)
[...]

This is my new Easterbrook Pen writing. I got it to-day for $1.00 and it is a smooth-writing honey.

———

Monday, December 1 (on the train)

Migraine—shot.

Slept until 10:00 a. m. on Pennsy "Golden Arrow."[44]

About noon developed a migraine which became very severe and was almost unbearable by the time I got to Strombecks'.[45] Took a "shot" right away and after getting very sick and vomiting I felt fine.

Had a good visit and left for home at 12:20. Went right to bed.

Tuesday, December 2 (on the train)
A fine trip all day on the train. Very comfortable. I had a rich time of Bible Study this afternoon—all afternoon.

I got to Bowie [Texas] on time & Maxine & the girlies met me. We had a swell time going back to Dallas.

Had a fine meeting of the Mitchell Club.

———

Jim did not often record historical events of the day in his journal. The start of World War II, however, is an exception. All three of Jim's brothers would serve in the military during the war, as would almost all of the young men in the first Young Life clubs.

---

[44] A train run by the Pennsylvania Railroad.

[45] J. Fred Strombeck (1881–1959). He was the president of Strombeck-Becker Manufacturing Company in Moline, Illinois. Strombeck, H. J. Taylor, and the Mitchell brothers were the most significant early backers of Young Life. Like the others, he would serve on Young Life's board for years. In fact, his death in 1959 was on his way home from a board meeting. Ted Benson introduced Jim to both Strombeck and Taylor.

Sunday, December 7

[...]

Went to Clyde's church to-night!

Japan attacks Hawaii! America now at war.

Monday, December 8 (Gainesville)

Maxine and the babes went to Gainesville with me. We had a fine time. Dinner at Bob's.[46]

The best meeting in a long, long time. 30 present.

Pres. Roosevelt asks Congress for Decl. of War. It is unanimous in Senate and only one woman pacifist dissenting in House.[47]

Sunday, December 14 (Ft. Worth)

230.

A wonderful time at Masonic Home this a.m. I spoke on "The Christian View of War" emphasizing a relationship with Christ as the ONLY way to please God—not dying for our country.

[...]

---

[46] While he attended DTS, Jim's brother Bob served as pastor of First Presbyterian Church in Gainesville, taking over after Clyde Kennedy left. (Kennedy began pastoring a church in the Dallas area.)

[47] The dissenting vote was from Montana Republican Jeannette Rankin, a lifelong pacifist.

1942

7300

Wednesday, April 15, 1942

105th Day—260 Days to Follow

Here I go again with a record of as happy a day as I have ever known. As I board the plane for Phoenix all I can think of is: "How wonderful is my Savior." I do not know how God could ever have used me as He has lately — especially to right with Persons gang of out & out Christian fellows and girls. (Ps. 71:16). Riding along in the plane to send my dear Maxine and Julia & home I feel that there couldn't be any fellow as happy as I am. And it is ALL from the Lord. Not a thing that has happened to make me happy could have been of myself. Persons and Rabbie and all the fellows was just right.

"… A RECORD OF AS HAPPY A DAY AS I HAVE EVER KNOWN."
Rayburn was winding up a very successful three-week speaking trip to the West and now had only one more stop before arriving back home in Dallas.

As the new year began, Jim resigned from the leadership of the Gainesville club, knowing that his increasing travel load would not allow him to lead more than three clubs a week (he was still leading clubs in Dallas, Houston, and Ft. Worth).

Several entries in early 1942 reflect a world very different from twenty-first century America. Doctors still made house calls, there were no computers to help with office work—all letters had to be written by hand, typewriter, or mimeograph machine—and most travel was by train. In addition, the nation's involvement in World War II was increasing by the day.

Friday, January 2
[...]

Ann & I arrived in Dallas at 7:00.[1]

I spent most of the day at the office and had a fine time of prayer & Bible study to-day. I am resolved that these matters are going to take precedence over everything this year & that no matter how busy the day I will not be TOO BUSY to PRAY & STUDY my Bible! I do pray that the Lord will specially enable me in this.

Gladys[2] left for Arizona to-day.

MANILA FELL TO THE JAPS.

I studied Galatians to-day.

—⁓—

[1] Jim and his daughter had been in Houston for a New Year's Eve "watch night service." In a letter he described the meeting: "We had a three-hour meeting climaxed by a time of testimony during which the young people spoke of the Lord's blessing in their own lives during the past year."

[2] Gladys Roche. She had been involved in Jim's early camping ministry in 1935 when she was a high school student in Coolidge, Arizona. She helped Jim in subsequent summers when he ran his "Mountain Top Conferences" in her home state. At the time of this entry she had graduated from Wheaton and was working in the Dallas headquarters of Young Life as a part-time secretary. In April 1943 she married Ed Phillips.

Saturday, January 24

Finished reading the Weymouth New Testament[3] since the first of the month. Had greatest blessing of any similar period of Bible reading & study.

Sunday, January 25

Maxine not well so we had a kind of hard day along with Ann being sick too.

Monday, January 26

Ann quite sick. We had to have the Dr. Maxine also feeling bad so the work at the office has had to be put off.

Tuesday, January 27

Maxine sick in bed. Had the Dr. for her. Took care of things around home most of day.

Monday, February 7

4th Migraine (R) "Shot"—compl. relief

One of the busiest days I ever had: Got out 850 letters to mailing list and 50 personal letters to various leaders. Really do not know how to tackle this stupendous job.

Took 'shot' after I got done at the office to-nite. Head never got real bad.

Monday, February 9 (Tyler, Texas)

Left on T & P[4] for Wills Point [Texas] this a.m. We are on the "daylight saving time" to-day so the train was an hour late.

A great day in Tyler with 50 kids in a fine** meeting to-night. A par-

---

[3] *The New Testament in Modern Speech* by Richard Francis Weymouth, originally published in 1903, although later editions had appeared by 1942.

[4] Texas & Pacific Railroad.

ticularly fine group of kids and the McKenzies[5] are particularly cordial and helpful.

Add & Loveta drove me to the R.R. & I went to bed.[6]

Tuesday, February 10

[…]

The #37 meeting was the best we have ever had and perhaps about the best club meeting I was ever in. The Holy Spirit was manifestly present and the whole program went over with the young people. One fellow accepted the Lord.

Tuesday, February 17

Dub Hedrick accepted the Lord Jesus after another excellent club meeting at #37. It was a <u>wonderful</u> climax to a good day. The Club is being greatly blessed of God.

Had dinner at Orville Mitchell's. Enjoyed <u>Sue Sue</u>.[7]

Wednesday, February 18 (Ft. Worth)

My best work at Masonic Home when I gave both clubs the Gospel very straight from[:]

Girls: John 2.

Boys: John 6:1–.

An amazing response to invitation to openly confess Christ: those who had received Him since the meetings began. 20 girls, 15 fellow[s] responded.

---

[5] Alex McKenzie was a successful banker and Presbyterian layman in Tyler. He joined the Young Life board of trustees in 1942 and served for the next sixteen years, many of them as the treasurer and a short stint as chairman.

[6] Add was leading the club in Tyler, as well as other clubs in East Texas.

[7] February 1942 entries are the first time Jim calls Mary Margaret "Sue." The Mitchells had kept Sue while Maxine and Ann were on a trip to Oklahoma.

Thursday, February 19 (Houston)

To Houston on the A.M. [train]

[...]

Ollie got out 13 letters for me.

A fine club meeting at #31. Good hearing 15 boys.

Prayed for each young person who professed faith in Christ this week by name, individually. I am sure there aren't many to pray for them.

J 4 "Nobleman's son" to-night!

Following the success of the "Rooftop Rallies" held the year before, Jim and the Young Life staff put on a week of "Mass Meetings" in February. The last week of the month saw seven meetings on seven nights in seven different cities—Dallas, Houston, New Orleans, Tyler, San Antonio, Wichita Falls, and Waco.

The wartime theme was "For Christ and Country," and the meetings were held in the most prestigious locations the cities had to offer—the Peacock Terrace of the Baker Hotel in Dallas, the Grand Ballroom of the Rice Hotel in Houston, the St. Charles Hotel in New Orleans, and similar venues in the other cities.

The meetings featured a thirty-voice men's chorus, plus Paul Beckwith and Bob Rayburn on grand pianos. Elroy Robinson, track star and owner of three world records, gave his stirring testimony. He was followed by Dawson Trotman, who gave a challenge to follow Christ. Reporting to H. J. Taylor a few weeks later, Jim called February, "the greatest month of our work."

Trotman, who had begun his discipleship ministry, The Navigators, a few years earlier, would become one of Jim's closest friends. One of the more immediate effects of Daws' time with Jim in February 1942 was encouraging Young Life to put an emphasis on "follow-up" with its young believers. It was around this time that Young Life began its discipleship program, which it dubbed "Campaigners," using material provided by The Navigators.

Monday, February 23
ROOF GARDEN RALLY [Dallas]

1500

Met Daws & Elroy in a.m. Had good—BUSY—time getting ready for 1st Mass Meeting!

The crowd was not so big as last year but the program was snappier and went over with a great "bang." Not quite the feeling of Victory and Joy over this meeting that we had hoped for but truly great blessing.

Tuesday, February 24 (Houston)

1000

A marvelous crowd of nearly 1000 practically filling the huge Rice Ball Room.

Friday, February 27 (San Antonio)[8]

500

The San Antonio Mass Meeting was "beyond that which we ask or think"[9]—a great time. Everyone very happy about the whole thing.

We had a wonderful time of fellowship driving down in the car.

I took a 11:00 P.M. train for home.

Sunday, March 1 (Waco, Texas)[10]

130+

500–600

A fine rest at Annie Scott's. Excellent service this morning at Bob's church.[11]

---

[8] There are no entries concerning the Mass Meetings on Wednesday and Thursday, other than noting attendance of 500 in New Orleans and 400 in Tyler.

[9] An allusion to Ephesians 3:20: "Now unto him that is able to do exceeding abundantly above all that we ask or think ..." (KJV).

[10] There is no entry for Saturday (the Wichita Falls Mass Meeting) other than noting attendance of "130+".

[11] On the way between Wichita Falls and Waco, the group stopped in Gainesville.

We had a delightful dinner at Mrs. McDaniel's and then rushed—thru snow-storm [—] to Dallas and on to Waco.

The closing service of the MASS MEETING week was a great thrill. The Lord greatly blessed & the after-meeting was wonderful. A large number of Baylor students really touched!

PRAISE THE LORD FOR HIS WONDER WORKING THIS WEEK.

Tuesday, March 3

A great meeting of #37 to-night. Robby[12] had a fine after-meeting with about 20 kids.

Nat Valkus[13] and I figured up the needs of the budget & Mass Meeting and it comes out about $250 short.

Maxine and I committed it to the Lord.

Wednesday, March 4

This is another of those RED LETTER DAYS! A check from Orville Mitchell—postmarked yesterday 3:00 P.M.!—Amt. $250. Just wipes out our deficit. It is AMAZING—to see how the LORD works.

Then to-night. How He did work at Masonic Home where 12 more girls accepted the Lord as Savior & Rob had a great time with the fellows.

The Masonic Home in Ft. Worth was about thirty-five miles from Jim's house in Dallas. It was a residential home for boys and girls. Jim led two clubs there each Wednesday—one for the girls and one for the boys.

During this time Rayburn was becoming increasingly close with Orville Mitchell and his wife Frances.

---

[12] Almost certainly Elroy Robinson.

[13] Nat Valkus was a Dallas businessman and early board member; at the time of this entry he was serving as treasurer for the fledgling organization.

Tuesday, March 10

A poor meeting at #37 to-night. Orville and Francis [*sic,* Frances] were there and I was very disappointed—as I had to get very tough with the kids about just silly horsing around.

———

Wednesday, March 18 (Ft. Worth)
                    Quite severe left hand headache—no shot, sedatives helped to bedtime.
We had another wonderful meeting at the girls club at Masonic Home. It was truly wonderful to see how they did their reading and memory and entered into their meeting with real enthusiasm.

4 more girls testified to being saved in the club, five others testified to having been previously saved!

Tuesday, March 24

Another RED LETTER experience with the young people. Jack Lindsay (for whom I prayed for months & John E [Mitchell] & Orville [Mitchell] & others prayed) stopped the meeting after I had dismissed them & said he wanted to say something. The first thing he said was "This week I thanked the Lord for dying for my sins ..." It was one of the most outstanding cases of witnessing I have ever seen.

———

From March 26–April 17, Jim travelled to the West Coast, speaking at thirty-seven different meetings, usually for young people. Almost all of the early expansion of Young Life came through DTS connections, and this trip was no exception. Much of his time was spent with his seminary friend Grant Whipple in the Bellingham, Washington, area, twenty miles from the Canadian border.

H. J. Taylor, who lived in Chicago, strongly encouraged Jim to expand Young Life beyond Texas. Jim was more than happy to oblige and used his travels to spread interest in the new ministry.

Tuesday, April 7 (Vancouver)

The service to-night was another of those times so characteristic of this trip when The Spirit seemed definitely to have full sway & my own heart was richly blessed in the ministry & people respond to experience real blessing. Spoke on "Peter"—(Lk 24:54–62).

Grant & I took a wonderful trip across Lions' Gate Bridge & up the Mt. for a beautiful view of Vancouver & environs.

Drove home after the service, to "The Firs."[14]

Tuesday, April 14 (Los Angeles)

16th Migraine (R)—Dev Late—Very Severe—shot, Relief, Interval 11 Days**[15]

Had a fine morning in Berkeley with Dee Small.

Then a beautiful plane trip to Los Angeles.

Felt rotten when we arrived but the Lord got me ready for perhaps the best message on the Gospel that I ever gave. The banquet of Christian men and their unsaved friends was held at the Hollywood Knickerbocker Hotel. Never have I been more sure, more real, more clear in delivering a message. I am happier to-night than I have ever been. The Holy Spirit blessed the Word and a Marine Pilot just recently saved from crash made his profession of Faith. Other rich opportunities with men.

Head bad by end.

Wednesday, April 15 (travelling)

7300 [for week]

Here I go again with a record of as happy a day as I have ever known. As I board the plane for Phoenix all I can think of is: "How wonderful is

---

[14] The Firs was the Christian camp run by the Whipple family.

[15] Jim often tracked the intervals between migraine episodes. His comments ranged in emotion from clinical, as in this one, to excited (September 7: "36 DAY INTERVAL! This is probably the longest I have gone since boyhood without a full-blown headache!!!"), and exasperated (February 9, 1948: "Don't understand this amazingly short 5 day interval."). The normal interval was about a week, although it varied over the years. The cause of Jim's migraines was never determined nor was it ever permanently solved.

my Savior." I do not know how He could ever have used me as He has lately—especially to-night with Dawson's gang of out & out Christian fellows and girls. (Ps. 71:16).[16]

Riding along in the plane toward my dear Maxie and girlies & home I feel that there couldn't be any fellow as happy as I am. And it is ALL from the Lord. Not a thing that has happened to make me happy could have been of myself. Dawson and Robbie and all his fellows were just right.

———~~~———

Sunday, May 3 (Chicago)
3000

[...]

I had the great honor of standing in Moody Church[17] pulpit to-night and preaching the Gospel. Felt led to urge upon that audience the necessity for evangelizing the young people—The Lord was mightily present—felt no tension or nervousness that would dishonor Him—but probably was not quite at my best—hope so—FOR HIS SAKE. 19 Texas kids present there.

Monday, May 4 (on the train)
[...] caught the Santa Fe Streamliner for Newton.—

Had a nice restful trip—saw a train wreck that occurred yesterday—got to Newton at 9:00 P.M. Good visit with the folks.

Tuesday, May 5 (Newton, Kansas)
Had a good rest and visit—saw most of the relatives—Boarded the Braniff Plane at Wichita airport, an hour late. Had a very rough trip to Okla. City and a smooth high trip above the clouds from there to Dallas.

---

[16] "With the mighty deeds of the Lord GOD I will come;
    I will remind them of your righteousness, yours alone."

[17] Moody Church on LaSalle Street in Chicago was the premiere congregation in the evangelical world of Jim's spiritual heritage. At the time, its pastor was Harry Ironside.

Taught the Dallas Club to-night. Maxine and the girlies were very sweet and I was glad to get back to them.

Tuesday, May 13 (Ft. Worth)

Absolutely ON TOP again! My time at Masonic Home was wonderful! Praise the Lord! Bob, Pinky, Granny**, Bill, Spunk & Brownie are really GOING ON I believe. I have a real burden for those kids.

Sunday, May 24

A good quiet restful day with much joy. Only someway to-night both Maxine and I seem troubled and not as joyous as we should be in the light of His wonderful grace. I have been convicted that we are not trusting things enough to Him (1 P 5:7)[18] Really want to BELIEVE Him for everything!

Friday, June 5

It seems to me like there is something very wrong to-day. Do not feel the fellowship with the Lord that I should and must to honor him.—Just can't get things really cast upon Him. (1 P 5:7.)

Saturday, June 6

A very good day at the office and in Fellowship with the Lord. It seems like the office work is in pretty good shape. Now to just WAIT on the Lord and watch Him work things out for the summer and the future.

"Cuss"[19] came in to-night and we had fine fellowship in the Lord and talked until very late.

---

[18] "Casting all your anxieties on him, because he cares for you."

[19] Dwight Custis. He served on Young Life staff for a time in the forties. Jim performed Custis' wedding to his wife Lucille seven months after this entry.

—⁓—

Friday, July 10 (Houston)
Saw Bro. Scott this a.m. Had lunch with Dustins & spent some time going over things with Ollie this p.m. This day would have been another 'bust' except for <u>one thing</u>:

Had one of the best times of prayer of my whole life to-night. Did not feel like praying but knew I needed to more than anything. Just took the Lord at His Word and went to Him with <u>everything</u> & He gave great peace.

As I study this thing I am more and more convinced that the times of coldness and unrest (such as I have had now for several days) are always due to failure in prayer and feeding on the Word—one or both.

—⁓—

Jim's love for Colorado, which would later come to play such an important role in Young Life, had begun when his family took vacations there during his boyhood. He decided to take his own family there in the summer of 1942. Ann was four-and-a-half and Sue was two.

After the vacation it was time to go back to Texas and begin Young Life's third school year. The Rayburns also bought their first house: 6010 Revere Place in Dallas. Jim's father made the down payment and the mortgage was $40 per month.

Monday, July 20 (Colorado Springs)
We went up Mt. Manitou for a picnic to-day. Enjoyed the trip immensely but the picnic was a bust due to rain, lightening [*sic*] and other things that girls don't like.

—⁓—

Wednesday, September 2
Couldn't have a finer, "fuller" day. The Lord blest, with great peace & joy, from the early morning time of prayer, on to the office pr[ayer] mtg.,

the letter of special imp. to Archer, all other correspondence, the abundance of wonderful mail and receipts, ($289.00 recpted. the first two days of the month), even to buying TWO suits and having a delightful dinner at "The Village" with the family and a swell evening at home.

Can never PRAISE THE LORD enough for the privilege of KNOWING HIM. Thanks be to God for Phil 4:19[20] and His daily "proof" of it. Oh to LIVE TOMORROW by BELIEVING GOD.

———

Tuesday, October 27

33rd (R) Migraine—Shot late p.m. relief. Feel terrible all day.

25

6—CAMP[AIGNER] TEST KIT![21]

Didn't do much but had a fine meeting to-night 20 boys, 2 girls. A wonderful time afterward just getting a group started on the Campaigner stuff.

———

Monday, November 2

Another real red-letter day—office work. Had the thrill of closing the books with a $270.00 balance for mo. of Oct. Total receipts about $1818.00 in this one month. Praise the Lord!!

Quiet evening at home.

The girlies are very sweet and I can never thank the Lord enough for them.

———

Continuing to plant seeds for future Young Life work, Jim trav-

---

[20] "And my God will supply every need of yours according to his riches in glory in Christ Jesus."

[21] The Campaigner Test Kit was a program of Bible memorization and other assignments inspired by The Navigators to help Young Life Campaigners grow in their faith. It required a significant commitment on the part of the high school student. Here, Jim is indicating that six kids came to his meeting to review their Campaigner Test Kit assignments for the week.

elled to the East Coast (primarily Pennsylvania and the Washington, D. C., area), speaking sixty-six times in twenty-three days.

Friday, December 4 (Bethesda, Maryland)

39th Migraine. Shot after mtg. right to sleep.

4550 [total for the week]

750 Chevy Chase [High School]!!!!

20 Busin. Girls

100

The finest high school assembly contact that I ever had—really thrilling the way the Lord led me and made the contact real—lots of fun and right down to business on "The Bible Merits Looking Into"—A general statement of ignorance concerning Word then Its claims & my testimony & others that it supports its claims to being God's Word, Message of Life, etc.

[...]

A high school lad came up after the evening mtg and said he had never understood Gospel—prayed "Lord I would have accepted sooner but I didn't understand..." Great.

Tuesday, December 8 (Chicago)

One of the grandest and MOST DEFINITE answers to prayer that I ever had. Just before leaving the room at 7:15 I prayed that the Lord would let me go home to-night. Had I gone without praying I would have missed the phone call telling me of a seat on the 9:10** Braniff to Dallas. PRAISE HIM. Deut. 32:4.[22]

Wednesday, December 9

Home at 7:00! Miserably tired—but very glad to be home.

---

[22] "The Rock, his work is perfect,
        for all his ways are justice.
    A God of faithfulness and without iniquity,
        just and upright is he."

—⁓—

Wednesday, December 30

A wonderful half hour of prayer at 5:00. I have been convicted more &
more about the many days that I do not really have much time ALONE
for prayer—so I have asked the Lord to get me up early and let me experience Ps 143:8[23]—He Answered and gave me a real time** this a.m.

Thursday, December 31

Ditto Wed. He got me up—in answer to definite prayer & I had the
most down to business time of prayer that I have had for a long time.
Now for the New Year—my main objective is that 1943 shall be a "prayer
year"—much more than ever before.

---

[23] "Let me hear in the morning of your steadfast love,
        for in you I trust.
  Make me know the way I should go,
        for to you I lift up my soul."

1943

COLLEGE STUDENT BILLY GRAHAM ACTS AS JIM'S CHAUFER

Rayburn began training a group of Wheaton College students in Young Life Methods during the 1943 school year. Billy Graham, the future evangelist, was one of the students. In this particular entry, Graham has drawn the duty to pick Jim up at the airport in the middle of the night.

Though he does not declare a New Year's resolution in his journal, it is obvious that as 1943 started, the thirty-three year old Rayburn was determined to stay in shape. For much of the year he often walked the three miles to his office (or a mile to the bus), and recorded doing exercises and bike riding, all of which stand out since Rayburn was normally not given to exercise regimens. Being a physically active person by nature (no one ever accused him of being sedentary), his normal routine typically kept him in good physical shape.

Jim was also preternaturally optimistic. Reading his reports to donors and staff one gets the impression that everything was always going not just great, but fantastic. He tended to only see the good things.

But he didn't choose to record everything. The largest average club in all of Young Life was only sixty-one kids—the average club attendance was less than thirty. Many of the new clubs did not last for more than just a few years. But statistics never stood in the way of Jim's following the increasingly clear vision of what God had for Young Life.

Friday, January 1

5:30 A.M. This has been the finest start I have ever made in a new year. Went to bed at 11:30 with a miserable headache (L). Had finished reading "The Raft."[1] With no effort on my part, simply comitting it to Him He woke me at 4:00 a.m. without any headache and gave me the sweetest time of fellowship with Himself that I have ever had—at least for a long time. My heart was open to confess my sin & failure and there was plenty of it. By His grace I knew that I really hated that sin & longed to

---

[1] Most likely *The Raft* by Robert Trumbull, which was a best-seller at the time. It was the true story of three United States Navy fliers who survived thirty-four days on a life raft in the Pacific.

be cleansed of it—and He kept His promise (1 J 1:9).[2] The Lord led me to really commit the year 1943 to Him & I prayed especially that my life might be more of a testimony to my own dear wife & kiddies & to the ones who work with me. THE WORD that was most blessed in my heart was Psa 143:8, 10[3]—my prayer for this new year. Prov 3:5, 6;[4] Rom 12:1, 2,[5] Ps 71:16[6] and others:

More definitely than ever I have <u>committed</u> the coming days, projects, growth, plans to Him. Now to LET GO & LET GOD.

The Lord was really with us all day. Maxine, Margaret & Dick Hillis[7] & I immensely enjoyed the Cottonbowl [*sic*, Cotton Bowl] Football Game—Texas vs Georgia Tech. Texas won 14–7.

Then our Staff Conference got going with dinner at Lakewood Cafeteria and the evening of fellowship and prayer at our house. The Lord

---

[2] "If we confess our sins, he is faithful and just to forgive us our sins and to cleanse us from all unrighteousness."

[3] "Let me hear in the morning of your steadfast love,
  for in you I trust.
Make me know the way I should go,
  for to you I lift up my soul …
Teach me to do your will,
  for you are my God!
Let your good Spirit lead me
  on level ground!"

[4] "Trust in the LORD with all your heart,
  and do not lean on your own understanding.
In all your ways acknowledge him,
  and he will make straight your paths."

[5] "I appeal to you therefore, brothers, by the mercies of God, to present your bodies as a living sacrifice, holy and acceptable to God, which is your spiritual worship. Do not be conformed to this world, but be transformed by the renewal of your mind, that by testing you may discern what is the will of God, what is good and acceptable and perfect."

[6] "With the mighty deeds of the Lord GOD I will come;
  I will remind them of your righteousness, yours alone."

[7] Charles Richard Hillis (1913–2005). At the time of this entry Hillis was a student at Dallas Seminary. He had an informal relationship with Young Life, occasionally speaking at events. He went on to become a well-known missionary, founding the ministry OC International, which eventually had missionaries in over fifty countries.

was with us & it was everything that could be desired.

Wednesday, January 6
Walked mile to bus** and got to office early. Great day—getting out more mail than we ever have before I believe.

Had one of the biggest disappointments since I got into the work to-night. Got to Masonic home and found that <u>Spunk</u>, <u>Pinky</u>, Charlie Torres**, Tom Brady and several others have enlisted in Marines & Navy. Some already gone.

———

Young Life activity at this point was not limited to weekly club meetings. Though Jim did see local clubs as the most important aspect of the work, there were several other regular activities under the banner of "Young Life Campaign." These included high school assemblies, which Jim addressed by the dozen every year for most of the forties and fifties; the previously discussed Mass Meetings; and Young Life Conferences, which were weekend trips taken by most areas in the spring. Gone for good were the summer tent campaigns; in their place there would be three weeks of summer camp in 1943.

As part of the plan to increase Young Life's ministry outside of Texas, Jim was travelling on a regular basis to Wheaton College in Wheaton, Illinois, just outside of Chicago. There he taught students in Young Life methods. Over two hundred signed up to be part of the program.

One of the young men who signed up was a lanky senior from North Carolina named Billy Graham. Though he enjoyed the classes and Rayburn, he chose not to join the Young Life staff. A short time after graduating from Wheaton, Graham became the first full-time employee of Youth for Christ. His involvement with Young Life was only peripheral, however he remained friends with Rayburn for decades. Upon Jim's death he wired the family, "[Jim]

was one of the greatest Christians I ever knew, and he had a pro-
found influence on my life ... It is now up to us to carry the torch
that Jim so courageously carried for so many years."

Thursday, January 14 (Wheaton, Illinois)

A very wonderful day—the Lord again really bestowed his Grace upon
the ministry & answered prayer. Arrived Chi Airport 2:15 a.m. in blizzard. Finally got in touch with Ted Benson & Billy Graham met me @
4:30. To bed at Dorm @ 6:15—Up at 10:00 & the day really clicked—
everything went off swell. (Offering for exp[enses]** $105.00)

Looking back over it undoubtedly it seems to be one of the outstanding days—I was not so hot in one or two meetings but how good
the Lord is to give His blessing & power.

———

The result of Jim's many speaking trips saw Young Life beginning
in Oklahoma, Tennessee, and Arkansas, as well as the Pacific
Northwest and Pennsylvania.

While these were heady times for Jim, he was very aware of
his own imperfection. His journal does not record the specifics, but
his dealings with the staff in February are an interesting insight
into his own failings; in this case he most likely took out some of his
frustration verbally on some of the office staff.

Monday, February 22

Just too pooped to do any good. Then on top of all that I am all flustered
about staff problems—this will be remembered as the day I pulled one
of the biggest boneheads of my life—and manifested that I have not
been LETTING the Holy Spirit fill me & empower me!

Tuesday, February 23

9th Migraine: VERY TOUGH—early. Reaction to "shot" very slow.

40

A wonderful time with the Lord this a.m. early.

The best mtg of the year at Club #37. I spoke on John 15:18–25. The
Lord blessed me. I have been feasting on the WORD in Jack's lectures[8]
& also convicted by James 5:16[9] so I made full confession of my sin to
Orville to-night and know that the Lord led me.

   [...]

Thursday, February 25
A good day for one thing—got a long private session with Glad[10] and
the Lord gave me the privilege of speaking openly to her of the wrong I
had done in acting so unwisely & "fleshly" on Monday. He brought us
to-gether————

   I do pray for a sufficient measure of His Grace to do what is pleasing
to Him in that office and in all dealings with the staff. Oh God get us
READY & WILLING to have no other purpose than to exalt Christ.

Friday, February 26
Our all-day Staff prayer-meeting. No doubt one of the greatest days of
prayer I have ever had.

   I believe the Lord clearly brought us to it and greatly used it and will
use it with all of us.

   Off to Ponca City [Oklahoma] on 10:00 P.M. Santa Fe.

Tuesday, April 6
[...]
   To Mitchells' for dinner and club. Then a wonderful time with the
Word & my old beaten-up copy of "He That Is Spiritual." To bed feeling

---

[8] Jack Mitchell's annual lectures at Dallas Theological Seminary.

[9] "Therefore, confess your sins to one another and pray for one another, that you may
be healed. The prayer of a righteous person has great power as it is working."

[10] Gladys Roche Phillips, who at that time was working as the secretary at Young
Life's headquarters office.

that the Lord really has all the answers to my problems.

———

One of the highlights of the spring was the Young Life Conference held at the end of April at Bachman Lake in Dallas. At the end of the weekend Jim's diary records the conference had been a success, but noted, "The Lord surely overruled a lot of things to make this a great time." He does not give any detail as to what problems there were, but a letter to the staff prior to the weekend may provide a clue. Describing the speakers, he wrote, "They are Mr. and Mrs. Gene Crapuchettes. In spite of the foul name they are really the stuff."

Three summer camps were held that year: Double Lake in Texas, Lake Ponca in Oklahoma, and Shelby Forest in Tennessee.

Saturday, August 28–Sunday, August 29 (Shelby Forest)
I believe these two days are the greatest I have ever had in the work. Apparently the Lord has seen fit to make me more effective than I have been heretofore—certainly I am as happy as I have ever been in my life & ALL my confidence is in HIM—My prayer life has been more real, love for the Lord & compassion for the kids more genuine than ever before.

Monday, August 30 (travelling)
We caught the 8:10** "Cotton Belt" for DALLAS. In spite of 17 hrs on the slowest train I have ever ridden THE JOY of the Lord is very REAL & ABIDING.

Murray Smoot counted 39 testimonies at the fagot service that definitely sounded like professions of faith at conf. 29 more were "maybe's." I had a deep spirit of prayer for the kids I dealt with over there.

———

Wednesday, September 15 (Wheaton, Illinois)

Jer 33:3[11]

Red letter [day] because of these Campaign kids on the campus. It is almost too much to believe—guys like Van[12] & Roy [Riviere], girls like Carleen[13] & Peg & Dotty—really hitting the ball for the Lord & out for Y.L.C. for all they are worth. Had hours with them to-day. Other good contacts. [...]

Saturday, September 18 (Chicago)

(II C 12:9)[14]

The interview with Mr. H. J. Taylor was the most satisfactory that I have ever had. He very favorable & granting us goodly increase in the support. Likewise the interview with Bob Van Kampen.—

Had a great time with Van, Roy & some of the gang this p.m. Then a swell meeting at Wheaton to-night. Bud Conner coming on the staff—fine prayer & interview with him & then with Don** Hoke.

Sunday, September 19 (Moline, Illinois)

What a day! I've been asking the Lord to really make it clear to me that I am in His Will—& praying specially about the interviews & contacts. Had a <u>delightful</u> time with Strombecks. They seem to really love me & I certainly do them: And then this. He had a $200 check written when I

---

[11] "Call unto me, and I will answer thee, and shew thee great and mighty things, which thou knowest not" (KJV).

[12] Van Clyne Nall. From Tyler, Texas, Nall was a former Young Lifer. Within two years of this entry he would enlist in the army, fight at the Battle of the Bulge, be captured by the Germans, become a prisoner of war, and be freed by the Allies. Upon his return to the United States he finished his schooling and served for a few years on Young Life staff.

[13] Probably Carleen Barclay, who went on staff three years later, after being involved as a leader at Wheaton.

[14] "But he said to me, 'My grace is sufficient for you, for my power is made perfect in weakness.' Therefore I will boast all the more gladly of my weaknesses, so that the power of Christ may rest upon me."

got there and the Lord just gave a clear open opportunity for me to talk
to them about the "Campaigners Plan" & while I was talking He spoke
to Mrs S. and went & got their personal check book & wrote another ck
to Campaign for $500 for materials.** [...]

1st time I ever closed the day with over an hour of intercession in a
Pullman berth!

———

*Young Life's second official fiscal year ended on September 30.[15] In
those first two years the staff had grown from five men in Texas to
twenty-one people in six states, including five women. Though the
majority of staff (twelve) were working in Texas, there were five
in Washington state, two in Tennessee (also leading club in Little
Rock, Arkansas), and one each in Oklahoma and Illinois.*

*The women on staff as the new fiscal year began were Ollie
Dustin, Wanda Ann Mercer (known as "Wam"), Annie Cheairs,
and Phyllis Rogers. Catherine Klein[16] was serving part-time.*

Friday, October 1

The fiscal year of the Campaign has closed—and what a close. Every bill
we could rake & scrape, <u>paid in full</u>—and a $237.00 cash balance in the
bank.

Wonderful time of prayer with several of the fellows to-day.

I can never thank the Lord enough for bringing us to this end-of-
year with such great blessing—spiritually & materially!

———

---

[15] Jim always pointed out that Young Life began when he left seminary in 1940.
However, Young Life did not begin as a legal and accounting entity until October
1941.

[16] Catherine Klein's husband Larry was serving in the military during the war. While
on the 1945 staff conference at The Firs she received word that he had been killed in
action in Europe. She then moved to Houston to work full-time with Young Life, and
subsequently to Dallas. There she met and married Clare Headington and left staff.
She remained involved as a donor and prayer warrior for Young Life for decades.

Wednesday, October 13 (Chicago)

Headache—uncomfortable but not severe from noon on but after meeting at night it became migraine and lasted most of night. Although I slept it off.

Got to Chi (downtown) at 5:00 a.m. Slept until 9:30** —had a good time of prayer, went to C W F[17] office—good interview with Bob Walker.

Out to Western Springs with Bob Van K.[18] Very nice evening and spoke at his church. Billy Graham very friendly. Delightful children that Bob has (Donnie**, Evelyn, Bobbie[19].) Feel very bum but the Lord gave me a good talk with Bob.

Friday, December 3 (St. Louis)

Got the FLU TO-DAY. Dr said I'd have to go to bed for several days.

Went out to Boettcher's. Though very sick I had them call me at message time and I went through with my part of the service.

[...]

Had bad chills all night. Felt very bum. Running quite a temperature. Do thank the Lord for getting me this nice place to be sick while I have to be. Real peace from Him about the whole thing.

Monday, December 6 (St. Louis)

2500 Normandy Hi
350 Wellston Hi
500 Mass Mtg.

---

[17] Christian Workers Foundation.

[18] Robert C. Van Kampen (1910–1989). Mentioned previously in the entry for September 18, Bob Van Kampen was an influential Chicago evangelical. As a deacon of Western Springs Baptist Church he had convinced Billy Graham to become their pastor upon his graduation from Wheaton earlier that year. It would be a short pastorate, with Graham leaving to become a full-time evangelist in 1945. Van Kampen served on Young Life's board from 1943–1947.

[19] Robert D. Van Kampen (1938–1999). "Bobbie" grew up to be a phenomenally successful businessman, founding what became Van Kampen Investments. At the time of his death it oversaw close to $100 billion in assets.

I "struggled through" all the meetings to-day. The Lord gave us very wonderful times in these high schools.

I also felt that His blessing and power was upon the evening meeting—although I was very sick. I went right home to bed.

Saturday, December 18 (Memphis)

100

MEMPHIS

Wally & Wam[20] & "Gang" meet me. Went to "Peabody" [Hotel]. Good day—mostly just talking to Wally.

Spoke to fine group to-night on "Personal Relationship With God."

Tuesday, December 28

Began at Acts to read thru the N.T. to-day!

Word 1 HR

Prayer 1¼ HR.

I have been getting about the greatest blessing of my whole life recently from a study of Pierson's "Life of George Mueller."[21] It has HIT ME HARD, and THE LORD has brought deep conviction about my own awful sin of prayerlessness & lack of Faith—lack of "continuing" [and lack of] "zeal and earnestness in prayer." By His grace I am asking for a real

---

[20] Wanda Ann Mercer, or Wam, graduated from college when she was only eighteen. She was just starting her fifteen-year staff career at the time of this entry. She also worked as personal assistant to both Donald Grey Barnhouse and Billy Graham. She eventually served on the faculty of the University of New Orleans in her native Louisiana. Wam never married, and died in 1989.

[21] The book's actual title was *George Müller of Bristol*, published in 1899 and written by Arthur T. Pierson. George Müller (1805–1898) has served as an inspiration to Bible-believing Christians since he began his orphanages in Bristol, England, in the 1830s. He is best known for his absolute dependence on prayer and faith to see to the material needs for the hundreds—eventually thousands—of orphans under his care. He never solicited funds nor revealed his needs to others, choosing to reveal them only to his heavenly Father.

turning pt. in my life. This time to "turn" up the path of "dead to Jim
R, his desires, comforts, etc and seeking to win no acclaim or approval
but God's!"

Friday, December 31

[…]

Maxine & I with Add were on our knees at midnight and '44 came
in as the Lord met us in a most wonderful season of heart searching &
fervent prayer. Oh for a year characterized by "prayer & the Word" in
my life & theirs.

1944

"ANOTHER UNBELIEVABLY WONDERFUL DAY."

Jim was invited by several pastors in the South Bend, Indiana, area, to speak at a weeklong series of evangelistic meetings. He spent much of the time in prayer and study, resulting in an even deeper committment to Christ.

As tremendous as the growth and success of Young Life had been so
far, what lay ahead in the next ten years would astound everyone.
God used 1944 to prepare Jim for what was to come. Although he
was just as busy as in other years, still leading three clubs a week
and travelling extensively, Jim spent literally hundreds of hours in
prayer in 1944, and almost as many hours studying God's Word.
It was no accident that Jim was able to hear the Lord's voice in
the years to come—his intimate fellowship with the Lord, which
reached a new level in this year, allowed him to recognize even the
faintest whisper of God's Spirit.

Saturday, January 1

Exactly 4 weeks since I have had a Migraine.
Only 23 in '43 as against 42 migraines in 42.

No doubt this is the greatest New Year's experience ever and one of
greatest exps. of my life. After Maxine went to bed Add and I continued
on in the most wonderful season of prayer until 4 a.m. Also great fellowship and sense of communion with the Lord. We (I) really turned things
over to Him. Asking def.—so definitely to really BELIEVE GOD for a
life of fervent - prevailing prayer and real feeding on the Word. The vss
that were up[p]ermost were Eph 3:20, 21,[1] II Tim 2:15,[2] II Cor 5:9, 5:14,
15.[3] There is great conviction of sin re Mt 7:7.[4] The awful fact that many
things we need from God we do not ASK FOR and do not stay with Him

---

[1] "Now to him who is able to do far more abundantly than all that we ask or think,
according to the power at work within us, to him be glory in the church and in Christ
Jesus throughout all generations, forever and ever. Amen."

[2] "Do your best to present yourself to God as one approved, a worker who has no
need to be ashamed, rightly handling the word of truth."

[3] "So whether we are at home or away, we make it our aim to please him ... For the
love of Christ controls us, because we have concluded this: that one has died for all,
therefore all have died; and he died for all, that those who live might no longer live for
themselves but for him who for their sake died and was raised."

[4] "Ask, and it will be given to you; seek, and you will find; knock, and it will be
opened to you."

when we do. DEEP Conviction also concerning Prayerlessness & Failure to Study the Word & love prayer & [the] Word. By HIS grace—not this year. Amazing answer to definite prayer: After less than two hours sleep we were able to work hard all day on "L-Rate"[5] without discomfort. A truly GREAT DAY!

Sunday, January 2
Another outstanding experience! Maxine and I met the Lord to-gether in a very precious time of confessing our faults and failures & committing ourselves, our girlies, our home, to Him in a new way. Very REAL— no doubt of His presence & leading.

Monday, January 3
This has been a great day and a rather hard day. I'm glad I've had Psalm 143:8[6] since I first woke up. If I don't really believe HIM I know I'll mess up. Never have I had such a complete understanding of my own worthlessness and hopelessness. I also know that the Lord Jesus has EVERYTHING a poor sinner needs—not just to be saved—but "TO ABOUND."

Had a good day at the office. Important mail gotten out. Also finished the "Y-RATE" & "C-Rate" set-up for the printer. Very thankful for this. But Maxine came down with a terrible back and also very despondent after our wonderful day yesterday when her victory contributed so much. But the Word still says to me "In EVERYTHING ..."[7] Thank God for the largest gift in history of our work from E——.

---

[5] "Y-Rate," "L-Rate," and "C-Rate" were all Campaigner materials being prepared in conjunction with The Navigators.

[6] "Let me hear in the morning of your steadfast love,
        for in you I trust.
    Make me know the way I should go,
        for to you I lift up my soul."

[7] Philippians 4:6 says, "Do not be anxious about anything, but in everything by prayer and supplication with thanksgiving let your requests be made known to God."

Wednesday, January 5

This has been a very good day—a lot of work turned out at the office and a fairly good meeting to-night. Encouraging group—not so many little squirts. "H" Harris[8] went with me.

Wednesday, January 12

Beyond doubt I am experiencing the most wonderful season of my Christian Life with respect to the FIRST thing: my personal relationship with the Lord. This day, from 12:30 AM until 5:00 was perhaps the most wonderful season of prayer I have ever had. And completely "beyond me." Almost the entire time on my knees—without weariness and a real sense of the Spirit of prayer. All thru the night Matt 7:7,[9] John 16:24,[10] Rom 8:26, 27.[11] Heb 4:16[12] were very precious and the Lord just thrilled my heart all day with Ps 16:11.[13] Oh to let Him show me this every step of the way.

A wonderful time of prayer with the girls[14] this a.m. Real burden for the** school. And the Lord is blessing the work so much—just in the

---

[8] Harlan Harris, who at the time was studying at DTS after graduating from Wheaton the year before. He joined the Young Life staff for a short while, and then went on to become a pastor and evangelist. Years later, he would attend Rayburn at his deathbed.

[9] "Ask, and it will be given to you; seek, and you will find; knock, and it will be opened to you."

[10] "Until now you have asked nothing in my name. Ask, and you will receive, that your joy may be full."

[11] "Likewise the Spirit helps us in our weakness. For we do not know what to pray for as we ought, but the Spirit himself intercedes for us with groanings too deep for words. And he who searches hearts knows what is the mind of the Spirit, because the Spirit intercedes for the saints according to the will of God."

[12] "Let us then with confidence draw near to the throne of grace, that we may receive mercy and find grace to help in time of need."

[13] "You make known to me the path of life;
in your presence there is fullness of joy;
at your right hand are pleasures forevermore."

[14] Most likely the staff women at the headquarters office.

matter of John 13:34, 35[15] specially.

Got stuck in mud on Concho St!

—◆—

Monday, January 31 (Cape Girardeau, Missouri, to Memphis)
365 chaps of Bible read in Jan. N.T. + Gen + Ex + 15 Chap-Lev.

Got up at 1:30 a.m. took train to MPHS.

Had breakfast and a brief visit with WAM and Carleen[16] then took the "train"—Cottonbelt for DL. 15 hrs. later we arrived. Outside of an hour of prayer made dif[ficult] by the circumstances and a couple hours of reading it was an uninteresting day.

Home at mid-night.

—◆—

Thursday, February 10
18.

Anne[17] and I went to Ft W. and had some good contacts with the kids this p.m.

The Lord greatly blessed the meeting. I asked them how we could know "He Lives" and the Lord really led & opened it up.

Best of all HE has given us a wonderful burden of prayer for the kids—

—◆—

---

[15] "A new commandment I give to you, that you love one another: just as I have loved you, you also are to love one another. By this all people will know that you are my disciples, if you have love for one another."

[16] Possibly Carleen Barclay.

[17] Anne Cheairs (1919–2006). She helped Jim in the Ft. Worth Riverside Club, as well as doing secretarial work at the Dallas headquarters office. Years later she recalled that the women would get to the office promptly at 8:30; Jim would arrive shortly thereafter. Jim was very particular, she recalled. "Our first duty every morning: we had to dust. Jim was very meticulous." Once Jim showed up, "we would begin praying. The first thing [we did] every morning was pray together." Cheairs was on staff for decades and one of the staff members Jim respected the most.

Jim speaking at one of the 1944 Mass Meetings. L–R: Howie Kee, Ted Bradley, George Sheffer, and Bill Pass.

Friday, February 18 (Memphis)

1000—So S.

1400—Central

1000—Tech.

500—(Treadwell-Quintet)

500**—Mass Mtg.

[…]

[Wonderful] chat w. Dr. Solteau (*sic*, Soltau)[18] this P.M.

(Sue is with me—very sweet all day!)

* WHAT A MASS Mtg! One of the greatest we have ever had! (Like the 1st Peacock Terrace) 500+ in attendance. I spoke on Nich Came to Jesus—"Personal" & "Born Again w. Numb 21"—One of the most effective messages I ever put on—all glory to the Lord. He gave the "Peace"

---

[18] Theodore Stanley Soltau, DD. He was the pastor of a large independent church in Memphis. His son was at Wheaton and became involved in Young Life leadership there. Dr. Soltau greatly encouraged Jim to use volunteer leaders. Up to this point, almost all the work was done by the full-time staff.

& "the Joy" & the Message. The Quintet was swell.[19] Worked hard but the meeting ROLLED.

───

Young Life's association with Dawson Trotman's ministry, The Navigators, reached a new peak in the mid-forties. Planning a joint staff conference to be held later that year, Jim and Add Sewell travelled to Los Angeles to visit Trotman at his home base. Grant Whipple, who at the time was heading Young Life in the Pacific Northwest, joined them. It had been decided the conference would be held at The Firs in Bellingham, Washington, a Christian conference grounds run by Whipple's family.

It is significant to note that in 1944 the combined ministries of both Young Life and The Navigators were only a fraction of what they would become in the coming decades, making Daws' and Jim's prayers in this next entry all the more prophetic.

Sunday, February 27–Monday, February 28 (Los Angeles)[20]

Getting better all the while—one of the best days of my life! This morning [Sunday] we went up on the hill near Dawson's place and it seemed like the Lord was very close as we looked out over all those dozens of cities in every direction and realized that with HIM leading we could have a very wonderful part in getting the Gospel to them—then, some fine fellowship in the afternoon and Grant took the train with us. A beautiful stateroom on the Golden State and we had a rich experience working straight thru from 6:30 p.m. to 2:30 this [Monday] a.m.—the last two hours was in prayer—as fine a time as we have ever had. How we did enjoy the PEACE that only HE can bring. We all went to bed in Yuma & got about 5 hrs. sleep.

[...]

───

[19] The Young Life Quintet, a singing group made up of five DTS men.

[20] This entry spills over onto two days. It begins in Los Angeles on Sunday and continues as Jim and party travel by train to Phoenix.

Thursday, March 2

24.

We had a hard mtg of the Riverside Club[21] to-night but I enjoyed getting over there again—

Took the Plane at 11:00 p.m. for Chicago—had to rush for it. "H"[22] drove me. Forgot my brief case—had to go back after it.

Monday, March 6

Read more in the Bible than I ever have before—60 chapters.

Saturday, March 10

[...]

My prayer life has been very definitely BELOW PAR this week and so has my reading of the WORD. I've got to get back at it in a big way.

Saturday, March 11 (Young Life Weekend Conference)

First mtg. of Dallas Wk End Conf. I spoke on Acts 26 "What Is A Christian." A very good mtg, I believe. Good spirit. Crowd of about 150.

Sunday, March 12 (Young Life Weekend Conference)

I flopped this afternoon on trying to bring a sequel message on Acts 26. It was a small crowd—not much Power in it I thought. I'm the NO. ONE REASON—just don't get going—very little prayer & the Word this past week.

Monday, March 13 (Young Life Weekend Conference)

After a day that was particularly hard for me a lot of "pressure" and "tension" that is indescribable—the Lord gave us a wonderful service to-night for the close of the week-end conf.

I spoke on Heb 11:6[23] emphasizing the two-fold application—1) to

---

[21] The club Jim was leading for Amon Carter Riverside High School in Ft. Worth.

[22] Harlan Harris.

[23] "And without faith it is impossible to please him, for whoever would draw near to

the Christian and 2) To the non-Christian. The Lord did it all—I was scared and would have been a mess. Six kids responded to the invitation. It was swell!!

Great prayer mtg with the fellows this aft.

———

In March Young Life produced the first issue of a monthly magazine for young people, Young Life. *The magazine was a staple of Young Life's ministry for the next twenty years. The first issue reported that there were twenty-seven staff members ministering to 2,000 high school students each week.*

From March 24–April 18, Jim travelled to Montana and the Pacific Northwest for more high school assemblies and other speaking engagements, addressing 14,000 students in twenty-two assemblies.

In the days of World War II, long-distance travel was extremely difficult. Long distance jets would not become common until a few years after the war, so all commercial flying was done in propeller-driven aircraft. As a result, most journeys required multiple stops. Often flights were cancelled after only one leg or delayed. Other factors in the difficulty of travel were the wartime rationing of gasoline and tires, and the prioritization of train travel for members of the military. It was not uncommon for Jim to mix trains, planes, and automobiles on a single trip during the war. He pushed for the board to purchase an airplane for Young Life's use, but they failed to share Jim's enthusiasm for the idea. Instead, as the following entries show, Jim's travel was a constant matter for prayer. As he liked to tell people when they asked him how he managed to get on so many flights when others were denied, "My Boss owns the air."

God must believe that he exists and that he rewards those who seek him."

Friday, March 24 (travelling)

[Airline] Called early—this a.m. Told we would only make Pueblo [Colorado] acct. weather.

A WONDERFUL DAY. It just seems that the Lord went beyond what could be expected to show me HIS divine hand in my plans and the events of this day. I was really LAYING HOLD of Ps 121:8[24] and Phil 4:6, 7[25] and the Lord was sure good to me. I got <u>scared</u> even though I was believing Him for the trip. <u>I don't like that!</u> After an hour of waiting at airport they called me and told me that I was <u>last non-priority pass[enger]</u> and was <u>sub.-hood**</u> at Ft. Worth. Couldn't feel that it would honor Him for these plans we had trusted Him for to go haywire. I prayed! Went through. All the way to Colo. Springs. Had swell talk with Dr. Hansen[26] & Mary Frances Redding.[27]——Arr DV in big snow-storm. (On the plane the Lord specially gave me Ps. 139:5, 6[28]—And my heart was full of PRAISE to Him) Called "Inland."[29] Said "no chance" for trip tomorrow. I grabbed Burlington [train] for Billings. DAY COACH ONLY. The Lord had a way for me. He ALWAYS has a way and I <u>want to walk in</u>

---

[24] "The LORD will keep
        your going out and your coming in
        from this time forth and forevermore."

[25] "Do not be anxious about anything, but in everything by prayer and supplication with thanksgiving let your requests be made known to God. And the peace of God, which surpasses all understanding, will guard your hearts and your minds in Christ Jesus."

[26] Dr. Howard E. Hansen was the pastor of First Presbyterian Church in Colorado Springs from 1938–1970. He became a great supporter of Young Life and was Rayburn's pastor from the time the family moved to Colorado Springs in 1947 until Jim's death in 1970.

[27] Mary Frances Redding was the Christian Education director of First Presbyterian Church in Colorado Springs.

[28] "You hem me in, behind and before,
        and lay your hand upon me.
    Such knowledge is too wonderful for me;
        it is high; I cannot attain it."

[29] Inland Air Lines.

it. One of the most wonderful days of my life in the matter of WATCH-
ING HIM work and realizing my own frailty in faith. Phil 3:10.[30]

Saturday, March 25 (travelling)

200

I got off at Casper and called "Inland Airways." [*sic*, Inland Air Lines]
The northbound trip for to-day is <u>clear out</u>. Will be at least 16 hours late.
It was a little extra blessing that I needed after my night in the day coach
and this beautiful flying weather. How wonderful it is to KNOW HIM
and to let Him have charge of all the arrangements. I am very anxious to
Let Him conquer completely this tendency of mine to get troubled and
excited by "bad circumstances."

A SUPERB time with Feelys. They really gave me a welcome—and
fine fellowship. N.W.A.[31] doesn't even have a reservation for me to Spokane. To bed just leaving it all to Him! Past midnight. Very much at
peace about it all—thanks to His love and grace.

Sunday, March 26 (Spokane)

A wonderful day. I got the thrill of a lifetime out of being waked at Billings this a.m. and told that NWA had space for me to Spokane. The
Lord has dealt wonderfully with me in all of this.

Fine meetings here in Spokane to-day. Arrived on time after a beautiful trip over the Rockies. Ted met me. Very good fellowship with the
Gills. Extremely weary to-night.

—⁓⁓⁓—

Wednesday, April 26

NOTE—Bible Reading.....

TO-NIGHT I FINISHED THE READING OF THE BIBLE THROUGH SINCE
CHRISTMAS.

---

[30] "That I may know him and the power of his resurrection, and may share his
sufferings, becoming like him in his death."

[31] Northwest Airlines.

A great club meeting at Brandts.

From June 21–July 6 Jim travelled east for meetings in Maryland, New York, Washington, and back home by way of Chicago.

Not long after returning to Texas, Young Life moved into its new headquarters at 2018 Commerce Street in Dallas. The John E. Mitchell Company (run by Young Life board members John E. Mitchell, Jr., and his brother Orville) had recently purchased the building, which they had previously been using as a warehouse. "They are turning over the front half of the second story to us," Jim wrote the staff. To a group of supporters he wrote, "Through all the months of our praying and looking for office space, we never once dreamed of anything so nice as the place the Lord has given us. Really, I cannot tell you how the staff and I feel about this. Personally, I am overwhelmed by it. To think that even though we would have been very well-satisfied with just a little larger quarters though they might be commonplace, yet the Lord has supplied us with a beautiful suite of offices comprising five rooms, four of them very large and all of it built to order for the Young Life Campaign."

Tuesday, June 20
An outstanding day at home. Just right. Maxine was sweet as could be as were the girlies. We played with the hose in the yard, and had a peck of fun.

Tuesday, June 27 (Camp Wabanna, Maryland)
Spoke on PROPITIATION—With liberty and punch and the same joy in preaching that I had on Sunday. Precious times of prayer, morning & evening. I am so thankful for the WARMTH that is in my soul—none of the tough coldness & battle to pray & keep with the Lord that I have experienced so much in the past two months. Praise Him. Oh to be "committed to Him" REALLY BELIEVING HIM! LOVING HIM BACK.

Swam a lot to-day.

Monday, July 3 (New York City)

[...]

Just fooled around—went up on the Empire State Building. Walked awhile on Broadway—Times Square and 5th Ave. I went to my Pullman at 9:30 and went to bed. Feel fine.

Tuesday, July 4 (travelling)

<u>NY Central—NY. to Chi</u> Liked the N.Y. Cent. very much—had roomette.

Slept late—very comfortable trip. Had the finest season of prayer that I have ever had on a train I believe.

Arr. Chi. on time.

Went straight to Morrison Hotel and didn't do anything. For some reason I didn't enjoy the evening at all.

Wednesday, July 5 (Chicago)

Had an excellent interview with Mr. Taylor, at dinner @ La Salle [Hotel]. I praise God for this man and for his warm interest in me and in the work. A great gift from the Lord.

Good interview with Bob Walker and Noel Lyons & chat with Dr. Smith.[32] Saw the Braves beat the Cubs 6–2. Tobin pitched—good!

Pain in back and legs—also bothering at nights. Apparently due to lack of ability to relax. Hardly slept at all last night and several other nights lately. For the record I should also include that I was badly handicapped with headache for 3 out of the 7 days at "Wabanna" and it climaxed with that very tough mig. on Sat that I was barely able to control even with a lot of pain and <u>too much</u> dope. Danger signals must surely be the Lord's warning to do something about it!

---

[32] Wilbur Moorehead Smith (1894–1976). A much-beloved Bible teacher. At the time of this journal entry he was teaching at Moody Bible Institute. He went on to help start Fuller Theological Seminary in California. Jim was talking to him about speaking at the upcoming Young Life Staff Conference.

*Some of the men at the 1944 Staff Conference with the Navigators.
Jim is standing in the center; Add Sewell is over Rayburn's right
shoulder; Dawson Trotman is in the dark jacket, front row, right.*

Wednesday, July 12

This is a gala day. We moved to our new offices at 2018 Commerce. The
new furniture was all in by 4:00 P.M. and it looks nicer** than anything
I ever dreamed of having for an office. I can never thank the Lord for
His overwhelming goodness in this—and how wonderful the Mitchells
have been to us as His "agents" in all this.

---

*Jim's diary does not record the events of the combined Navigators
and Young Life staff conference in August, although other con-
temporary sources indicate it was a success. When the Rayburns
returned home to Dallas they had been gone for weeks. Jim was
ready for the new school year. When he wasn't travelling, he would
be helping lead the North Dallas, Woodrow Wilson, and Terrell
Prep clubs in Dallas, as well as the Riverside club in Fort Worth.*

Friday, September 22 (travelling)

Arrived home at 11:00 P.M. after a very comfortable trip to-day. No heat. Stayed in Amarillo until after lunch. We have never had such a fine trip. Enjoyable all the way and <u>no trouble</u> at all—2000 miles on an old Ford tire after the blowout in Oregon. My heart has been more full of gratitude to our wonderful Lord with each mile that we have come closer to home. Oh to be more like He would have me and do a JOB for Him this year.[33]

Tuesday, September 26

44.

Started the North Dallas Club. Very fine bunch. Best starting meeting that I ever saw. Of the 44 present 19 were boys.

Began with "Why a Young Life Club—What is it supposed to do."

Wednesday, September 27

Started the Woodrow[34] Club to-night 28** present. Not a very promising outfit.

Used same theme as Tues.

Thursday, September 28

Dallas–Ft Worth.

16.

Started the Riverside Club. They listened this time—What a contrast to a year ago.

Used same opening there as Tues. Worked good here & Tues. Not so good Wed.

---

[33] In a letter to Grant Whipple he wrote a few days later, Jim provided a little more detail about the trip home: "We came all the way home from that little dump in eastern Oregon, nearly 2000 miles, on that old Ford tire that we put on there. It was really wonderful coming all that way with not a minute of trouble from any source. God is good."

[34] Woodrow Wilson High School in Dallas, known by most students by its "first name."

Saturday, September 30

A wonderful Board of Directors Mtg—Bank Bal. of $1026.00 after all bills paid for the year. $42,600.00 receipts to the general fund this year. To everything about $50,000.00. That is the third year of the work. I know my heart is full of deep gratitude to God for ever overcoming all my failures and permitting such wonderful growth & blessing.

———

At the invitation of Mary Frances Redding and Dr. Howard E. Hansen, Christian Education Director and Minister, respectively, of First Presbyterian Church in Colorado Springs, Jim and some of the men travelled to Colorado to put on a series of meetings in October. It would be the beginning of a long connection between Jim Rayburn, Young Life, and the community of Colorado Springs.

In addition to Jim's speaking, the Mass Meetings featured the Young Life Quartet (or in the case of the Colorado Springs meeting, the Young Life Quintet)—a group of talented singers whose membership changed from year to year. Members were usually recruited from Dallas Seminary. One of them was George Sheffer. Sheffer joined Young Life's staff full-time after graduating from DTS in 1945 and, along with his wife Martie, became beloved leaders of the mission, pioneering Young Life's suburban work, urban work, camping ministry, and helping start Young Life's ministry in Africa before his death in 1987.

To get a feeling for the appeal Rayburn had with crowds, it is helpful to read what Jim's old mentor and president of Dallas Seminary, Lewis Sperry Chafer, had to say about him. In a letter he wrote in September to a friend who was looking for someone to speak to young people. Chafer wrote, "The best man we have available in the United States for just this kind of thing is James Rayburn... Rayburn graduated here in 1940 and took the Young Life work which now is sweeping our country; especially designed for high school students. We have had rallies here that have run up to

1,800 high school students intensely interested in the Gospel. Rayburn is almost supernatural in his appeal and power with these young people ... Follow his instructions and you will see miracles on a very large scale on a most blessedly true Gospel foundation ..."

It wasn't just Chafer who felt that way. After the Colorado Springs meetings, one of the high school students wrote to Jim: "I personally saw seven of the eleven starters on [our] football team at the Young Life mass meeting last Monday. I was also impressed by the number of kids who talked the meeting up the next few days. Being the grandson of a minister, I was amazed at what interest you stirred up. I never saw anything like it in this town before. I would like to thank you for the good that it did me, too."

Or, as one high school girl put it more simply, "If that's religion, I could go for it."

Thursday, October 12

A busy morning and just barely got away to get the train. Fine afternoon on the train—restful.

Geo. [Sheffer] and I had a grand conversation about the things of the Lord and he told me that he was definitely committed to the Campaign Staff for at least a year or two—the only other consideration being the foreign mission field.

Monday, October 16 (Colorado Springs)

1200—Colo. Spgs Hi.
670—North Jr.
300—South Jr.
300—West Jr.
230—Manitou Hi.
1200+ To-night's Mass Mtg
[Total:] 3900
The "Red Letter" of "Red-Letter-Days"

What a day! Five assemblies. Every one of them just rolled. Can never THANK THE LORD enough for HIS grace & power to make us acceptable to these kids.

I cannot write of to-night. Surely I have never been privileged to see anything like it. In one day's time—this great throng of young people. And the presence and power of the Lord by the Holy Spirit every moment of the way. By His Grace alone I was enabled to produce the best day's ministry of my life—To-night I preached the most forceful Gospel message I have ever preached. At the end the kids were so quiet and attentive & all prayed 'till it was like nothing I ever saw. All the boys agree: OUR GREATEST DAY IN Y.L.C. I have gone in deep sincerity anew to I J 1:9[35] & I Cor 10:13[36] to-n[ight]. I <u>know</u> God hears & answers prayer.

Tuesday, October 17 (Colorado Springs)

I began this day just after midnight seeking the Lord's face in grateful PRAISE for yesterday and with all my heart dedicating myself anew to the proposition of being absolutely all out for Him all the time.

[...]

Friday, October 20

Worked hard at office and then went with Elna Ann to her school dinner and carnival to-night. A mob—enjoyed doing it with the kiddies.

Too tired for any good to-night!

Saturday, October 21

Took the kids to the circus this aft. Enjoyed it greatly.

Very weary. Have been extremely worn out ever since getting home— to the point of exhaustion every evening. Way below par on prayer, study et. al. Believe this is a spiritual problem that I must deal with.

---

[35] "If we confess our sins, he is faithful and just to forgive us our sins and to cleanse us from all unrighteousness."

[36] "No temptation has overtaken you that is not common to man. God is faithful, and he will not let you be tempted beyond your ability, but with the temptation he will also provide the way of escape, that you may be able to endure it."

Sunday, October 22

A good day—too[k] girls to S.S. at Scofield.[37] Had swell hour at my office. Home all aft. Reading & Studying "Youth Seeks A MASTER."[38]

Only 4 guys at Campaigners Meeting To-day.

Monday, October 23

Up at 6:30 this a.m. and got down to b. with the Lord about the Work
& the Main Job of Praying & Studying.

[...]

Had a good evening at home and a swell time of prayer.

———

*One of the interesting things to see in Jim's journals is how he went
from speaking to a meeting of several hundred one day, to a meeting of only a few students the next. Yet he rarely commented or
complained about the disparity. On October 16 he spoke to 3,900
students; three days later his Riverside club in Fort Worth had
only a dozen, But, ever the optimist, he recorded, "Only 12 kids but
[once] again they listened."*

*Jim's clubs during the 1944–45 school year tended to have
small attendance, no doubt due in part to his frequent and lengthy
absences. But Add Sewell was having much better success with his
three clubs in East Texas. As Jim pointed out to the staff, the secret
to Add's success was his spending time with kids at football practices and other places where they gathered; a practice that would
later be called "contact work." It would be a hallmark of the kind
of ministry the Lord was leading Jim to pioneer: communicating
God's love to non-Christians by caring about them and getting to
know them.*

---

[37] Scofield Memorial Church.

[38] *Youth Seeks a Master* by Louis Hadley Evans, 1941. Evans was the pastor of the
influential First Presbyterian Church of Hollywood, California.

In early November Jim travelled to the South Bend, Indiana, area, where he had been invited by the ministers of twelve different churches to speak at a series of meetings for young people. His journal entries during his time there are some of his most poignant—and would prove tragically prophetic.

Tuesday, November 7 (Mishawaka, Indiana)

I cannot understand the sweet Peace the Lord has ministered to my heart to-day. I have great problems—enough to bring TURMOIL and He ministers sweet Peace. Oh to KNOW my SAVIOR and to WALK w. Him. Phil 3:10.[39]

[...]

Wednesday, November 8 (Mishawaka, Indiana)

This has been one of the truly great days of my life. Shortly after going to bed last night about 1:00 a.m. I became very restless. Soon got up. Read the Word & Prayed and the Lord met me in such a strange and warm way as I just bared my heart before Him until nearly 5:00 a.m. Then up at 6:30 and out to pray with the men and right back here where I spent the whole morning & much of the afternoon in intimate fellowship with the Lord in prayer & study of the Victorious Life. Oh the joy of realizing that He is RIGHT HERE!

[...]

Thursday, November 9 (Mishawaka, Indiana)

[...]

Another unbelievably wonderful day. The Lord is doing something to me that has never happened before—giving me such a desire to be absolutely sold out to Jesus Christ and completely dead to self & all else that the world holds. I spent almost all day in prayer yesterday and

---

[39] "That I may know him and the power of his resurrection, and may share his sufferings, becoming like him in his death."

to-day—most all the time I had to myself—in prayer and the Word. It seems that my heart is almost to break just to completely enter into the truth of ALL THINGS IN JESUS I FIND. Now it is 1:30 a.m. I have lost much sleep this week and have not experienced THE LEAST BIT of weariness in my work. The LORD Jesus is more precious to me than ever before. I want to know what it means to SUFFER FOR JESUS' SAKE. May the Lord Jesus by His Spirit deal with me until truly "Christ be FORMED IN ME" Gal 4:19.[40]

Tuesday, November 14

60.

Left Chicago at 7:30 a.m. and had a beautiful and pleasant trip to DL arriving at 3:00 p.m.

Had a good tho difficult Club meeting to-night.

The Lord has been very precious to-day & I have had a great blessing from His Word. Still believe this past week has brought me through the greatest crises of my spiritual life.

———

His journal does not shed light on the details or even the nature of the various crises he was facing, however it is obvious what got Jim through them: dependence on His Savior, and hours upon hours spent in His presence. Jim's prayer to suffer for Jesus' sake would be answered in many ways over the coming years.

---

[40] "My little children, for whom I am again in the anguish of childbirth until Christ is formed in you!"

1945

77 - 25

Slept late. Feel swell. Thankful
to the Lord for the big change in
my feelings over last night. Had conf.
at office with whole crew - Grant, Norm
Warn. Then to Nat. V with Norm. Then
to Seattle by bus. Had supper with
Ruby Goth... Then beautiful plane
trip to Portland. Wally met
me + we had a nice chat and
bite to eat before I went to hotel.
Good day. Feel close to the
Lord to-night. Oh may I LIVE
close to Him Regardless of how
I "feel"!

"FEEL CLOSE TO THE LORD TO-NIGHT."

Jim was thirty-five years old and Maxine was about to turn thir-
ty-three as the new year rolled in. The ministry of Young Life con-
tinued to grow and develop at an exciting clip. Always looking for
new ways to appeal to high school students, in February Jim made
an extensive tour of the country with track star Gil Dodds.[1]

Monday, January 1

Again I can say as last year—perhaps this is the finest beginning to a
new yr I have ever had. Entirely different—not the "joyous experience"
of last year—but (In spite of terrific weariness of the body) I feel that
when I met the Lord at midnight it was as a Christian who has grown
in HIM & by His grace stands READY to go on with Him. Know my
own "unreliability" better—sense NEED much more personally & pow-
erfully—BELIEVE GOD more definitely. Am more thankful than ever
for JESUS my SAVIOR—more sure that His hand is on my life—these
are just some random thoughts not well stated but coming out of the
greatest crisis of my life perhaps & Praise God I believe HE DOETH ALL
THINGS WELL.[2]

Although I did not get near as much time alone with the Lord as I
had hoped I did feel a distinct sense of the Lord's <u>presence</u> <u>all</u> <u>day</u> and I
believe it was to an extent which was "different." He has made me feel
that I mean business with Him and more personal with Him than ever
before.

[...]

Tuesday, January 2

Hard to report the truly significant facts of to-day. While awake in the

---

[1] Gilbert Lothair "Gil" Dodds (1918–1977). Known as "The Flying Parson," Dodds
had broken the world record for the indoor mile (4:06.4 minutes) on March 18, 1944.
He went on to coach the track team at Wheaton.

[2] Most likely a reference to Mark 7:37: "And were beyond measure astonished,
saying, He hath done all things well: he maketh both the deaf to hear, and the dumb
to speak" (KJV).

night I had a real spirit of prayer as far as I can tell—tho very weary had good short time this a.m.—on way to office same.

For second straight day—as far as I know I have not spoken sharply or manifested any spirit of unlove to anyone—nor criticized anyone. PRAISE THE LORD.

I went to Harlan [*sic*, Harlin] Roper[3] this afternoon and openly confessed my sin of criticism and lack of love. Thanks be to God. He made both of us very warm tow. each other. All day I have felt a Spirit of Prayer. Believe physical weariness—esp. from 3:00 p.m.-on is proving a big handicap.

Friday, January 5

A very outstanding day. Extremely weary so got off to a late start but from 9:30 on it was all business and definitely conscious of the Lord's presence in several hours of Bible Study and prayer. The thing that is signif. to me about the day is that which is happening more & more of late—Praise God—namely, my communion is very personal in HIM and based upon HIS WORD more than ever. The consciousness that "He is right here" continues to keep me aware of His Presence in a wonderful way. So far as I can possibly tell I am "in fellowship" & do not know why the prom[ise] of Phil 4:7[4] has not been complete unless it is a case of I Pet 1:6, 7.[5] We had a Bible Study Session at the house to-night. Staff girls, Barbara, Rosie, Saundy and Mildred.

---

[3] Harlin Roper was the pastor of Scofield Memorial Church in Dallas from 1927–1972. The church had significant connections with Dallas Seminary and was the Rayburns' church home during their years in Dallas.

[4] "And the peace of God, which surpasses all understanding, will guard your hearts and your minds in Christ Jesus."

[5] "In this you rejoice, though now for a little while, if necessary, you have been grieved by various trials, so that the tested genuineness of your faith—more precious than gold that perishes though it is tested by fire—may be found to result in praise and glory and honor at the revelation of Jesus Christ."

Saturday, January 6

Read Mt, Mk, Lk, John to-day. Real blessing. Got a better picture than ever before.

Word from Gil Dodds came to-day that we can have him Feb 4–24.

Monday, January 8

1st Mig. Hdache for '45—(10 day interval) Shot.
Not a very good day. We were badly interrupted at the office by the failure of the furnace as it was hard to concentrate on anything. Did have a very good short season of prayer with the crew this a.m. and alone to-night in spite of severe mig. symptoms.

Friday, January 12

Had splendid conv. with Dr. Criswell[6] this afternoon. Very friendly. Believes the Word. Thank God.

Have had a lot of intimate personal conversations with the Lord to-day. The Gil Dodds itinerary seems now to be definitely set.

[...]

It is strange how this aparently [*sic*] "important business" (and headache) has crowded out the Word & interfered with prayer life this wk. Oh Lord how to put those <u>always</u> first. And to live up to my privileges along line of "peace"—"joy."

Jim had been invited a few months earlier to speak in Winnipeg for a series of meetings at Elim Chapel. His visit there in January appears to be the first time he met Sid Smith, a leading Canadian businessman with whom he quickly developed a deep friendship.

Saturday, January 20

An excellent trip. Arrived more weary than I've ever been it seems. FEEL

---

6   Wallie Amos Criswell (1909–2002). Criswell had been appointed pastor of Dallas's First Baptist Church three months earlier; he served in that role until 1995. He and Rayburn were the same age.

VERY "LOW."

Graciously received by Mr. [Frank] Frogley—Levi Loewen, and Mr. Sidney Smith.

Spoke with great liberty & joy to CBMC banquet.[7] Spoke on "WALK IN WISDOM …" Royal reception! And at IVF[8] rally.

———

Gil Dodds and Jim travelled together for much of February. After that tour, Jim continued with some speaking engagements of his own. Altogether, his 1945 diary records fifty-three airplane trips and ninety-four days out of town for the year (as well as thirty-seven migraine headaches).

The last stop on the Dodds tour was Bellingham, Washington. The staff man there, Norm Robbins, had been hired by Jim on the recommendation of Grant Whipple, even though Robbins had never seen a Young Life club. He served on staff for almost thirty years. (One of his first club kids was Jim Elliot, who later became famous after being martyred for his faith while serving as a missionary in Ecuador.)

Things at home continued to be difficult as Maxine fought depression and other health problems.

Sunday, February 4

First day I have def. not prayed an hour or more for several months—since last Oct 10—I believe.

The Lord gave Gil & I a great time over at E. Dallas Christian men's class. Left for LR [Little Rock] to-night.

———

---

[7] Jim described this meeting in a letter as "the Christian businessmen's committee annual banquet—about 400 businessmen and wives there."

[8] Most likely Inter-Varsity Christian Fellowship.

Wednesday, February 28 (Bellingham, Washington)
Slept late. Feel swell. Thankful to the Lord for this big change in my feelings over last night. Had conf. at office with whole crew—Grant, Norm, Wam. Then to Mt.** V[ernon] with Norm. Then to Seattle by bus. Had supper with Rudy Goth ... Then beautiful plane trip to Portland. Wally met me & we had a nice chat and bite to eat before I went to hotel. Good day. Feel close to the Lord to-night. Oh may I LIVE close to HIM Regardless of how I "feel"!

Saturday, March 31
CAMP[AIG]N DAY OF PRAYER—
I was greatly blessed by the time we had to-gether before the Lord to-day, altho it was shorter than usual. We prayed very definitely for all our workers and their needs. It seems that the past two weeks have been the most difficult of my life. I just can't get strung out. Am a "misfit" at home, at the office, and every way. Feel miserable but for some reason the main trouble is I won't get down to business with the Lord. Thank God ..."He changes NOT ..."[9]

Sunday, April 1 (Easter)
A difficult Easter Sunday—Maxine too ill to go to church—I took the girlies. Dr. L. Sale-Harrison[10] was good. Feeling very bum and things indeed at a low ebb around home to-day. Don't know what to do. Need the Lord's help very much. Have failed Maxine so and do not know how to help her it seems. Prayed personally for each member of the staff to-night. Hard to get down to much of a season of prayer it seems.

Saturday, April 7 (Camp Parthenia, Oklahoma)
They picked me up in town at 8:00. I spoke at 9:00 on "The Urgency of

---

[9] Perhaps a reference to Malachi 3:6, "For I am the LORD, I change not ..." (KJV)

[10] Visiting speaker L. Sale-Harrison was known for his books and messages on biblical prophecy.

the Gospel" or receiving it. Using Isa. 64:6.[11] Again well pleased with the response and believe the Lord was with me. Had a wonderful time alone in the woods on the other side of the lake—met the Lord in a wonderful way—thru His Word. Specially Phil 1, 2, 3, 4. Believe this day marks a big new step forward in my dependence upon HIM for EVERYTHING.

[...]

—⁓—

Young Life was finally making some headway in Pennsylvania and Chicago, and Jim's trips there became increasingly frequent.

Sunday, April 22 (Chester, Pennsylvania)
A truly wonderful day in Chester. The people were so nice to me. In the Morning I spoke on J 4 & J 8 using "them t. are without" as a text.[12] Evening on [Greek lettering].[13] Both times the Lord gave me liberty & joy in speaking. Went to "Broad Street" to get my Pullman—left for Chi at 11:15.

Monday, April 23 (Chicago)
Had to change in Pittsburg[h] early this a.m. Got a Pullman seat into Chi & had a good day—especially in the afternoon in a season of prayer at which time I prayed for all the workers in the Campaign.

---

[11] "We have all become like one who is unclean,
    and all our righteous deeds are like a polluted garment.
We all fade like a leaf,
    and our iniquities, like the wind, take us away."

[12] Colossians 4:5—"Walk in wisdom toward them that are without, redeeming the time" (KJV)—was a favorite verse of Jim's. The phrase "them that are without" is used four other times in the New Testament, each time meaning people who are outside the Christian faith. Sensitivity to such people was a hallmark of Jim's life and Young Life's ministry.

[13] Though he knew both Greek and Hebrew, this is one of only a few times in his journals that Jim wrote in either language. In this case, it appears that he spoke to the evening crowd about "archegos" ("author" or "founder") as used about Jesus is Acts 3:15 and 5:31; and Hebrews 2:10 and 12:2.

Had a wonderful time with Chub Andrews and Margie[14] to-night. They met me & took me out to dinner.

—⁓—

With the increasing Young Life presence at Wheaton, Add Sewell (then the Chicago area director), Wally Howard, and Jim were invited to lead a two-week inter-session course on Young Life methods at the school, from June 12–22. Jim brought with him Orville & Frances Mitchell's son, Bob. "Mitch" as he became known by generations of Young Lifers, had just graduated from high school in Dallas, and was about to begin Wheaton in the fall.

But the biggest event of the summer, and certainly the one that had the most significant impact on Young Life's future, was a two-week staff conference at the Navajo Hotel in Manitou Springs, Colorado, just outside of Colorado Springs. (Bob Mitchell was brought along for the staff conference.)

It was also at the conference that, for the first time, Jim exposed his staff to the Colorado Rockies and shared with them his dream of Young Life owning its own camp. Jim later said that the time at Manitou Springs was "where this camp project idea really crystallized in my own prayer life and my own thinking."

He even already had a place in mind—a property named Crystal Park near Colorado Springs—and led the staff on a hike to the property.

Friday, June 8

Really got a lot accomplished at the office to-day. "Say G."[15] and a lot of imp. mail taken care of. Had a swell brief parting visit with the Mitchell men.

Last night and the night before I slept all night and breathed thru

---

[14] Dr. William F. "Chub" Andrews and his wife, Margie.

[15] "Say, Gang!" was Jim's monthly column in the *Young Life* magazine.

my nose the whole time—7½ hrs or more asleep both nights—The first time this has occurred since sometime last fall. The improvement has been gradual, almost imperceptible for the past month.

Thursday, June 21 (Chicago)

Watched Dr. Nelson Percy operate: Apendectomy [*sic*], Histerectomy [*sic*], Goiter—great stuff—amazing to me. Could hardly take some of it but VERY glad I went.

Met Mr. Taylor. Had a wonderful chat with him. He did a wonderful thing for us. Gave Maxine and me 100 shares of Club Aluminum Stock as an Education Fund for our children.

Had our closing conference session this aft. Feel that it went well.

[...]

Saturday, June 23 (Chicago)

Chub & Margie came to "Augustana"** and picked us up. We had breakfast at The Triangle to-gether. Bob [Mitchell] & I took the plane at 10:30. Good trip to Wichita. Arr. 4:00. Earnest, Pearl & Flossie there.[16] Swell visit. Then Flossie went w. us. Had grand trip via "Continental" to Colo. Spgs. arr. at 9:30. I helped the stewardess, Susan Ann Potter serve dinner, both Bob & I had swell talks with her about the work & the Lord. It was a pleasant & restful day & the Lord seemed very near. Our Manitou hotel set-up is "funny."[17]

Tuesday, July 10 (Colorado Springs)

Howard Hansen and I went to see the attorney for the Broadmoor peo-

---

[16] Earnest M. Wetmore, his wife Pearl, and their daughter Florence, of Tonkawa, Oklahoma. E. M. Wetmore was on the national board of trustees. Florence, known to all as Flossie, was on staff at the time.

[17] He might be referring to the fact that the bathrooms were not in the rooms, but down the hall on each floor.

ple—about Crystal Park. I was thrilled to learn that he is quite open to the idea of selling it to us and suggested cutting the announced price of $30,000.00 somewhat. I am very enthused about the prospect. Intend to keep before the Lord about it and see what He has in mind for us on this.

Walter Guy[18] took us to the train. We left Colo. Springs in a downpour of rain. Fine dinner on the train. Our two bedrooms thrown together make excellent accommodations.

―⁓―

After the successful staff conference, the Rayburn family left Colorado Springs for vacation at his new friend Sid Smith's summer home in Minnesota. Jim no doubt spent much time during those two weeks praying and thinking about Young Life's future camping ministry. Unbeknownst to him, the very property he was enjoying—Sid Smith's vacation home—would one day become a Young Life property itself, Castaway Club, when the Smith family gave it to Young Life in 1963.

Most of the Smith clan—Mr. and Mrs. Smith and their sons and grandchildren—was there to welcome the Rayburns.

Thursday, July 12 (Detroit Lakes, Minnesota)

19th Migraine: Came in night from yesterday's headache which I couldn't stop. S[top]** time very early this a.m.

Had a bustling time getting on the train to Detroit Lakes but it was a comfortable journey. Harold & Mrs. Smith met us at the train.

We came right out to Smiths'. Truly a beautiful place—and there were 20 of us at the big house for dinner. Harold's family, Clancy's, Gordon's without Gordon—

―⁓―

---

[18] Guy was, according to a letter Jim wrote to the staff before the trip, "an out and out Christian, [who] is feeding us—at a very special rate."

Wednesday, September 19 (Colorado Springs)

A MEMORABLE DAY.

Fog this morning. Howard Hansen drove us to Crystal Park. It was completely engulfed in the clouds from about 8000′ on up. We couldn't see the scenery at all—nevertheless Mr. Taylor was SOLD on the project and after a conf. with Mr. Carruthers[19] he said he would buy it or practically said that—if the terms are right. I can't see how we could have made more progress on this deal in such a short time. Boarded plane for DL @ 5:15. (Hansen very happy about the project too!)

Home at 11:30 p.m.

———

Despite Mr. Taylor's generous offer, Crystal Park was not destined to become a Young Life property. Without explanation, its owners sold it—for the same amount Taylor offered—to someone else. Jim was heartbroken, but he was now convinced that God wanted Young Life to have its own camping program.

The war now over, a new day was dawning in America. A new day was dawning in Young Life, as well. Now beginning its sixth year of club work, the staff had learned that "the key is personal contact," as Jim told the board members in September. As Jim and the other leaders helping him in the Riverside and North Dallas clubs got to know kids personally (rather than just put on events for them), the attendance at club began to pick up in a dramatic fashion. North Dallas hit 132 in attendance, and Riverside in Ft. Worth hit 139, Jim's biggest clubs up to that point.

As autumn came, the Rayburn family was about to be expanded for a third and final time. Maxine gave birth to James Chalmers Rayburn III, on October 31.

---

[19] The attorney representing the owners of the property.

Friday, October 5 (travelling)

[…]

This has been a great day. One of the very best. Practically the whole day spent in prayer and Bible Study. The Lord surely spoke to me & seemed very close all day. In fact I haven't experienced anything comparable to this[,] this whole year of '45. Wonder why? Prayer is so real to-day. There is "peace." A real love for the Word to-day. Thank God. Why am I so cool so much of the time[?]

[…]

———

Monday, October 29

A much better start than I have had for days. Exc. time of prayer at the office too. Boy how the Lord helped me tackle the Board & Staff letters and the acknowledgments and other correspondence. Feel that I have really been close to the Lord to-day.

Still Maxine is at home—2½ weeks since we expected the babe's arrival.

A good time with the officers of the N. Dallas Club to-night. What a chance I have. Oh that God will make me the leader that these kids need.

Tuesday, October 30

90

Got a lot done at office and then home most of afternoon.

Great club mtg to-night.

Maxine began to have pretty strong pains about 10:00. I called Art[20] & he went & got Rosella** & Lyndora. We went to the hospital at about 12:30. Maxine was having bad pains about 6 or 7 min. apart.

---

[20] Most likely Art Rech. At the time of this entry, Rech was doing post-graduate work at DTS, after graduating from Wheaton and Princeton Theological Seminary. He and his wife Jean were welcome additions to the Young Life family when he joined the full-time staff in 1946.

Wednesday, October 31

32nd Migraine. Afternoon. Shot @ 4:00.

80.

My little son was born at 4 A.M.!

I was very surprised when it happened so soon. Expected a longer wait. I waited around to see him but didn't get to. Home about 5. Had a good time of prayer and then went to the office for a fine hour of prayer. Then home to breakfast & bed. Couldn't sleep much. Back up about 12:30.

Saw Maxine for awhile. Then to Ft. Worth. Felt very sick at stomach all day. Migraine pain very bad after 1:00.

Wonderful mtg at Riverside in spite of Halloween. A great day.

Thursday, November 8

1650 N. Dallas H. Assembly

This rates as one of my truly great days because of the marvelous way the Lord enabled me & blessed me in the eyes of all those kids at North Dallas Hi. As so many times He made the whole thing go over, and oh how I pray that He may get the glory—all of it! Oh to follow it with a smashing** offensive with the Gospel. Never have we had such an opport[unity]. Lord show me how to evangelize LOST KIDS—how to present CHRIST in His Beauty & Great Power.

Took the kids to Fair Park to-night—Great!

Worked hard at office all afternoon. Worked 'till after midnight here at home.

[...]

Monday, December 24

Considerable R-side pain. Thot mig coming but did not materialize.

A happy day at home—specially helping the "kiddies" get ready for Christmas. Their anticipation of it was a very heart-warming thing.

Tuesday, December 25
A truly grand Christmas—all of us had many nice gifts—the children were loaded down with them—but seemed to go for the skates far more than anything else.

1946

STAR RANCH IN THE PINES
The main building (above). A club meeting at Star (below).

Unfortunately, even though it proved to be one of the most impor-
tant years in Jim's life, the whereabouts of his journal for this year
are unknown.

The key event of that year was one of the great miracles of
Young Life history: the acquisition of Star Ranch, Young Life's
first property.

Fortunately, however, when Jim told the story five years later,
his message was transcribed. What follows is that account.

The Story of Star Ranch, as told by Jim Rayburn to the Leadership Training Institute, August 30, 1951

Young Life began in Dallas, Texas, in 1940. One of the first things we did was to have camps down in Texas—using any old kind we could get (that's the kind there are in Texas). [We] branched out to Tennessee, where we had our camps in state parks. Then we started in the Northwest—at Bellingham, Washington.

Work spread out until in 1944 we had a quartet which travelled—composed of George Sheffer and Wally Howard and two others. We were up in Colorado. [I] got to thinking as we were called to hold meetings what a wonderful thing it would be to have a camp of our own—instead of going around, instead of renting everyone's ramshackle places. Something located right geographically—for the Texas work as well as the Northwest. [It] seemed [a] wonderful idea if camping facilities could be found in the Colorado Rockies. [You could] bring kids from both places.

We had (and have) a wonderful friend in Dr. Howard Hansen, pastor of the First Presbyterian Church in Colorado Springs. [He has been a] lot of help—one of the finest friends we have in the nation. He encouraged us greatly. And he got busy himself looking for camp facilities. Little plot of ground by some stream. Pitch tents—any old lean-to would do. ([He had been] brought up in traditional fashion—like other fundamentalists accustomed to doing the Lord's work. Lean-to's!) No vision for what the Lord had in mind.

[We] learned quite a few things accidentally; some things on purpose. But this we had nothing to do with at all—just fell into it. [The] Lord led us in ways we did not know. We came through Colorado Springs once in a while, and every time went with Mr. Guss Hill[1] of Colorado Springs ([he is] on our national board) and Mr. Hansen to look at places.

We found one suitable spot in Manitou,[2] but the deal fell through. I was discouraged! On the way back, Mr. Hill mentioned that he didn't know much about the work. He would like to know. None of it here in Colorado. [That] started quite a conversation—for an hour. I told how we went after kids. How we felt that every kid—tough, society— all kinds—those too smart for religion—had a right to know the facts concerning the person of Christ and what He had done. We deliberately went out after him. We didn't exclude anybody. [We] talked methods; he was very interested. He said as we came down West Colorado Avenue, "I know a place which is just the thing you're looking for. Of course, the trouble is, it costs $50,000." I said, "That *is* a great *deal* of trouble!" Thought I knew where I could get someone to spend $1,000 or $2,000 to get started. Wouldn't hurt anything to dream. So, we drove up Cheyenne Mountain, the ride familiar to many of you—[the] road to Star Ranch.

The gate was locked—buttoned up! The caretaker was fussy, and the owner was away. He had given definite orders that no one should look through the ranch. And so we looked through the fence. "About the most beautiful place I ever saw," was all I thought about [it].

---

[1] Guss D. Hill was the owner of Hill Realty & Investment Co., in Colorado Springs. Hill and his wife Millie became close friends of the Rayburns. He served on the board of trustees from 1949–1958 and 1963–1966. His most important contribution to Young Life, however, was his role as "God's Real Estate Agent": he was instrumental in the acquisition of Star Ranch, Silver Cliff Ranch, and Frontier Ranch for Young Life, as well as The Navigators' purchase of Glen Eyrie in Colorado Springs. Hill died in 1996.

[2] He is referring to the Crystal Park property.

Then we went to town. I said, "Thanks for the ride," and went to my hotel. I prepared to leave Colorado Springs.

Here again ... you folks believe in God. So many things happened that can't be accounted for, except for the leading of the Lord. The laws of mathematical probability would prove it. God led.

I wrote a letter to a Christian friend in the East[3] who wanted to know if we ran into anything. He hadn't said that he would help. I wrote him (I had already written my wife that day!). Told him that we had seen the most beautiful place. A millionaire's summer home. He never used it. That was all I said.

Then to Tennessee—way out in the weeds—Union City, Tennessee—for meetings in [a] church for the kids. We were going along. Suddenly [I] got a letter, telegram, or telephone call, from this friend. "My wife and I are going through Colorado Springs next Monday. Can you meet us?"

I took a plane—for Colorado Springs, via Amarillo, Texas, where we were grounded, as usual. ([Thanks to jets, we] now fly over it at 20,000 feet!) Something happened—wind blew [the] wings off, or an ice storm, or something. [I] stayed four hours there, listening to fellows cuss Amarillo because they were spending hours there, too. [...]

Finally got to Colorado Springs—six hours late! Feeling pretty low. Not even a chance to meet with [my] wealthy, prominent friend. [I] couldn't have felt any lower down than then. Went to my hotel and called him at his hotel—quite a different hotel![4] He asked me if I could come out to the Broadmoor and have dinner with him. I went there, and he said, "Well, Jim, I've got a surprise for you. The Mrs. and I have been out to Star Ranch. Mr. Hill took us around. Sorry you couldn't make it."

I said, "I'm sorry, too."

---

[3] H. J. Taylor.

[4] The Taylors were staying at The Broadmoor, Colorado Springs' finest hotel.

"Beautiful place."

"Yeah."

I went on slurping my soup, disheartened. Things just hadn't gone right. Nothing was right that didn't turn out according to *my* calculations. The lady was apparently in good humor. Ate a square meal. Smiling as ladies do. [...]

We weren't very far along in the meal until this eminent gentleman turned to me and said to me, "Do you think you could use Star Ranch for Young Life work? [Is it the] kind of thing you want?"

[I told him] I'd never seen anything in my life like that. [It was a] dream spot! [I] never imagined there could be anything so wonderful. Then he looked at his wife and said, "We've decided to buy it for you."

Half of the crew of the Broadmoor waiters dug me out!

We talked happily about this great project. How we could use Star Ranch. [That's] precisely all I had to do about it! Never [even] got around to praying for it! Seemed clear out of reach. I was not so much as counting on it. Certainly thought if we got it that this man would say, "We will give $5,000, and if you can raise the other $45,000, it's yours."

Reminds me of a verse of Scripture: "Now unto him that is able to do exceeding abundantly above all that we can ask or think" (Ephesians 3:20).

The growth of Young Life Campaign and [the] acquisition of other things is characterized by those words from the pen of Paul. God has put in us His great divine power, the Holy Spirit. That Holy Spirit works in ways we do not know. [It] always appeals to me about the way the Lord has led in getting far more than we intended to have. [...]

———

Star Ranch in the Pines, as it was known when the Taylors obtained it, had been used as a private home by its three previous owners. It boasted a breathtaking view of Cheyenne Mountain, an immaculate lawn dotted by granite boulders, and buildings made of stone and log. It was truly a showplace.

Herb Taylor and Jim.

Believing as Jim did that God wanted Young Life to be in the camping ministry, the Taylors leased Star Ranch to Young Life for $1 a year.

Decades later, when Maxine Rayburn was asked what Jim considered his greatest triumph, she did not hesitate: "Getting our first camp. I believe that would be it, his greatest triumph." No doubt the hundreds of thousands of high school students who have experienced "the greatest week of their lives" at a Young Life property would agree.

1947

Monday, July 7, 1947
188th Day—177 Days to Follow

Our camp started well to-night — Counting all the staff and work crew we have just about a capacity with only 45 regist. campers.

I spoke to-night on "What's It all About." Jer 9 23, 24.

YOUNG LIFE CAMPING BEGINS

Even though Young Life obtained Star Ranch in 1946, the camping season for that year did not get off the ground due to a polio scare. The above entry is from the first day of the first week of outreach camp at a Young Life-owned property. The forty-five campers would be followed by hundreds of thousands in the decades to come.

The Taylors and Young Life took possession of Star Ranch in May 1946. Rayburn had hoped to have at least some outreach camping at the new property that summer, but a polio outbreak cancelled any such hopes. The staff did gather there for their annual two-week conference in June, however, and christened the place.

As 1947 began, there were thirty-two full- and part-time staff in ten areas in seven states. Jim was anxious to make the move from Dallas to Colorado Springs and Star Ranch. Understandably, he wanted to put the ranch to good use, as well as "show it off." With that in mind, he put together a trip to Star Ranch for the Ft. Worth Amon Carter Riverside High School basketball team in February to play Colorado teams. Sammy Adams and Pancho Page were two of the Riverside players; coaches Low and Goldstein were the boys' coaches.

During the Texas years, Jim was often on the radio, usually as a part of the Dallas Seminary Quartet's regular program or a guest of another broadcast. He never had his own program.

Wednesday, January 15

An important day. Hard work in office—then to Ft. Worth. Exc[ellent] contacts with Sammy, Pancho, Ed, et al. Coaches Low & Goldstein. Mr. Browning.

Have peaceful feeling about the work & see clearly the hand of God upon it—Getting more burden for the kids & more vision of the tremendous opportunity God is giving and the great responsibility attached to such leadership.

Saturday, January 18

Good A.M. at office.

KRLD Broadcast @ 2:00. Went good!

Home all evening.

For the third January in a row, Jim and several others travelled to Winnipeg for Sid Smith's Elim Chapel meetings. The depth of Rayburn and Smith's relationship can clearly be seen in this next series of entries.

Wednesday, January 29 (Winnipeg)

Just don't see how the Lord can bless me so much & this work which is so dear to my heart. This evening mtg was by far the best yet—a really big crowd—larger than any wk nite—I spoke—with much liberty and sense of the Lord's blessing—upon Ro. 5:1–10 ("The Four Things We Are Without Christ") with a long intro. concerning the FACT of the CRUCIFIXION & RESURRECTION.

To a great Rotary Club this noon—poss[ibly] 250 men on—"The American Way"—the me[aning] of standing guard over our freedoms [...] then on Bible as source of ALL such PRINCIPLES. Very well received. Sid & I had one of those sweet intimate times of fellowship such as I never had with any but him I believe. Thank God for it ALL!

Thursday, January 30 (Winnipeg)

The same wonderful story. I could say of to-day all that I said of these other days. The Lord is <u>Good</u> (Ex. 34:6,[1] Ps. 86:15,[2] Joel 2:13b).[3] He has done it all. I see it & see HIM more clearly than ever before. Nothing I have or am that is any good but He gave it to me. I'm <u>sure</u> I really love the Savior and He has given me much <u>peace</u>. Oh to be more for Him! A larger crowd again to-night. Big downstairs practically full. I think the

---

[1] "The LORD passed before him and proclaimed, 'The LORD, the LORD, a God merciful and gracious, slow to anger, and abounding in steadfast love and faithfulness.'"

[2] "But you, O Lord, are a God merciful and gracious,
    slow to anger and abounding in steadfast love and faithfulness."

[3] "Return to the LORD, your God,
    for he is gracious and merciful,
slow to anger, and abounding in steadfast love;
    and he relents over disaster."

thing that has drawn my heart out to the Lord Jesus more than anything
else is the way these people love me & believe in me so that it makes me
ashamed. I could not have such warmth & love apart from His Grace.
I Preached "Reconciliation"** to-night. II Cor. 5, Colossians 1:20, 21,[4]
Romans 5:10.[5] Story of HERB.[6]

---

*In a bizarre, unpredictable turn of events, Sid Smith died sud-
denly the next day. He hosted a luncheon for six businessmen at
which Rayburn spoke, and then he passed away peacefully while
being driven home later that afternoon from his office. In a letter
to the Young Life staff, Jim wrote,*

> Mr. Smith was very happy, and spoke with great enthusiasm of
> the privilege of giving these men [at the luncheon] the Gospel
> in a simple, tactful way. (He often arranged such luncheons as
> this just for the purpose of getting the Word of God to men
> who would not go to church.)
> About the last thing he ever said to any of us was that as
> long as we are in this life there is really nothing half so impor-
> tant as getting the Word of Life to other men.

*Smith's death came before the week's meetings ended, with sev-
eral more still to be held by Rayburn and his crew.*

Friday, January 31 (Winnipeg)

SID went HOME to-day. Quickly and quietly at 5pm., HE was caught away
to meet the Saviour he loved. OF all the sweet memories that I shall carry
thru life of this dearest friend GOD ever gave me—this is paramount.

---

[4] "And through him to reconcile to himself all things, whether on earth or in heaven,
making peace by the blood of his cross. And you, who once were alienated and hostile
in mind, doing evil deeds..."

[5] "For if while we were enemies we were reconciled to God by the death of his Son,
much more, now that we are reconciled, shall we be saved by his life."

[6] Possibly H. J. Taylor.

SID LOVED JESUS! Like JOHN of old he loved Him because He KNEW HIM.—"Because He first loved me"—. Sid taught me of Jesus' great love as no other man ever did. He taught me what friendship means. He was my friend. I could never forget. He loved me. My heart rejoices in that. I wonder why it was so? He often told me so sincerely, "Jim, no matter what you did I would love you," "No matter what you say I will stand by you." He meant it! WHAT A GUY! His last week on earth was the happiest week of my life. God's wonderful GRACE shining through SID SMITH made it so! I want to love Jesus like SID did. He loved the SAV-IOUR so much that he even loved the LITTLE GUYS TOO. LIKE JESUS DID!

We carried on at the chapel to-night for God and for Sid. It was lonely up there. The Lord gave us a great mtg with more young people accepting Christ than at any other time. I spoke on I Cor 15: 1–4. Wonderful time at Gordon Bell School this noon. A grand luncheon at Ft. Gary. Sid was there, happy & pulling for me as always.

Monday, February 3 (Winnipeg)

We buried Sid to-day. John Bellingham Jr.[7] spoke briefly & read scripture, then I spoke before leading in prayer—I was conscious of a great desire to say what Sid would have wanted there stating the Gospel as clearly as I could. I felt that the whole service was effective & fitting. Mallis gave a closing word—the cong[regation] sang 3 vss of "The Sands of Time Are Sinking"—a soloist did beautifully—it was all just 30 min. Church almost full in spite of worst weather in years. I experienced the worst cold weather of my life at the cemetery. There was a big crowd at the house until 9:30 p. Then I showed Emy,[8] Gordon, Izzy et. al., some slides of Star Ranch & family.

---

[7] Bellingham's father, John Bellingham, Sr., had co-founded Elim Chapel with Smith, and had passed away ten years earlier.

[8] Sid Smith's wife, Emily.

Ann and Mary Margaret ("Sue").

—⁓—

After a few days back in Dallas, Jim next headed to Waco. At this time, Ann was nine years old and Sue was almost seven.

Saturday, February 8

Migraine (R) late to-night—Shot. Relief without sickness.

This aft. Maxine & the girlies & I went to Waco. Dinner with Jack Franklin & wife. Then I spoke to 75 Baylor U kids @ Sat. Night Bible Study. It was wonderful. I started out to speak on Matthew 8, "faith"—but intro. by saying the three big words in the N.T. are Life—Love—Faith. Spent a full half-hour on Life—hammering away at "pure grace" for Salvation & detoured a lot—ending with the Suffering of Christ on the Cross.

—⁓—

Later that month Jim travelled to St. Louis for speaking engagements and on the way home he felt convicted by God about his spiritual life.

Sunday, February 23 (St. Louis)

Spoke @ West Pk. Baptist Ch. this a.m. 1st to Y.P. church & then to reg. A.M. Service.

A.M. on Acts 17. To kids on Believing—"Life."

Aft. Rally grand about 150 y.p. Really amazed at how much the Lord has done with our work here almost entirely through Will Brunk.[9]

Left for home at 10:30 p. Arr. 1:30 a.

In a very earnest & heart-searching time of prayer on the plane the Lord spoke to me of the urgency of devoting myself more earnestly than ever before to prayer and a close walk with Him—finding His Will in every particular of my life—careful not to move apart from that!

Monday, February 24

Very severe L & R mig both—altern[ating] thru the night. Worked hard around house all day. Maxine still sick. Got quite sick in aft. Lost my supper & felt very miserable to-night. Severe pain in head. This day seemed to make it almost if not really impossible to devote myself to prayer as I purposed. I have great confidence in God. Oh how faithful & merciful I see Him to be—Now to really go on with Him.

Tuesday, February 25

Not much done to-day. Felt terrible in a.m. Very severe pain in my head. Don't understand it. Maxine quite ill.

Had lunch & interview with Ed Phillips—[10]

Fine club mtg to-night.

A tough set of circumstances. Surely the Devil is contesting me all along the line in regard to the prayer life.

Wednesday, February 26

Up @ 4:30 a. Dick[11] drove me to Longview—bless him. I spoke twice at LeTourneau's[12] plant—nothing else happened. Neither of LeT's there.

---

[9] Will Brunk was a volunteer leader who was heading up the effort in St. Louis.

[10] Ed Phillips was married to Gladys Roche, Jim's old club kid from Arizona who is mentioned often in his 1935 journal.

[11] Almost certainly Dick Langford, Young Life's business manager at the time.

[12] R. G. LeTourneau held chapel services at his factories; see note on the March 16, 1941, entry.

Home at 3:30.

Cancelled my trip to Ft. W. to-night—sent Marty[13] for me. Maxine & I decided it was the Lord's will for me to go to Knoxville Fri. so felt I must stay home for the evening. Quite weary. A sense of loss to-night at not getting in the prayer for all the urgent matters facing me.

———

Jim spent almost the entire month of March on the road, much of it in the Pacific Northwest.

Wednesday, March 12 (on Pacific Northwest trip)
This has been a grand day—largely because the dear Lord has helped me greatly to get d.t.b. in real intercession. Oh how I want to pray—really pray—not just say prayers. To-night the burden of intercession was real and I sense some real <u>Trust</u> in His marvelous promises in my stony heart.

Thursday, March 13 (on Pacific Northwest trip)
Mig (R.) Very tough—on trip to Mt. Hood. Shot, quick relief. Unsurpassed beauty and a thrilling time of skiing at Timberline Lodge on Mt. Hood to-day. But the terrible migraine hit me hard before we left the mt. Nuf said.

Grand mtg at Vancouver to-night. 25 or so swell needy kids.

Wednesday, March 19 (on Pacific Northwest trip)
Very Rough Mig (R) Sympt. on waking—weathered 'till 1 pm. Shot, slow relief w. much sickness—pain gone in 4 hrs.

Plenty sick most of day. Radio bdcst at noon. I felt tough. Shot & complete rest this aft. Ate at 5:30 but still not very well.

Grand time with Murray [Smoot] at Hockey Game to-night, Seattle beat Portland 2–0.

---

[13] Martin "Marty" Walt. At this time he was a student at Dallas Bible Institute, following military service in World War II. He served on staff in Portland, Oregon, for the remainder of the decade, leaving Young Life in 1950.

Then—Praise the Lord—a wonderful time of prayer. How sweet to find the Lord so ready to listen to me. Oh that my stony heart will give HIM more chance to lead me out in much prayer.

Had a pleasant surprise this aft @ 4:30 when Maxine called & I got to talk to her & hear the sweet voices of my three precious little ones.

———

After being gone for several weeks, Rayburn found himself swamped by office work. Much of his mental and spiritual energy was directed at moving Young Life's headquarters to Star Ranch. He had obtained permission from Herb Taylor, the legal owner of Star Ranch, to make the move. Now he was working on the other board members.

Monday, April 7
A good day—tho not much work done as far as "catching-up" is concerned.

A long conference with Mitchells at lunch—again the Lord seems to be confirming in every possible way the matter of our move. Oh to WAIT ON HIM—find His will—and then do it with all His might. I'm thankful that I KNOW He is great enough to lead us and having led us to enable us to live for His glory in the place of His choosing. I feel very prayerful about all these great matters.

———

Having obtained the go-ahead from the board, in late April the Rayburn family made the move to Star Ranch. Due to the severity of migraine attacks and other attendant problems, Jim was ordered by his doctor to take several weeks off from work. He did so from April 24–June 9. During that time Jim and his family travelled to the West Coast, not returning to Star Ranch until Young Life's first summer camping season was to begin.

The first full summer season at Star Ranch consisted of just three weeks of Young Life camp. The first was for Christian kids;

only the latter two were outreach camps. Jim recorded a few thoughts during the first of the two outreach weeks.

Monday, July 7

Our camp started well to-night—Counting all the staff and work crew we have just about a capacity with only 45 regist[ered] campers.

I spoke to-night on "What's It All About." Jer 9:23, 24.[14]

Tuesday, July 8

Camp progressing well. I spoke to the Gideons to-night—on Lk 18 "The Imperialistic Christ."

Bob[15] gave the evening message at camp.

Wednesday, July 9

A very good day. I preached for 30 min. to-night on Isa 64:6[16] & really got going thanks only to the Lord!

⸺⁓⸺

Sunday, August 24

Art[17] & I et. al. went to Rose Point for breakfast this a.m. It was a grand climb. Slow but everyone took it swell & there was no one getting squeemish [*sic*] or griping. We left at 5:00 a.m. & arrived on top at 8:00.

⸺⁓⸺

---

[14] "Thus says the LORD: 'Let not the wise man boast in his wisdom, let not the mighty man boast in his might, let not the rich man boast in his riches, but let him who boasts boast in this, that he understands and knows me, that I am the LORD who practices steadfast love, justice, and righteousness in the earth. For in these things I delight, declares the LORD.'"

[15] Possibly Jim's brother Bob.

[16] "We have all become like one who is unclean,
        and all our righteous deeds are like a polluted garment.
    We all fade like a leaf,
        and our iniquities, like the wind, take us away."

[17] Art Rech, an early staff member who, during the summer of 1947 was acting as the Ranch Manager of Star Ranch.

Tuesday, September 2

Feel very bum—to-night have achy feeling all over particularly in lower back and legs. Have had migraine type pain all day but no actual migraine headache. Just strong symptoms.

Add & Sheff[18] were here & we spent the morning & lot of aft on problems in re the executive committee[19] that they brought up.

Wednesday, September 3

Again to-night I am just about flattened out with severe achy pain all over me. Maxine helped me greatly to-night. In some ways these have been the two hardest days I've ever had I believe. But the Lord is Near. He may be gradually leading to some change—I've always had a dread of being in young people's work too long—after I got too old to fit in and to "take it."

97 days since "shot"—only symptoms to-day—No actual pain.

———

In addition to serving as Young Life's first camp, Star Ranch was also the Rayburns' home and the headquarters of the growing ministry. The local Colorado Springs Young Life club, which Jim was leading on the weeks when he was in town, also met there.

They located the administrative operations of Young Life in a small log cabin on the property. Jim would crow about the fact that his was the only executive office in Colorado Springs with a fireplace in it; never mind the fact that the fireplace was the only heat in the building, Jim thought it was classy! It would snow 127 inches that winter, and the little building didn't have running water—but it did have a fireplace!

---

[18] George Sheffer.

[19] The executive committee was made up of Jim and his top lieutenants, and dealt with personnel and policy matters.

Monday, September 29

In a pouring Rain 32 boys & 37 girls came to Y.L. Club to-night in I.Q.[20] This was the best of the three meetings. [G]reat spirit—fun & d.t.b. att[ention] to the Word. I spoke on the general theme of Y.L. & that kids HAD to have a chance to KNOW what God says & Bible the only way to KNOW and closed with John 20:31.[21] Thought I got the right touch on it by His Grace & want to follow-up from there next week.

Moved into Log Cabin Office to-day!

—⁓—

Living at the ranch along with the Rayburns were Bob "Pancho" Page, Bill Pinner, Hal White, and James "Frog" Sullivan, all for-mer Young Life kids. Only recently out of high school, Frog had moved to Colorado from Memphis where he had been dramati-cally converted. Years later, after a successful Young Life career, he would dedicate his memoir, The Frog Who Never Became a Prince, *to Jim Rayburn, "who gave so much of God's love, and himself, to so many of us."*

While Rayburn had moved to Colorado, the headquarters of-fice remained in Dallas until December. One of the Dallas staff was Kay McDonald, also known as "Kay Mac" (or "Kay Mc"). She had come to work for Young Life in 1945, after serving as a volun-teer leader in Memphis. Along with Wanda Ann Mercer, she was one of the first women to serve as an area director.

In October Jim travelled to Dallas for the semi-annual board meeting.

---

[20] Jim often used codes for city names in his journal. IQ was the abbreviation he sometimes used for Colorado Springs.

[21] "But these are written so that you may believe that Jesus is the Christ, the Son of God, and that by believing you may have life in his name."

Friday, October 3

Frog and I had a wonderful climb up to Rose Point over a new precipitous route. Grand trip. Up in 2 hours—Down in record time 28½ minutes.

Brooklyn beat Yankees 3–2 in fourth game of world's [*sic*] series. LAVACETTO [*sic*, Lavagetto] A PINCH HITTER HIT A DOUBLE WITH TWO OUT IN THE NINTH & BEVENS ONE OUT FROM RECORD NO HIT GAME. Pinch Runners on 1st & 2nd both scored. I believe this is the most exciting incident ever to happen in World Series History.

Thursday, October 9 (Dallas)

Arr. DL on Zephyr this A.M. Kay Mc[22] & I worked hard on Board Report & kept at it until we were done at mid-night—all the office crew working hard 'til late. A very good day with fine esprit de corps manifest. I thank the Lord for the crew & the fine spirit He has brought. Staying at Mitchells'.

Friday, October 10 (Dallas)

A long talk with Mr. Taylor. Then an executive comm. meeting until late in afternoon.

Saturday, October 11 (Dallas)

A grand Board meeting. John E., Orville, E. M., H.J., Ted, Gene Gillis,[23] Fred S., Alex McK present.[24] They really went to town. Voted heartily on the move to the ranch—raised the salaries all through the work. Gave great backing to me in everything. John E. elected Pres. of the Board[.]

---

[22] Katherine "Kay" McDonald (1914–2000). Jim's high opinion of her is evidenced by his April 30, 1945, journal entry: "KAY MAC IS COMING TO THE WORK!" (emphasis Jim's). McDonald, who never married, stayed involved with Young Life long after she left the payroll. At the time of her death she was helping train new staff in the San Francisco Bay area—at age eighty-six!

[23] Gene Gillis served on Young Life's board of trustees from 1946–1958. He also served on the board of Dallas Theological Seminary. Gillis was in the furniture manufacturing business in Memphis.

[24] John E. Mitchell, Jr., Orville Mitchell, Earnest M. Wetmore, Herbert J. Taylor, Ted Benson, Gene Gillis, Fred Strombeck, and Alex McKenzie.

—·w—

One of the newest staff members at the time was John Miller. He
went on to become the first person to ever retire from Young Life (in
1982 at age sixty-four), after pioneering Young Life in four states.
In his retirement he wrote Back to the Basics of Young Life, *a*
book Young Life used to train new leaders for many years.

Star Ranch hosted various Young Life groups for weekends
during the school year, including one four-day camp in October.

Thursday, October 23

Camp began this afternoon on rather a low note for me. It just seemed
to me that we have drawn a crowd of kids that will be awfully tough. I've
often felt that way before—now to watch the Lord work.

I spoke to-night.

Friday, October 24

Camp moving along well. Geo.[25] got here this a.m. I spoke this a.m. also
John Miller[26] and Geo. to-night.

Colorado Springs 6 – Cañon City 7.

Saturday, October 25

Centennial 40 Trinidad 6.

I spoke morning & evening. Geo. also spoke.

Very good personal contacts with Centennial kids.

Sunday, October 26

I spoke this a.m. on II Cor 5:14a[27] with I J 4:10[28] on the "love of God,"

---

[25] Most likely George Sheffer.

[26] John N. Miller, Jr. (1918–2001). At this time he was on staff in Colorado, after
moving there from Washington, D. C.

[27] "For the love of Christ controls us ..."

[28] "In this is love, not that we have loved God but that he loved us and sent his Son to
be the propitiation for our sins."

also emphasizing the cost of our Salvation as** II Pet 2:24 (*sic*).[29]

This camp closed in an unbelievably good fashion—it is hard to believe that it could have come out so well—especially with the Centennial Crowd. Those kids seem definitely changed—born again. Our total crowd of kids hit 75 for the week-end.

[...]

Thursday, October 30
Frog & Pancho & I had a wonderful prayer mtg this morning—praying for a lot of staff and kids.

———

Jim put Frog Sullivan and Pancho Page to work, not just around the ranch, but also in starting a Young Life club in Peyton, Colorado, a small town about twenty-five miles from Colorado Springs.

The club didn't last long, however. Not long out of high school himself, and from a rough background, Frog was still immature in his faith. While he was trying to deliver the message at one of the meetings, a high school boy in the crowd wouldn't keep quiet. Sullivan tried asking him from up front to be quiet and listen, but to no avail—the boy continued to interrupt the message. Finally Frog lost all patience, took the boy outside and decked him. The club was discontinued after that.

The entire extended Rayburn clan—Jim's parents, his brothers, Paul, Bob, and Frank along with their families—came to Star Ranch for Thanksgiving. Though he often visited his parents and brothers over the years, it was rare for them to all be together, as they lived in different states.

---

[29] Since there is no verse twenty-four in the second chapter of 2 Peter, Jim probably meant 1 Peter 2:24: "He himself bore our sins in his body on the tree, that we might die to sin and live to righteousness. By his wounds you have been healed."

THANKSGIVING 1947
The entire Rayburn family
spent the holiday at Star Ranch.
The Rayburn brothers (left):
Bob, Paul, Frank, and Jim. The
whole family, including Jim's
parents (below).

Thursday, November 27 (Thanksgiving Day)

Arr. I.Q. at 8:30. Frank & the Folks already here. Paul arrived about 11:00 a.

Big Thanksgiving Dinner & fine time. First time whole family & all the kids have been to-gether since we got any kids—10 years or more.

1948

Tuesday, August 24, 1948
237th Day—129 Days to Follow

About 5:00 p.m. as we were leaving the ball-field lightning struck, killed Tom Henderson + knocked out Bud Carpenter and me. I woke up in the Squirrel House shortly before Dr. Karabin came. Had terrible pain in my head and legs felt peculiar. Doc gave me a shot of M.E. #5 but it did no good. Relief later with Jim medicine. Very thankful to the Lord for sparing me. Can't help thinking a lot about His leaving me here when I was so close.

TRAGEDY STRIKES AT STAR RANCH
Rayburn, Bud Carpenter, and Tom Henderson were hit by lightning following a ball game. Henderson, a camper from Wichita, Kansas, was killed. Rayburn and Carpenter recovered fully.

Jim's diary for 1948 has fewer entries than most—only 128 for the entire year, and no single month has more than seventeen entries.

Rayburn was as busy as ever travelling and speaking, and when he wasn't on the road he continued to help lead the Colorado Springs Young Life club. In January he, along with other staff, began leading a club in Pueblo, forty-five miles south of Colorado Springs.

By February, the administrative staff of Young Life had all moved to Colorado and the official headquarters of the ministry became the old log cabin at Star Ranch. The Rayburns, of course, were living on the property.

Migraine headaches continued to dog Jim, and doctors prescribed various medications to help control them. None solved the problem permanently, nor did any seem to give consistent relief. Jim was constantly trying and analyzing treatments.

Monday, February 2 (Minneapolis)
L-side Mig-type pain—very disagreeable most of day after noon. Rode NWA to Minneapolis with Howie,[1] Murray, Ted. Then on to Chicago alone. To the Stephens'. Felt bum** upon arrival so took some pills and stayed in all evening.

Monday, February 9
3rd (R) Mig—Very tough—don't understand this amazingly short 5 day inter[val]. May be due to my ab[s]cess & having tooth pulled. Took no shot & it really wrecked me—altho I took several Dermatol** it was very, very rough all day and until nearly morning Tues.—
Had to miss club to-night. Frog spoke. Had 101 present.

―――――

Nineteen forty-eight proved to be a very difficult year for Maxine.

---

[1] Howard Clark Kee. A brilliant, diminutive man, Kee was the unlikely club leader of "toughs" like Frog Sullivan in Memphis. A staff member for several years, he went on to become a professor at Boston University and a respected Bible scholar.

*Three different times she went under the doctor's knife: in Febru-
ary it was for back trouble, in July it was for varicose veins, and in
December she had to have an emergency hemorrhoid procedure.*

*Unfortunately, the February surgery did not solve Maxine's
back problem. Instead, it led to something even worse. Maxine
described it in her son's book,* From Bondage to Liberty: Dance,
Children, Dance—

> I was naive about drugs; it had never occurred to me to ask for
> a painkiller. But after the surgery I was given a large supply of
> Seconal to help me sleep. Soon I was reaching for a pill every
> time I felt pain, or discouragement. Before long, I was hooked.
> I had no idea of the devastation this would cause my family.
> By the time I recognized my dependence on these drugs, it
> was too late to stop. I felt I couldn't face life without them.

*Sadly, it was a battle she would not win until almost a decade
after Jim's death.*

Saturday, February 21
Maxine operated on this a.m. 1½ to 2 hrs. She has extreme post-operative
pain but they are keeping her well doped & she sleeps most of the time.
Thank the Lord it is over with. Believe it will do the job.

———

*Tragedy of another kind happened in April. On Saturday, April
10, a fire threatened Star Ranch and everyone there. Strangely,
Jim's journal makes no mention of it. He did, however, write a
lengthy letter explaining the ordeal (all emphasis Jim's):*

The Fire on Cheyenne Mountain (account by Jim Rayburn, written in April 1948)
Thick grey billows of smoke were pouring up all around the cabin area.
Great sheets of flame were leaping out above the tops of the pine trees,
60 or 80 feet above the ground. Through the smoke and flashes of flame
I caught glimpses of the little headquarters building. Those flames

seemed to melt down my heart. It was almost impossible to believe, standing there within a few feet of that roaring inferno, that our beautiful little office building with all of its furnishings, national records, correspondence—everything that we used to carry on the work—was there going up in a blast of flame and smoke.

The families and staff were evacuated; the only thing left for them to do was pray. Jim continued his narrative:

All kinds of reports came from the fire area. Several different ones reported that all buildings had been burned and that the butane tank had exploded. I can honestly say that I felt that the Lord was letting this beautiful property be destroyed. In it all I was searching my heart, and once again I know I speak for the rest when I say that we were brought very close to Him and brought face to face with the positive necessity of trusting implicitly in His way, regardless of the circumstances. The loss that we felt we were sustaining was far and away too great to bear apart from Him.

The first word of the miraculous deliverances that God had wrought for us came as I shouted to a passing truck of soldiers being shifted to another arm of the fire area. Two or three of them heard me above the din of the motors and yelled back that the main buildings were still there. My heart leaped for joy, but I still expected great destruction.

Much to everyone's relief, a true miracle—wrought by the fervent prayers of all involved—had occurred. The fire had not damaged Star Ranch.

The feeling of relief, and the praise and inner peace and joy that welled up in me will not be properly described this side of heaven. One after another of those who later gave their eye witness accounts of the fire in the headquarters area, told of seeing the same thing that I had seen ... giant flames roaring all over, apparently consuming the cabin, and yet not so. The cabin stood in the midst of this inferno with the fire licking at its walls on three sides, and did not burn.

A Captain directing the firefighters said later, "I don't see why that cabin did not burn." He also said, "I thought the fire was going clear on over the mountain, when suddenly it just stopped." [...]

Fires were still breaking out everywhere when we made our way back into the area, but there was not a scar of any kind along the road. *All the beautiful trees within the landscaped area were untouched. Not a building was harmed. The athletic area, the Cheyenne House area, everything used by the camp is exactly as it was before. There is no sign of the fire.* [...]

I paced from the stone fence, surrounding our lawn area, straight across the road into the woods and found that the fire raged up to within 35 yards of the lawn and stopped. Where it stopped there was nothing to break a fire, just deep pine needles and oak leaves such as you would expect to find in a forest area. *But it stopped.*

All along the line it was that way. As it leaped toward the athletic area it just stopped. As it raced toward the Cheyenne House area, it just stopped. As it started down across to the main ranch buildings, it just stopped. I have never seen such a vivid and impelling illustration of the phrase, "Thus far and no farther."

> *It was truly a miracle. The Colorado Springs Gazette-Telegraph reported the next day that the fire had taken 600 firefighters to control and had swept through 1,500 acres of timber, but Star Ranch had remained unharmed.*

⸺

> *Jim began teaching the "Mr. and Mrs." Sunday School class at First Presbyterian Church in Colorado Springs in 1948 and continued to teach it for the next fourteen years.*
>
> *He and Maxine took a rare vacation to Glenwood Springs, Colorado, in May.*

Sunday, May 9

I taught the 10th Chap Acts to my S.S. class with apparently the best blessing from God I've ever had in that pleasant task. HE surely seemed to speak to those people.

MAXINE and I left at 3:00 p for Glenwood Springs after I hastily dictated all my answers to current mail and Board & Staff Bulletins.[2] We had a superb trip through this favorite part of the mountains and arrived at the Hotel Colorado at 9:30 p where we quickly got "bedded down" in a nice big room.

Monday, May 10 (Glenwood Springs, Colorado)

Slept late this a.m. Had a delicious breakfast here and then I fooled around town getting my car greased & the brakes fixed. Then we went up to Aspen for lunch. I was greatly impressed by the chair lift.[3] Then we drove Back to Basalt and went up the "Frying Pan" to where Maxine camped as a child—then we went to Redstone & Crystal River Lodge. I gathered some Marble. We were back to the hotel at 6:30 and rested before going to dinner about 8:00. Really a grand day.

[...]

—⁓—

Unfortunately, the Rayburns' Glenwood Springs getaway did not turn out well for Maxine. After Jim left for meetings in Chicago, she stayed on for a few days. The placidity was violently interrupted by a series of explosions in a gasoline storage area nearby. Between the explosions and the Star Ranch fire, Maxine's nerves were badly

---

[2] For the first dozen years of Young Life, communication to the staff and board was primarily taken care of in periodic "bulletins." Beginning in 1952 and for the next twenty-five years thereafter, that function was taken care of in a weekly one-page newsletter called *Monday Morning*. Whereas the bulletins were typically written entirely by Jim himself, in *Monday Morning* he was only responsible for a small column.

[3] When the first runs at Aspen opened less than two years earlier the ski area boasted "the world's longest chairlift." This is probably what impressed Jim.

frazzled. In July her medical ordeals continued as she went in for surgery on varicose veins. Camp was being held at Star Ranch, and Jim was the speaker.

Monday, July 12

Took Maxine to hospital this aft.

Had dinner this evening with Cunnings.

Tuesday, July 13

The Lord gave me an exceptionally fine time in the Word & Prayer this a.m. Awoke at 4:45 a. Decided to get up. Bath** got me awake for a real time of fellowship with the Lord—the best in many a day.

Maxine was operated on at 10:15 a for varicose veins. On table an hour. Much severe pain afterward.

I had dinner with Karabins[+] to-night—then the Lord gave us a wonderful closing night for the week's camp. Quite a number of kids definitely coming thru for the Lord.

Wednesday, July 14

Another day in which the Lord has privileged me & enabled me to spend an unusual amount of time with Him. Up at 5:30.

Maxine couldn't come home from the hospital because of stomach acting up & too much pain in legs.

I spoke on Acts 18 "Gallio" to-night for first time in years. Have forgotten the old outline on the passage. Camp off to a good start.

Little kids very sweet to-night. Wonderful, warm fellowship with Ed[5] into the wee hours.

I thank the Lord for this good day.

[+] Dr. John Karabin was a general surgeon in Colorado Springs. He and his wife became good friends of the Rayburns.

[5] Most likely staff man Ed Wichern, but there were at least three other "Eds" in Jim's world at the time—Ed Headington, Ed Landrum, and Ed Phillips—and this could be referring to one of them.

Thursday, July 15

Mig (R) Shot DHE 45⁶ @ 2:45 a. Slow, complete relief, while sleeping—26 Day interval
since last real Mig & shot!

Up at 6:45 in spite of my very bad night. Doubt if I slept more than 2 or 3 hours.

Brought Maxine home this p.m. She has a lot of bad pain—

I spoke on "Christianity—The Most Attractive Prop[osition] in [the] World." Outline—made up of attractive things. Life, Love, Faith,—Relationship to Jesus Christ, who Himself far most attractive.

Very, very weary to-day but thankful to the Lord specially for to-night.

———

Surgeries, forest fires, and explosions had already beset the Rayburns in 1948, but the closest brush with death was yet to come.

Robert "Bud" Carpenter was a college student at Whitworth in Spokane, and Tom Henderson was a sixteen-year-old camper from Wichita, Kansas. Both were at Star Ranch in August, along with Jim, when tragedy struck.

Tuesday, August 24

About 5:00 p.m. as we were leaving the ball-field lightning struck, killed Tom Henderson & knocked out Bud Carpenter and me. I woke up in the Squirrel House shortly before Dr. Karabin came. Had terrible pain in my head and legs felt peculiar. Doc gave me a shot of DHE 45 but it did no good. Relief later with pain medicine. Very thankful to the Lord for sparing me. Can't help thinking a lot about Him leaving me here when I was so close.

Wednesday, August 25

In bed all day. Pain receding in a.m. Comfortable in afternoon and evening. Maxine's condition set back bad by this shock.

---

⁶ DHE-45 is a form of ergotamine administered by injection.

*The Star Ranch playing field, where Tom Henderson,
Bud Carpenter, and Jim were struck by lightning.*

Bud Carpenter was the least effected by the lightning strike and
recovered quickly. (Carpenter's Young Life career was just beginning. He served for about twenty years with the ministry, mostly
living on and managing the Young Life properties). Rayburn suffered burns on his shoulders and experienced excruciating pain in
his head, legs, and back for twenty-four hours.

Within forty-eight hours of the strike, however, he was on the
road again, this time for three weeks of speaking engagements in
the East. This included speaking at his friend Jack Wyrtzen's Word
of Life Camp at Schroon Lake, New York.[7] Jim often spoke to non-
Young Life groups in those days.

---

[7] Jack Wyrtzen (1913–1996). Wyrtzen became a Christian at age nineteen. In 1940
he began the Word of Life ministry, including a New York-area radio program. His
rallies for young people in the 1940s drew thousands.

Sunday, September 5 (Word of Life Camp, Schroon Lake)

Back to camp & I had the closing service to-night. Spoke on "The Love of God" II Cor 5:14, 15[8] and I J 4:10.[9]

I have been greatly impressed with the warm quality of devotion to the Lord here & the lives of the kids. In fact I am sure the Lord has begun a real revival in my own heart. I am not getting missionaries out to the world—and I'm not building these dear kids up as I ought to be. My own life is sorely lacking in real deep prayer & study & this is SIN. By God's grace I shall get going for Him.

In spite of all the trials of the year, Young Life continued to thrive, as the next entries show. Jim continued to help lead both the Colorado Springs and Pueblo clubs each week.

His description of the board meetings in October reveals an insight into the way he kept his diary up to date. It is apparent that occasionally (as in this case) he did not record the day's events the day they happened, but went back and filled them in later.

Saturday, October 16 (Dallas)

I should certainly have written up the annual Board Meeting without waiting several days. It was great. The fellowship was grand—the vision of the work increasing—so much to thank the Lord for—the great outreach to the kids, the tremendous expansion of the Volunteer Leaders program. The fellowship with Orville and John[10] has been better than ever all thru the past week.

---

[8] "For the love of Christ controls us, because we have concluded this: that one has died for all, therefore all have died; and he died for all, that those who live might no longer live for themselves but for him who for their sake died and was raised."

[9] "In this is love, not that we have loved God but that he loved us and sent his Son to be the propitiation for our sins."

[10] Orville and John Mitchell.

Sunday, October 17 (Dallas)

Spoke at Bro Hawkins[11] broadcast @ 7:30 and took plane for home at 9:30. Arrived just in time for dinner at the ranch with Dr. Warren[12] of Whitworth. Excellent contact.

—~~—

Tuesday, October 26

187 at the Colorado Springs Club at Hendee's Home to-night. Makes average attendance for the fall season 170 per week.

—~~—

In November Jim travelled to the East Coast. He spent a week on Long Island leading evangelistic meetings at Dr. Frank Gae-belein's Stony Brook School for Boys. Gaebelein[13] took a shining to Jim as a result and became an enthusiastic backer of Young Life.

Monday, November 1 (Stony Brook, New York)

[…]

Seemed to get off to a good start with the boys and Dr. Gabelein [*sic*] said he was pleased. Confidentially, I was disappointed—not feeling at my best and trust the Lord to over-rule.

[…]

---

[11] Brother E. W. Hawkins was a preacher and radio minister who had a regular broadcast in the Dallas/Ft. Worth area. He was an early supporter of Jim and his work.

[12] Dr. Frank F. Warren (1899–1963). Warren served as president of Whitworth College from 1940 until his death in 1963. At his inauguration he declared "Knowledge with Christian character is the eternal hope of today and the radiant glory of our tomorrows." He and Rayburn got along wonderfully; this appears to be their first meeting.

[13] Dr. Frank Ely Gaebelein (1899–1983). He was a Christian educator of great renown. In addition to founding Stony Brook School, Gaebelein was an associate editor of *Christianity Today*, served on the translation committee for the New International Version of the Bible, and authored dozens of books. Raised with an appreciation for art and music, he was the sort of sophisticated Christian that Jim Rayburn greatly admired. Gaebelein's father, Arno C. Gaebelein, had helped Lewis Sperry Chafer found Dallas Theological Seminary.

The Rayburns at Star Ranch.

Friday, November 5 (Stony Brook, New York)
[...]

   Frank Gabelein [*sic*] very cordial—very complimentary—so glad I came. We have had steadily deepening fellowship.

1949

A BUSY WEEK IN CALIFORNIA, OCTOBER 1949

Rayburn's time on the West Coast included visits to Henrietta Mears' camp, Forest Home, Billy Graham's history-making Los Angeles Crusade, the two-year-old Fuller Seminary, and one of the first Young Life club meetings to ever be held in Southern California.

Most of the diaries Jim used measured 3½ inches by 6 inches and featured a blank page for each day. The diary he used for 1949, however, was much smaller—only 3 inches by 5 inches—and had two days per page. Therefore, Jim's entries for this year are all very short.

God was at work in a mighty way in the United States in the late 1940s, shaping the evangelical movement that would impact Christendom for the next several decades. The city of Los Angeles was the epicenter of much of the action: Henrietta Mears was in her prime in her work with First Presbyterian Church of Hollywood and her camp, Forest Home (both ministries would impact thousands directly, and hundreds of thousands indirectly). One of the members of her Sunday School program, Bill Bright, was about to begin his own ministry, Campus Crusade for Christ. Dawson Trotman, Jim's good friend, was seeing tremendous growth and blessing on his ministry, The Navigators, based at that time in Los Angeles. Later that year, Billy Graham would be vaulted onto the national scene as he held his watershed crusade in the City of the Angels.

But the most influential of all of the evangelicals in southern California, indeed, in all the nation, was Charles E. Fuller, host of the phenomenally popular radio program "Old Fashioned Revival Hour" with its weekly audience of about twenty million. In addition to the radio ministry, the evangelist had just started a new seminary, Fuller Theological Seminary[1] (Bill Bright was one of its students).

There was also growing interest in Young Life beginning a ministry in the area. In March, Jim and Maxine made a trip to Los Angeles to lay the groundwork.

---

[1] Fuller Theological Seminary, begun two years earlier, was named after Charles Fuller's father, Henry Fuller. H. J. Taylor served as one of its founding board members.

Tuesday, March 8

83 @ Club in a snowstorm. Maxine & I got stuck on the hill coming to town to take train to L.A. Frog took us on in the Jeep. We made it just in time & went to bed in our comfortable compartment.

Thursday, March 10 (Los Angeles)

Arr. L.A. o.t. [on time] 7:13 (Pasadena).

Grand day just fooling around with Daws & Co. I was at the Sem[inary] for a while.

Saturday, March 12 (Los Angeles)

This was the best day since here. Maxine & I had a wonderful visit with Dr. & Mrs. Chas. E. Fuller & Dan[2] in their home. This was a great treat & blessing. They were very cordial about our work.

Then to-night a[t] Daws' we all had grand fellowship with Bob & Dorothy Van Kampen.

———

Young Life was able to begin its work in southern California when the new school year began in the fall. This was thanks in large part to the participation of Fuller Seminary students. Another major area of expansion for Young Life was Knoxville, Tennessee, which also started that fall.

Tuesday, April 12

Arr. 5:45 a. No one to meet me [at the train station] so I decided to walk to Ranch. Took 1½ hours. […] A truly wonderful club mtg at lodge to-night. 12 kids professed salvation.

Sunday, April 17 (Easter)

EASTER

A great day! Our two little girls were baptized and joined the church in

---

[2] Son of Charles and Grace Fuller, Daniel P. Fuller went on to a long and distinguished career at the seminary and as an author.

a beautiful afternoon service in which 146 joined our church.

Monday, April 18
Good day @ home & office.

Very interesting morning devotions with the girlies—and what a
blessing to be in our own home having our own home-cooked meals.[3]

---

*Though Rayburn preferred flying, trains were still the primary
means of long distance travel in the United States. He typically put
the time on the train to good use, catching up on reading, studying,
and resting, as in the case of this next entry as he travelled to the
West Coast to speak at a Young Life weekend camp.*

*The California Zephyr was a train that ran between Chicago
and San Francisco, passing through Denver along the way. Jim
rode it often. Its inaugural run had been only six weeks before this
next entry, and this was almost certainly Jim's first trip on the
state-of-the-art train, complete with its Vista Dome viewing cars
and onboard hostesses, the "Zephyrettes."*

Tuesday, April 26 (on the train)
Up at 3:50A. Shower & to the office to dictate for hour.

Took 5:45 [a.m.] train to DV. Talked to Harlan[4] about Cheyenne
House.[5] Took "California Zephyr"[6] and had most restful & enjoyable
trip I ever had on a train—all day.

---

[3] This is probably referring to the fact that Maxine's illnesses often kept her from
cooking for the family and a recent improvement in her condition had allowed her to
return to the kitchen.

[4] Harlan E. Rathbun was a Denver architect who Young Life used to make
improvements on Star Ranch.

[5] Cheyenne House was the boys' dormitory at the camp.

[6] With his frequent trips to Chicago, Rayburn would travel on the Zephyr dozens of
times in the coming years. However, other than this entry, he almost never spelled it
correctly, styling it "Zypher," a rare misspelling for the normally punctilious Rayburn.

Wednesday, April 27 (on the train)

Up before 6:00.

A very fine restful day. Enjoyable & helpful—I got a lot of reading and "thinking" done. Felt the Lord very much with me to-day.

Walked around Oakland Pier an hour before catching "The Cascade" for Portland. Tried to call Bob Munger[7]—wasn't at home.

———

Finances were almost always a problem in the young mission. No matter how much God blessed, He never seemed to provide so much that Jim and the staff took His provision for granted.

In May, Jim called for "an all-day session of prayer" for the headquarters staff, with the primary need being funds to pay "back salaries" owed to staff. (In those days, fundraising shortfalls were distributed equally across the mission. If only eighty percent of the salary needs were raised in a given month, then each staff member received only eighty percent of his salary. By September 30, the close of the fiscal year, whatever back salaries were still owed were simply written off.)

Friday, May 20

Day of prayer—9 of us to-gether with Major Billing. Personally I had every conceivable interruption & had to fight to get in at all. The Lord gave a lot of assurance that our great needs will be met. We feel much confidence in praying for the total sum needed tho it is $17,000.00.

Eighteen days later Jim was informed that since their day of prayer $16,292.16 had come in (out of an annual budget of about $80,000) and that other donors had indicated they were sending the rest

———

7 Robert Boyd Munger (1911–2001). Munger was a Presbyterian minister and author (his 1954 booklet *My Heart—Christ's Home* has sold over eleven million copies). At the time of this entry he was the pastor of First Presbyterian Church of Berkeley, California. He was an ardent supporter of Young Life.

needed to meet the $17,000 goal. Jim wrote to H. J. Taylor, "Our
hearts are filled with deep gratitude to God for this very evident
answer to prayer—the greatest along financial lines that we have
had in our work ... It is humbling to repeatedly learn from our
God how gracious and faithful He is in the face of all our frailty.
All back salaries have been paid in full. All Campaign bills have
been completely met ..."

———

God's miraculous supply had an interesting effect on Rayburn: it
encouraged him to pray for even bigger things. Over the years his
prayers and vision continued to increase.

The summer of 1949 saw the largest attendance yet at Star
Ranch. It was apparent that soon the camp's capacity would not be
enough for Young Life.

Remembering his family visits to Chaffee County, two hours
west of Star Ranch, Jim found a property there on the side of Mount
Princeton that seemed just right. Chalk Cliff Lodge's asking price
was $76,000—far more than Star Ranch had cost, and certainly
more than Young Life could humanly afford.

But Jim, along with a group of young businessmen called the
Star Ranch Executive Committee that helped him oversee the op-
eration at Star, prayed that God would work a miracle.

Rayburn felt led to talk to Herbert Taylor in Chicago about
Chalk Cliff. He also went to see Coleman Crowell, a fairly new
friend to Young Life. Crowell's father, Henry P. Crowell, was the
founder of the Quaker Oats Company and had set up the Crowell
Trust to support evangelistic ministries. Three years after his father's
death, Coleman Crowell was now in charge of the foundation.

Monday, September 26 (Chicago)

Very weary this A. M. And very backward about doing what I felt I should—go see Mr. Taylor & Mr. Crowell about "Chalk Cliff."[8] When I did the Lord rewarded me greatly with very refreshing fellowship with both men.

A restful afternoon on the train with Maxine for home.

Monday, October 3 (Yuma, Colorado)

A grand day in Yuma.

[…] Wonderful reception by business men and a grand club mtg— 60 present. Drove home after mtg. A <u>good</u> 22 hour day.

Friday, October 7

> Sick all night with L-Side pain.

Rough day but Good.

This day we reached our great goal of all back salaries being paid.[9] How can we ever thank the Lord?

Saturday, October 8

A wonderful morning of prayer with the staff @ headquarters.

A hard afternoon—Maxine sick & I sure feel bum.

Saturday, October 15 (Dallas)

This is Board Mtg Day in Dallas.

A grand time with the men. We took another big step with the Lord in raising the salary budget by $20,000.00 and everything else proportionately. Impossible apart from the Lord.

Maxine & all the party to Cotton Bowl to-night. S.M.U. 28 Rice 41.

Wednesday, October 19

> Up a lot with Ann and bad nose condition.

Feel very beat-up this morning. The weariness and almost daily conflict with pain in my head is certainly making serious inroads into my

---

[8]   This is the first time Chalk Cliff Lodge is mentioned in the journals, though Jim does mention a visit to the general area in April.

[9]   Young Life's fiscal year had just concluded.

devotional life again. Very THANKFUL to the Lord tho—for His great blessing.

[...]

Sunday, October 23 (Los Angeles)

At LAKE AVE CONG. THIS A.M.[10] "The Church's Place Among Modern Y.P." II C 4:1–6. Good hearing.—

Went to hear Billy Graham @ Tent Mtg. Afternoon.[11]

To-night very cordially received by Dr. McCullough @ Lincoln Ave. Presby, where I preached on work from II Cor 5:17–20.[12]

To "Nav" house[13] for night and rest of my stay here.

———————

Almost two months had passed since Rayburn had visited Coleman Crowell in Chicago about Chalk Cliff Lodge. While Jim had just about given up on the Crowell Trust, he had not given up on praying that the Lord would deliver Chalk Cliff into Young Life's hands.

On November 18, a letter from the trust arrived just after an

———————————————————————

[10] Lake Avenue Congregational Church, in addition to being an influential evangelical congregation, was the home in those days of Fuller Seminary, until the school was able to construct its own facilities.

[11] This was no ordinary tent meeting (though it was, indeed, held in a tent). The crusade was supposed to have ended a week earlier after three weeks of services, but due to phenomenal response it ran until November 20. Historians, secular and Christian alike, point to this series of meetings as the event that propelled Billy Graham to national fame.

[12] "Therefore, if anyone is in Christ, he is a new creation. The old has passed away; behold, the new has come. All this is from God, who through Christ reconciled us to himself and gave us the ministry of reconciliation; that is, in Christ God was reconciling the world to himself, not counting their trespasses against them, and entrusting to us the message of reconciliation. Therefore, we are ambassadors for Christ, God making his appeal through us. We implore you on behalf of Christ, be reconciled to God."

[13] Six years earlier Charles Fuller's ministry had bought a large home for use by The Navigators as a hospitality center for their ministry. Dawson Trotman and his family also lived there and often hosted guests like Rayburn in the turn-of-the-century mansion.

extended session of prayer about the project. Enclosed in the letter
was a check for $5,000, with the explanation, "This is a check to en-
able you to get an option; and we will pay $20,000 more if you are
able to get the deal through."

Friday, November 18

Our day of prayer. It was hard for me to get into it much this time because of outside pressure.

[...]

The letter announcing the marvelous gift from the Crowell Fund for
purchase of "Chalk Cliff Lodge" arr. to-day. Thank the Lord!

Saturday, November 19

Rough going again to-day.

Star Ranch [Executive] Committee came for dinner—we had a great
Bible Study time with about 70 adults—then a committee meeting for
two hours about Chalk Cliff.

Sunday, November 20

Feel very bad—and Maxine very ill—rough day.

Record crowd of 82 @ Sunday School Class.

Monday, November 21

Much time with Guss [Hill] & Ferd Bollman[14] about Chalk Cliff. Have
talked to John E. M. & E. Wetmore.[15] Agree to go ahead with effort to
establish price & seek funds.

With the incredible start provided by the Crowell Trust, by the
end of the year the staff were able to raise the rest of the money
needed to take possession of Chalk Cliff Lodge, which Young Life

---

[14] Ferdinand O. Bollman (1892–1971). "Ferd" Bollman was a Colorado Springs real
estate agent.

[15] Board members John E. Mitchell, Jr., and Earnest Wetmore.

Silver Cliff Ranch, Young Life's second property.

rechristened "Star Lodge."

The new property sat on ninety-six acres at the bottom of breathtaking silver cliffs. The facility had sixteen log cabins for guests, a naturally heated swimming pool, a dining hall and main lodge building, a stable, and ten horses. The novelty of having two camps with "Star" in their names wore off quickly, and Star Lodge was quickly renamed Silver Cliff Ranch.

1951

"ONE OF THE GREATEST THINGS THE LORD EVER DID FOR ME."
The Crowell Trust surprised Rayburn with a pledge of $100,000 toward the purchase of Round-Up Lodge for Boys—almost half of the entire amount needed. The largest gift in Young Life's history prior to this was $5,000.

There were seventy-eight *Young Life* clubs scattered around the country by *1950*. After several years of finding their way, the staff had settled on a basic format for club meetings that would remain essentially the same for decades to come. As Jim had pioneered in Gainesville ten years earlier, club meetings were held weekly during the school year in members' homes. Music was lively, usually to the accompaniment of a piano (the change to guitar would not occur until the mid-*1960s*).

There was an emphasis on good, tasteful humor, and on keeping the meetings to an hour. Messages were simple in the sense that they focused on one main point of the gospel each week, and leaders avoided the use of Christian clichés. The goal for *Young Life* clubs, and by all indications it was successfully met, was to be an inviting and exciting place for non-Christians to come and hear about Christ.

By *1950*, Campaigners was firmly established as *Young Life's* discipleship arm. Those meetings were also held weekly, although their intended audience was Christian students who wanted to deepen their faith. The meetings were smaller than "club" and centered around studying Scripture.

Unfortunately, Jim's journal for *1950*, if he kept one, has been lost. The year started with a second fire that threatened Star Ranch. Yet again, the ranch was spared serious damage in miraculous fashion.

Maxine had another difficult year. Jim took her to Johns Hopkins University Clinic for treatment for her drug addiction, but whatever help they were able to provide was short-lived. She also had a hysterectomy that year. In October, Jim took the family on a vacation on a World War II-era minesweeper being used as a missionary hospital ship in Alaska. The cruise was one comical mishap after another, but the dangerous conditions were not so funny to Maxine, whose nervous condition was no laughing matter.

The new year began with "life as usual," if there was such a thing for the Rayburns. Jim continued to help lead the Colorado Springs and Pueblo Young Life clubs, as well as travel frequently.

Two significant additions to the full-time staff around the time were Bill Starr in Portland, and Bob Mitchell ("Mitch") in Colorado Springs. Both men would follow Rayburn as president of Young Life. Starr, the youngest man to be commissioned an officer in the U.S. Navy during World War II, had first gotten involved in Young Life while a student at Wheaton after the war. Mitchell, of course, was the son of Orville and Frances, Jim's longtime friends and supporters from Dallas.

Monday, January 1

STAR RANCH

A beautiful snowy day—the first good snow of the winter—about 3 or 4 inches. We were disappointed that it quit so soon—need moisture badly.

We will never be able to thank the Lord enough for the wonderful Holiday Camps that closed yesterday. Great results in the hearts of kids at both ranches.

Maxine quite ill to-day.

Tuesday, January 2

A busy, good day at the office getting caught up on correspondence.

Wednesday, January 3

Another fine office day—conference with the boys regarding Ranch work and the mail finished up. Didn't get to Pueblo—Mitch took it instead.[1]

---

[1] Jim's evangelistic background is showing here: preachers like his father often spoke of "taking a meeting" when referring to leading it.

Thursday, January 4 (Denver)

Finished up my work in good shape for leaving. [...]

Mitch drove me to DV this aft. after I had stopped at school & found that the girls did well showing the Alaska slides to-day.

Mitch & I had a very enjoyable trip thru Hathaway Instrument Co. Then I had dinner & evening at Claude's plus looking over lapidary equipment they are going to do for me.[2]

Friday, January 5 (Portland, Oregon)

First Migr. of year** —a full 8 day interval after only 3 day [interval] before.

Claude took me to airport at 3:30a. I waited 'til 5:15 to leave. Slept fairly well on plane—

Arrived PDX @ 9:00a.

[...] Add came, we got out to camp and started L.T.I. [Leadership Training Institute] @ 6:00. [...]

I gave a little Historic background of the work to-night.

Saturday, January 6 (Portland, Oregon)

This leadership tr. conf. seems to be going very well—one can't help wondering what a lot of these Multnomah[3] kids can do.—

A wonderful meeting to-night—with our local committee with us.[4] Felt that the Lord was really working.

---

[2] Claude and Hazel Hathaway were enthusiastic supporters of Young Life who lived in Denver. He was an electrical engineer and founder of Hathaway Instrument Company.

[3] Multnomah Bible College, then Multnomah School of the Bible. The school had been started thirteen years earlier by Rayburn's friend Dr. John G. "Jack" Mitchell.

[4] Local committees had been a part of the picture since almost the very beginning of Young Life, but they served only as boards of reference. Portland's committee, which Rayburn instructed Bill Starr to begin, was taking a much more direct role, specifically in the area of fundraising. Up to this point, the great bulk of Young Life's fundraising was still done by Jim. The newness of this kind of committee is perhaps demonstrated by the fact that Jim had originally written "Board of Directors" and then replaced it with "local committee."

Monday, January 8 (Portland, Oregon)

A wonderful day—more d.t.b. prayer than for a long time. Spoke on Mt. 8 at the Milwaukee [*sic*, Milwaukie] Club this evening. Good fellowship with Bill and Ruthie.[5]

Tuesday, January 9 (Portland, Oregon)

The thing that has made this day good was the times of prayer—alone & with Bill. The problems in Portland seem larger than ever—the progress plain discouraging—but the Lord is with us and He knows the way. Oh to find His way. The opposition and ill will of [another ministry's] leaders is disheartening. I pray that all of us will trust the Holy Spirit for strength to <u>love our brethren</u> wherever we find them.

Left for Spokane via train @ 9:45.

Saturday, January 13 (Spokane)

A great L.T.I. [Leadership Training Institute] day. 70 or more here— I spoke with very gracious & enthusiastic reception—almost all day on Mk 4:11,[6] Col 4:5[7] etc., I Cor 9, 10:31, 32, 33[8] et. al.

Wonderful crowd of kids.

As far as Young Life was concerned, the most important develop-
ments of 1950 had been a series of seemingly unrelated events, the
first of which happened that summer. Two boys serving on the work
crew at Silver Cliff Ranch happened upon a much larger camp just

---

5   Bill Starr and his wife Ruth. This is the first time Starr is mentioned in Jim's diary.

6   "And he said unto them, Unto you it is given to know the mystery of the kingdom of God: but unto them that are without, all these things are done in parables" (KJV).

7   "Walk in wisdom toward them that are without, redeeming the time" (KJV).

8   "So, whether you eat or drink, or whatever you do, do all to the glory of God. Give no offense to Jews or to Greeks or to the church of God, just as I try to please everyone in everything I do, not seeking my own advantage, but that of many, that they may be saved."

ROUND-UP LODGE FOR BOYS
The pool, game room, and The Lookout in a photo taken several years before Young Life obtained the property (left). The camp brochure cover (right).

above Silver Cliff on Mt. Princeton. Cy Burress and Jerry Kirk decided they should pray for God to give Young Life the camp, Round-Up Lodge for Boys.

The second event happened a few weeks later. Dr. Alfred E. Marquard, the owner of Round-Up Lodge, asked Jim to speak at the camp's closing banquet for the summer. He had spent twenty-five years of his life developing and building Round-Up, which was known far and wide as one of the best camps in the entire country. Jim had heard of the camp's splendor going all the way back to his own childhood vacations in the area.

As Jim and Maxine drove out of the camp after the banquet, Jim said to Maxine, "Well, he doesn't know it yet, but this doesn't belong to him anymore. I'm real sorry, but it doesn't belong to him anymore, because I asked the Lord for it."

Maxine thought he was joking at first.

"I'm not kidding you," Jim told her.

Years later she recalled, "I knew him well enough by then to know that you don't question when Jim says something like that, because he had the faith."

Round-Up Lodge for Boys was not up for sale, nor had there been any discussion of that happening any time soon, but that didn't keep Jim from believing that God wanted Young Life to have it.

And then the third event happened: Ted Benson read his copy of the October 7 issue of The New Yorker *magazine. Benson, Jim's old friend from Dallas Seminary days, was then working for Young Life at the headquarters. He saw a small ad in the back of the magazine that caught his eye and passed it on to Rayburn. "Do you have $250,000 to invest?" the ad asked. "I have a boys' summer camp in the high Continental Divide country of Colorado that is paying a good return on the investment …" Benson passed it on to Jim as a joke. "Let's you and I go 50-50 on it," he said in the attached note to Rayburn.*

The ad did not mention any other details, but Rayburn knew instinctively that it could only be one place: Round-Up Lodge for Boys. "I didn't know what to do," he told a group of leaders ten months later. "I just felt here's the opportunity of opportunities! The most wonderful camp I've ever seen or heard of, and it's for sale! It's wonderful!"

The real estate agent listed in the ad was Ferd Bollman, with whom Jim had worked a year earlier in the acquisition of Silver Cliff. With Guss Hill, Jim went to Bollman and ascertained that the property was indeed Round-Up Lodge. The next hurdle was to get the Young Life board's approval. He went to the next board meeting directly after speaking at a weekend camp for Young Life in southern California.

Sunday, January 28 (San Bernardino, California)

A surprisingly wonderful closing to the camp.

Many kids closed in [with the Lord]. Grand testimony mtg at close this a.m. Many key kids testified to finding the Lord at the Ranch. More & more evidence that we must hit the ranches program harder—I wonder if all this down here & in the N.W.[9] is to lead me on about Round-up & a large expansion program.

Left for Chicago via A.A. @ 7:15p. [...]

Monday, January 29 (Chicago)

Very bad mig—dev. thru day—severe—shot @ 5 p.m.
7 day interval.

Only 5½ hrs to Chicago. In bed at La Salle Hotel before 4 A.M. Up at 9. Breakfast with Guss & Millie Hill. Met Hathaways, talked to Frank Taylor[10]—went to Board mtg.

A great mtg. I was bowled over at the last when they voted to approve the expansion program & authorize me to seek the funds.

Altho very ill with headache I went out to see Coleman Crowell & he took me to the train.

Left at 7:15p. for Mphs. Very cold in Chicago. 8° below.

———

The board's approval came with one condition: since the ministry was having a tough time raising that year's regular budget (which was only half as much as the asking price for Round-Up Lodge), they wanted Rayburn to get the funds only from foundations and large donors. That did not deter Jim—he felt more confident than

---

[9] Jim is referring to the rapidly expanding work in southern California and the Pacific Northwest.

[10] Frank Taylor was the chairman of the board for the Moody Bible Institute and the vice president of the Continental Illinois Bank in Chicago, as well as a trustee for the Crowell Trust. He was an important supporter of Young Life's work. Jim's comment about him in his diary entry on October 30, 1948, is very telling: "He is a great man and a great Christian—one of the very few men I've ever met who make me think, 'I'd like to be like him.'"

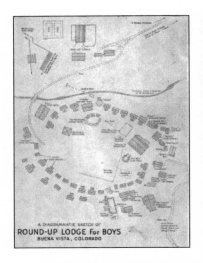

DR. MARQUARD'S ROUND-UP LODGE

Round-Up Lodge consisted of dozens of log cabins forming a circle around the softball field, as shown in the schematic from the camp's brochure (top left). Alfred Marquard and his wife Mabel enjoy a horseback ride at the ranch (top right). The sumptuous appointments of the dining hall were typical of Round-Up (below).

ever that acquiring this "most wonderful camp" was God's will.

When he did meet with Dr. Marquard on February 15 and 16, the St. Louis dentist added another hurdle: he would only hold off other potential buyers for thirty days. Jim set off on a whirlwind month of prayer, travel, and wonder as he watched God work a seemingly impossible miracle. His journal records the tale, step by step. (The donors who participated wished for anonymity, so though Jim's journal gives their names, this account uses only initials.)

Friday, February 9

Another good day in the office marked by an especially good time of prayer to-gether about all the work and particularly the expansion plans.

Almost got out from under the big pile of correspondence. Maxine & the crew went to Mich–CC Hockey game—I stayed with the kids.

[…]

Tuesday, February 13

Worked hard on the long Staff Bulletin to-day: re: The Expansion Project involving Round-up Lodge and Ranch—First notice of projected plans for most of staff.

Great club mtg to-night. Spoke on "Noah's Ark."

Wednesday, February 14

Cleared up correspondence and prepared to leave.

Maxine & I left for St Louis at 6 p.m. to see Dr. Marquardt [*sic*] about Round-Up. Ferd Bollman with us.

Thursday, February 15 (St. Louis)

Arr. St L. @ noon.

Lunch & conference with Dr. Marquard.[11] Very cordial. He won't come below $250,000.00 for Lodge, $325,000. for Lodge & Ranch.

Maxine & I staying at Statler Hotel. Nice evening.

Friday, February 16 (St. Louis)

Slept late. Luncheon with Dr. Marquard at Miss[ouri] Athletic Club. His tax man—Joe Sestric** there. (St L. City Assessor.)

[…]

Saturday, February 17 (St. Louis)

Visiting with Barkers & Snelsons. Took train for home at 4 p.m. after I had another cordial telephone conversation with Dr. Marquard.

Pleasant eve. on train. Very satisfactory visit to St L. Still feel very positive that the Lord is leading definitely in all this.

Tuesday, February 20

Hated to miss club but after our prayer session this a.m. it was decided I should catch the "Rocket" and go to Chicago to see the trustees[12] about purchase of "Round-up."

Wednesday, February 21 (Chicago)

Migraine—dev. thru morning—could have** aborted but for exhausting conference. Shot at 6 p.m. Ill. Relief in 2 hrs.

A gruelling but a wonderful day. Arr. Chi @ 9A. Went right out to see Coleman Crowell. After 1½ hrs. he called mtg of trustees at Cont. Bank. We went all afternoon! Talked every angle. It did not look too favorable when we broke up for the night but the Lord gave me a wonderful peace! After being violently ill I got a good night's rest.

[…]

---

[11] Alfred E. "Doc" Marquard, DDS (1895–1958). Marquard was an imposing figure at 6′4″ and had been a college athlete at Washington University in St. Louis. He and his wife Mabel had been the owners of Round-Up Lodge for Boys since 1928, and associated with it even earlier.

[12] The trustees of the Crowell Trust.

Thursday, February 22 (Chicago)

What a day! This is the day the trustees voted to give $100,000.00 to us for Expansion project. What can I say[?] One of the greatest things the Lord ever did for me. And truly He did it all. Without Him it would be folly to attempt such things. Now to follow Him for the next step.

Lunch with George [Sheffer] at the Union League Club—then rushed to the Rocket.

Friday, February 23

Arr C.S. @ 8:30A. Guss Hill & Ferd met me—talked joyously about the big deal. Called Doc[13] in St. L. He very favorably impressed.

Wonderful time with Maxie and later with the kids. What a joy to see her so much better. All thanks to the Lord!

I banged thru as hard as I could all day in the office. With the splendid assistance of Kay, Roy, and Millie[14] I got almost finished—

Very worn out.

Saturday, February 24 (Denver)

First time I ever began to write my day's account at 9 AM. The Praise, and Thanks and peace & joy that I am experiencing near overwhelms me. Never has the dear Heavenly Father permitted me in His Grace to ex- perience so much tangible evidence of His gracious dealings & sovereign leading in my life as the last three days. Left C.S. at 5:45 A.M. Met dear friend C. H. & H—— at Denver station. Had a precious hour of fellow- ship. We rejoiced to-gether about all that is happening! Then those dear people pledged $50,000.00 to the Expans. project! What can I or anyone say? They further said that if their foundation can be formed they will give $100,000.00 this year and next! A total of $200,000.00 in 2 yrs that they hope to give! I just had time to grab the Calif. Zypher [sic] @ 8:40.

---

[13] Dr. Marquard.

[14] Millie Sisco (later Carter). At the time she was working in the Colorado Springs headquarters.

Sunday, February 25 (San Francisco)
A restful day on train except for headache discomfort. Couldn't sleep last night. Too keyed up I guess. Feel very, very thankful to the Lord & realize better than ever my utter dependence upon His love & grace for everything.

[...]

Saturday, March 3 (Portland, Oregon)
Couldn't get any kind of a place on the train to-day—so flew to Portland. Mrs. P—— in Hawaii—[so I] stayed overnite in Hotel.

Sunday, March 4 (Seattle)
Went to Seattle on 10 a.m. train. Conferred with R. O. F—— & Add.
Felt bad most of day.
Took train for St. Paul at 9:00 P.M.

Monday, March 5 (on the train)
A pleasant restful day aboard the "North Coast Limited." Meals superb.

Tuesday, March 6 (on the train)
Another nice day on train. Met Dr. O. O. Van Steenberg** of Belgium. Had good fellowship.
Arr. St. Paul O.T. [on time] 10 p m.

Wednesday, March 7 (St. Paul, Minnesota)
Good day with Mrs. W—— and Mrs. C—— No definite results.

Thursday, March 8 (St. Paul, Minnesota)
Fine conversation with F. W.—He Assured me of continued interest and support but nothing definite.
Dinner with Stan Olsen [*sic*, Olson].[15]

---

[15] Dr. Stanley W. Olson. He was at the time associated with the Mayo Clinic in Rochester, Minnesota. Later he would become the Dean of Baylor College of

Took train to K. C.

Friday, March 9 (Kansas City)
Uneventful day in K. C. [Mr.] L—— not here.
   Enjoyed being with Frank & Dorothy[16] & their new little "Scotty."
   Took train for home.

Saturday, March 10
Glad to get home but sure feel low to-day. Can't figure anything out.

Monday, March 12
Good season of prayer with the gang this a.m.

Tuesday, March 13
Sue is 11 to-day. Had a big party. Went swell.
   An excellent time of fellowship with Claude and 7 or 8 other members of the committee[17] to-night. The Lord made us know of His Presence. Wonderful, prayerful spirit**—I feel better about the whole project & closer to Him than for two weeks.

Saturday, March 17
Wonderful day of skiing with the Girlies to-day. Best ever! Hans was very complimentary about my skiing.
   To SILVER CLIFF to-night—good swim.

Sunday, March 18 (Round-Up Lodge)
With Joe went to Round-up Ranch & Lodge this a.m.
   Lunch with Shultes.
   Home in aft. Called several of Board men.

Medicine in Houston and a member of the board for the Young Life Institute.

[16] Jim's brother and his wife.

[17] The Colorado Ranches Committee, most likely, which had taken the place of the Star Ranch Executive Committee once Silver Cliff was added.

Monday, March 19

Talked to Ferd & Guss. Ready & waiting for Dr. Marquard to arrive.

Paul[18] came in on way to Newton.

Dr. Barnhouse[19] here for lunch. All greatly enjoyed him.

Tuesday, March 20

To-day was the day! We closed the deal for "Round-up" after a long, hard day with Dr. Marquart [*sic*].

What can I possibly say. The Lord is <u>so</u> <u>wonderful</u> & has done such a superabundant thing for us in this—I want always to PRAISE & THANK HIM.

Talked to Crowell trustees. Talked to [board members] Wetmore, Weyerh.,[20] Mitchell, Gillis. All agreed we go ahead. Great spirit of one-ness.—I grabbed the 3:00p train for Newton.

Mrs. P—— made a splendid pledge to-day to take us over $300,000.00.

> *From the prayers of two work crew boys to the closing on the property had been less than nine months. Now Young Life had a third camp—the finest and largest of them all. Only nine donors had participated, and the fundraising had all occurred in a single month's time, despite tremendous odds. Jim loved to tell this story, explaining to one audience, "[I] told you in the hope that it will be a blessing to you and that you will share it with others and spread the word among the Lord's people as to how God can work."*

---

[18] Jim's brother Paul, travelling to see their ailing father.

[19] Donald Grey Barnhouse (1895–1960). Influential radio preacher and pastor of Tenth Presbyterian Church of Philadelphia. Barnhouse knew Rayburn from their mutual connections to Dallas Seminary. Wanda Ann Mercer, after leaving Young Life in the late 1950s, went to work for Barnhouse.

[20] Charles Davis Weyerhaeuser (1909–1999). Scion of the famous timber family. Dave Weyerhaeuser had joined the Young Life board in 1943 and served until his death fifty-six years later.

Jim's father, now seventy-five, was hospitalized in Newton following a massive stroke in March, causing the family to reunite once again. Though his father did not die right away, he never left the hospital, and passed away eight months later.

Wednesday, March 21 (Newton, Kansas)
Arr. Newton 1:30a. To bed after visit with Mother & Paul.

To hospital at 8:30. Dad very bad. Much pain and didn't know me…

To K. C. this aft. Dinner at Frank's.[21]

[…]

To Chicago to-night.

Sunday, March 25 (Easter) (Newton, Kansas)
Arr. Newton 4:15A. With Mother & Dad all day. Left for home after midnight.

Tuesday, March 27
Wrote letters to all my contacts seen on this trip.

Left for Round-up & Silver Cliff after supper with Guss, Kay & Maxine. Ran into big snow storm. Didn't arrive until after midnight.

Wednesday, March 28 (Round-Up Lodge)
At Round-up all day!

———

Jim took all the available staff to Round-Up Lodge to dedicate the new camp to the Lord. Structure by structure—over fifty in all—they inspected the buildings and prayed over each one. They renamed the property "Frontier Ranch."

With three camps now, Rayburn hired Parker Woolmington to help run them. Woolmington's background was in food service and he was a welcome addition to the Young Life family.

---

[21] Jim's brother.

In May, Jim brought together many of the staff for a week of prayer. His journal entries for that week, included here in their entirety, list how much time he and the staff prayed each day.

Tuesday, May 15
5 Hours

Wednesday, May 16
6 Hours

Thursday, May 17
4 Hours

Friday, May 18
4 Hours

Saturday, May 19
5 Hours.

The degree of fellowship and the earnestness of prayer at a very high peak as our week of prayer is closed. Probably nothing we have ever done so valuable or of such eternal significance—. The Lord is near.

Sunday, May 20 (Frontier Ranch)
The past week has undoubtedly been one of the greatest of my life—and the greatest week in the history of our work.

I was busy at FRONTIER until supper time.[22] Had supper at Silver Cliff then home—about 9:30.

Saturday, May 26
Parker Woolmington arr. 7:45a. Took him around the ranch[23]—then with family to Frontier. (First showed him briefly around Silver Cliff.)

We had a great open house at Frontier. Particularly enjoyed showing

---

[22] This is the first time Rayburn calls Round-Up Lodge by its new name in his diary.

[23] Star Ranch.

around Dr. & Mrs. Geo. White and Dr. & Mrs. Martin Anderson and son, Martin Jr.

Monday, May 28 (Silver Cliff Ranch and Frontier Ranch)

Spent day at Silver [Cliff] & Frontier with Parker. Had prayer with him about the big decision of his coming. Believe the Lord is leading in that direction.[24]

We drove home leisurely with the top down via Royal Gorge, Skyline Drive**. A delightful trip. Impressed with Parker's enthusiasm for the country.

June saw the first campers arrive at Frontier. Jim's diary tersely records three days of the historic week.

Monday, June 11 (Frontier Ranch)

First camp at "Frontier Ranch" got under way at 8:00 p.m. Grand crowd of kids—over 100 counting work crew kids. Excellent start.

Wednesday, June 13 (Frontier Ranch)

A smooth running camp.

Saturday, June 16 (Frontier Ranch)

J——S——of New Trier High closed in with the Lord to-day or yesterday. Great camp!

In the middle of the summer Young Life held its annual staff conference at Frontier. The fall saw the start of another school year

---

[24] Jim was certainly correct that the Lord was leading the Woolmington family to Colorado. Woolmington sold his catering business in Pennsylvania and moved to Chaffee County later that year to work at Silver Cliff and Frontier. But he only stayed in Young Life's employ for a short while, choosing to venture into his own camping ministry with Deer Valley, a resort he developed next to Silver Cliff Ranch. The Woolmingtons remain good friends and neighbors of Frontier Ranch to this day, more than fifty years later.

Mt. Princeton and Chimney Rock.

with Jim helping lead the club in Colorado Springs, as well as continuing his frequent travels.

Monday, July 9 (Frontier Ranch).
Climbed Mt. Princeton this a.m. Wonderful experience. Sue went all the way to summit. We took the horses to timberline.

Tuesday, September 25
Having awful pain in my head to-nite.

This was the day. Our third Young Life meeting of the year was the largest in history for the 2nd straight week—308 present at Star Ranch. Wonderful meeting. One senior lad said he had closed in with the Lord. Had a nice talk with him.

Thursday, September 27
Still some pain in my head to-day.

Got quite a bit done at the office and then had wonderful contacts at the football field with coaches and boys. I know the Lord has given this great "in" for a purpose." I Pray that we may make the most of it.

Thursday, November 29 (on the train)

Good meeting with Claude & Denver Ranches Committeemen at breakfast btwn trains in Denver.

Quiet pleasant day on Calif. Zypher [*sic*]. Some fine study in Soteriology[25] & other subjects.

---

[25] The theology of salvation.

1952

2 - 1 - 1 - 1 - 1.

I feel greatly constrained to pray more + seek from the Lord all that He has for us of guidance for our lives (solutions to our problems), + spiritual power in our ministry. A very good day at the office. Earnest prayer for the back salaries.

1 - 3 - 1 1

Y.L. Mtg to-night the largest in history! At Swan Funeral Home — 410 present. Great meeting — I spoke on the Bible — "How We Know It is The Word of God" - authors unity etc. Excellent hearing.

ENTRIES FROM SEPTEMBER 22 AND 23, 1952

These entries are good examples of Jim's use of numeric notations at the top of many pages. It is unclear what the codes meant, but Rayburn used them for many years.

With Young Life's rapid growth, training became a significant concern. Jim and the other ministry leaders were determined that Young Life not grow at the expense of quality. The first part of the solution was in holding Leadership Training Institutes for volunteer leaders. For full-time staff, in September 1951 the Young Life Institute was started (first called the Graduate Training Program). With only seven students to begin with, it was decided that the students would go to the faculty, hence the graduate-level program was dubbed "the Station Wagon Institute," as its members drove to leading scholars around the country for intensive theological studies. When they weren't on the road, they were at Star Ranch and Jim was one of their teachers.

In addition to teaching the graduate students, Jim continued to teach the "Mr. and Mrs." Sunday School class when he was in town (and sometimes even if he wasn't, as in the case on March 9 when he drove the four-hour round trip from Silver Cliff to Colorado Springs).

Wednesday, January 2

Terrible post-nasal blocking. Altho I had a very good day at the office I feel terrifically under the weather & specially to-night can't do anything.

2 fine hrs. with the Graduate Trainees.

Thursday, January 3

Got quite a bit done in the office even tho I sure have a very bum nose.

Lunch with Guss.

Friday, January 4

Worked with mail and had a good time with the Graduates this a.m. Have loaded with anti-histamine but it doesn't do much.

I have fixed up a "study" in the pantry downstairs—which I like and believe it will give me much more time for quiet study & prayer.

The family all enjoyed seeing C. C. Hockey team best Minn U 5–3.

Sunday, January 20

[…]

Taught Rev 6 to my class this a.m. with all time record 125 present. A very wonderful hearing for the Word. Truly a heart-warming privilege for me.

————

Monday, January 28 (Chicago)

Ten present for Y. L. Board Mtg. Dave Weyerhaeuser presiding—a splendid mtg. specially with the local staff people for reports at noon. Someway I felt that I failed the men & again I longed to be Spirit-filled—so that my leadership & decisions will be HIS & the Lord Jesus honored in what I present.

Saturday, February 2 (Chicago)

To wk-end L. T. I.[1]

60 Wheaton students.

Dr. Kanzer [sic, Kantzer][2] of college fine.

Spoke on Mk 2. "We're roof men" was a key idea that went over.[3]

————

[1] Leadership Training Institute.

[2] Almost certainly Dr. Kenneth S. Kantzer (1917–2002). Kantzer had received his doctorate from Harvard two years earlier and was teaching at Wheaton. He later taught at the Young Life Institute, served as dean of Trinity Evangelical Divinity School, and editor of *Christianity Today*. In the context of this entry, he has spoken that day at the Leadership Training retreat.

[3] "Roof men" refers to the young paralytic's friends in Mark 2 who brought him to the feet of Jesus by lowering him through the roof. Rayburn called the paralytic "a fortunate fellow" because he had friends who cared enough about him to do whatever it took to give him a chance to meet Christ.

Sunday, March 9 (Silver Cliff Ranch)

Drove from Silver Cliff to teach SS Class. Fine time on Rev 13.

Back for dinner & grand committee meeting.

Staying over night.

———

With fifty-two men and women on staff in eight different states, Young Life—and Jim—were becoming more and more well-known around the country. Nowhere was this more true than in the Pacific Northwest. On a trip to the region in March Jim met with two politicians who became great friends of Young Life: Washington governor Arthur Langlie, and Oregonian Mark Hatfield. Hatfield, then a state representative, was later elected to two terms as governor of Oregon and then to five terms in the United States Senate. He served on Young Life's board for many years.

The most significant "meeting" Jim had on this particular trip to the Northwest, however, was with a place, not a person. A chance comment by the parent of a Young Lifer led to the discovery by Jim of Malibu Club, a breathtakingly beautiful resort originally built for the Hollywood crowd.

Wednesday, March 19 (Salem, Oregon)

A good day in Salem. Splendid interview at lunch with Mark Hatfield (?)[+] Very well received at 1st Baptist Church this eve. Spoke on the work.

Offering from this area totalled over $700.00 during this brief visit.

In every way this was my best visit to Portland in all the years.

[+] The question mark is Jim's, indicating that he was unsure of how to spell the name. Hatfield was on Young Life's board of trustees from 1961–1975; his wife Antoinette also served on the board from 1980–1984.

Monday, March 24 (Spokane)

Headache (R.)

[…]

A wonderful kids mtg at the Spokane Hotel—350 present—the program <u>rolled</u>. Spoke on Mt. 8.

Took train to Seattle. Very sick to-night, most of night.

Tuesday, March 25 (Seattle)

Fine time with Dave W[eyerhaeuser] in Tacoma at lunch.

Very fine interview with Gov. Aurthur [*sic*, Arthur] B. Langlie.[5]

To-nite saw Kansas U beat Santa Clara & St. Johns beat Illinois in NCAA Semi-finals.

Wednesday, March 26 (Seattle)

This was a pleasant, restful, thrilling day. Flew in Jim Campbell's Seabee with Jim, Elaine [*sic*, Elsie] & Add to Malibu Club in Canada. Spectacular place! Then back by Vancouver Island & Friday Harbor.

Saw K.U. beat St. J. 80–63 to become Natl. Champs. Grand day.

Bad headache developing thru the day. (L-side.)

———

Rayburn's short entry does not tell the whole story, of course. Jim and Elsie Campbell's son had been a camper at Star Ranch in 1951. When the Campbells met Rayburn at Add and Loveta Sewell's home in Seattle, Jim Campbell told Rayburn about a property that Young Life might be interested in: Malibu Club in British Columbia.

The only problem was that this exclusive resort was only reachable by a long boat ride or a seaplane. It just so happened that Campbell had such a plane, and Rayburn insisted on a tour of the place.

---

5 Arthur Bernard Langlie (1900–1966). Republican governor of Washington (1941–1945 and 1949–1957).

In typical Rayburn style, as they first approached the spectacu-
lar property from the air, he said, "There is Young Life's next prop-
erty." It would take almost two years of prayer and hard work be-
fore Rayburn's pronouncement came true, and the diaries tell the
story. Until 1953, however, the above entry is all that is mentioned
about Malibu in Jim's journals.

Jim took a rare vacation in April with Claude Hathaway
and several other men to Utah's Monument Valley, where the
stunning scenery gave Jim a chance to practice one of his hobbies,
photography.

Saturday, April 26 (Monument Valley, Utah)

This was one of those once-in-a-lifetime days. Harry Goulding[6] took us
out and we shot pictures of <u>everything</u> we came to get & a lot more too.
Indian Children—a whole sand-painting ceremony—goats, cooking,
rug-weaving, shearing, etc., etc.

I shot 60 Stereo's[7] & 25 kodachromes & had the kind of day that
kept me thinking of and thanking the Lord.

Those little kids & their need touched our hearts.

—⁓—

Jim's diary is silent from April 28 until September 8, one of the
longest such periods in all of his journals. Coincidentally, he was
ordered by his doctors to take time off that summer, which he did
as he and his family spent the summer at The Lookout at Frontier.
The Lookout had been Dr. Marquard's private residence when he

---

[6] Harry Goulding was responsible for Hollywood's discovery of Monument Valley
when he convinced the director John Ford to film the John Wayne epic "Stagecoach"
there in 1939. Rayburn had been to Goulding's trading post on a previous trip to the
area in April 1951.

[7] A Stereo Realist camera had recently been given to Young Life. As it was explained
to the staff, the camera "takes a pair of pictures, one picture corresponding to the
viewpoint of each eye. ... Jim has found these 'third dimension' pictures invaluable in
numerous deputation contacts."

The Lookout at Frontier.

owned the property, and Rayburn adopted the beautiful log cabin as his own, as well. In many ways, it was the house he felt most "at home" in.

From May 20–25 Jim once again called the men of the staff to Colorado for a week of prayer.

With the close of Young Life's fiscal year on September 30, that month almost always found Rayburn praying and working fever-ishly for the Lord to meet the ministry's financial needs. That was certainly the case in September 1952. At the same time that Jim was praying for miracles on the financial front, he watched God perform miracles in the Colorado Springs High School Young Life club. Below are all of his entries, in their entirety, for the second half of September.

Saturday, September 13

To-day we sent out letters telling the mailing list that we were nearly $40,000 in need for salaries to end the year this mo.

Tuesday, September 16

Club to-night at the ranch—over 300 present. Gave a very introductory message on the Gospel with the intro. along the lines of how little we think of these great things. Went well!

Monday, September 22

I feel greatly constrained to pray more & seek from the Lord all that He has for us of guidance for our lives, solutions to our problems, & spiritual power in our ministry. A very good day at the office. Earnest prayer for the back salaries.

Tuesday, September 23

Y. L. Mtg to-night the largest in History! At Swan Funeral Home—410 present. Great meeting. I spoke on "The Bible—How We Know It is The Word of God"—Authors unity etc. Excellent hearing.

Saturday, September 27 (Frontier Ranch)

Over 200 from Colo. Spgs Hi in camp. Pretty rowdy but going well.

Monday, September 29

How warm and thankful my heart is to-day. In addition to the big $10,000 gift that we knew was coming we rec'd $7,000.00 in smaller amounts—to just about put us over the top for the year. Unbelievable! Lk 1:37!![8] Praise the Lord.

Tuesday, September 30

Outdoor meeting at Hallenbecks. Btween 325 & 375 present for perhaps the best meeting we ever had here. I spoke on Romans 1:18–End. & "No Fear Of God ..." Intro. about "fear." Have you ever been afraid of God? of leaving Him out, etc? Went every well.

To-day was one of the greatest experiences. We had all the money for the back salaries. Over $45,000 came in. It is "impossible" except for our wonderful God. All praise & thanks to Him.

—◦—

In October Jim travelled to Dallas for the semi-annual board meeting, and then on to a series of meetings California.

---

[8]   "For with God nothing shall be impossible" (KJV).

In Los Angeles Jim took part in a fundraising banquet for the ministry there. The Portland, Oregon, committee had begun the idea of putting on a banquet to raise support for Young Life a little earlier, and Jim was warming to the idea.

Roy Riviere, mentioned already in previous journal entries, was by now the area director for Northern California, which included the San Francisco Bay area. First introduced to Young Life as a high school student in Tyler, Texas, Roy was yet another Wheaton alum, where he had met his wife Doris. Riviere served as a senior leader for over twenty years, many of them directly at Jim's side as one of his most trusted and valued lieutenants.

Saturday, October 11 (Dallas)

The Board meeting went very well. All the men were pleased & very thankful to the Lord for the wonder-working way that He has blessed us.

Highlights—Total income to all our** work "51–52"—$321,000.00 Hundreds of new donors. Much larger clubs & camps.

I greatly enjoyed the OU Texas game—OU 49–TU [*sic*] 20. 1st quarter the greatest football I ever saw OU scored 28 pts.

Thursday, October 16 (on the train)

I left for LA via the Santa Fe at 1:25 a.m. After a swell sleep I had a wonderful restful day—the best day in prayer and the Word that I have had in a long time. I will be much more ready for my work out west.

Saturday, October 18 (Los Angeles)

A very odd combination of things this morning—I awoke about 5:30 with advanced mig. symptoms & really severe pain (R.) Took Caf.,[9] went to bed for 20 min. & just lying there meditating I got started on a wonderful season of prayer—the kind I feel such a great need of. The <u>Lord</u> is very real, and every close.—

---

[9] Caffeine. Then as now, used as a headache reliever.

Now the day is over and I cannot express the joy of it, nor my thanks to the Lord. Every prayer on my list that could be answered by now has been abundantly answered. Fine L.T. [Leadership Training] this a.m., wonderful fellowship with Dick H.[10] & his men at the luncheon & game. (UCLA 24 Stanford 14!)

[...]

Dictated until midnight—cleared up all the correspondence Betty[11] sent & more. Great!

Tuesday, October 21 (Los Angeles)
Great time at Fuller Chapel. Spoke on John 1—"come & see."

Wonderful Chinese luncheon and fellowship with Wilbur Smith at noon. And a meeting to-night that makes this one of the greatest days of my life. How can I ever thank the Lord. 200 at our beautiful "promotion dinner" & what a warm, enthus[iastic] crowd! They gave gifts in cash & pledges totalling over $7,000.00!! Nothing like that ever happened before. Wonder if that's the way to go about it [—] must pray.

Home to pack @ 1:00 a. Writing this at 2:15—to bed!!

Wednesday, October 22 (San Francisco)
Left L.A. @ 8AM. Arr. Frisco 9:30. Went to see Mr. B.—he chatted & offered to give us at least $1000 before first of year. I can't thank the Lord enough that he is giving us all this wonderful indication of His blessing & provision in finances.

A splendid time with Roy & June[12] & Doris & a good mtg. at 1st Presby in Berkeley.

---

[10] Probably Dick Hillis (see January 1, 1943, entry).

[11] Betty Lee Duncan. Jim's secretary from 1951–1954, she also helped out in the Colorado Springs club. As a high school student she had been in the Peyton, Colorado, Young Life club when Frog Sullivan was its leader. She later married Will Wyatt.

[12] June Gadske, who, along with Roy Riviere, was the other staff person in northern California.

James Chalmers Rayburn, Sr., and Elna Ann Rayburn.

---

*Lewis Sperry Chafer, Jim's mentor from Dallas Theological Semi-
nary, died in August. Sadly, he was not the only father figure Jim
would lose that fall. After being hospitalized for eight months,
James Rayburn, Sr., died on November 1 at age seventy-six.*

Friday, October 31

Mig (R)

Mild mig. symptoms progressing slowly from early morning. Knocked it out in aft.
with 1 #3 & 2 Caf.

Voted to-day.[13] Shopped for Jamie's birthday. Caught train for Newton
at 3:55 p.

---

[13] Jim took his duties as a citizen seriously and was a staunchly patriotic American. It
is likely that he is referring here to voting absentee in the 1952 presidential election, as
he knew he would be out of town on election day speaking at two school assemblies in
Wichita, Kansas.

Saturday, November 1 (Newton, Kansas)

Dad died this morning at 1:45. Just 20 minutes before my train arrived. Frank met me. We brought mother home from the hospital & sat around & talked until 4:30 or so. Made all funeral arrangements this a.m.

[...]

Monday, November 3 (Newton, Kansas)

Father's funeral to-day. Bob & I conducted it. The Lord gave us a very good day. All the relatives were in.

Tuesday, November 4 (Wichita, Kansas)

Mig at 3:00 A.M. Caf & #3 fixed by morning.

[...]

Took train for Chicago at 10:00 P. Listened to IKE get elected PRESIDENT.

Maxine had surgery in November but did not want to miss the opportunity to travel with Jim and several others to be Billy Graham's invited guests at his Albuquerque crusade.

Wednesday, November 19

A very busy day.—at office & bringing Maxine home.

Frank & Mrs. Ga[e]belein are here & we are enjoying them.

Put Maxine on the train at 1:25A to Las Vegas [New Mexico].

Thursday, November 20 (Albuquerque)

We left at 7:00 A.M. Fine trip. Picked up Maxine in Vegas at noon. She [is] feeling very bad. Lunch at the La Fonda in Santa Fe. To Albu. & the Hilton. To the Billy Graham mtgs. I was very cordially received by Billy after the mtg & by the whole crowd.

Friday, November 21 (Albuquerque)

A pleasant day in Albu except for Maxine who is having a very painful time. Ate Mex food & shopped in the old plaza district. Att[ended] the Graham mtg. Sat on the platform & enjoyed it. Afterward had a wonderful late Supper party with Billy & Ruth, Cliff & Billie Barrows, Bev Shea et. al.[14] They were all most cordial & Billy presented me with a beautiful Bible & Bev with several of his records. He is my favorite.

Thursday, November 27 (Thanksgiving Day) (on the train)

Some strange Thanksgiving day. Arr. in St Louis a little late[15] & left at 1 p.m. on the "Spirit of St L." for Philly. Had steak for my "Thanksgiving Dinner" alone on the diner.

Saturday, December 13

All time record attendance at S.S. Mr. & Mrs. Class (160).

Thursday, December 25

I think the whole family is agreed that this has been our best Christmas. The girls got the ski equipment they so wanted and many other beautiful things. Jamie is very happy with his ice skates, hockey stick, & record player. It was a beautiful, restful day, with so much for which to thank the Lord.

Wednesday, December 31

I should have kept a faithful record of this month as a number of interesting and important things have happened.

The fireside testimony mtg of the camp[16] lasted until nearly mid-

---

[14] The Billy Graham team: Billy and Ruth Graham, Cliff and Wilma "Billie" Barrows, and George Beverly Shea. The team by this time had already worked together for several years—Barrows as the music and program director, Shea as the soloist—and would remain together until Graham's retirement in 2006.

[15] He was travelling from Dallas to the East Coast.

[16] One of the highlights of early Young Life camping trips was a fireside meeting where kids were encouraged to share what the time at camp had meant to them. In this case, it was a snow camp at Star Ranch.

night and many fine kids testified that they have invited the Saviour into their hearts. It has been a good camp-time. Both here[17] & at Silver Cliff.

How faithful the Lord is. How wonderful He has moved us forward. Oh, to be all that He can make me—that what we do, where we go, who we touch may be in the fullness of the blessing of the Gospel of Christ.

---

[17] Star Ranch.

1953

Monday, December 21, 1953
355th Day—10 Days to Follow

This will go down as a very historic day. We went into escrow on the Malibu transaction this morning! Everybody very happy. Gene phoned that the Board gave approval.

Gus + I left LA at 8:30 p. Uneventful trip home. Arr. DU 1:30 a.m. Cos 3°. Cold!!

"THIS WILL GO DOWN AS A VERY HISTORIC DAY."
The purchase of Malibu Club, Young Life's fourth property.

Thursday, January 8

The first day of our two day area staff conference—we spent the entire day in prayer with great blessing from the Lord.

[...]

Tuesday, January 13

Had a very wonderful time of prayer btwn 3 & 5 A.M. because my head was so painful I couldn't sleep.

Good day at office. Fine parents mtg to-night at club—altho only about 30–35 parents.

———

In addition to using his journals to record his health problems and significant events, he also used it to record short outlines of some of his messages. His entries from a Young Life weekend camp in California exemplify this.

Friday, February 6 (Crestline, California)

Arr. LA. 10:30 A.

Went to Halverson's,[1] then with him to luncheon @ Calif. Club[2]—The Lord blessed our time with about a dozen key** men—

To Crestline (Thousand Pines). A remarkable opening of camp. Everything went far better than expected. I spoke on:

    I. "Who Are You Afraid Of."—Rom 3:18[3] and "Fear of Lord beg. of

---

[1]   Richard Halverson (1916–1995). At the time of this entry he was on the staff of First Presbyterian Church in Hollywood, serving alongside Henrietta Mears and Louis Evans. Halverson became a beloved leader, not just in his own Presbyterian denomination, but in the American church. After a successful career pastoring flocks in three states he spent the last fourteen years of his life as the chaplain of the United States Senate. He counted Rayburn as "one of the few authentic heroes in my life. From our first meeting to the last, he was for me the prototype of what a servant of Christ should be."

[2]   Located in downtown Los Angeles, the California Club was the oldest private club in southern California.

[3]   "There is no fear of God before their eyes."

FRONTIER RANCH, 1953
*Top row: Jim, Wanda Ann Mercer ("Wam"), Marge Stone (later Peterson), Digger
Langford, Dr. Vernon Grounds. Bottom row: Wally Howard, Roy Riviere.*

wisdom."[4] Everyone afraid of something. Big loud mouths afraid too ...
But not of God ... (I'm <u>brave</u>—watch me—not afraid of Texas Zypher
[*sic*])

Fear Him—means—reverence Him, be afraid to go against His
way, His power. <u>Put</u> Him in <u>His</u> <u>Rightful</u> <u>Place</u>.

Went very, very well—should be developed!!

Saturday, February 7 (Crestline, California)

Another unusually fine meeting this a.m. Both last night and this a.m. I
have enjoyed wonderful liberty from the Lord.

II. From I. I recaped [*sic*] on "Fear" for 4 or 5 minutes—(Afraid of
Alphalpa [*sic*]—No! Sun No!—Air. No. All of 'em kill people.) Gotta
keep them in their right place! Then headed** right into John 5—Once
you realize truth of I—ready to consider Him & take Him—first He
must demonstrate who He is & second you must see your need of
Him—(Exc approach!!) Both I & II 27 min long.

III. Did brief recap. especially on "helplessness"—then to Lk 23 "Je-
sus & Two Criminals"—One said "Don't you fear God ..." <u>Ties</u> <u>in</u> <u>beau-</u>
<u>tifully</u>. Grand reception. Fine day!!

+   Proverbs 9:10.

Sunday, February 8 (Crestline, California)

A great closing—I dropped back to a simple message on "How To Become a Christian." J. 20:31,[5] J 1:12[6] & Rev 3:20.[7] Went well!! The Testimony time was one of the greatest. Don [*sic*, Donn] Moomaw was great![8]

Bad trip to town—traffic!! Grand dinner at Daws'. Splendid mtg at 1st Presby Glendale. Then wonderful fellowship with Daws, Dick H., et. al.

Migraines continued to plague Rayburn; 1953 proved to be a particularly tough year in that regard.

Thursday, February 19

11 out of the last 18 days I have had bad headache. 5 of these were very severe attacks. What to do? That is the question.

[...]

Tuesday, February 24

In bed all day with terrible mig. Caf. & #3 did no good. Finally as last resort Dr. knocked me out with Demerol.**

Went to club. Did not speak. Mitch spoke on Gen 22. Good. 145 present.

---

[5] "But these are written so that you may believe that Jesus is the Christ, the Son of God, and that by believing you may have life in his name."

[6] "But to all who did receive him, who believed in his name, he gave the right to become children of God."

[7] "Behold, I stand at the door and knock. If anyone hears my voice and opens the door, I will come in to him and eat with him, and he with me."

[8] Donn D. Moomaw. Former All-American at UCLA (he had just graduated), Moomaw had been dramatically reached for Christ while in college and was very much in demand by various ministries to give his testimony. He later became pastor of Bel Air Presbyterian Church and counted Ronald and Nancy Reagan as members of his flock.

While Jim thrilled at being in the thick of Young Life activities—whether it was training young leaders or presenting the ministry to a Lions Club meeting—he still found church meetings to be a bore.

In late March and early April the Rayburn family took a ski vacation.

Wednesday, March 25 (Seattle)

The Lions Club luncheon was the best mtg. of the kind I ever had. Tone was excellent and I did absolutely the best job I am capable of doing—truly a grand experience.

A dull dinner & a dull mtg afterward at 1st Pres in Bremerton.

Thursday, March 26 (Tacoma, Washington)

Fine luncheon in Tacoma.

Dave [Weyerhaeuser] flew us to Portland.

Here again both Tom [Raley] & I did our best & the Portland banquet exceeded anything of the kind we have ever done. About 500 present & beautifully done.

Sunday, March 29–Monday, March 30 (Sun Valley, Idaho)

[This entry is written across two days.]
Arr. Sun Valley about mid-afternoon.

The next seven days was a wonderful experience for all of us. We greatly enjoyed the whole thing—every member of the family. First vacation of the sort, I think. I was not as good at skiing as I thot—the steep slopes showed me up badly. But I made considerable progress. Jimmy did fine beginning. The girls did very well.

Not everything Rayburn touched turned to gold, of course. For instance, occasionally donors' intentions did not match their ability to follow through with their gifts, as was the case with one friend of the ministry who had made a significant pledge to the work. (The donor's name and city have been obscured to protect his anonymity.)

Monday, August 31 (city in Colorado)

Left ranch about 9:00 A.

Tried all aft & eve. to see X——. He was there but wouldn't see me. Very tired & sick with headache to-n. Went to tourist court.

Tuesday, September 1 (city in Colorado)

Finally saw X—— for about 2 min. this a.m. He wouldn't talk. Said he was broke & his house & business were for sale—I said I didn't believe it. We'll see. To [another city] to see Bankers.

Back to Frontier later.

[...]

In September, Rayburn was given the opportunity to participate as part of the Billy Graham team during their crusade in Detroit.

At the same time that the Detroit meetings were going on, Dawson Trotman and The Navigators were in the process of buying a property in Colorado Springs to serve as their national headquarters. The move was precipitated by Trotman's desire to be closer to Rayburn. Guss Hill, Jim's good friend and real estate agent, first suggested Glen Eyrie for Billy Graham's use. When Graham turned it down, Trotman and his crew realized it would be just right for them. Built by the founder of Colorado Springs, General William Palmer, for his homesick British wife, it was a complete English castle. The move solidified the good relationship Young Life enjoyed with The Navigators.

Though the Graham crusade lasted through October, Jim did not stay the entire time, leaving for the middle two weeks and coming back to fill in one night for Graham.

Sunday, September 27 (Detroit)

My first day with Billy Graham in Detroit. Response fine from the whole team as far as making me feel welcome, etc. A great crowd completely overflowing the building. Perhaps 20,000 in all.

[...]

Monday, September 28 (Detroit)

Went with Billy to a big Kiwanis luncheon (500). At eve mtg—close to capacity crowd—around 9000.

Good day. Felt fine with no pain in my head at any time.

Got a lot of correspondence handled to-day.

Tuesday, September 29 (Detroit)

Headachy in a.m.—& thru day. No bad pain—no medicine. Breakfast with the Graham team. Read, studied, rested. & didn't go to mtg to-night because of way I've been feeling.

Good conference with Cliff Barrows to-day & also with Lorne Sanny.[9] "Navigators" closed the deal for "Glen Eyrie" to-day.

Wednesday, September 30 (Detroit)

Studied a lot.

Thursday, October 1 (Detroit)

A good day—

Some valuable contacts made. Talked to home office—We are <u>over the top</u>—for another year—Praise & Thanks to God! It is all of Him!

Saturday, October 3 (Detroit)

[...]

Inside studying and resting this aft.

---

[9] Lorne Charles Sanny (1920–2005). Sanny was Dawson Trotman's top lieutenant and succeeded him as leader of The Navigators after Trotman's death in 1956 and served in that capacity for thirty years. Like Trotman, he was an enthusiastic backer of Young Life.

Monday, October 5 (Detroit)

A wonderful day.

Pastors breakfast this a.m. was grand. Many excellent contacts.

A splendid interview with Bishop Russel[l] Hubbard[10]—Episcopal Diocese of Mich—

Very fine Chinese dinner and chance to talk about the work with Billy, Cliff, Grady & Jerry.[11]

Tuesday, October 6 (Detroit)

Another very fine day—Good contacts at Presbytery of Detroit—

Also at DTS Alumni luncheon.

And with Billy—another long conference. Also Jerry Bevan [*sic*, Beavan] & the Maddox[es].[12]

Overflow crowd to-nite.

———

Monday, October 26 (Detroit)

This was a great day. Grand fellowship with the team.

I preached to-nite—near 10,000 people present, at least half of them young!

Rushed to Willow Run Airport with George and Wam[13] & on home—changed in Chicago.

DV at 5. Home at 7.

The great story of the year for Jim would be what happened next:

---

[10] Russell Hubbard was a ranking Episcopal clergyman who maintained a good relationship with Young Life for many years.

[11] Billy Graham, Cliff Barrows, Grady Wilson, and Jerry Beavan. Wilson was Graham's right hand man and Beavan worked for many years on the crusade team.

[12] Probably Paul Maddox and his wife. Maddox had been the chief of U.S. Army chaplains in Europe after World War II and served several years on the Billy Graham team.

[13] George Sheffer and Wanda Ann Mercer, both then on staff in Chicago.

the miraculous acquisition of Malibu Club.

Tom Hamilton, who had made a fortune in the aviation industry, had spent a large part of that fortune building his resort on the Jervis Inlet in British Columbia. It lacked for nothing—save guests. Shortly after he built it, World War II began and dried up any potential business. When the war ended Hamilton reopened the facility but he was never able to make a go of it as a business. When Rayburn visited it the previous year Hamilton had put it on the market for $1,000,000.

The property was certainly worth that, even in 1953 dollars. The 645 acres were some of the most dramatic scenery in North America as the mountains plunged into the sea, and the facilities were first-rate.

After Rayburn left the Graham crusade in Detroit he headed for southern California where Hamilton lived, to begin negotiating.

Friday, October 30 (Los Angeles)

ARR. 9:45 AM (L.A.)

Went to Suttons & got a car from John Woudenberg.[14] To Miss Mears' home.[15] Wonderful time there.

---

[14] John Woudenberg (1918–2005). Former college and NFL football player, including four years with the San Francisco 49ers, during which he played on both the offensive and defensive lines, as well as special teams, becoming known as a "60-minute man." A strong Christian, when he left football he became an auto dealer and often helped provide Jim with new cars (in the case of this entry, the car was a loaner while Jim was in Los Angeles).

[15] Henrietta C. Mears (1890–1963). Christian Education director at First Presbyterian Church of Hollywood. During the time she was there the Sunday School enrollment grew from 400 to more than 6,000. She founded Gospel Light Publications in 1933 and Forest Home Christian Conference Center in 1938. She also significantly impacted many Christian leaders, chief among them Bill and Vonette Bright of Campus Crusade for Christ, and Billy Graham. Rayburn, too, considered her an influence and was very fond of her. Her importance to evangelical Christianity in the late twentieth century was summed up by the cover of the September 1996 issue of *Christianity Today* which called her "The Grandmother of Us All." The home Rayburn is referring to was her recently-purchased house at 110 Stone Canyon Road

Tom Hamilton came by this evening.

Saturday, October 31 (Los Angeles)
Mig came early 5 A.M. 2 Caf. 1 #3 stopped it.

Saw UCLA beat Cal 20–7.

Good fellowship with Miss Mears, Vonette Bright,[16] Jim Ferguson et. al.

A fine time to-night. Dinner at the Beverly Hills Hotel with Tom Hamilton. [...]

Monday, November 2 (Los Angeles)
Felt "low" and generally bad to-day. Worried about to-nite & ashamed that I am.

[...]

The [Los Angeles Young Life] banquet was great & we all thank God for it. Over 250 present. Tom Hamilton was there.

Tuesday, November 3 (Los Angeles)
Lunch with Vaughan [*sic*] Antablin[17] & John Woudenberg—Vaughan was complimentary about last night. Can't help but feel that something great may come of this—

A wonderful conference with Tom Hamilton this aft. Am I right in feeling like Malibu is about to be ours[?] I humbly thank God for all He is doing.

Dinner alone at the Calif Club to-night. One of the best I ever ate— 'specially the buffet.

---

in the tony Bel-Air section of Los Angeles.

[16] Vonette Zachary Bright. Wife of Bill Bright and co-founder with him of Campus Crusade for Christ. At the time, the Brights were living with Miss Mears.

[17] Vaughn Antablin was a lawyer on the Los Angeles Young Life committee.

Wednesday, November 4 (Los Angeles)

Had a fine conference with Tom Hamilton and Calder MacKay.[18] Looks better all the time—I seem to have a sense of the Lord's sovereignity [*sic*] & omniscience in this. How little I have done. Nothing! But wonderful things continue to happen, things that I believe God initiates.

Great kids rally in Pasadena. 900 present.

[...]

Thursday, November 5 (Los Angeles)

Who knows—We may look back on this as a very historic day in Young Life. Tom Hamilton came to the [California] Club while I was breakfasting with Jim McMillan. We quickly got into the Malibu deal and signed the agreement binding him to sell at the phenomenal price of $300,000 & binding me only to TRY. He is willing to take $150,000 or less down & make further concessions. How I do thank God. I've seldom felt so deeply grateful to Him.

Flew to Portland—Great banquet to-nite—300 or more present.

The Lord had used the Internal Revenue Service to lower the price of Malibu by seventy percent: Hamilton also owned the famous Beverly Hills Hotel and when he sold the hotel earlier in the year, he became willing to sell Malibu at a loss to offset his capital gain on the hotel, putting Malibu's price in striking distance for Young Life.

But in order for it to be advantageous for Hamilton, the deal had to be concluded by the end of the year, only fifty-six days away. For the second time in as many years, Jim found himself making a mad dash around the country to raise a seemingly impossible amount of money.

At the same time that he was raising money for Malibu, Jim

---

[18] Calder MacKay was a prominent Los Angeles attorney, here representing Tom Hamilton's interests.

*was also raising money for two other items: the Pine Valley Club,
a former country club in Colorado Springs that he hoped to make
a new headquarters facility for Young Life; and the "Future Unlimited" fundraising campaign for general expansion needs of the
ministry. The latter two fundraising efforts were not successful, but
Malibu was a different story. (As with the Frontier account, the
anonymity of the people Jim solicited has been preserved.)*

*In addition to raising the funds, he also needed to obtain board
approval since the next official meeting of the board would not be
until almost a month after the deadline.*

Friday, November 6 (Portland, Oregon)
Breakfast with Paul.[19]

    To Salem. Great assembly—really rolled. [...]

    Wonderful time with the boys who met the Lord at the ranches.
Great banquet!

    Hurried to Portland to talk to Mrs. P—— about the Malibu Club
project.

Saturday, November 7 (Portland, Oregon)
Got up & talked to Mrs. P. on way to airport—didn't get far.

    Off to Spokane 7:45 A Arr 10 A.

    Saw TCU 21 – WSC 7.

    Very poor mtg to-nite.

    Took train for Everett with Bill Starr.

Sunday, November 8 (Malibu Club)
Got of[f] at Everett—early.

    To Malibu with Jim Campbell in Seabee.

    Add—Bill & I (again) completely bowled over with the possibilities

---

[19] Jim's brother Paul who was establishing himself as a successful businessman in
Portland after serving as a pilot in the war.

Jim speaking at a Seattle banquet in the early fifties, most likely the one mentioned in his November 9, 1953, entry. Flanking Jim are Richard Halverson (left) and Washington Governor Arthur B. Langlie (right).

it presents. Didn't even remember it was so beautiful and <u>complete</u>.

Came back late aft. to wonderful Campaigners mtg in Seattle.

Ate dinner, went to Univ. Presby.—and to bed—thanking and praising the Lord for His unfathomable goodness to us.

Monday, November 9 (Seattle)

A whole lot of miracles to-day! Talked Malibu with Dave W. this a.m. <u>by phone</u>. He expressed interest and favor and asked me to talk to committee. They in turn very impressed—Clarence[20] too. Both Dave & Clarence vote FOR!

Our greatest promotion banquet to-night! Gov Langley [*sic*, Langlie] et. al. did a wonderful job. Top $7,600.00 offering in cash & pledges.

Left for home at midnight—This has been one of my greatest days!!

---

[20] Clarence A. Black. Both Black and Weyerhaeuser were serving at the time on the Young Life board of trustees, and being from the Pacific Northwest, it was especially important for Jim to have their support for the project. Weyerhaeuser was married to Black's sister Annette.

Thursday, November 12

Worked hard & "conferred hard" with the office crew this a.m. on the "5354 Project."[21]

Very thankful for the guys' reaction.

Friday, November 13 (Dallas)

Mig. early—1 Caf. 2 #3. Slow relief but complete by noon.

A grand day in Dallas. Went right with E——C——to see his mother & they are going to stand true on this deal. Put up $10,000 this a.m. Say rest of pledge firm & sure!

John E. enthused. He & (Orv. & O. T., & Alex)[22] (by proxy) vote "yes"! Everything about this deal has the hand of the Lord upon it, as far as my feeble understanding can tell. Praise Him!

Tuesday, November 17 (Knoxville, Tennessee)

A memorable day in Knoxville. J——C——gave $3000—1000 each for Malibu, Pine Valley & "Future Unlimited"

Great "parents nite" club. Much good will. How I do thank & praise the Lord these days!

Thursday, November 19 (Chicago)

Arose late & had a hard, long day at Trust Mtg.[23]

They came thru, thanks only to the Lord, for 50,000 Pine V. and 15/yr for 5 yrs on Malibu.

Vi & Lillian took me to the plane—lock on trunk broke—I'll never forget that. All luggage inside.

Restful trip to N. Y. Feel calm assurance of the presence & guidance of the Lord. Larry[24] met me at La Guardia & we talked late!!

---

[21] Another name for the "Future Unlimited" fundraising campaign.

[22] Texas board members John E. Mitchell, Orville Mitchell, O. T. Goldsmith, and Alex McKenzie.

[23] The Crowell Trust.

[24] Probably board member Larry Kulp.

Friday, November 20 (New York City)

A great, great day. Mr. R——M—— very cordial. I am extremely hopeful that he will throw his weight behind us. This could mean—who knows. Thanks be to God only & may He lead in what is to follow. U. S. Senator _____ of Nebr.[25] also very cordial. Good chance at him thru R.M.

Monday, November 23

Worked hard in the office.

M—— called—said if I would get another $50,000 he would attempt to raise rem[aining] $100,000!!

Larry called. Had just talked to M——. Felt fine about it. Said about the same as R.M. did. Whoops!

Talked to S——K—— He said come Wednesday. Let me never forget that there has never been a season where everything fit to-gether like this for me. Every day evidence of Psa 32:8,[26] 121:8.[27] I thank the Lord & look to Him!

Thursday, November 26 (Thanksgiving Day) (Chicago)

Arr. in Chi very ill. Had taken Caf. Codine [sic] & a sleeping pill—I suppose the comb. made me so sick. Went to Union Sta[tion] Hostess @ Fred Harvey's[28] [she] guided me to Emerg.** Hosp. where a very kind person let me go to bed & called H. J. Taylor.

Gradually got well. Went to Winnetka. Had Turkey dinner with

---

[25] Jim has left the senator's name blank. At the time, Hugh Butler and Dwight Griswold were the officeholders from Nebraska.

[26] "I will instruct you and teach you in the way you should go;
    I will counsel you with my eye upon you."

[27] "The LORD will keep
    your going out and your coming in
    from this time forth and forevermore."

[28] The Fred Harvey Company ran a chain of train station restaurants called Harvey Houses.

Gloria Taylor's folks & sisters. Talked long time to H. J. Went to loop &
to bed on train about 10.

Friday, November 27 (St. Paul, Minnesota)
Arr. St. Paul 7:30 A.

A grand conference with F——. He pledged generously to the PV[29]
project.

Wonderful evening with H—— W——. She too will give. Had to
run for train.

Saturday, November 28 (Winnipeg)
Arr. Winnipeg. G—— very cordial and will give to new
project—Malibu.

Monday, November 30 (Winnipeg)
Pleasant morning with G——. He will give $5,000 for expenses & see
other [donors] about the 25,000 pledge to Malibu Project.

Off on CPR[30] to Vancouver. Nice restful aft.

Thursday, December 3 (Seattle)
LV Vanc 8:30

ARR Seattle 12:10.

[...]

To Tacoma to see Dave.

Not much enthus. here for Malibu. D—— gave $10,000 to P. V.

I will be more prayerful & cautious. Ask the Lord again & again to
keep us on His road. He will! That I know.

ARR Portland 9:15.

Friday, December 4 (Portland, Oregon)
Fine luncheon with J—— M——, then terribly sick with Mig, rest of day.

---

[29] Pine Valley Club.

[30] Canadian Pacific Railway.

Saturday, December 5 (Portland, Oregon)
Luncheon w. Portland comm.

    More funds collected (Mrs. P's $.)

    To train at 4:30. Off to Berkeley.

—~~~—

Sunday, December 13 (Dallas)
Late out of Mphs. Arr. DL about 3:00 P. Spent all afternoon with Orv, Alex and Wally—They are enthu[siastic] about the Malibu deal. The thing seems to be the Lord's leading. I do so desire to be cautious and not go "ahead."

    Flew home to-nite.

Friday, December 18 (Los Angeles)
Up at 3 A.M.

    To DV. 3 hrs late out.

    Into LA at Noon.

    To Statler [Hotel]. Good. talk with Tom Hamilton. Things continue to shape up. I can't begin to <u>thank</u> the Lord for all of this.

Saturday, December 19 (Los Angeles)
A lot of phone conversations with Tom and Vaughan about the big deal. Stayed in or near the room all day. To bed early.

Sunday, December 20 (Los Angeles)
Dean Stephan,[31] Guss Hill, Frank Muncy,[32] Vaughan Antiblin [*sic*] and I had lunch at "Bev Hills Hotel" with Tom H. and then went to see Calder MacKay. Everything went along smoothly and the negotiations are complete. We go into escrow—with what Vaughan & Frank con-

---

[31] Los Angeles area board member Dean E. Stephan. At the time he was a district sales manager for Chicago Bridge & Iron Company.

[32] San Francisco accountant Frank Muncy, who would later serve on the board of trustees.

sider a very favorable deal—to-morrow. John Woudenberg and Vaughan
came up to room to-night.

Monday, December 21 (Los Angeles)

This will go down as a very historic day. We went into escrow on the
Malibu transaction this morning! Everybody very happy. Gene[33] phoned
that the Board gave approval.

Guss & I left LA at 8:30 p. Uneventful trip home Arr. DV 1:30 A.
Cos [Colorado Springs] 3:30. Cold!!

*When it was all said and done, Jim had made twenty-seven trips
by air or rail since September 1.* Monday Morning, *Young Life's
weekly bulletin for the staff, reported on December 31, "JCR is quietly catching up on desk work, sleep and family life after his thirty
thousand miles of travel since the middle of September." He was
also speaking to a snow camp full of kids.*

Wednesday, December 30 (Silver Cliff Ranch)

Skied at Cooper Hill to-day & had one of the best days ever. The girls
are skiing beautifully and I am doing much better. It was a perfect day.

Very good hearing on John 5 to-nite. Several fine fellows closed in.

Thursday, December 31 (Silver Cliff Ranch)

Camp wound up with great blessing from the Lord. Otherwise it was
a very difficult day. The Lord has been wonderfully good this year in
permitting us great forward strides. Now to follow Him & see what
significance is attached to acquiring Malibu, getting to know K——,
M——, etc.

*What had seemed impossible had once again been accomplished
through faith and prayer. After the heady experiences of the past*

---

[33] Gene Gillis, then serving as chairman of the board.

several years, it is no surprise that one of Jim's favorite hymns was "Come, My Soul, Thy Suit Prepare" by John Newton:

> Come my soul, thy suit prepare.
> Jesus loves to answer prayer ...
> Thou art coming to a King,
> Large petitions with thee bring;
> For His grace and pow'r are such
> None can ever ask too much.

1954

Some pain early — no real mtg

Saturday, December 4, 1954
338th Day—27 Days to Follow

This is the memorable morning that I was awaked by the storm — near Cyprus. Read Acts 27. The Lord's presence was a curious reality. Had a grand day. We ran out of the gale in the afternoon.

FOLLOWING IN PAUL'S FOOTSTEPS

Rayburn encountered rough weather as he sailed the Mediterranean during his round-the-world tour in 1954, just as the Apostle Paul did as recorded in Acts 27.

The first half of 1954 was a difficult time for the Rayburn family. The January 4 entry sums up much of the stress Jim faced on a regular basis: "During this whole week my work at the office almost unbearably tough for me—Maxine sick all week. No word from [a potential donor]—no encouragement from any quarter—no money for back salaries—For me at least this must be a terrific time of testing."

Though the Lord yet again miraculously provided for the salary needs, Maxine's troubles with depression and other ailments caused her to spend more than a month in the hospital in the early part of the year. With three children (Ann was sixteen, Sue was thirteen, and Jim III was eight as the new year began), the Rayburns were fortunate to have the help of the Star Ranch staff to pick up some of the slack during the tough times.

While the Malibu acquisition had shown many instances of God's blessing, the board had their doubts, even after they met at the new property in July.

One of their concerns was the area's climate: could the coast of British Columbia provide a pleasant (and sufficiently dry) atmosphere conducive to a week of high adventure? The camp opened that summer just after the board meeting and Jim was the main speaker for the week. His journal includes a daily weather report, perhaps kept to use as evidence that Malibu could indeed work as a Young Life camp. History, of course, has proven Jim correct, as tens of thousands of kids have enjoyed "the best week of their lives" at Malibu since that first summer.

Monday, July 5 (Malibu Club)

The Board Mtg continued until 3 p.m. Good spirit. Lots of good work done. The men not as enthused about Malibu as I had hoped but undoubtedly the interest is growing.

I had a wonderful time up the Inlet with Orv. & Frances this af-

Malibu Club, British Columbia.

ternoon. The head of the Inlet must be one of the most beautiful spots there is.

Weather beautiful—cloudy in morning—sunny in aft. no rain.

Tuesday, July 6 (Malibu Club)
Camp started at Malibu tonight.

Weather overcast—some sun. Light rain during lunch and at 10 p.m. Did not interfere with any activity.

Wednesday, July 7 (Malibu Club)
A very hard day for me. Pressure from all directions. In spite of this the day went wonderfully well with the kids & I had a grand time with them after speaking on Mark 2.

Rain all morning. Quit at noon ex. for sporadic showers none of which interf. with afternoon program outdoors.

Thursday, July 8 (Malibu Club)
The camping program really rolled to-day. All meetings and activities went wonderfully well.

We made a fairly high climb on the other side of the inlet & the kids got a big bang out of it.

A beautiful, warm—sunshiny day. Perfect weather.

Friday, July 9 (Malibu Club)

Mac at the head** of PLI[1] loaned us his boat and we had some wonderful water skiing.

I spoke on What is FAITH from Matt 8—The Lord helped me much & greatly blessed the whole mtg.

Cloudy, cool—all activities went off as scheduled. Light rain after 5:30 P.

Saturday, July 10 (Malibu Club)

A very rainy day. Spirit in camp seems excellent. I spoke on "Reconcitiation" [*sic*] using mostly the Ro 5 passage. Not as good as last night.—

The "Carnival" went swell to-night.

Rained all last night & until after 3pm to-day without stopping. Then on & off thru the day—everybody happy. Camp going very well.

Sunday, July 11 (Malibu Club)

A good, good day in spite of the weather.

I felt great blessing from the Lord on speaking on "Calvary—Why Three Crosses" to-night.

Rained most of A.M.—light & sporadic in p.m. Most of outside rec. washed out. Very cool still.

Monday, July 12 (Malibu Club)

Camp ended.

[…]

Beautiful day—sunny & warm; the prettiest night I ever saw.

———

[1] Princess Louisa Inlet.

Weather concerns aside, Malibu was off to a great start, with over
700 guests for the summer. (Interestingly, over the years Malibu
has seen many "drop-in" guests who happen upon the isolated
spot in their yachts. That first summer saw a visit from United
States Senator Henry "Scoop" Jackson and his wife, along with an-
other first-term senator and his young wife: John and Jacqueline
Kennedy.)

The breakneck pace of Young Life's expansion—the miracles of
Star Ranch, Silver Cliff, Frontier, and Malibu had all occurred in
a mere eight years—as well as the stresses of home life had taken a
toll on Jim. Maxine wanted to do something to help her husband.
Her thoughts are recorded in their son's book, From Bondage to
Liberty: Dance, Children, Dance: *"Jim was totally exhausted and*
sinking fast. I knew he needed help. I wasn't in any position to assist
him as I was having such a struggle in my own right, but I could
see he was in trouble; someone had to come to his aid. I contacted
some friends who gave the money for Jim to take a trip around the
world. He left in October and was gone for three months."

Before Rayburn left, he visited his seventy-four year old mother
in California. She had moved there to live with Jim's brother Bob
after her husband died. She was ailing from cancer and Jim knew
that it might be the last time he would see her.

Sunday, October 10 (San Francisco)

What a surprise I got upon arrival at Oakland Pier. Roy had "the band"
out. A lot of swell kids. Some Cal guys playing instruments & a big
hoop-la in the station.

Then to hotel & "New Joes" for a swell dinner with Roy & Doris,
Sid & _____, Ronnie and _____²

They gave me some very fine books.

---

² Jim has left blank spaces for the names.

Tuesday, October 12 (at sea)

I'm off! Roy & Doris came aboard with me—Frank[3] came down later.
The ship is no luxury liner, but very nice & big. Most interesting part
of day: The tugs. What a sight—three [...] powerful little red "water-
wagons" fussing around pushing & pulling on the big boat & finally
circling of[f] with whistles blowing in a beautiful "formation." Lots of
roll after we get outside the gate.

Slept an hour before dinner.

Sunday, October 17 (Hawaii)

Headachy to-nite—relief with Emp 1 & 3 No Ergot for 4 days.
A truly wonderful day! I was called at 6:30. Went on deck & witnessed
our approach to the Island of Oahu. Beautiful sunrise & the lighting
effect on the green hills of the islands was superb. Then the harbor and
a long, beautiful and very educational trip around the island. Highlight:
stopping in the midst of the Dole Pineapple Plantation & eating huge
chunks of fresh pineapple. Called Maxine. We embarked & left the harbor just at sunset—the beauty & the whole process of getting away—
skin divers, tugs, "Aloha"—formed a never-to-be forgotten experience.

Monday, October 18 (at sea)

Early AM.—Bad Mig 2 #1; 2 #3—2 Caf Good relief by noon.
In spite of severe pain this a.m. I had a wonderful day—perhaps the
best yet on shipboard. The medicine brought complete relief in a.m. & I
loafed in my cabin all day.

A strong east wind has kicked off quite a swell & we have rolled
more than any day. I slept some. The breeze is cool but away from the
breeze it is hot. We are nearing the equator. 16° N Lat. this noon.

Wednesday, October 20 (at sea)

Headachy—bad—lots of Emp to stop it. Can't understand this?!
Rec'd the message about mother's death this am. She died on the 19th.

---

[3] Probably Jim's brother Frank or possibly San Francisco donor Frank Muncy.

Felt bum all day.

[...]

Friday, October 22 (at sea)

[Jim has crossed out the date and offered this explanation:]

Crossed the International Date Line in the night so this date does not exist for us.

Monday, October 25 (Fiji Islands)

No headache—no medicine

Fiji—truly a most interesting and enjoyable day. Colorful, friendly, smiling natives, mixed with about equal numbers of East Indians.

Walked all over town—specially enjoyed the native market-place. Went to a Catholic boys high school. They were swell. Gave me a big welcome. Talked to them awhile—half the school speaks 3 to 5 languages. All speak 2.[4]

Thursday, October 28 (Auckland, New Zealand)

A very interesting day in Auckland. The city is just plain—quaint! Looks like Denver in 1919, only more so.[5] Went on a drive out into the N.Z. "bush" this a.m. "The Waitaki Range." Good views of town & harbor.

[...]

Sunday, October 31 (at sea)

Aft Headache—2 #3—1 Caf.

After a good morning I got a terrible pain in my head while napping after lunch. Stopped it before dinner. Went to "Divine Services" this morning. Episcop. or rather Ch of England with the Captain leading

---

[4] This was not a pre-arranged assembly. According to a letter to the staff, Rayburn hopped in a cab and asked to be taken to the nearest high school, which turned out to be this Catholic boys school.

[5] In a letter to the staff, Jim explained this further: "I wrote in my diary concerning [Auckland] that it was about like Denver in 1919. That's no exaggeration either. They are at least 30 years behind us. I get a bit of nostalgia walking around. It is so much like the civilization of my boyhood days."

the service and another officer reading the 14th Chapter of John.

First leg of my journey about over. It's been great! In spite of disappointingly bad health. Looking for better days soon now.

Monday, November 1 (Sydney, Australia)

Arr Sydney 8 AM. I was up at 5:00. Saw us thru the "heads." Beautiful harbor & the Sydney Harbor Bridge is a marvelous cantilever truss 1650 yards(?) long.

Customs was a mess. Out at 12:30. To the Australia [Hotel]. Comfortable room. Out to Troutmans.[6]

Saturday, November 13 (at sea)

A troublesome pain I was able to control with nothing but Alka & Emp #1.
A calm restful day—in fact a bit boring, but I am beginning to be most hopeful about the headaches. Nothing serious enough to require Ergot or Codeine for 3 days. The attacks start as usual almost every day but are easily controlled with a little Alka-Seltzer and regular Emperin. I think that def. means the beginning of the end of the things.

Saturday, November 20 (at sea)

Took 2 Caf. early—no Cod.—attack not nearly like of old.
I tried to stave it off but all thru the early hours of the morning the right side pain was just too persistent so I took some Caf. Made for a sleepless night—(took at 2A). Then I had a very comfortable and restful day in spite of the heat and humidity—and the Lord seemed very near, like old times and I prayed earnestly and read His Word.

Monday, November 22 (at sea)

A good lazy day—feel fine—still very hot and muggy.

Watching the coast of India slide by.

---

[6] Charles Henry Troutman, Jr. (1914–1990). Troutman at that time was serving as the General Director of Inter-Varsity Christian Fellowship in Australia. He would later fill the same role for Inter-Varsity in the United States.

Saturday, November 27 (at sea)

A wonderful day—felt good—took better to resting—had some real times of fellowship with the Lord in His Word.

Tuesday, November 30 (at sea)

9 Days without Mig. only 2 Bad days out of the last 30.

On up the Red Sea—passing many ships—often the Coast line is visible on the Arabian side.

Wednesday, December 1 (at sea)

10th day—no pain—feel great!

Entered the Gulf of Suez at noon. One of the most interesting parts of the trip—rugged Mts. of the Sinai Penn. on the Starboard Side—almost as rugged on the African coast. The passing ships are interesting. Completely loafed all day—and must say I'm getting tired of it—4 days to Marsielle [*sic*, Marseille].

Saturday, December 4

Some pain early—no real mig.

This is the memorable morning that I was awaked by the storm—near Cyprus. Read Acts 27.[7] The Lord's presence was a warm reality. Had a grand day. We ran out of the gale in the afternoon.

Sunday, December 5

A very pleasant day—my last on the ship—my friends[8] are being very kind, and seem genuinely sorry that I am leaving.

———

Before making it to Europe, Rayburn had visited Hawaii, the Fiji Islands, New Zealand, Australia, Sri Lanka (then known as Ceylon), India, Yemen, and Egypt. The European portion of his trip

---

[7] The biblical account of Paul's sailing in the same area of the Mediterranean Sea and enduring a tremendous storm.

[8] The friends he had made aboard ship.

was given mostly to skiing in Switzerland.

In Switzerland Rayburn met up with Rod Johnston. Rod and his wife Fran were starting Young Life in France.

Monday, December 6 (Marseille, France)

Arr. Marseille at 3 p. Went to LE GRAND [Hotel] and met** Rex[9] & did we ever have a meal—at the hotel. Went down to the ship with the crowd late to-nite, then came back to bed.

Tuesday, December 7 (Marseille, France)

Did a lot of walking around Marseille. Feel very strange here when I can't talk to anyone. Arranged my trip on to-night's train to Geneva. Went to the station & boarded at mid-night. Have a fine room in a beautiful car.

Wednesday, December 8 (Geneva, Switzerland)

ARR. GENEVA 8:45 A. Awoke this morning with the train winding along high above the Rhone. It was very cloudy but beautiful. Geneva is wonderful!

Thursday, December 9 (Geneva, Switzerland)

No money from home yet—can't leave. […]

Friday, December 10 (Geneva, Switzerland)

Around Hotel most of day. Got my money from home and did some "Christmas shopping" at a big dept. store.

Thursday, December 16 (Davos, Switzerland)

Davos—Got my ski equipment this a.m. and got on the ski school hill this afternoon. Did very well for a first day—on quite steep slopes. Enjoyed it immensely. Came in at 4:00 p & had a swell nap before dinner.

---

[9] One of his fellow passengers, Rex Knight. A few days earlier he had noted, "Had a long talk with Rex Knight this morning about Young Life. He has more 'savvy' than anyone aboard."

Enjoying my friends George & Peggy Haghen**—of Johannesburg […]

—⁓—

Saturday, December 25 (Davos, Switzerland)

The strangest Christmas I ever spent. No Christmas spirit here at the Gr. Belvedere. First Christmas Carol I've heard all season was to-nite at dinner when the orch. played "Silent Night." I had a wonderful time with the Lord this a.m. & specially remembered my home & loved ones & fellow-workers.

Sunday, December 26 (Davos, Switzerland)

Talked to Maxine this a.m. at 8. Had a very good morning just praying & reading the Word & skied the Schatz-Strella Hill this afternoon. "Powder" almost to my hips at times. I didn't fall once. Must be getting better!

Tuesday, December 28 (Zermatt, Switzerland)

Lv Davos 7:20A Arr ZERMATT 8:30P

A glorious day. More beautiful & spectacular scenery specially coming thru the Bernese Oberland & Lotchburg [sic, Lotschberg] Tunnel.

But most of all—it was the best day of prayer I've had for years. Certainly the Lord was very near—and brought much peace.

Thursday, December 30 (Zermatt, Switzerland)

A wonderful day! Rod & I took the train to the GORNERGRAT this a.m. and skied back to town—about 10 miles! From 11,300′ to 5000′. What sport! The greatest ski run I ever saw—even better than yesterday—and faster. Again I made it without the slightest mishap. Sure enjoyed it.

Spent the afternoon in prayer & fellowship with Rod.

1955

ENTRIES FROM JANUARY 1955

Still on his round-the-world tour, Jim did not have a new diary for 1955 so he wrote entries for most of January on three pages in the back of his 1954 journal. Above is the first of those pages. The numeric entries on each day are typical, but their meaning is uncertain.

Rayburn did not buy a new diary until after he had arrived back in the United States; therefore the first few weeks of January 1955 were recorded in the back of his 1954 journal. The entries are typically just one line per day, so details—including his whereabouts—are scarce.

Saturday, January 1 (Zermatt, Switzerland)
Skiid [*sic*] hard this AM. Saw Rod & Boys¹ off & had a grand afternoon in prayer & the Word.

Sunday, January 2 (Europe)
Read the Word several hrs to-day.

Monday, January 3 (Europe)
Read Word & "Miracles" by C.S. Lewis.

Tuesday, January 4 (Europe)
Prayer was hard to-day. (? ? ?)

Wednesday, January 5 (Europe)
Wonderful time in prayer. Word precious.

Saturday, January 8 (Europe)
Good time in the Word again.

Sunday, January 9 (Europe)
The impr. in my dev life last 2 wks very real and impt. to me.

Tuesday, January 11 (Paris)
Very Import[ant] Paris Parents Night—J. 14 Recp Exc.

Wednesday, January 12 (Paris)
A wonderful, never-to-be-forgotten French Campaigners Mtg at Jacque's house.²

---

¹ Johnston had brought some Paris high school students with him.

² Describing this event to the staff, Jim wrote, "We met in the home of Jacques, who

Thursday, January 13 (Paris)
Amer. Camp. at "Koki" Leisure's [*sic*, Leasure's] house.[3]

Friday, January 14 (travelling)
Bad day on train & Ferry to London.

Saturday, January 15 (London)
Hard but finished strong.

Sunday, January 16 (London)
Rain & snow & smog.

Monday, January 17 (London)
WITH SANNY THIS P.M![4]

Tuesday, January 18 (London)
Lv London for S[outh]hampton & "Q Mary."

Wednesday, January 19 (at sea)
Cherbourg—got my luggage & fine cabin.

Thursday, January 20 (at sea)
Sea getting rough.

Friday, January 21 (at sea)
Studied the Word & prayed this whole day thru. A great day.

---

was at Frontier last summer. Only one of the lads spoke English and I don't speak French, so the meeting was conducted by translation. My message, the questions and answers were translated by Art [Johnston, Rod's brother]. By the way, [Art] is getting to be real Frenchy. Sounds more Frenchy than the French do to me.... One of the great joys was to have fellowship with Jacques' father who is an industrial engineer in Paris and has given his heart to the Lord Jesus Christ in the past few months."

3 Koki Leasure was an American high school student in Paris who had attended Frontier the previous summer. This gathering was a Campaigners meeting for American students in Paris.

4 Lorne Sanny of The Navigators. He played a key role in Billy Graham's All-Scotland Crusade which began several weeks later, and was probably in London on crusade business.

Saturday, January 22 (at sea)
One of greatest days in prayer & The Word—O. Hallesby "Rel. or Chr."[5]

Sunday, January 23 (at sea)
Another grand day of worship and prayer.

Monday, January 24
ARR N.Y. 10A. Norm[6] & East Staff met me. Hard, lonesome day.

—∿∿—

Immediately upon returning—even before making it home to Colorado—Jim had a board meeting to attend in Chicago.

Wednesday, January 26 (Chicago)[7]
Board Mtg. in Chicago. Wish I hadn't come. Could just as well have gone home for all the good it did. Very disappointed—prone** to be discouraged about condition of the work. But that means the Lord must take a larger place with me. His Will is ALL that matters.

Friday, January 28
ARR Home 10:30 A. Greeted by headquarters crew & Navs. Big luncheon at home with all the crew. Great to be back.

Sunday, January 30
Taught the class this A.M. 160 present! Went to church with the family. Harlan[8] came down and we went out to the lot and made plans for the house.

---

[5] *Religious or Christian* by Norwegian theologian and author Ole Kristian Hallesby (1879–1961). The book was a call for Christians to return to the basic essentials of the faith.

[6] Norm Robbins, who at the time was in charge of all Young Life on the East Coast.

[7] From here on the entries are found in Rayburn's 1955 diary.

[8] Denver architect Harlan Rathbun.

—···—

After living at Star Ranch since 1947, the Rayburns built their own home at 1006 Mesa Terrace in Colorado Springs.⁹ Ann and Sue, now in high school, particularly welcomed the move into town where they could be closer to their friends.

Once again, Young Life was in a difficult financial situation in the spring. Rayburn went to Chicago to enlist the aid of the Crowell Trust one more time. He also had several engagements on the East Coast.

Tragically, a classmate and friend of Sue's, Joey Hatton, was struck and killed by a car on March 16. The boy's parents were friends of Jim and Maxine.

Wednesday, March 16

A very fine day of special prayer with the area crew.

Thursday, March 17 (on the train)

Lv CS for Chi & Phila.

Joey Hatton died last nite after being hit by a car. I spent most of the morning with Joe & Lucy—so sad.

Had a hectic time getting off—rushing through a lot of mail—made the train just barely & had a restful afternoon.

Friday, March 18 (Chicago)

Bad L-side pain. 1st in months. Gyn at midnight relieved.

What a day. ARR. 9A. Went to Palmer House looking for Howard Hansen.—Then to mtg at bank.¹⁰ Long session there—but Lord greatly blessed. Received (20 G) for back salaries. So thankful to Him I don't know what to say or do. Last two days too tough for me I guess. Felt mig. symptoms on way to train. Came on late.

---

9   After Colorado Springs was replatted the address changed to 1455 Mesa Road.

10   A meeting of the Crowell Trust at Continental Bank.

Tuesday, March 22 (Philadelphia)

Union League luncheon—great! Did my best job yet of presenting work to men's group. Theme: "Juvenile Delinq.—The Answer." Intro. Amer. History—what made us free: God, Bible, Church—fought for freedom because preachers taught the Bible—"freedom more important than life." Free enterprise, whole way of life endangered by neglect of y.p. spiritually—have to do more to reach—that's where Y. L. comes in—for pers. faith, church, nation—cause of freedom everywhere. Our future depend[s] upon God—"righteousness exalteth a nation."[11]

Good mtg at Rex Clements'[12] to-nite.

Fine fellowship with Charles & Madeleine McClary [sic, Maclary][13] to-nite—invited to Malibu.

Saturday, March 26 (Pocono Manor Inn, Pennsylvania)

[...]

Message to-nite on "Basic Facts of Christianity," "Incarnation, Atonement, Resurrection" with Acts 3:1–11, or 12, for closing went well, I think.

Sunday, March 27 (Pocono Manor Inn, Pennsylvania)

The week-end had a very impressive closing. I spoke on J 3. A large number including the president of Dormont Hi in Pittsburg[h][14] professed conversion. The spirit was very good. All seemed pleased.

Bud Bylsma[15] drove me to Paoli. Called home & waited for train.

---

[11] Proverbs 14:34: "Righteousness exalteth a nation: but sin is a reproach to any people" (KJV.).

[12] Rex Clements was the pastor of Bryn Mawr Presbyterian Church near Philadelphia.

[13] Charles T. Maclary was the minister of music at Bryn Mawr Presbyterian Church.

[14] Over the years Jim consistently misspelled the name of Pennsylvania's second largest city, always leaving off the "h"—perhaps because of his earlier association with Pittsburg, Texas, one of Young Life's earliest areas of ministry.

[15] Bud Bylsma was on Young Life staff from 1950–1981 in a variety of roles and

The Lord must have specially helped and answered my prayers. I feel that I was as effective in presentation of the Gospel as I know how to be this week-end.

———

Jim was the speaker that summer for several weeks at both Frontier and Malibu. The first session at Frontier began June 20; after spending the first few weeks of the camping season there, he and Sue travelled to Malibu, arriving on July 20.

One of the staff mentioned in these entries is Tom Raley (previously mentioned in the March 26, 1953, entry). Raley was the young area director in Portland. He had become a Christian in Add Sewell's club in Pittsburg, Texas, in the earliest days of Young Life. He and his wife Recie, a former staff woman herself, were married in 1950. The Raleys continued serving in Young Life for more than fifty years, including many years as "Ministers-At-Large," ministering to staff all over the country.

Jim's brief entries describing the second summer of camping at Malibu continue to include his daily weather report.

Saturday, July 30 (Malibu Club)
Laid off to-night. First night in camp all summer that I haven't spoken.

Cloudy & rainy all day.

Sunday, July 31 (Malibu Club)
This day started of[f] well with a wonderful time of fellowship with the Lord & was my best day of the summer.

Camp went very well in spite of the steady bad weather. Spoke with marked blessing on Ro 3.

Staff to-gether for fellowship & prayer to-night.

Steady rain all day.

---

locations. At this time he was in his first year as area director of Baltimore, the first staff person there.

Tom Raley, Bill Starr, Bob Mitchell, Rayburn, and Tom Bade at Malibu.

Monday, August 1 (Malibu Club)

I skied hard to-day.

Spoke on "Propitiation" for the first time this summer. Camp going well.

Cloudy & sunny by spurts; a clearing day—good.

Tuesday, August 2 (Malibu Club)

The program went great.

And the "Say So" mtg was <u>one of the best</u>!¹⁶

A fine sunny day.

Thursday, August 4 (Malibu Club)

An excellent day—practiced water skiing & went on one several times for a mile or so. Great sport.

---

¹⁶ "Say So" was an opportunity for campers to stand up and testify in front of the rest of the camp what the Lord had done for them. The name came from Psalm 107:2: "Let the redeemed of the LORD say so, whom he hath redeemed from the hand of the enemy" (KJV).

Spoke on "The Claims of Christ" using John 3, John 8, Col 1. Went just tops–great favorable reaction from key kids.

A beautiful warm sunny day.

Friday, August 5 (Malibu Club)

Another swell day. I just plain <u>had fun</u> for the first time in ages. Worked more at skiing. Mitch, Raley, Starr & I went all four behind the big speedboat. Rode a long way into the Jervis. Rudy[17] took a lot of pictures.

Took the evening off.

[Weather:] Same as yesterday.

———

While the Rayburns finished building their new house, they lived for a while at Glen Eyrie, the estate The Navigators had purchased to serve as their headquarters. Finally, in October, the new home was ready to be moved into.

As another fiscal year came to an end, the Lord provided another miracle to meet the financial obligations of the ministry.

Wednesday, October 5 (Chicago)

<u>Lv St Paul</u> 7:30 (Rain)**

<u>Arr Chi.</u> 10:00 A. To Continental Bank for meeting.[18]

Recvd the bal. needed for ('54–'55 fiscal year) How can I ever thank the Lord for this wonderful faithfulness.

Lv Chi 9 P.

Arr Dv 11:30

[…] Home late but very happy about the way the Lord blessed.

Thursday, October 6

Just about to get into the house. Very difficult days these.

---

[17] Rudy Vetter. Vetter was a professional photographer in Memphis whose photos Young Life often used in promotional material and the *Young Life* magazine.

[18] A meeting of the Crowell Trust at Continental Bank.

Rayburn speaking at Frontier Ranch sometime in the fifties.

Friday, October 7

Maxine ill & the house not completely furnished** & I have to leave. A hard set of problems to cope with. Left for Dallas at 1:30 p.

Open house at Dallas Headquarters to-night.

—⁓—

Monday, October 31 (Philadelphia)

ARR. Philly 9:50 A.

Committee luncheon.

Staff meeting.

Enjoyable & profitable visits with Dr. "Chick" Koop[19] & Dr. Gene Spitz,[20] & Dick James. One of the <u>best</u> days I've had! Everything to encourage. I do thank the Lord for such a wonderful day!

—⁓—

After celebrating Christmas in their new home, Jim took Ann and Sue to Chicago. Maxine joined them a few days later.

---

[19] C. Everett Koop (born 1916). Renowned physician and surgeon-in-chief of the Children's Hospital of Philadelphia, Koop was also a committed Christian. He later gained fame as Surgeon General of the United States from 1982–1989.

[20] Eugene Spitz was a prominent neurosurgeon in Philadelphia. Earlier that year he had co-invented the Spitz-Holter valve for use in the treatment of hydrocephalus.

Jim and his teenage daughters, Sue and Ann.

Sunday, December 25

This our first Christmas in our new home was a very happy one. I am thankful to God that the children were well pleased.

Monday, December 26 (on the train)

After an hour or so of office work Ann, Sue & I caught the Rocket for Chicago.

Had a very nice afternoon.

Tuesday, December 27 (Chicago)

Bad Mig came slowly yest. afternoon—took shot of Gyn. just after midnight this a.m. ARR Chi—9A.

This was a swell day. We went directly to the Palmer House—then rode the subway, came back to Marshall Fields, then had a huge lunch at the "Chicago Room"—the kids slept some this p.m.—we went to "Cinerama Holiday"[21] to-nite. It was superb.

Wednesday, December 28 (Chicago)
Another swell day with the kids.

Shopped—walked all over the loop hunting lunch & finally came back to the hotel.

Went to the Empire Room to-night.

Thursday, December 29 (Chicago)
Went to Marshall Fields then the new Prudential Bldg.—lunch with Lillian Edman.

Maxine's train 6 hrs. late.

The girlies went to Wheaton to-night.

Maxine & I had dinner at the hotel.

---

[21] "Cinerama Holiday" was a documentary filmed using the then-revolutionary cinerama photography process.

1956

On this day Mama went to the
hospital and we are all very sad.
She is so sad and disappointed in me
that I think I can't stand it. Can only
pray that she will someday come to
know what is in my heart — that I would
never wilfully hurt her + that I want to
be loved by her + have her aware of my
great love for her, more than anything.
Sue did the washing — Anne + Jim + I
the shopping, dinner + dishes and
we got along.
Harry Bickford, Mrs Warth + Sister —
came to see us to-night.

A SAD DAY FOR THE RAYBURN FAMILY

*Still fighting depression and addiction to prescription drugs,
Maxine was sent to the hospital for several weeks in 1956.*

Ann was in her final semester of high school in the spring of 1956;
Sue was a sophomore, and Jim III was finishing fourth grade.

The stresses and strains of raising a family, Maxine's medical
and psychological problems, Jim's ongoing migraines, travel, and
the challenges of running Young Life all made the Rayburns' mar-
riage a difficult one.

Friday, January 27

This day (after a terrible week) will always be in my memory as a great
& wonderful day. Maxine talked to me for hours about my problems &
our problems & we had such warmth & fellowship & understanding in
it as we have not known for years. She was wonderful—and the Lord is
more real & wonderful thru it.

Sunday, February 5

150 at S. S. Taught Eph 5 & 6. Enjoyed it and felt that the Lord blessed
me greatly. I know I've never faced my personal failures as squarely as
in the last week & I will not alibi or rationalize but look to the Lord to
make me the kind of a Christian in Eph 6—operating according to His
resources—not my measly ones. Always have wanted that. Wonder why
I'm such a failure—

Friday, February 10 (Memphis)

[...]

The Lord seems near and has blessed me here. Called Maxie, mostly
to tell her I loved her. She says stay for that medical exam in the a.m.

Saturday, February 11 (Memphis)

The examination by Chub,[1] Mack & Dr. John Wilson was rough.

Went home on the Braniff milk run this aft.

---

[1] Rayburn's friend, Dr. William F. "Chub" Andrews.

—w—

With over 100 people on the staff roster, by 1956 Young Life was experiencing organizational and managerial difficulties—it had grown too large for any one man to run single-handedly. Many senior staff were beginning to express to Jim their dissatisfaction with his leadership style. At Jim's request, several of these men wrote him letters sharing their concerns. The February 20 entry is perhaps indicative of the strain this placed on Rayburn as he was in the process of responding to those letters that day. However, since he often used "bum" in reference to his headaches, it could also have been related to an oncoming migraine.

As always, Jim continued his heavy travel schedule, including a chance reunion of the Rayburn brothers in California.

Monday, February 20
Worked away in the office—feeling kinda bum.

Tuesday, February 21
Got sick at the office to-day—dizzy, nauseated and a strange kind of headache. Went home & spent the rest of the day in bed.

—w—

Saturday, March 24 (San Francisco)
With Roy to John _____² for conference & lunch—all day with contacts. Dinner at Roy's with Raleys present.

    […]

Sunday, March 25 (San Francisco)
Preached on the Y.L. work & the Sacrifice of Christ at Oakland Neighborhood Church this a.m.

    A little time for rest & study this afternoon.

---

² Rayburn has drawn the blank space, indicating he did not remember the man's last name.

Preached for Dr. Munger this evening on "The Cross." A wonderful service.

Back to hotel about midnight—

A very hard week just past with much tribulation and much blessing & help from the Lord.

Monday, March 26 (Los Angeles)
Up early (6A) and to L.A. for a busy day of contacts.

(Met Frank in lobby of Statler & had lunch with him & Paul & Bob. Quite a coincidence.)

Dinner with Paul & Edith.[3] A very good day & I am thankful to the Lord.

—⁓—

The annual staff conference was held at Star Ranch in April, with Richard Halverson as the speaker. Larry Kulp, who was professor of biophysics and director of the Lamont Geological Observatory at Columbia University, was a member of Young Life's board and was also helping oversee the new Young Life Institute.

To help better administer the growing ministry, Young Life now was divided into four regions: Northern, Southern, Southwestern, and Northwestern.

The discouragement Jim mentions on April 9 was probably due to his dealings with his Presbyterian denomination. Wanting to keep his clergy status in good order, he had to submit himself to the local presbytery, based in Pueblo, Colorado. This group of ministers, for the most part, was suspicious of Young Life and wanted Jim to submit all of his activities in Young Life—his travel and speaking, for instance—to them for approval. He fought this battle for years.

---

[3] Jim's brother Paul and his wife Edith.

Friday, April 6

Staff Conference ended at dinner to-nite on a high plane of spiritual blessing and fellowship. Dedication of Staff and address by Larry Kulp in the last session at 5 p.

24 people dedicated for staff work—a really "historic" occassion [*sic*] as Bill Starr and Roy Riviere become Regional Directors. Mitch to San F Bay Area.

[...]

Monday, April 9

Worked in office this a.m. & went to Presbytery Mtg this aft. in Canon City.

A very hard and discouraging day. May God help me not to be discouraged when the Word is <u>plain</u> that I do not need to be.

Wednesday, April 18 (Los Angeles)

Severe Mig. [...]

This day was full of the knowledge of the presence of the Lord. He was with us—as He always is—to help and guide & bless—but somehow I was much more AWARE of Him than usual to-day: "carrying with me thru this day a real sense of Thy Power and Thy Glory."[4]

As he had with his daughters a few months earlier, in April Jim took his son to Chicago.

When they returned, the Rayburn men worked on the land-scaping of their home with the help of Dawson Trotman.

---

[4] From John Baillie's book, *A Diary of Private Prayer*: "Almighty God, who art ever present in the world without me, in my spirit within me, and in the unseen world above me, let me carry with me through this day's life a most real sense of Thy power and Thy glory." Rayburn often used Baillie's book in his personal devotions. The book, published in 1949, has morning and evening devotions for thirty-one days. This particular passage is from the morning devotional for the seventeenth day.

Sunday, April 29 (Chicago)

L-side pain—bad late—went away after bedtime**.

Slept almost all morning. Took Jim to the Field Museum and the Aquarium. He has been just great on this trip. Oh yes, also rode the "L" for Jim's first time. Got him up front where he could see.

Took Denver Zypter [*sic*] for home at 5 p. Had a fine chicken dinner and a nice evening.

Saturday, May 5

Daws & I went up the Rampart Range Road for rock. Got some good stuff for finishing the front walks.[5]

Sunday, May 6

Finished Col[ossians] with the S.S. Class this a.m.

Had a good time of prayer with the office crew.

Maxine's back continues very bad—this attack has been a week now.

———

Maxine's back troubles (for which she would undergo yet another surgery in July), were not the only troubles facing her. Her depression and other psychological issues forced the family to hospitalize her for several weeks.

Tuesday, May 22

Mig sympts strong to-nite.

On this day Maxine went to the hospital and we are all very sad. She is so sad and disappointed in me that I think I can't stand it. Can only pray that she will someday come to know what is in my heart—that I would

---

5   Years later Maxine remembered, "Jim wanted that [front walk] done so much and he was never good around the house repairing anything or building [anything], so this was very typical—he got Daws Trotman to help him." She further recalled that before Jim finished the project, he also recruited Cliff Barrows from the Billy Graham team to help. "It was so cute, when he couldn't do something ... he'd always get the big names to come out."

never willfully hurt her & that I want to be loved by her & have her sure of my great love for her, more than anything.

Sue did the washing—Ann & Jim & I the shopping, dinner & dishes and we got along.

[...]

Friday, May 25
Really got a lot of work done at the office, for the first time in a long time. Millie Carter a big factor in this.[6]

Went to High School Choir Concert that Sue was in to-night. It was marvelous.

Saturday, May 26
Good restful day at home—rain, again—we've had lots!

The girls did well with the work—Ann did especially well preparing a Roast Beef Dinner!

———

On June 18, Jim's dear friend Dawson Trotman died suddenly. While in New York speaking at Jack Wyrtzen's Word of Life camp (where Rayburn had spoken in 1948), Trotman was in a boat on Schroon Lake that threw him and another passenger out when it hit a wave. Daws helped the other passenger, who could not swim, until the boat was able to return. While she was helped back into the craft, Trotman sank beneath the surface. His body was recovered two days later.

Rayburn, along with Billy Graham, Wyrtzen, and other evangelical luminaries, spoke at Trotman's memorial service at Glen Eyrie on June 27. Jim's journal is silent for most of June, so his thoughts on the events were not recorded.

---

[6] Millie Carter (formerly Sisco) had been Jim's secretary, but left full-time work when she married John Carter a few years earlier. In this instance she was filling in part-time. She and her husband would be two of the longest tenured staff in Young Life's history.

Thursday, July 12 (Frontier Ranch)

Mitch, Phil Mc,[7] Frog, Carl N.,[8] Shef & I spent the night at "The Saddle" on Princeton trail and had a wonderful time of prayer & fellowship. About 5 hrs of prayer last night & this a.m.

Camp started very well to-nite.

Tuesday, July 17

Maxine had spinal surgery this a.m. Was in surgery & recovery room 6 hours. Still pretty knocked out rest of day.

I went home to dinner with the girlies, leaving about 3:30.

Wednesday, July 18

Back to DV to be with Maxine this p.m.

Saturday, July 21[9]

Jimmy sold "chipmunks" & bought me nice cuff links for my birthday & Ann fixed a wonderful barbecued chicken dinner last night for birthday dinner.

Maxine still hurting badly to-day.

As the summer ended, Maxine was able to join the rest of the family at Frontier for her recuperation. Lila Trotman was also there, getting away for a while in the wake of her husband's death.

For many years, the last event of the summer at Frontier was a week of training for volunteer leaders, known as the Leadership Seminar, or Seminar for short.

---

[7] Phil McDonald was in the process of taking over the Young Life work in the Twin Cities area. He served on staff for many years, becoming Midwest Division vice president. He was a talented program director at camps.

[8] Carl Nelson at this time was heading up Young Life in Knoxville; he eventually became the Mid-South regional director for Young Life. A gifted communicator, he wrote a book, *Just the Greatest*, that was a series of his club messages about Christ.

[9] Jim's forty-seventh birthday.

Thursday, August 16

Went home to-day.[10] The past three or four days have been wonderful. Blessing on the work. Great time with kids & work-crew & staff. A sense of the Lord's presence & blessing that is unusually real & important.

Lila Trotman has been at Frontier.

Sunday, August 19

Taught the Class on Heb 8.

Maxine & I came to Frontier on the "Royal Gorge." Had a compartment & bed for her. It was a fine trip & I was so glad she could come.

Monday, August 20 (Frontier Ranch)

This was a fine enjoyable day at the beautiful "Look-Out." Maxine seemed to enjoy it a lot.

We had red raspberries.

Thursday, August 23 (Frontier Ranch)

Leadership Seminar began to-night with what looks to me like the best crowd of leaders we have ever had. Excellent college age.

[...]

The Lord greatly blessed the opening mtg.

Lila Trotman & "Joyce" over staying with us a few days.

Friday, August 24 (Frontier Ranch)

Seminar going very well. I spoke on Mark 2 "them without" for 35 min & quit without going to the rest of the material.

Again the Lord gave unusual liberty & blessing. It is the best I have done.

Gave intro. about our beginning "in the dark"—experimentation—close [with] rel[ationship] to the church.

---

10 From Frontier.

Jim relaxing at Frontier in the living room at The Lookout.

Saturday, August 25 (Frontier Ranch)
Spoke to-nite on Col. 4:5[11] et. al.

I have never experienced anything like this in Leadership. The openness of the audience—the heart preparation. I cannot thank God enough. Felt so bad I didn't think I could go to the meeting & then in some way He poured out the blessing.

Sunday, August 26 (Frontier Ranch)
Another good day & fine evening service—Spoke on Acts 17.

Monday, August 27 (travelling)
Maxie & the children went home this a.m. & I left for Malibu on the aft. train for Salt Lake City.

It is the end of a blessed summer. Almost cried when Ann & Jimmy & "Jet"[12] left. They have been so wonderful to me & I've had such good "fellowship" with the children this summer. Will always remember Jet's

---

[11] "Walk in wisdom toward them that are without, redeeming the time" (KJV).

[12] "Jet" was the Rayburns' dog, a jet-black half border collie mix.

extreme loyalty to Jimbo.[13]

Between the four properties, Young Life hosted twenty-seven weeks of camp that summer, with a total of 4,290 guests in attendance.

Monday, September 24 (St. Paul, Minnesota)

What a grand day. Went to see F.W. He gladly gave $10,000 for the present emergency. The Lord certainly "went before."[14] [...]

Monday, October 1

What a glorious day! We went away over the top on the 55–56 budget (called C.—got 12,000 to wind it up.) First time we have closed on Oct 1st for probably 10 or 12 yrs. It was "impossible" but it happened. How great & loving our God is!

---

[13] One of Jim's nicknames for his son.

[14] Probably an allusion to Exodus 13:21: "And the LORD went before them by day in a pillar of a cloud, to lead them the way; and by night in a pillar of fire, to give them light; to go by day and night" (KJV).

1957

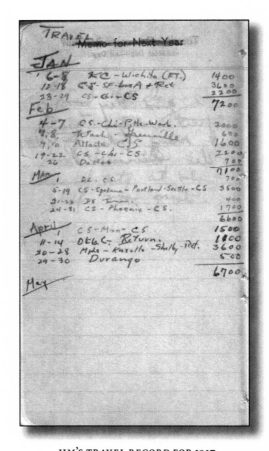

JIM'S TRAVEL RECORD FOR 1957

Rayburn often kept a running total of his travelling mileage during the year. The above page shows he travelled 27,600 miles during the first four months of 1957.

Jim loved sports, particularly football and baseball. Once bowl games became nationally televised, his New Year's Day was filled with watching as many as he could.

Never that interested in money, and certainly no business-man, Rayburn nonetheless desired to secure a comfortable future for his family. Toward that end he pursued an oil venture with two brothers he had known from his days in Texas, Clare and Ed Headington. The venture never bore financial fruit, however.

Tuesday, January 1
Got home from Silver Cliff about mid-night.[1] Watched TV Games:
Orange Bowl: Col. 27–Clemson 20.
Rose Bowl: Iowa 34–OSC[2] 19
Cotton Bowl: TCU 28–Syrc. 27.
Sugar: Baylor 13–Tenn 7.

Sunday, January 6 (travelling)
Leaving at 9:30A. Ted & I had a very pleasant trip driving to Kansas City—we read & discussed Theology most of the way, and the time passed very rapidly. Arr @ Frank's home about 11 p.

Monday, January 7 (Kansas City)
A very good all day session with Frank[3] and the Headington Bros. discussing the oil company proposition.

A fine luncheon of men at noon at University Club where I introduced Norm[4] and the work.

---

[1] Rayburn had been speaking at the annual snow camp.

[2] Oregon State College, later Oregon State University.

[3] Jim's brother, an attorney.

[4] Norm Robbins, who was serving as the area director for Young Life in Kansas City.

Rayburn made a new friend when he met Sam Shoemaker, the prominent Episcopal priest who, at the time, was the rector of Calvary Episcopal Church in Pittsburgh.

The unique role Young Life filled—and Rayburn's ability to get along with different types of people—is seen in the February 8 entry when he met with fundamentalist Bob Jones, Jr., president of Bob Jones University, just two days after meeting Shoemaker. From progressive northeastern Episcopalian to rock-ribbed southern conservative in just two days' time!

Wednesday, February 6 (Pittsburgh, Pennsylvania)

A great day in Pittsburg[h]! Best of all was getting acquainted with Sam Shoemaker[5] and the wholesome happy fellowship we had to-gether.

[…]

To train late.

Friday, February 8 (Greenville, South Carolina)

Mig came on suddenly in middle of last night—thought I had it licked with Emp & Codine [*sic*] but finally had to take shot of "Gyn" this afternoon.
—Full 15 day interval again—

Arr. Greenville 11:30 A.

Good sleep on train—fine day here.

Conf. with Bob Jones Jr.[6] this aft.

Excellent dinner for 40 at hotel to-night. Fine representative crowd. Cliff & Billie Barrows were hosts & really pushed the work.

---

[5]   Dr. Samuel Moor Shoemaker (1893–1963). An Episcopal priest, he was once listed by *Newsweek* magazine as one of the ten most outstanding preachers in the country. He was instrumental in the forming of Alcoholics Anonymous and was the founder of *Faith at Work* magazine. He was also a prolific author. He and Rayburn remained close friends until Shoemaker's death.

[6]   Robert Reynolds Jones, Jr. (1911–1997). Jones was the son of Bob Jones, Sr., a famous evangelist who had begun Bob Jones University in 1927. Bob Jones, Jr., served as the school's president from 1947–1971.

Monday, February 25

A hard productive day at the office.

[...]

A grand evening at home—played with Jimmy—watched T.V. We are "21" fans for sure, Prof Charlie Van Doren—up to $143,000 and up against a brilliant lady.[7]

———

Rayburn was no longer involved in leading a weekly club, but he still enjoyed nothing more than presenting the gospel to a group of high school kids and did so whenever he was asked. As always, he continued to crisscross the country speaking at banquets and promotional meetings for Young Life.

He was also still having to justify his ministry to the Pueblo Presbytery in Colorado.

Saturday, April 27 (Kentucky Lake, Tennessee)

The morning & evening meeting were very well received. Good group of adults.

Excellent fellowship.

I stayed mostly on the Person of Christ—I J 5:11, 12;[8] J 20:31[9] & related truths.

---

[7] Charles Van Doren was a Columbia University professor of English who gained national fame on the phenomenally popular game show, "Twenty-One." Unbeknownst to the Rayburns and the millions of other Americans watching the show, the thirty-year old professor was being fed the answers by the show's producers. The episode mentioned here was one of Van Doren's last, as he was finally beaten by Vivienne Nearing, the "brilliant lady" Rayburn mentioned. Two years later when game shows were being investigated by Congress, he dramatically admitted before the House Committee on Interstate and Foreign Commerce, "I was involved, deeply involved, in a deception."

[8] "And this is the testimony, that God gave us eternal life, and this life is in his Son. Whoever has the Son has life; whoever does not have the Son of God does not have life."

[9] "But these are written so that you may believe that Jesus is the Christ, the Son of God, and that by believing you may have life in his name."

Sunday, April 28 (Kentucky Lake, Tennessee)

"Propitiation" this a.m. Great meeting. Left very encouraged that the Lord has touched many hearts.

_____[10] flew me to the Memphis airport whence I departed on Braniff for the long tiresome run to C.S.

Home at 7:30.

Monday, April 29 (Durango, Colorado)

To Durango, with Howard Hansen & four others.[11]

Tuesday, April 30 (Durango, Colorado)

Last night: 1cc Gyn @ Midnight after only 3 days. Presby[tery] voted to approve my ministry as Exec[utive] Sec. of Young Life for another year.

A beautiful trip home via the Silverton, Ouray route. In fact the most beautiful mt trip I have ever seen in the US. Snow pack very deep—nothing like it.

———

One of Rayburn's favorite things to do with kids was to take them snow sliding at Frontier. His son described it in From Bondage to Liberty: Dance, Children, Dance: *"Jim would gather the crowd, give a brief set of instructions, and slowly start inching out on the [snow] cornice while everybody watched. When the snow could no longer support his weight, he simply disappeared through a small hole, screaming and hollering all the way ... Person number two would reluctantly inch toward the edge of the cornice. Eventually ... the snow would give way—whoosh! After hitting the snow, one could slide a thousand feet down the mountain in thirty seconds."*

---

[10] The blank spaces are Rayburn's—he has forgotten the person's name.

[11] For the annual meeting of the presbytery.

Goldbrick Delaney, Bill Starr, and Jim take a break while leading a snow slide in the early sixties.

Friday, July 19 (Frontier Ranch)

Hurt my knee badly coming off of Mt. Princeton.

35 kids—mostly Morgan Park[12] had a great time on whole trip.

Mile long snow slide below summit.

Best ever.

I got a big blessing out of taking them in spite of the injury.

Saturday, August 31 (Frontier Ranch)

A grand summer came to a close to-day.

70 colleges, Universities & Seminaries represented at Leadership this year in crowd of 200.

4000—total crowds of kids for the summer.[13]

Tuesday, September 24 (Star Ranch)

This was our day of prayer.

A fine time with the staff to-gether at the ranch from 7A until afternoon.

---

[12] Morgan Park is an area of Chicago that had kids at Frontier for the week.

[13] This figure is the total for all four Young Life camps.

The close of the 1957 fiscal year was one of the most dramatic yet. When October 1 rolled around, there was still a serious deficit. It meant that over $10,000 of back salaries would simply be wiped off the books.

The new committee structure pioneered earlier in Portland had taken hold in Memphis, and that area had raised their share of the budget for the year. When the Tennessee crowd heard of the salary deficit they took action.

Monday, October 14 (Memphis)

One of the greatest days of my life. 200 men—by far the best crowd I've ever had in Memphis—for lunch @ Peabody [Hotel]. I spoke on "Young Life." H——H——& T——W——L——very complimentary. Then the barbecue at night & H——'s offer to "match" a gift for our deficit. It was "electrifying." Can't thank the Lord enough.

At the meeting described above, the matching donor's challenge was met with pledges of $5,000. Within a few days, still more Memphis money had come in, resulting in a total of $13,000—enough to pay the back salaries. The books were re-opened and the salaries were paid. Describing the situation, Rayburn wrote it was "one of the great dates in Young Life history. To me, personally, it was one of my very greatest days in the Gospel ministry. It was a day made possible by magnificent teamwork on the part of the Memphis Committee and staff on the one hand and the exceeding abundant blessing of God on the other hand."

Sunday, December 8 (St. Paul, Minnesota)

This was the greatest day for "personal" blessing that I have had in a long long time. A perfect visit & dinner at Mrs. W——'s with [her son, daughter, and grandson].

Goldbrick Delaney.

Then to Mrs. C——'s for a wonderful visit & "out of the blue" with no discussion of any finances she gave me a huge check for Christmas. Such a great answer to prayer & supply of need that I am helpless when I try to express to the dear Lord my gratitude.

—⁓—

A very important presence in the Rayburns' lives was Andy "Gold-brick" Delaney and his wife, Gerry. They were hired as the cooks for Frontier for the summer of 1951 and ended up moving to Colorado full-time. They lived at Star Ranch in the non-summer months, running the kitchen there. They also played a hand in raising the Rayburn children, since Maxine was debilitated much of the time and Jim was on the road so much. "I liked Jim right from the beginning," Andy recalled. "He was an unusual man, he just had a way about him. He was a good man, he was demanding. He was just a leader and he had a way of drawing people to him. I didn't know the Lord in those first days. That's how I met Him, through Young Life."

Monday, December 16

Arr DV 11:30 p.

[Arr] CS 1:30 A

Felt very bum to-day and had a hard day—both at the office & at home.

Andy[14] & I put up the tree to-night & I enjoyed that in spite of illness.

Had fever.

——᭡m——

Wednesday, December 25

A happy, peaceful day—the best Christmas I can remember in a long time.

Thursday, December 26

Our 25th Wedding Anniversary—we had a very nice day. 60 or 70 of our friends in this afternoon.

---

[14] Andrew "Goldbrick" Delaney. Loved by generations of Young Lifers, Delaney and his wife Geraldine ("Gerry") were the first black members of the Young Life staff. They retired from Young Life in 1975 to open their own restaurant in Buena Vista. Goldbrick died in 1998; Gerry passed away in 2005.

1958

Saturday, February 22, 1958
53rd Day—312 Days to Follow

Washington's Birthday

To Ashville.

After a poor noon meeting with leaders in Greenville this turned out to be a very good day.

A fine dinner party at the hotel with Ashville Committee – then the evening meeting was very profitable. At the end Billy Graham asked to speak & gave a hearty endorsement of Y.L. and pledged his full support of the work there. Committee very pleased. I was too.

A BANQUET TO REMEMBER

The 1958 Asheville, North Carolina, Young Life banquet included both Jim Rayburn and Billy Graham as speakers. Graham was there as a parent.

Add Sewell (on Jim's left) and dignitaries at a Seattle Young Life banquet.

Jim's diary entries from the early part of February 1958 show one of his typical whirlwind tours.

Thursday, January 30
Lv CS 9:05 P on "The Chief" for Calif.

Friday, January 31 (on the train)
Good day on the train.

Saturday, February 1–Sunday, February 2 (Southern California)
[This entry is written across two days.]
Good time in Palm Desert visiting with the Harold Smiths.[1]

Monday, February 3 (Southern California)
A discouraging day—
   Poor committee meeting and nothing at all at the evening meeting in [blank space][2]
   Dinner at Paul's—good time.

Tuesday, February 4 (Southern California)
A very good day. An inspirational kind of visit with Ron White (his son, his commitment, his vision for Y.L.).
   Good noon meeting at Riverside.

---

[1] One of Sid Smith's sons.

[2] Jim has left the location blank.

Excellent meeting at Covina to-night. Grand crowd 60—mostly parents—looks like this area will go.

Oh yes! A great mothers "coffee" in Riverside this a.m.[3]

Wednesday, February 5 (travelling)

> Mig dev. on trip. 1cc Gyn in Aft. hit me hard but stopped pain.
> 18 Day Interval.

Lv. L.A. 9:30 A

ARR SEATTLE 3 P.M.

Dull flight—getting sick.

Good thing I had the evening off.

Thursday, February 6 (Tacoma, Washington)

Another great Tacoma Meeting—like last year.

I spoke.

Larry Kulp finished. Did a grand job.

Friday, February 7 (Seattle)

Seattle Comm** Luncheon

Seattle Banquet—

964 Present. Grand Affair. $19,500.00 In cash & Pledges.

Rev. Bob Richards and Larry Kulp spoke.

Saturday, February 8 (travelling)

Lv Sea 10A

Arr Chi 5:15 P

To Bismarck [Hotel].[4] Very weary—went to bed.[5]

---

[3] Afternoon "coffees" for mothers of club kids were a common promotional event at this time.

[4] Now known as the Hotel Allegro Chicago.

[5] Jim often complained in his journal about being weary—but he seldom lost his sense of humor. His son quotes him in *From Bondage to Liberty: Dance, Children, Dance* as being overhead saying, "Why, I'm so tired, the seat of my pants is wiping out my footprints."

Sunday, February 9 (Chicago)
A wonderful day. Best time of prayer in a long time.

Monday, February 10 (Chicago)
A good day—but impossible without Him.

The Trust[6] meeting was better than usual even with the build-up of pressure within me—My presentation requesting $100,000 for Capital funds was, as usual, last. It was not approved—in the absence of Mr. Taylor, but was well received. I left very thankful to the Lord for letting me present it and felt His presence—Reached the train exhausted—conferred with two Rock Is[land] men about summer transport.[7]

Arnie Jacobs, at the time a young area director, was able to boast of something no one else would ever be able to claim: his 1958 Asheville, North Carolina, banquet featured both Jim Rayburn and Billy Graham as speakers.

Saturday, February 22 (Asheville, North Carolina)
To Ashville [*sic*].

After a poor noon meeting with leaders in Greenville [South Carolina] this turned out to be a very good day.

A fine dinner party at the hotel with Ashville [*sic*] Committee—then the evening meeting was very profitable. At the end Billy Graham asked to speak & gave a hearty endorsement of Y.L. and pledged his full support of the work there. Committee very pleased. I was too.

Jim's troubles with the Pueblo Presbytery were resolved somewhat in the spring. After two days' of meetings the "Committee on Minis-

---

[6] A meeting of the Crowell Trust.

[7] Rayburn was probably trying to arrange a deal for Young Life groups to travel to the Colorado ranches on the Rock Island Railroad.

terial Relations" determined that though he frequently ministered outside of Colorado he was never in any other specific presbytery long enough to be considered to be "laboring" there.

Such bureaucratic red tape was a source of irritation to Rayburn. From his perspective, he was doing God's work—something the church should accept gladly. Instead, he had to seek their permission year after year in order to keep his ordination.

Dealing with the local governing body of his denomination was not the only thing Rayburn was finding aggravating. He was willing to put up with almost constant travel, but as long as he was on the road, he wanted his time to be well-spent. Several times this year he makes comments about how he should no longer accept certain engagements again.

Monday, March 3–Tuesday, March 4 (Star Ranch)
[This entry is written across two days.]
Conf with Presbyterian Comm. on Ministerial Rel[ations]. Went very well and I was pleased with the group & very pleasantly surprised.

Tuesday, April 22 (Salida, Colorado)
The Presbytery treated me very cordially. Of course there are a few— maybe only one or two that are disgrundled [*sic*].

Returned home at 1 p m.

Wednesday, April 23
Andy and I worked on the rock wall until nearly noon.

Took the "Rocket" to Chicago.

Thursday, April 24 (Chicago)
Chicago

A great Red Letter Day

The Trust voted us a $100,000.00 grant on the specifications I requested. How can I thank the Lord. He made the project smooth. Now to work—matching the first $50,000.00—then getting the rest.

Met Gene Gillis—had dinner on the train to Memphis with him. To bed early.

Saturday, April 26 (Kentucky Lake, Tennessee)[8]
I'm going to cut out this assignment for a year or two. Too much output for the volume & results.

Jim's propensity for daredevil behavior took its toll when he broke his knee just a few days before his forty-ninth birthday.

Despite his infirmity, he kept most of his summer appointments, including hosting Dr. Emile Cailliet and his wife Vera at Frontier. Cailliet would become a great supporter of Young Life and a confidant of Rayburn's. Cailliet was a professor at Princeton Theological Seminary and was teaching that summer at the Young Life Institute in Colorado Springs. He later authored the first book about the ministry, Young Life, *published in 1963.*

Tuesday, July 15 (Malibu Club)
A great meeting to-night—best reception I've ever had. [...]

Wednesday, July 16 (Malibu Club)
Add & I went up the Inlet & had some wonderful slalom skiing—then in a moment of complete forgetfulness I tried a water start on the one ski—put too much strain on the bad left knee & something popped—guess it is a torn or strained ligament—can't walk—much pain.

Great meeting to-night—Used Mk 2 & some new slants.** Terrific attention & response.

Thursday, July 17 (Malibu Club)
Mig—1cc Gyn. (Think acct.** of accident)

---

[8] Jim was there addressing a weekend retreat for adults for the second year in a row.

Had another grand time with the kids—particularly impressed with the Calif. youngsters. Very sharp, well trained, appreciative & receptive.

Friday, July 18 (travelling)
I flew into Vancouver & caught train to Seattle—just made connection for Portland. At Portland I had 20 minutes—got a bedroom to Cheyenne.

Saturday, July 19 (on the train)
Comfortable day on train—mostly in bed—leg bad.
    Arr Cheyenne 7 P. Called home.

Sunday, July 20 (Cheyenne, Wyoming)
Flew home this A.M. Dr. Krauser** examined me—have a broken knee.**

Sunday, July 27 (Frontier Ranch)
Having Dr. & Mrs. Emil Cailliett [sic, Emile Cailliet][9] of Princeton here at the Look-Out for the week-end has been a great source of blessing & encouragement to me. They have taken in everything. Have vision for our task—very helpful suggestions.

Tuesday, August 12 (Frontier Ranch)
                                          Severe Mig. to-nite—early AM [...]
Lots of pain in my leg—Didn't feel like speaking to-nite.

Wednesday, August 13
Went home. Dr. Christensen took off cast & put me in hospital with "Phlibitus" [sic, phlebitis].

---

[9] Emile Cailliet (1894–1981). Born in France, Cailliet was wounded as an infantryman in the French army during World War I. He became an American citizen in 1937. He served at four different universities as a professor of French Literature before becoming Professor of Christian Philosophy at Princeton Theological Seminary. Though he enjoyed his time around Young Life staff, it is said he did not appreciate being called "Yippee Cailliet" by program directors.

With three ranches in Colorado, Young Life had acquired quite a string of horses. Seeking a place to winter the horses and to grow hay for them, Rayburn was pursuing further acreage near Frontier and Silver Cliff. Called the "Round-Up Ranch" originally, the land would eventually be named "Rancho Caballo."

At the same time that Jim was pursuing Round-Up Ranch, he was making plans for a trip to Europe the next spring with Maxine.

Thursday, August 21 (Chicago)

Had a great time with M——M——@ lunch. He went for the "Round-Up Ranch" idea in a big way. Will give his money to close the deal.

Got some fine travel info. for the European trip. Ready to make final plans.

More every day it looks like the Lord is leading us to the** "Round-Up" deal.

For several years Andy "Goldbrick" Delaney would travel around the country putting on barbecues for Young Life areas. These events would feature Young Life entertainment as well.

As the new school year began, Jim continued his normal travels. On the family front, the Rayburns' daughter Sue had graduated from high school and was beginning her college career at Westmont College in Santa Barbara, California; Ann was married to her high school sweetheart Jim Patterson; and Jim III was in seventh grade and would turn thirteen in October.

Monday, September 22 (Wichita, Kansas)

Lv Colo Spgs 8A.

Arr Wichita 11A

A grand afternoon of study & prayer & an exceptionally fine mtg tonite. 480 present. Goldbrick Barbequed. Program enthusiastically received.

Tuesday, September 23 (Omaha, Nebraska)
Good mtg in Omaha. About 90. Everything was too long—except my speech—kept that under 30.

[...]

Didn't sleep at all last night. Got a 2 hour nap this p.m.

Tuesday, September 30
To-day (with one wk of "grace") we have come to within $10,000.00 of meeting our huge budget. The balance is almost assured.** How to be thankful enough! The Lord's faithfulness & love is so great—we will never comprehend it. Eighteen years—the same "miracle of supply."

Left at 2:30 P to drive my car to Phoenix. Hated to leave Maxine and it's a long drive.

Arr. Albu[querque] about 9 P. Went to bed at a little motel on w. side.

Sunday, October 5 (Los Angeles)
Sue & I drove to Santa Barbara with Starrs. I went to bed right after early dinner at Edie Benson's.[10]

Budget for '57–'58 met in full. Another "miracle of supply"—very very thankful to our wonderful Lord.

———

Jim's hectic schedule is exemplified in the following entries: Portland all day on Monday, a banquet there that night, followed by the "red-eye" flight to Minneapolis, arriving on Tuesday morning. After speaking at a meeting there, it was on to the train for Chicago for meetings there on Wednesday.

Monday, October 20 (Portland, Oregon)
A good day. Lunch with the staff & Hil Holstrom.

———

[10] Benson's husband Jack had been an early member of the Star Ranch Committee when they lived in Colorado.

Big Banquet to-night. Went well.

A fine time of fellowship at the "Oyster Bar" with Ed & Mrs. Back-strant [*sic*, Backstrand],[11] Tom & Recie, Jack & Marge,[12] Brent Johnson[13] before leaving on the plane.

Tuesday, October 21 (Minneapolis)

Lv PD 1:30 A

Arr Min 9 A

Good time with Frank Walters[14]—feel that we really got someplace.

Only fair mtg to-nite. Disappointing crowd.

To Pullman & bed right after mtg. Very weary.

Monday, November 3 (Los Angeles)

A great day in the work. The "Mothers Coffee" @ Nelsons' this a.m. was very good. These affairs are top-notch, & essential for our pub. relations.

To-night the Statler banquet—sponsored by B——J——. An out-standing event in every way. I was proud & happy to have Maxine & Sue with me. Over 500 present, $12,500 in cash & pledges. Along with Van-couver & the two Chicago luncheons this makes the fourth very out-standing pub. relations & promotion affairs [*sic*] this fall. Very thankful

---

[11] Dr. S. Edward Backstrand and his wife Ester. Backstrand was a Portland dentist and had served on the board of trustees from 1954–1957.

[12] Jack and Marj Potts. Marjorie Wright was an early club kid in Tyler, Texas, and married staff man Jack Potts.

[13] Brent Johnson was a young staff man in Portland. Originally from California, he later served as area director of Wichita, Kansas, and then Houston.

[14] Frank W. Walters was a business executive who had conducted an extensive organizational study of Young Life beginning in 1955 at the board's request. His suggestions, adopted in 1957, had resulted in major structural changes for the ministry. Walters served on the board himself, from 1957–1972.

to the Lord for the wonderful response from Committee & parents.

---

*Last mentioned in these excerpts on January 15, 1947, "Sammy"
Adams, one of Jim's old club kids from Fort Worth, was now Coach
Sam Adams and building a successful football program at Whit-
worth College.*

Sunday, December 7 (Spokane)
Another fine day, with these attractive Whitworth kids.

Big snow last night.

Late dinner at Sam Adams' home to-night. He has certainly developed. I believe is a real leader of men now.

1959

Tuesday, September 1, 1959
244th Day—121 Days to Follow

THE VISION FOR TRAIL WEST IS SHARED
Jim took committee members and their wives to Rancho Caballo to show them where he wanted to build a first-class guest lodge for adults. Rayburn's vision would come to fruition several years later when Trail West opened in 1964.

In January Maxine and Jim entered a new phase of their lives when they became grandparents when Ann and her husband Jim Patterson had their first son.

Thursday, January 1

Coming home from Silver Cliff after closing meeting of holiday camp. Prayed earnestly as I could and was greatly bothered by this coldness or difficulty in prayer that has troubled me so much in recent months. Know of no revealed reason why I shouldn't have more liberty in prayer. God has been so GOOD—such a Great year past. I will earnestly seek it!!

Listened to all the Bowl Games.

Okla 21 Syracuse 6.

LSU 7 Clemson 0

A.F.A. 0 TCU 0

Iowa 38 Cal 12.

Saturday, January 10

Ann phoned that "labor" started.

Drove to Boulder early. There all day. Ann with rather intermittent labor. She was swell about it & we had a good day.

I went home about 7:30 p when it seemed nothing would happen— but they took Ann to Hospital [...]

Sunday, January 11

Our Grandson—"Mark Rayburn Patterson" born @ 1P to-day.

I taught my S.S. Class—180 Present—my largest.—Then rushed to Boulder & got there for the big event.

We saw Ann & the baby afterward. A wonderful experience. The Lord answered all our prayers so wonderfully. Ann very "groggy" & happy.

We drove home.

Monday, January 26 (travelling)
To DV on Texas Zypher [*sic*] @ 4:50A! Had to wait until nearly 1p. for the Calif Zyph. [*sic*] but didn't mind as I was so interested in John Bright's "Kingdom of God" and another book.

Had a very good aft & evening on the train.

Sue was not doing well in college, so Jim and Maxine had her accompany them on a two-month trip to Europe. The trip was part vacation and part work, as Jim explored opportunities for the expansion of Young Life overseas.

A few days before they left, the Navigators held a Bon Voyage party for them, giving Maxine new luggage and Jim the money for a new pair of skis. The crossing was through rough seas.

Saturday, February 21 (New York City)
Cold Day.

We sailed on "Saturnia" at Noon. Beautiful tho cold sailing. The "America" followed us down the river.

Good cabins—very happy and thankful to be off. The ship is old and far from luxurious but I am satisfied.

Photogs took pictures of Sue before sailing.

Movie this afternoon.

[...]

Monday, February 23 (at sea)
At sea.

Rough & stormy.

All the family good sailors.

Captain's party turns into a hilarious fiasco by flying hors d'oeuvres, cocktails, & people—oh yes & furniture. Funny.

A scene that played out hundreds of times over the years:
Rayburn returns home from one of his trips.

Wednesday, February 25 (at sea)

Same—good days at sea. Sleeping a lot—enjoying the rough weather.

Thursday, February 26 (at sea)

Same.

> Getting tired of the rough weather.
> Got out of it this evening passing some of the Azores.

———

Rayburn's diary entries during the trip offer few insights into the trip itself; they are mostly just itineraries (for instance, the entire entry for March 13 reads, "Milano—Saw 'The Last Supper'"). In all, they visited eleven countries.

The part of the visit that had the most lasting impact on Jim was his first-ever visit to East Berlin. Seeing the stark contrast between free West Berlin and communist-controlled East Berlin haunted Rayburn. Always a proud American, he became even more fiercely anti-communist after he witnessed firsthand the oppression brought on by a system of government that counted atheism as one of its main pillars.

Tuesday, April 21 (New York City)

Home! Disembarked at 3P. Thru customs and checked in at Statler-Hilton by 5P. Long conference with Wam, who met us at the Ship.

Went to "My Fair Lady" to-nite.[1] It was great!

Friday, April 24 (Chicago)

Stayed in all day and feel better.

The Chicago Banquet at the Morrison was great but missed as far as getting support & pledges right on the spot. Believe we have to watch this.

———

Summer brought the now-familiar routine of staying at Frontier and speaking there and at Malibu.

Jim was increasingly burdened to see that high school kids in other countries had the opportunity to hear about Christ in the way Young Life had pioneered. His June 13 entry is the first mention in the journals of visiting with foreign exchange students in The Lookout at Frontier, a tradition he continued for the next several years. His heart broke for these kids, many of whom went home to environments that were literally hostile to Christians and the Christian faith.

Tuesday, June 9 (Frontier Ranch)

Night (early this a.m.) Severe Mig—1cc Gyn. fast, complete relief.

Opening night of camp at Frontier—went very well—nearly full—kids enthusiastic and responsive. Entertainment crew did well.

Lorne Sanny with me.

Thursday, June 11 (Frontier Ranch)

Took 55 kids up Chimney Rock[2] this aft. Jimmy with me.

---

[1] The original Broadway production, which was three years into its 2,717-performance run at the Mark Hellinger Theater.

[2] Chimney Rock is a rock outcropping visible from the "infield" at Frontier. Now the camp's rappelling site, it was a common day-hike during the first four decades of Frontier's history.

*Jim and Maxine
at Frontier Ranch.*

(Otherwise a very hard day for me.)

Took the evening off. Bill Starr spoke!

Friday, June 12 (Frontier Ranch)

Jim III[3] & Bill & I took 105 kids to the snow-slides to-day. Beautiful day—lots of snow—great time.

Ann, Jim[4] & little Mark arrived about 9:30 p. Just great to have them.

Saturday, June 13 (Frontier Ranch)

The Camp going very well. We had the 12 Exchange (Foreign) students with us at the Lookout to-nite.

(Heard that [...] the Denmark girl became a Christian tonight.)

---

*A new wrinkle to the summer routine was a national gathering
for committee members and their wives. Known as the Commit-*

---

[3] This is the first time in the journals that Jim refers to his son as "Jim III."

[4] Jim Patterson, Ann's husband.

teemen's Conference (committees in those days were men-only af-
fairs), the second annual conference was held at Frontier and Sil-
ver Cliff ranches in August.

When Young Life bought Rancho Caballo earlier in the year,
Jim began making trips to the 640-acre property in his World War
II-vintage Jeep. In order to obtain the good pastureland, Young
Life had to buy the "worthless" mountain land above it. Jim spent
hours in the beautiful "worthless" acreage praying about what he
believed the Lord was leading him to next: an adult facility to
showcase Young Life.

Sunday, August 30 (Frontier and Silver Cliff)
The Committeemen's conference is splendid and the fellowship with
friends great.

The entire crowd at "Lookout" to-nite—about 70.

Tuesday, September 1 (Frontier and Silver Cliff)
Viewed the proposed adult "Guest Ranch" site at Rancho Caballo this
aft. The entire group enthused about plans & site.

Sue fixed an array of goodies & we entertained 25 after mtg
to-night.

Thursday, September 3 (Frontier Ranch)
Left Frontier for the season—drove the Jeep home—had a flat.

Wednesday, September 9
Inaugurated weekly conf. with Roy, John, Orien. Very good two hour
session preceeded [sic] by a fine time of prayer.

For about a year, Roy Riviere had been working at the headquar-
ters as Administrator of Young Life (a title later changed to Man-
aging Director). His hard work greatly freed up Rayburn from the
administrative work which was so vital to the growing ministry

*but which had never been Jim's strength. Rounding out the head-
quarters crew of executives were Business Manager John Carter
and* Young Life *magazine editor Orien Johnson.*

Tuesday, September 22
To Okla City—8:40A Braniff.

An excellent mtg to-nite [—] $1,000 offering too. About 300 pres-
ent—our largest hearing so far in Okla City.

Wednesday, September 23 (Oklahoma City)
Breakfast with Bill Yinger.[5]

Lunch with a small group.

Otherwise restful day.

Monday, September 28 (Minneapolis)
Late to-nite—took 2 Migral—again not a full grown mig.

Arr. 9A. (Minn.)

Dinner with Phil, Joan,[6] & Dick Lowey.[7]

A great mtg to-nite—over 500 present.

Report from Hdqts:

Hear that the money is almost in! Need less than $4000 to top!
How thankful to God I am. It doesn't seem possible.

——

Tuesday, October 20
Arr DV 3 A.M.

Arr Home 5 A.M.

---

[5] William Yinger was an Oklahoma oilman who would later join the Young Life
board of trustees.

[6] Phil and Joan McDonald. Phil was the Twin Cities area director.

[7] Dick Lowey had been on staff about four years at this time. He continued with
Young Life for many years and, along with McDonald, was one of Young Life's great
camp program directors.

Slept until 10A and got quite a bit of office work done before getting Jim at school. We played with the "Frisby" [*sic*, Frisbee].[8]

Saturday, October 24 (Pittsburgh, Pennsylvania)

ARR. PITTSBURG[H].

Coffee at Harry & Hope's.[9]

To Game with Bill & Grace Kiesewetter.[10] An unusually happy time. These people are "regular guys"—enjoy being with 'em. Pitt 3–T.C.U. 13. Chuck Reinhold[11] made a beautiful 55 yrd run & otherwise played the best for Pitt. Visited with him & others after the game.

(Walked 3 miles this p.m.)

Dinner at Kiesewetters' & to bed early.

———

When Jim came home from his second trip to Europe he approached his contacts at the Kresge Foundation in Detroit to underwrite a trip for him and several of the top men in Young Life to go to Berlin to study the effects of communism. The hope was that the staff men would then be able to use their firsthand knowledge as a tool to address school assemblies, thus furthering Young Life's work. The Kresge Foundation liked the idea.

Jim and ten others—Roy Riviere, John Carter, Orien John-

---

[8] Wham-O's flying discs had just come out two years earlier and were becoming a national sensation.

[9] Harry and Hope MacDonald. Harry MacDonald was the first Student Staff member for Young Life during his college days in the 1940s. He then came on the full-time staff and served in various capacities until 1980, leaving to become a Presbyterian pastor. Hope wrote several books, including *Discovering How To Pray* (1976).

[10] William and Grace Kiesewetter were a prominent Pittsburgh couple. Bill Kiesewetter joined Young Life's board this year, eventually becoming a Life Member. He was an associate of C. Everett Koop and, like Koop, was a highly regarded surgeon.

[11] Chuck Reinhold, then a college football star, later joined the Young Life staff and served for decades, including a long tenure as senior vice president in the 1990s.

son, *Tom Raley, George Sheffer, Wally Howard, Bob Mitchell, Bill Starr, Pittsburgh area director Harry MacDonald, and Los Angeles area director Tom Bade—set sail from New York in No- vember on the S.S. *Rotterdam.

Their primary contacts were with the American military in West Germany, but they also spent time in France and England. Two of the men (Sheffer and Riviere) stayed on several more days and made a trip to the Soviet Union.

Saturday, November 7 (Dallas)
Much of Board mtg was good but I left rather disappointed at the lack of vision & warmth to-ward the staff problems of finance and the big needs for the advance.

[...]

Thursday, November 12 (New York City)
Very tough mig in aft. 2 Ergone** & 2 #3 dulled pain but very slow relief.
8 DAY INTERVAL.

Sailed for Europe 2 hours late @ 2 p m.

S.S. Rotterdam.

The N.J., Conn., & Penn. Y.L. crowd down to see us.

Beautiful day.

Short conference with the boys @ 3:30 then rest—dinner—movie.

Very calm sea.

Sitting at 1st Officer's table with Mitch & some English people.

Friday, November 13 (at sea)
A restful day.

Food wonderful—sea unbelievably calm—boys getting big kick out of it—ship & service perfect in every way.

No work for the group to-day.

They looked swell "dressed" for dinner.

Saturday, November 14 (at sea)
Up @ 9.

Three hr. conference with the men this A.M.

1 hr. Advisory Comm.[12] mtg. this aft.

Got very sick at dinner time—the "Indonesian" luncheon dish still on my stomach.

Rough evening.

Sunday, November 15 (at sea)

Ill all last night & very shaky & weak to-day. Finally got some tea & cakes to go down & stay in aft. & went to dinner & ate very lightly.

Stayed very quiet & enjoyed the evening visiting with the boys & playing a little "42."

Had a call from Maxine about noon—could hear surprisingly well.

Monday, November 16 (at sea)

Fine night of sleep—the first. Slept 'till 11A. Breakfast in room. Great conference with the men about the Board mtg. & our organizational structure.

Pleasant evening doing nothing—but a little "42." To bed early with a very interesting book from ship's library.

Tuesday, November 17 (at sea)

No sleep last night—even Carbital didn't help […]. Toured "Tourist" section of ship. Unbelievable. Luxurious. More beautiful lounges than 1st. Better than 1st on any other ship.

Conf (mostly on "Image of America") with the men.

Wednesday, November 18 (at sea)

Good day—met with the fellows for conf. & time of prayer—otherwise just loafed.

---

[12] The Advisory Committee was made up of the top staff in Young Life (all of whom happened to be on the trip, with the exception of Add Sewell) and served as Rayburn's cabinet, regularly advising him on matters of personnel and policy.

*Staff men Harry MacDonald, Bill Starr, Wally Howard,
and John Carter on the trip to Europe.*

Thursday, November 19 (at sea)
A good, restful last day on the ship but for some unaccountable reason
I couldn't sleep to-nite.

Called @ So. Hampton @ 7:30A at LeHavre @ 3:30.

Friday, November 20 (travelling)
Arr. Rotterdam 7:30A.

Beautiful trip up the river to dock.

Rotterdam–Delft–Amsterdam–Brussels

Saturday, November 21 (West Germany)
Brussels to Frankfort [*sic*][13]—stop @ Cologne—Weisbaden Mtg. Co-
burn**, "Andy" Anderson, King & one other chaplain there. Tough
mtg—that came out so well it is worth the whole trip.

Sunday, November 22 (West Germany)
The Great, great day @ Rhein-Main.[14]

---

[13] In all of his travels to West Germany, Jim consistently spelled "Frankfurt" this way.

[14] Rhein-Main Air Base, located just outside of Frankfurt and operated for years by

Met Col. Amen** for breakfast—he stayed right with me 'till 1P—went to church to-gether. Then** to his office for Berlin calls.

Toured the base with all the guys—enjoyed getting up in a "Globe-Master."[5]

Arr. Berlin @ 6:10 p. Dr Reinartz[16] elated to see party. Air Force (Capt. John Reynolds) met us—bus to Hotel; Walked—to bed . . .

Monday, November 23 (Berlin)

To Templehof [sic, Tempelhof] USAF Operations** @ 9A. Met Chaplain Ellis. Pictures—the "Helfen"** Operations—Capt. Reynolds brought me a flock of candy, gum & stuff.

To East Berlin with the whole crowd all afternoon.

At Bob Voth's** to-nite with two East German (Sov. Sector) Christian Teen-agers. A powerful experience. None of us will ever forget the 19 ye[a]r old's moving prayer "Will never see each other here . . . in the Kingdom . . ." (Not money—"we have money") ("seal off Soviet Sector.")

Tuesday, November 24 (Berlin)

Another tremendous day—where but in Berlin could one have such heart searching experiences. We went to the Marionfeld** Rec. Center this a.m. Sat in on a "trial" of young E. German who has tried for 2 yrs. to reach his wife in the west—gave up everything—but has "got it made" now. Lunch. Took pictures of "Director of Center"—then of dozens of little kindergarten kids—they called me "Uncle Jim"—Bill S, Tim Nuveen[17] & Orien with me—the kids & mothers awed & over-

---

the United States Air Force and NATO.

[15] The Globemaster was a large military transport plane.

[16] Dr. Hilde Reinartz, a German academic and Christian who had become a supporter of Young Life's efforts.

[17] Tim Nuveen had been a club kid in Chicago. He would later accompany Jim on his round-the-world trip in 1963.

joyed at pictures. Briefed by Pastor Shultz—interviewed a 19 yr. old girl, just escaped from Leipzig. To Hotel—weary—cold. Dinner with Tim Nuveen for 3 hrs! Good talk. Can't sleep—2 A.M.

Wednesday, November 25 (Berlin)

Headachy this a.m. Went away with only anacin.

A great experience this a.m. in a teen-age boys' camp. Grand case-histories by personal account. Took about 40 pictures—others took 40.

Climax of trip: An hour-long con. with Mayor Willy Brant [sic][18]—small personal chat & pictures.

This evening a big meeting of German Church Y.P.—very impressive—Bishop of Coventry & Bishop Dibelius spoke. Met them both. Bishop D. very impressive—is no doubt a real man of God.[19] Meeting was at Templehof [sic] Church. 10:30 p. Dinner with Mitch and Bill S.

Thursday, November 26 (Thanksgiving Day) (Berlin)

Thanksgiving Day! Every Year More!

Briefing at Gov.** House this a.m. Shocking official Communist Film—

A very moving experience at lunch with Supt. Ahme, Dr R., Pastor Schultz. Ahme gave a great talk. I responded with a "Thanks & Farewell"—

Had a visit with Bishop Dibelius at his home this evening. The boys went to Soviet Sector for mtg with y.p. Brought them back to hotel—we took pictures in the lobby.

---

[18] Willy Brandt was the mayor of West Berlin and an international figure. He would later become chancellor of West Germany.

[19] Friedrich Karl Otto Dibelius (1880–1967). As the German Evangelical Church's bishop for Berlin, he was viewed by most as the head of the Protestant church in Germany.

Friday, November 27 (Berlin)

Slept late. At 10A to two camps[20]—at second one [for families] took a lot of pictures and received a warm response. Old man in bed, never well after starving & brutality in Concen. Camp. Got a "masterpiece" photo of the cab driver & me. To hotel—lunch with Johnny O'Niel [sic, O'Neil].[21] Shopped for my girlies—to Templehof [sic] @ 4:00.

Arr Frankfort [sic] (Rhein-Main) @ 6:20 P Col Amen** had arranged for us to use Clipper-Club Room at PAA.[22] Had a great mtg. All the men spoke on "Impressions"—some very good.

Lv. Rh.-M @ 2100—Air France Arr Paris 2205 (Caravelle Jet) Art & Rod met us. To Rod's for Late snack—Cheeses.

To Royale Hotel for bed 12:30A.

Saturday, November 28 (Paris)

Slept late. Met group @ Arch of Triumph—with Tim to see "Corots**" @ Place d' le Concord [sic]—then walked along the Seine to le Grand Palais & saw an exhibition.

Lunch with the men @ Le Pergola** on the Champs Elleysee [sic].

They went to The Louvre—I went to bed.

At 6 p.m. went to the Seine for Amer. Y.L. Club boat trip & meeting.

Beautiful night views of Notre Dame, Eiffel Tower (lighted) Place de la Concord[e] et. al.

The Communist Youth (Leaders) 15–30 from all France and N. Africa—200—taking boat from same wharf for outing on river!

Sunday, November 29 (London)

Rod came for me @ 7A. To Orly Airfield.

---

[20] Refugee camps.

[21] Chicago staff man John O'Neil had just recently been transferred to Germany to head up the work there.

[22] Pan American Airways.

Lv. Paris 8A. Arr London 8:15 G.T. We checked in at the Strand Palace—fine hotel—reasonable rates. Taxied to "All Souls Church"—heard John Stott,[23] attended luncheon there—Stott very friendly—walked down Regent Street to Picadilly Circus, Haymarket, Trafalgar to Hotel. Rested.

Took Cabs to Buckingham, Parliament, West. Abbey, St Paul's, London Tower, London Bridge—etc.

Conferred for an hour with Mitch & Bade then they left for home.

Slept an hour & had dinner with the rest of the men. Stayed in my room to-night while the other guys walked**. Very thankful to the Lord for all this trip—beside the "mission accomplished" the fellowship with the men has been ideal.

Monday, November 30 (travelling)

Up at 7:45A. Fine breakfast at the hotel with the men—To London Central Airport.

Lv London 11A PAA JET—because of weather had to take long southerly route—575 mi per hr.—crowded, but not too bad—Arr Idlewild (N.Y.)[24] @ 2:30 P.

Lv Idlw. on United #735 @ 4 P.

Riding over the mid-west now 6 P.M. it is hard to realize that breakfast at the Strand Palace was this A.M!

Arr DV on time @ 8:30 p.m.

On** home Arr @ 10 P.

Picture & interview by "Free Press"[25] and then home with Jim & Maxine. Sue sick from tooth extraction.

---

[23] John R. W. Stott. Considered by many to be the leading evangelical in all of England, Stott was the Anglican rector of All Souls Church, Langham Place, in the heart of London.

[24] Now known as John F. Kennedy International Airport, or JFK.

[25] The *Free Press* was one of Colorado Springs' daily newspapers. The article and photo appeared in the paper the next day.

Jim had a wonderful sense of humor which, unfortunately, is not as present in his journals as it was in his day-to-day dealings with people. From Bondage to Liberty: Dance, Children, Dance *recounts that upon his return from one of his trips to Europe (very likely this one) he reported to his Sunday School class: "Why, the carpets on that ship were so plush, I ran around all day without my pants on, and nobody knew the difference."*

The stated purpose of the trip had been to investigate the effects of communism and to report their findings in high school assemblies around the country. Almost none of the men had much success with this, although Rayburn did have some.

As the ministry grew, the need for a headquarters facility separate from Star Ranch was becoming increasingly obvious. Jim's journal records the finding of the eventual site, 720 W. Monument, which would serve as Young Life's home office until 1996.

Monday, December 7

A very profitable day at the office. Got off letter to J.E.H.[26] Talked a long time to Gov. Mark Hatfield—also to Stan Kresge[27] and Amos Gregory in Detroit. Got out a lot of other correspondence.

With O. L. Clark[28] viewed the first good prospect for a Natl. Headquarters site on W. Monument.

A great "Annual Y.L. Banquet" to-nite at Alamo Hotel—our best. 300 present—representative citizens. Spoke on Communism & Christianity—the Berlin experiences.

---

[26] Almost certainly J. Edgar Hoover. Rayburn was an admirer of the FBI director, and had been trying for years to meet him.

[27] Stanley Sebastian Kresge (1900–1985). Kresge's foundation had sponsored the Berlin trip. His Kresge Stores were the forerunner of K Mart.

[28] Orrin L. Clark was a Colorado Springs builder who was on the board of trustees.

Monday, December 14 (St. Paul, Minnesota)
The best thing about this day was a long visit with Mrs. C———. She is
a true friend and exhibits more perception regarding problems and the
progress of the work than one would expect—why don't more people, is
what I mean.

Flew to Chicago.

Took train for Pittsburg [*sic*].

1960

Saturday, September 3, 1960
247th Day—119 Days to Follow

Slowly packed up for home — after spending some enjoyable hours up on the Princeton Trail & at Cabin site with Bill Mitchell & Lawrence Bender. We surveyed the route for extension of road from present Timberline Camp to proposed cabin site.

Left Frontier late afternoon. Every year it is harder to leave. Such a grand place, so many wonderful memories — a grand summer! Very thankful to God for these last 10 summers at "The Lookout."

"EVERY YEAR IT IS HARDER TO LEAVE."
Jim left Frontier and "The Lookout" for the 1960 summer season after making plans to build "The Chalet"—a cabin to be used for overnight stays by Young Lifers on Mt. Princeton. (The "100" at the bottom of the page refers to the number of miles he travelled that day as he drove home to Colorado Springs.)

For years Young Life had hoped to receive favorable publicity in a national magazine like Saturday Evening Post *or* Life *but had not had any luck. When national publicity finally came their way, it was certainly no "puff piece." In its January 4, 1960, issue,* Time *magazine published an article, complete with a dour-looking photo of Jim, titled, "Teen-Age Church?"*

The reason for the article was "a stern denunciation" of Young Life by several Connecticut ministers issued at the end of 1959. The ministers warned parents away from Young Life.

Monday, January 18 (Los Angeles)
Bad Mig late to-nite—2 Ergomar & 2 #3 Emp. stopped it. only**

Worked all morning with Mitch & Bade on the Drafts for our Assembly addresses.[1]

Good time at Lunch with Committee & leaders—talked on 1) Their important work for Y.L. 2) The New Headq. 3) The "Time" publicity.

Tuesday, January 19 (Los Angeles)
Up late—bad night with the headache.

[...]

To Fuller [Seminary]. Conf with Paul Jewett.[2]

To Y.L. office for mtg with our young leaders. They are the best group we have ever had—about 16 of them, headed for the work.[3]

[...]

———

Rayburn travelled to Connecticut to meet personally with the New

---

[1] For the "Freedom Speeches" they were hoping to deliver to high school assemblies about their experiences in Berlin.

[2] Paul King Jewett was a professor at Fuller Theological Seminary from its early days until his death in 1991. He served for many years as the dean of the Young Life Institute.

[3] One of these young leaders was Mal McSwain, who did indeed come on staff full-time after completing Fuller Seminary. He served on staff for almost fifty years.

Canaan ministers in late February.

The Connecticut episode aside, most news for Young Life was positive, including an endorsement of the "Freedom Speeches" (as the Berlin trip assemblies were called) by Vice President (and soon-to-be presidential candidate) Richard Nixon.

Saturday, February 20
Feel real bad.

Finished correspondence—John & Millie [Carter] came over & Maxine picked a beautiful carpet for Kachina Lodge.[4]

To DV. Zyphr [*sic*] 1:00 p.

Slept some—had dinner early—went to bed.

Friday, February 26 (Washington, D. C.)
A great day. I had a very warm & friendly talk of nearly 20 minutes with Vice-Pres. Nixon at noon. He liked the idea of my big project with the high school assemblies—and will endorse it just as I suggested. I'm to write the idea up for him. Talked a long time to Charlie McWhorter—legislative Asst. to Nixon. Think he's with it too. Calls for Symington & Humphries' [*sic*][5] secs., saying "Next time." Called Maxine to report.

Took train late for Boston.

Very thankful to the Lord—

Monday, February 29 (New Canaan, Connecticut)
A wonderful time of prayer and preparation & meditation these days. Do hope I am getting stronger in these areas. Seems some definite improvement in late weeks.

[…] Conf. & prayer with Frank Cicero. Long conf with Rev. Grant

---

[4] The Kachina was the new clubroom being built at Frontier Ranch. It opened that summer.

[5] Senators Stuart Symington of Missouri and Hubert Humphrey of Minnesota.

Morrill & short time with Presby. Spears [*sic*, Speers].[6]

To Knectle's** [*sic*, Knechtle][7] @ 4:00 P. Talked to Ann K (Grace Kiesewetter's** sister) and Peggy Winpenny.

Dinner with Comm.

Successful Publ. Rel. mtg for Parents, preachers, et. al.

Long talk with Emilio** & Ann Knectle [*sic*] before bed at midnight.

Very fine day.

———

After being with Young Life for the first twenty years, Wally How-ard decided to pursue other ministry opportunities, most notably eighteen years as editor of Faith At Work *magazine.*

Friday, April 1 (Washington, D. C.)

Tough Mig dev late 2 Ergomar & #3 All night the pain continued. Don't get it??! Long conf. with Wally—apparently he is going to resign.

Several talks with Bud,[8] Add, Roy.

1) Aft. Short interview with Sen. Symington.

2) Grand chat with Charlie McWhorter.

3) A most pleasant & interesting surprise at the warm reception & response from Warren Elliot, Legis[lative] Asst. to Sen Gordon Allott,[9] he took

4) me to Senate, got Allott & we had a great chat. Real rapport!

Took train for Chi.

---

[6] Grant Morrill and T. Guthrie Speers, Jr., were two of the clergymen who had signed the anti-Young Life statement.

[7] Emilio Knechtle was an importer and friend of Dave Weyerhaeuser's who was on the local committee.

[8] Local staff man Bud Bylsma.

[9] United States Senator from Colorado, Gordon Allott.

*Jim addresses students at Fuller
Theological Seminary in California,
ca. 1960, as staff men Bob Frey (left) and
Ken Wright (right) enjoy listening in.*

Saturday, April 2 (Chicago)

[...]

Arr. Chi 8:30A.

Mostly loafed & got some much needed rest this aft.

For two months now I have carefully studied my prayer life & kept record of various responses. The wide discrepancy—in degree of openness to prayer & ability to stick to it—(from day to day) is a matter of considerable perplexity. Witness numerous days when heart and mind is responsive to idea & prayer is relatively easy—and equal number of days when there is little or no predisposition to pray & the act is more like a matter of just hanging on & plowing through. Goodly number of apparent ANSWERS—rewarding & inspirational—other petitions seem to go unheard. Yet it cannot be so! Ability to "praise" & "thank" & "meditate" seems generally on the increase. Biggest question ?—Why the days of relative prayerlessness??

Monday, April 18 (Knoxville, Tennessee)

Another WONDERFUL DAY. So good I can't believe it and can't thank the Lord enough. Very tense before assembly at So. Hi. The Lord gave me one of the great responses—students (specially some fine big boys) Principal, Bruce, cool before […] effusive in his praise afterward. Teachers, too.

Then lunch & a great time of prayer with Geo.[10] & Charlie Scott. Charlie is a choice trophy. Then Dr. Andy Holt[11] picked me up—to his home for dinner. I loved the guy right off. The whole family very nice.

Fine evening meeting—disappointing crowd but some excellent new adults & kids.

———

Charlie Scott was indeed "a choice trophy"—after college he came on Young Life staff, where he continues to serve to the present day.

The annual staff conference was set to begin May 1 at Silver Cliff. Jim felt compelled to call a Staff Day of Prayer for April 28. The primary concern was staffing. He wrote to the staff and board: "Perhaps one of the greatest crises in our history—the issue is LEADERSHIP, recruiting, training, assigning, moving, leaders. We are stepping into the greatest panorama of opportunity ever afforded us."

He continued, "The Advisory Committee faces its most serious responsibility in preparing recommendations for Staff Conference discussion. Our only hope of being right and finding the way is the guidance of the Holy Spirit."

Thursday, April 28 (Star Ranch)
Day of Prayer—the greatest, for me at least, in years. Office force in A.M.—warmth and liberty—I put emphasis upon meditations.

Advisory Comm. in afternoon. Same spirit.

---

[10] Knoxville area director George Blood.

[11] Andrew David Holt, PhD (1904–1987). Holt was president of the University of Tennessee from 1959–1970. In addition to his academic accomplishments, he was known for his sense of humor and strong Christian faith.

Good evening mtg. Geo Sheffer spoke—Staff Prayer Mtg. Excellent spirit in camp.

Sunday, May 1
Great Class—221. John 21 & some more on "The Christian's** Privilege in Prayer."

To Frontier after Dinner**¹² with Anne Cheairs & Mitch.

The greatest opening ever** for Staff Conference. I broke in to Song Service for half hour of MEDITATION and prayer.—Then spoke to them on the church & the pastor's¹³ role in starting Y.L.

—⁓—

While much good was happening with the Young Life work around the country, Jim's personal life continued to be troubled. Maxine's various health problems seemed never to end, nor did the Rayburns' financial difficulties. On a trip to Minnesota in May, Jim had some severe health troubles of his own.

From Minnesota he went to New York City where Young Life was trying to establish a foothold. As soon as he returned home, however, the top priority became his health.

Thursday, May 12
                    Bad Mig—Dev fast enroute Bldr. 3 Ergomar aborted by dinner time. Worked hard at the office. Had lunch with Gus[s] Hill.

Home for a few minutes then Drove to Boulder—Altho I got sick enroute I had a wonderful time with little Mark and Ann—then a nice dinner with Jim, Ann & Mark—Visited awhile with Ann then drove to Denver—"Cosmo"¹⁴ & to bed.

Good day in spite of pain in head. Very prayerful about the Board Mtg.

---

¹² Sunday dinner, that is, lunch.

¹³ First Presbyterian Church of Gainesville and Clyde Kennedy.

¹⁴ The Cosmopolitan Hotel in Denver.

Friday, May 13 (Denver)

An unexpected blessing to-day. The long hours with the Finance Committee was [*sic*] enjoyable & productive—the spirit was excellent—obviously the evidence of the Holy Spirit overcoming some of the weaknesses of former sessions. [...] Exec Comm. good during lunch. Ann & Mark came for Dinner with Don Mitchell[15] & me. A truly great day.

Saturday, May 14 (Denver)

Up early after very restless night—Talked to D—— before breakfast—but, after very earnest prayer—He agreed to give $25,000 for Headquarters—I'm so very thankful to God!

All day in Board Mtg. was just great—my report better—& better received than in years.

[...]

Long & very cordial talk with Larry Kulp until 11:30 p. Couldn't eat to-day. Ate late in room. Tired!

Sunday, May 15 (Denver)

Severe Mig—Aft. 3 Ergomar—slow relief.

The Board Mtg continued & closed on a fine note. Nothing said about my pers. financial problems—I am close to discouragement—and pray that I may remember—Another looks after me & mine.[16]

Arr home at 4 P. Found Maxine very ill.

Tuesday, May 17 (St. Paul, Minnesota)

Arr St Paul 8:15.

Called F——. He couldn't see me—wonder why.

Went to see Mrs. C——. That dear lady always showers the blessing

---

[15] Donald F. Mitchell was the younger brother of John and Orville Mitchell. At the time of this entry he was serving on the board of trustees.

[16] Another was indeed looking out for Jim and his. As a surprise gift the staff raised $6,000 for the Rayburns. Prior to this magnanimous gesture, Maxine and Jim were considering selling their home.

of friendship & help on me. Felt very bad. She sent me to her Cardiologist. Car[d]iogram, Fluoroscope, Chest X-Rays—have some trouble in Aorta, accounting for my pain. Missed appt. with Mrs. W.

Tom Starr[17] took me to train.

Friday, May 20 (New York City)
This was a great day. Up at 8.

To N.Y.C. with Harve** [sic, Harv][18] at 9:00. Had a very fine talk with Roger Hull[19] at his office. He thinks budget of $35,000.00 for City Area (Includ. Conn. & Jersey suburbs) is feasible. Offered to help with luncheon for men ("Two or three times if you want")!

Excellent talk with Harve** [sic]. Right at the main tensions—good response in fact extremely encouraging. Believe we can work him. Want to give it a TRY! [...]

Thursday, May 26
Called John Karabin**. Arranged to go to Glockner** & have the tests here instead of Denver or Memphis.

Entered Penrose Hospital 2pm.

Friday, May 27 (Penrose Hospital, Colorado Springs)
Started tests

Upper G.I. to-day

Saturday, May 28 (Penrose Hospital, Colorado Springs)
Lower G.I. tests to-day.

[Drs.] Charlie Fisher, [blank space][20]

---

17 Bill Starr's brother.

18 Staff man Harv Oostdyk.

19 James Roger Hull (1907–1972). Hull was a senior executive with Mutual of New York, taking over the company the next year. He had been instrumental in Billy Graham's Madison Square Garden Crusade three years earlier.

20 Jim has left a blank space, probably because he did not catch the name of the fourth

John Karabin, Jim McMullen giving me a lot of attention.

Very pleased to have them working on this—and to be here!

Sunday, May 29 (Penrose Hospital, Colorado Springs)
Just resting.

Monday, May 30 (Penrose Hospital, Colorado Springs)
Drs. conferred here in my room. No heart or vascular disease—definite "internal organic disease"—unknown as yet. Will continue tests & repeat some.

Tuesday, May 31 (Penrose Hospital, Colorado Springs)
Back at the Upper G.I. tests. They found it! Gastric Ulcer—large—I'm relieved that they know now, & the Drs are pleased as kids. Now have to try to determine if it is benign & treat—if it doesn't clear up quickly has to come out.

Wednesday, June 1 (Penrose Hospital, Colorado Springs)
Dr. Bob Smith did the Gastroscopy this a.m. A very rough & trying proceedure [*sic*]. In operating room over an hour for prep et. al. They said the Gastroscope was only in me a little over 10 minutes.

Found the ulcer—Bob says "a giant one." Looked small to me. Very sore throat but they gave me plenty of Demerol.

Had a fine long talk with Dr. Lloyd Lunsten** to-night.

Thursday, June 2 (Penrose Hospital, Colorado Springs)
A comfortable day. Just read a lot & fooled around. Enjoying the TV. Glad Maxine had me get it.

Sure have had the fine Drs.[:] Karabin, Fisher, Smith, McMullen, Lunsten.

---

doctor. It was probably Bob Smith or Lloyd Lunsten, both mentioned later.

Friday, June 3 (Penrose Hospital, Colorado Springs)

Mig to-nite—2 Ergomar

Drs said I could leave to-morrow and go to Frontier—complete rest—
Charlie says he wants me to be a "complete bum" for the next month.

A nother good visit with Dr. Lloyd Lunsten to-nite.

---

*In a letter to the staff, Maxine explained Jim's health situation.
"Jim's present illness (mainly severe chest pain, great fatigue, and
general feeling of illness) started about 15 days ago during the Board
Meeting. Last July he did have an acute attack of this same thing
but not so severely. . . . Monday, May 30, [the doctors] told him they
wanted him to stay for more tests and X-rays, since they had not
found the cause of what they termed as 'definite internal organic
disease'. They now think surgery may be a possibility if the new
series of tests etc. do not prove conclusive. Such surgery would be
'exploratory'—they do suspect cancer of course, and we are thankful they are so thorough."*

*While recuperating at Frontier and Malibu Jim took an extra
interest in the work crew.*

Monday, June 20 (Frontier Ranch)

Great closing service for second week of camp. Several of the Foreign
Exchange students strongly affected, perhaps some even closed in with
the Lord.

Tuesday, June 21 (Frontier Ranch)

Lv. Camp at 3:30 P. Took the whole work crew to the Timberline Camp.
32 on horseback.

Walked them to the saddle to see the Chalk Creek Gulch & Antero,
etc.

Prepared dinner for the entire 47—hamburgers, hash-browns, fruit,
cookies, milk.

A wonderful time of devotions around the fire—cold, windy—a rough night at Timberline.

Wednesday, June 22 (Frontier Ranch)

Arose at 5:30A after a practically sleepless night. Prepared breakfast for all and had everyone properly fed at 7:30.

Drove the jeep down the trail—fully loaded—arr. in camp about 9:30.

———

Though still recuperating, Jim was able to travel to Canada for his annual visit to Malibu, this time during a week for adults. Then it was back to Frontier for the third annual Committeemen's Conference.

Saturday, July 9 (Malibu Club)

This was the best day of rest, fun, exercise & good fellowship that I have had in many a moon. I skied five times for a total of about eight miles and did not get as tired as the first three minutes made me five days ago. The friendship of the work-crew and my fellowship with them is a constant source of joy and inspiration. Also the counsellors. And a number of the adults are fun to be with.

Nothing at all to-night. Went to bed early—after a beautiful evening ride on Jervis Inlet in the speedboat.

———

Sunday, July 17 (Frontier Ranch)

Planning session & prayer with staff about Committeemens Conf.

Pleasant day.

Conference started at dinner 7p. About 75 here.

In spite of several complimentary remarks afterward I honestly felt that I did very poorly on opening address. Felt badly about it. Prayed. Trust that the dear Lord will overrule & use it for some good purpose.

Tuesday, July 19 (Frontier Ranch)

Highlight of the day was taking the committeemen & wives to Caballo—where I got the same impression as last year—that they are thrilled at the prospect of the new adult ranch—and it seemed to me that the Lord wanted us to have it and that He will work it out.

Wednesday, July 20 (Frontier Ranch)

A fine closing day of the conference. Excellent spirit. I did much better to-nite on the closing address—

    Drove to Colo Spgs after midnight.

Thursday, July 21[21]

My Two Months X-Rays. & visit with Dr. Fisher. Prognosis Good!

    Back to Frontier about 3P.

Friday, July 22 (Frontier Ranch)

Left at noon to take 68 work crew kids (a few counselors) to the "Bear Lake" Country on Mt. Harvard.

    Rode horseback—a great trip—beautiful.

    Wonderful evening with the kids around the campfire.

Saturday, July 23 (Frontier Ranch)

Up at 6:30. Most of the kids too cold to sleep last night.

    Led the entire crowd above "Bear Lake" & then went to try some scaling but found no routes I wanted to use with the kids.

    Hiked all the way back to the road. Rained some. Very pleasant trip. In fact "inspirational."**

    [...]

Tuesday, July 26 (Frontier Ranch)

Up at 6—completely awake. The best time of prayer & med. in some time—but I am still very troubled about my weakness along this line.

---

[21] Jim's fifty-first birthday.

Wednesday, August 3 (Malibu Club)

Specially thankful to God for this wonderful day.

Spoke at evening round-up[22] on "No one ever spoke ... no one ever did ... LIKE HE DID." Got a tremendous reception—just bowled me over—altho I was an hour long the response was terrific. A girl—hi school grad from one of the boats—accepted the Lord wonderfully after the mtg.

A great time with the work crew this aft. on "Love, etc."

Long evening of fellowship with Rog, Loy[23] & Jim Shelton[24] after mtg.

Saturday, September 3 (Frontier Ranch)

Slowly packed up for home—after spending some enjoyable hours up on the Princeton Trail & at Cabin site with Bill Mitchell & Laurence** Bender. We surveyed the route for extension of road from present Timberline Camp to proposed cabin site.[25]

Left Frontier late afternoon.

Every year it is harder to leave. Such a grand place, so many wonderful memories—a grand summer. Very thankful to God for these last 10 summers at "The Lookout."

---

[22] The nightly club meeting.

[23] G. Rogers "Rog" and Loy Ann Carrington. His father, Glenn Carrington, was a significant Young Life donor. Rog became a Christian as a Seattle high school student at a Young Life camp (Add Sewell was his leader). The younger couple became close friends of Jim's.

[24] Jim Shelton was a long-time California staff man, just starting his career when this entry was written.

[25] The cabin was eventually built and was named "The Chalet," based on its Swiss-style design.

Summer gave way to the regular school year routine, including the race to finish Young Life's fiscal year in the black.

Jim and Maxine became grandparents a second time when Ann and Jim Patterson's second son, Matt, was born on September 14.

In other family news, Sue had spent a semester in Mexico City at the University of Mexico. By the time the new academic year rolled around, however, she had decided to pursue a career as a flight attendant with Braniff Airways.

Wednesday, September 28
A very good day at the office. We need only $17,000 to complete the annual financial need! It was about $85,000 at the beginning of Sept.

Took a good nap at home this aft.

Friday, September 30 (on the train)
Only $10,000 needed to complete the year. D—— offered his Dec. $5,000 which, if I decide to use would reduce to 5.

Took train for Chi to-day.

Saturday, October 1 (Chicago)
Went to Iowa 42–North W. 0 game with Herb Taylor. To Ldrs Wk End Camp with Bill Starr.

Good time with the kids to-night.

Sunday, October 2 (Chicago)
A great wk-end with the leaders.

Took "United" Jet to DV. Arr. home about 7 pm.

Monday, October 3
Tried to get office work done—it's slow. Too many entirely different things!

Tuesday, October 4
X-Rays at Penrose.

Nice staff picnic in the Aspen this noon.

Conf. with Charlie Fisher. Thinks my stomach o k.

Wednesday, October 5 (travelling)

We finally discovered that we have made the budget again this year! Got out the official announcement just before leaving after a "frantic" morning in the office trying to get ready to leave.

Home to pack & lunch. Goodbye to Sue who will be gone to "Braniff" before I get back.

Lv C.S. 2:00. First Stop Las Vegas 265 miles 6:35

Decided to drive on Left Albu 8:35.

Arr. Gallup [New Mexico] 11P Ate supper Lv 11:20.

Arr Show Low [Arizona] 1:30A.

Sunday, October 9 (Southern California)

This was another day for which I have special reason to thank the Lord. Mtg in Glendale this aft. 85 leaders! and to-night at Paul's house** about 25 of crowd of 50 were college leaders. I was "flat" all day & my brain was weary—had a hard time keeping my thoughts tracking—yet Tom Bade [...] and a number of others said I was effective & the young leaders told them so. Only the Lord!

Watched Pirates beat Yankees 3–2 in very thrilling game.

World Series now 2–2.

Wednesday, October 19 (Vancouver)

Slept late—good rest.

[...]

25 mtgs in last 12 days—over 4000 miles of travel included—only day off—had to travel 1000 mi L.A. to Portland with a stop to see Ann.[26]

---

[26] Ann and her family were now living in the San Jose area.

—∾—

In November Rayburn sailed for a fourth time to Europe. This time he took eight committeemen on the twenty-day trip. The journey had much the same agenda as had his previous trip with the staff men, with most of their time spent in West Germany.

After visiting France, Denmark, and Sweden, Rayburn returned to America.

Tuesday, December 6

Better at the office work this a.m. There is such a staggering pile of it.

Spent an hour reporting to the office crew about the trip[27]—glad I did. Feel that it was worthwhile.

Oh how we need to pray—for oppressed people—for those without hope of the LIGHT—for the path ahead—the FUTURE of our work.

—∾—

Sunday, December 25

A good Christmas day in spite of the normal** sense of loss that our girlies couldn't be with us—for the first time in 23 years!

Tuesday, December 27

Spent the morning in the office—it is hard to see how to approach the job now & get the most necessary things accomplished and eliminate some of the present work. Advisory Committee must prayerfully find the answer to this—if possible—at Feb. 6, 7 mtg.

---

[27] His just-completed trip to Europe.

1961

Memoranda

'61 Mileage Record.

Jan.	11,300
Feb.	9,600
Mar.	10,050
Apr.	7,400
May	13,700+
Five Month Total.	52,050
June, July, Aug	10,000
Sept.	6,450
Oct.	10,100
Nov.	9,000
Dec.	8,000
	43,500
'61 Total.	95,550

JIM'S MILEAGE RECORD FOR 1961

Jim's diary for 1961 is one of his longest, and for good reason: it was an intense year for Rayburn. Young Life continued to increase in prestige and exposure, and Jim was very much the face of the ministry, resulting in almost 100,000 miles of travel. The year also saw tremendous health problems for Jim, as well as an increased focus on prayer toward the end of the year.

Though Jim did not like to use statistics as a justification for the ministry, an April article in Eternity *magazine noted that Young Life had a full-time staff of 120 who, along with 450 volunteer leaders, reached a total of 50,000 high school students a year.*

The year started with Sue marrying Milford Smith (known as "Smitty") in Dallas in February.

Thursday, February 16 (San Jose, California)

Spent several hours with Ann & babes—took Mark for a long walk. What a joy the little boys are.

To Mt Hermon[1] with Mitch.

The Evening Mtg "The Past—Corners We've Rounded On The Way To To-Day," was great & exceeded my expectations—just got thru 4 of 8 pt outline & quit while I was way** ahead[:]

1) The influence of L.S.[2] emphasis upon Person of Christ & Gospel of Grace.

2) The Fellowship & Encouragement of great men.

3) The Personal-Contact Ministry (Development.)

4) Dev. of the "Importance of People"-Concept.

Sunday, February 19

Lv San Frans. 8:20A

Arr DV 11:20A

---

[1] The Mount Hermon Christian Conference Center in Mount Hermon, California. Jim was addressing a staff gathering.

[2] Lewis Sperry Chafer.

Sue & Milford met me. We had a pleasant, interesting visit and a very nice day. Reception at the house for them, with lots of our dear friends in. A surprisingly pleasant & enjoyable occassion [*sic*].

[...]

Bone weary to-night. To bed early & could not sleep.

———

As Young Life continued to hit its stride, its prestige was evident in the fact that two popular governors joined its board. Frank Morrison was the governor of Nebraska, while Mark Hatfield held the position in Oregon.

Monday, March 27 (Eugene, Oregon)

Personal—for me only. This morning started in a most unusual way—at 5A had headache—took a little Emperin—at 6:30 free of pain & awake—with no "strain" went directly to prayer—had the best hour of prayer I've had in years (morning, that is).

The mysterious thing called "liberty"—communication—the Lord greatly helped & blessed me.

Lv Pd³ 8:35 Good fellowship with Jack Potts on the plane.

Arr. Eugene 9:35 Fine time w. Jack & Bill Green.

Called Mark Hatfield. So friendly & gracious! He enthusiastically agreed to come on the Board of Directors. I can't thank the Lord enough!

Very worthwhile time with Committee (lunch). Heartwarming fellowship with Bill Bright.

Good fellowship & prayer with Bill Green, Tom Raley, Jack & Margie Potts. Then the big banquet—200 [—] went very well! Gov. Morrison made a hit—sure is for us. Coffee time at Greens'—exc[ellent] contacts. (Sue Chalmers—Dr. Glen Gordon's wife from Gainesville club). Don Rogers**, a County Supt. School—great backer.

---

³ Jim had been in Portland.

A blessed, wonderful day! God was in <u>it</u>!

—∾∾—

In April Jim addressed a conference in Philadelphia of East Coast committee members.

Later that month, Rayburn and the headquarters staff moved into new offices in Colorado Springs. Jim was proud of the ultra-modern facility he had helped design at 720 West Monument.

Increasingly, his health was becoming a problem.

Friday, April 14 (Philadelphia)
Lv N.Y. 9A

Great luncheon at Philly—Union League Club. I again emphasized the uniqueness of Y.L and the imperative nature of the task. 1) No other work does this. 2) Only effective approach at area of greatest need. 3) Main thrust & principal impact among uncommitted. 4) Works across whole spectrum of adolescent society.

Again I did a better job in this essential area—best I've done—good practice—very thankful to God. Exc[ellent] contact with Allen [*sic*, Allyn] Bell.[4] Amazing afternoon.

Opening night of Eastern Reg. Comm. Conference—"What's Happening In Y.L." Emphasis upon long-range look (21 yrs) at evidence of this "thrust" & impact. [Moe, Vinnie et al.][5]

A wonderful evening—much evidence, internal & external of Presence & Power of the Holy Spirit. Again great thankfulness that He enabled me to do the "best I can do." Wonderful conf. with Coe,[6] [Bob]

---

[4] Allyn R. Bell, Jr., was the head of the Pew Foundation Trust.

[5] Moe and Vinnie were two young men who had experienced dramatic conversions through Young Life. Vinnie Pasquale, a former drug addict from Newark, New Jersey, had given his life to Christ at Frontier in 1956, and shared his testimony at the 1957 Billy Graham Crusade in Madison Square Garden.

[6] Doug Coe. Coe was a former staff man for Salem, Oregon. His club was even larger than Rayburn's Colorado Springs chapter, reaching a record attendance of 452 kids from Salem High School. After he left Young Life in the mid-1950s he began his

Patton**, Add, afterward.

Saturday, April 15 (Philadelphia)

A.M. Address on "Uniqueness in Y.L."

1) "Contact"—emphasis & development—"personal friendship evangelism." "Win the right ..." ++

2) Y.L. "Club." Pioneer, creative exploration & development of Christian <u>mtgs</u> for <u>non-Christians</u>—only ones—not "clubs"—not "club leaders"—"People leaders." (N.T. "flavor & example"—primitive Christianity—our Lord's attitude & example. "teaching situations**.")

3) Communications (Semantic problem) (Early emphasis on modern English transl[ations]) Early "light" "sin to bore ..." Probably best I've done. <u>Board & Staff</u> needs <u>more of</u> this!—

Spoke on "<u>Y.L. & The Church</u>" to-nite. Went well. [...]

Memorable day that the Lord enabled me to confess to Doug Coe my neglect & lack of appreciation. His response overwhelming.

Sunday, April 16 (Philadelphia)

I thought the conference closed well—very good spirit—just wonder what will come of it. So hard to know if Christians will change—got to!

To Princeton—in spite of extreme weariness had a wonderful time of fellowship with <u>Don Williams</u>, Charlie & <u>Caroline</u> Brown, <u>Burt</u> & <u>Ruthie</u> Chamberlin, <u>Rog</u> & Loy Carrington, Add & <u>Vetie</u>. (Those underlined are Y.L. "converts") [...]

Wednesday, April 19

Called at 7A. "<u>Staggering</u>." Lv. Det. 9A.

I got very ill out of Chicago—could hardly change planes at Denver.

Home to bed about noon.

---

ministry with The Fellowship Foundation in Washington, D. C.

Dr. Fisher came—apparently nothing wrong with me to speak of. Seems funny.

Thursday, April 20

First day at my new office! Just marvelous. I had a good time reporting to the office crew for an hour—spent the rest of the day reading my mail.

Restful evening at home.

Friday, April 21

A productive and joyous day at my beautiful new office—in spite of lots of work that is hard for me now because of my extreme weariness.

Saturday, April 22

Couldn't get to sleep last night. Passed up my "sleeping spell" about 8P. Slept only about 2A to 6A. I've got to get some way to rest.

Sunday, April 23

An hour of prayer with the staff before Sunday School. Good class. Spoke on Matt. 17. Particularly "Faith ... mustard seed ... move mountain." (Don't really believe God for anything in particular.)

A good time of prayer this aft. at the office (above)—another fine time with the hdqts. crew 4:30–7P.

Monday, April 24

An early morning prayer session that was definite and down to business.

Much dictation—all the old stuff!

Rec'd the first contribution from the Pew Foundation—$5000.00 for the general fund.

The new hdqts continues to bless & inspire. How very thankful to God I am for this "exceeding abundantly, above ..."[7]

---

[7] From Ephesians 3:20–21: "Now unto him that is able to do exceeding abundantly above all that we ask or think, according to the power that worketh in us, unto him be glory ..." (KJV).

Thursday, April 27

Feel awful bad. Finished up office work pretty well—so thankful for the new office!

Had to take codiene [*sic*] for stomach & chest pain before leaving home at 4:30p.

LV DV 7 p.

Arr San F 8:30.

Wonderful dinner & evening with Ann, Jim, Mark & Matt.

Wednesday, May 3

Good time of prayer with the men—and a good day of work—easier to get the job done at this beautiful new office.

A lot more pain—specially around noon.

Friday, May 5

To Penrose for X-Rays. Jim McMullen showed me the pictures. Have the ulcer back—same place.

Did considerable work at office tho felt very bum.

To [Dr.] Charlie Fisher ... home for dinner.

To Penrose Hospital ...

Saturday, May 6–Sunday, May 7

[This entry is written across two days.]

In hospital very restless. Can't enjoy reading or anything, really. No pain except for mild mig headache.

[...]

In a letter to the staff, Roy Riviere explained that Jim's doctors had decided to treat the ulcer non-surgically. If that did not work, they would have to remove the affected part of Jim's stomach.

Riviere explained Jim's attitude: "The boss begrudges the nuisance and the inevitable restraint this puts on his activities for Young Life, but otherwise he's his usual self—kidding the hospital staff, and raring to be gone."

*Immediately upon leaving the hospital, Rayburn attended
the spring board meeting, being held in Colorado so the members
could see the new headquarters.*

Friday, May 12

Awoke at 4:45, quite rested. Fresh enough & "open" enough to enjoy a
wonderful hour of med. and prayer.

The day with the Board (mostly Comm. mtgs.) went very well. In
fact they had already given me what I asked before it came up. Never had
a more relaxed & pleasant day with the Board of Directors.

Note from Heindrick [*sic*, Hendrick] Kraemer[8] thrilled me. Gave
appt.** asked.

Saturday, May 13

Excellent Board mtg. Enjoyed all of it. Much talk by Bill K[iesewetter],
Dave [Weyerhaeuser], et. al. about getting my stomach operated on.
Guess I'll have to.

Sue & Milford arr. & went to dinner with the Board to-nite.

Talked to the Board at close of eve. session on Psa 121:8.[9]

Tuesday, May 16

[…]

Went to [Dr.] Charlie Fisher & [Dr.] John Karabin**. The stomach
surgery is scheduled for June 5th.

Friday, May 19 (Baltimore)

7:00A

To Baltimore** for a preacher's** [*sic*] meeting. Didn't amount to much.

---

[8] Dr. Hendrick Kraemer (1888–1965). Kraemer was a renowned Dutch theologian.
Jim had read some of his work and was excited that the elderly professor had agreed
to meet with him on his upcoming trip to Europe. The two men had a lengthy visit at
Kraemer's home in Holland less than three weeks later on May 29.

[9] "The LORD will keep
your going out and your coming in
from this time forth and forevermore."

To Washington for a long conference with Dr. John MacKay[10] which <u>did</u> amount to very much. Most interesting, instructive & cordial.

To Baltimore** for banquet—I had Add & Rog Carrington speak at points in my address which took the strain off of my speaking engagement.

To Princeton for the nite.

———

From May 20–31, Jim made his fifth trip to Europe, continuing to help establish the work in France and Germany, and looking into possibilities for other countries.

According to Jim Rayburn III in From Bondage to Liberty: Dance, Children, Dance, *Jim's health troubles were due in part to a drug he had been prescribed, Dexamyl. "By the early sixties Jim was beginning to experience adverse reactions to the new 'wonder drug' that he'd been taking ... Dexamyl, an amphetamine known several decades later as a type of 'speed,' causes marked insomnia, irritability, hyperactivity, and personality changes. Dizziness, tremors, headaches, dryness of the mouth, diarrhea, and various gastrointestinal disturbances are other adverse reactions. At one time or another, Jim experienced every one of these symptoms, yet no one suspected the cause, least of all his doctors." (The Dexamyl prescription most likely came from a physician in Washington state, not one of his regular doctors.)*

It was decided that Jim should have over half of his stomach removed. Though not an uncommon procedure at the time, it is no longer practiced, and for good reason—Rayburn was rarely able to digest food properly for the remainder of his life.

---

[10] Dr. John Alexander Mackay (1889–1983). A former missionary, the Scottish-born Mackay became president of Princeton Seminary in 1936, the same year that Rayburn applied (and was rejected). He retired from that position in 1959 and began teaching Spanish at American University in Washington. Mackay coined the phrase, "winning the right to be heard," to describe Young Life's method.

As soon as he could, Jim retreated to Frontier to recuperate.
His journal is mostly silent for the summer. All of his entries from
June 4–July 23 are recorded here in their entirety.

Sunday, June 4
To Penrose Hospital this p m for surgery.

Monday, June 5
Stomach surgery this A.M.

—⁓—

Thursday, June 15
Out of the hospital to-day. Shaky but feeling good.

Friday, June 16
Around home.

Saturday, June 17 (Frontier Ranch)
Maxine & I went to Frontier this aft. Very happy to get back to "The Lookout."

—⁓—

Sunday, July 23 (Frontier Ranch)
A wonderful evening of prayer & fellowship up at "The Chalet" site with Mitch & Bill. The most perfect weather I've ever experienced at night at high altitude—almost balmy, calm, moonlite—spectacular beauty.

—⁓—

Rayburn, Starr, and Mitchell did not know it as they prayed together on Mt. Princeton, but each of them would serve as the head of Young Life. Altogether, the three of them led the mission of Young Life for a staggering forty-six years, from its beginning until Mitch left the president's office in 1986.

Jim was increasingly feeling the need for concerted prayer on the part of the staff. Twenty Septembers of seeing God's miraculous provision for Young Life's end-of-the-fiscal-year financial needs led him to invite all staff men with over four years of tenure to join him at Frontier for three days of prayer.

The staff remaining at home were apprised of the agenda and invited to pray themselves, specifically for "direction for our future, September finances, and power for the club year now beginning."

Sunday, September 10

Exc. time with the Class this A.M. on "Pastoral Epistles." More enthus. response than I've had for _____.[11]

To Frontier with carload of the men this aft.

Very fine time of discussion & fellowship regarding the Prayer Meeting that is to begin in the morning.

Monday, September 11 (Frontier Ranch)

Psa 63, Eph 1, Eph 3

45 or 50 staff men began our 3 Day session for Prayer this a.m.

There was considerable blessing—difficult to evaluate—and a surprising amount of time spent in actual prayer. Good attention.

Tuesday, September 12 (Frontier Ranch)

AN AMAZING DAY. Up at 4:55A. All the group praying to-gether at 5:30A. First half hour praise & thanks—then I was impelled to speak to them of our MISSION & the great things—admonishing it was time to thing [*sic*] positively—not always "what is wrong." Amazing, unexpected response & an "inspired" time of prayer before breakfast.

The rest of the day was outstanding—it is hard to know what to say about a time like this.

---

[11] Blank space is Jim's.

Wednesday, September 13 (Frontier Ranch)

> Mig—early—2 Ergomar (under tongue) slow relief.
> First Mig req[uiring] ergot in at least six weeks I believe. ??

Another great early morning session. And the best prayer meeting about "money" that I ever attended, I believe—10A till 12.

The morning times** of prayer were particularly** meaningful for me. I got very weary—surprisingly enough, for the first time—aft & evening.

Excellent spirit at the close. Communion service.

Thursday, September 14

Drove home with 5 guys 9A–11. Good prayer time in the car.

Worked at office.

Went to [Dr.] John Karabin.

Pooped out! Went home for rest of the day.

—·———

The focused time of prayer at Frontier had an impact on Rayburn's personal spiritual life. For the rest of the year he was more diligent than he had been in the previous months about spending extended amounts of time with the Lord.

One of the things the Lord was increasingly putting on Jim's heart was Young Life's relationship to the larger church. Toward that end he had determined to bring together leading Protestant churchmen from around the country to discuss Young Life, young people, and the church. Eventually the meetings would be called the Chicago Fellowship and be the apex of Jim's career as a leader of leaders. While in its planning stages, Jim referred to it as "the National Pastors' Conference."

Sunday, September 24 (New York City)

(Good time of thanksgiving and prayer on the plane)

Up at 6:30A. Pretty weary.

To train at 8A.

John O'N.[12] joined me at Trenton—good trip.

Arr. Wash. 11:45

To Rudy Vetter's for dinner.

A wonderful afternoon with Dr. & Mrs. MacKay—took Rudy & John with me. Dr. MacK very interested, "committed" to the Natl. Pastors Conference. So interested I cancelled my plane to Pittsburg[h]— got one at 8:30p. To Pitts.-Hilton @ 10:30. Talked to Harry Mac, Bill Kiesewetter, Sam Shoemaker & to bed—so weary I can hardly stand or see!

Supper in room @ 12M & to bed.

Monday, September 25 (Pittsburgh, Pennsylvania)

Headachy a.m.

Up at 7:30. (Still awfully early—considering yesterday) BY FAR THE BEST HOUR OF PRAYER (ALONE) THAT I CAN REMEMBER. More concentration—more ground covered—God is greatly helping me!

Breakfast in the room.

A long talk with Harry MacDonald. Then a chat with Steve Jenks. Lunch with Max Lightner & John Alter. Then a wonderful time with Sam Shoemaker. He will go on the Pastors Conference! Very thankful. Back to the hotel—very beat, and off to N.Y. Good Day!

Plane late—arr. N.Y. 8:15.

Bert & Rog met me—To "Intern[ational] Hotel" for conferences— very "beat" but thankful to the Lord for this day.

Tuesday, September 26 (New York City)

Tough to get up shortly after 7:30A but it turned out well & I had good time before leaving for Mr. Hull's office.

Good conf. with Roger Hull. Again he promised to help organize a committee and raise next yrs. budget.

[…] Add took me back to hotel & to airport—we had a long confer-

---

12 Staff member John O'Neil.

ence about the preachers Natl. Conf...

Lv N.Y 5P Arr DL 6:15. E——C——failed to meet me. To Baker [Hotel.] Too tired to do anything.

Wednesday, September 27 (Dallas)

Awoke @ 5A w Headache. 2 Emp #3 & sleep aborted it.

What a day. Tried hard but couldn't do anything well. Prayer time in a.m. was poor. Breakfast with E——. She couldn't (or wouldn't) give anything. Talked to E——C——. He said he'd "try" to get something but never showed up. Talked to Sheff. Then to John E. [Mitchell.]

Went to train Lv DL 1:30p.

Read & slept all afternoon.

Thursday, September 28

A good time of prayer on the train before 5A arrival & at home—and a good time of prayer with Maxine. To office—read lots of mail—checked income—$40,000 to go!

Briefed the office men & prayer with them.

[...]

Monday, October 2

A great day—full & complicated but so much for which to thank the Lord.

We still needed over $26,000 for Sept. Receipts postmarked Sept 30 & before apply. Over $17,000 came in to-day!

Tuesday, October 3

This was the great day. Sept. Income reached $100,000 completing our '60–'61 budget of $700,000.

Needing $7,000 I called (as req. by him) H. H.—he gave $2,500—such great fellowship over the phone—and told me to use it as "incentive gift" to get the rest. $3,000 finally came in from D——S—— as promised & the rest came from here & there—giving us (with H. H.'s promised gift) $7,600! & we closed the books on '60–'61. Over

$100,000.00 income for September. Over $700,000.00 income for year '60–'61. Thanks be to God. And I'm not forgetting PRAISE for <u>what</u> <u>He</u> <u>is</u>—regardless of income or ans. prayer or anything.

Wednesday, October 4

Tough getting started. Will I ever understand why it is often so hard to get down to business & pray—specially when I have so very much for which to be thankful.

Prayer with the office crew.

Letter to Board & Staff notifying them of the marvelous wind-up of our fiscal year.

Home to look at World Series N.Y 2–Cincin 0.

To Office—fast work on a lot of letters.

To "Eagle" 5:55** p. Dinner—an excellent time of prayer.

Monday, October 9 (Lincoln, Nebraska)

After going to my room @ midnight was sleepless & had a wonderful time of prayer and reading the Word. Art Slaikeu[13] was—great blessing. He "went for" the Preachers Conf.

Finally slept about 2:30A. Exceptionally good time of prayer & reading first. Awoke at 7:30 for another good "quiet time." Breakfast with the Gov. Then to his office & downtown**. Conf & prayer with Rex @ 11A. To Ministers Luncheon. Rev V——W——(Pres) & a M.E. [Methodist Episcopal] gave me a bad time—I felt sorry for them & for those they lead & the Lord greatly helped me. Somewhat more satisf. time with the city's C.E. Dirs.[14]—Then a swell meeting with our Nebr. U. leaders.

Dinner @ the [Governor's] Mansion.

---

[13] Dr. Arthur L. Slaikeu. He was the pastor of First Baptist Church in Lincoln. A year earlier Jim had written about him in his journal: "He is CHOICE. A rare find for whom I deeply thank the Lord."

[14] Christian Education Directors.

Fine Mtg w. Committee.

Visit with the Gov. To bed @ 12M.

Almost a 24 hr. day. An excellent one!

—⁓—

The annual fall board meeting was held in Dallas in November. Later that month, Sue and her husband "Smitty" welcomed their first child (and Maxine and Jim's third grandson), Milford Harland Smith III, later known as Trey.

Sadly, Ann and her husband Jim were having a difficult time in their marriage. They eventually divorced after the birth of their third son, Mike.[15]

Wednesday, November 1 (on the train)

Since I was headachy & wide awake began again at midnight—had a very warm time of prayer—specially prayed for all the Board individually.

Good sleep. Awake @ 6:10 rested and had a good time of prayer & meditation before Arr DL 7:30.

Conf. with Geo. [Sheffer] Preparation & prayer in my room until 11:30A.

Oak Cliff Lions Club—largest in U.S. The Lord greatly helped me—I think it was as good as I can do.

Rest this aft. Exhausted.

Dinner with the Staff at Lakewood Country Club. Great time!

A truly fine day. My rapport with staff people continues improved.[16]

---

[15] In 1980 Jim Patterson founded the technology giant Quantum Corporation, a leader in the then-emerging world of digital storage.

[16] Over the years Jim had been warned by senior staff that the younger staff found him intimidating. This was always a shock to Jim as he sincerely cared about all the staff—in fact, up to this point he had had a hand in hiring each of them.

Friday, November 3 (Dallas)

Again sleepless at 12:00A, so went at praying, and the time was so sweet & amazing over an hour passed before I knew it. God "initiates" & enables & the mystery remains—why so different now—after the long struggle and with no "human" reasons. Sovereignty that's it!

Finally slept at 5A. Up at 7. Good Conf. with Roy & John [Carter] at breakfast. Wonderful warm fellowship with John E [Mitchell] et. al.

A few preliminary minutes of prayer & talk with Board then return to hotel to prepare <u>Noon</u> & Board Rept. Oh God ... Choice audience of 300+. John E. thought I did the best I've ever done. Very thankful. Board mtg good—me, extremely weary. Report to-night on the new work of God in our hearts—and "Theology of Grace"[:] The Root of all we do—better than I could have hoped.

Thursday, November 9

Good start to-day.

Hurried hour or less at the office but got a lot done.

Sue's baby boy "Milton III" [*sic*, Milford III] born at 1:26 p.m. I stayed at the hospital couple of hours before.

LV C.S. 4:30 p.

Arr Okla C.

Wednesday, November 15 (on the train)

Another amazing experience. After midnight I was both wakeful & alert and had a very meaningful and fervent time of prayer. Awoke** two hours before ARR. Another unusually blessed experience in prayer before breakfast—characterized by unnatural peace, specially in the face of the pressure deal I am going to to-day & the heartache about Ann & Jim. After breakfast a thrilling time reading the Gospel of John—with new lessons learned & important ideas for messages. ARR Chi 9:10 A.M. Hurried to Bismark [*sic*][17]—called Coleman [Crowell], and got ready

---

[17] The Bismarck Hotel.

for [Crowell] Trust Mtg @ Union League Club. Ran into discouraging obstacles there. Lowest cash for disb[ursement] ever, and lowest reserves. Long docket. Asked for more than 100. Got passed down too
far (75). Ask them not to vote. Sugg[ested]: 30/yr—total 90. Hesitant.
Ask them again not to vote. Then, the Lord led me to think—"we could
spread over four** calendar years by a gift now & last only 26 mo. from
now. They agreed. Just what we all asked—the whole $100,000. Tried to
THANK THE LORD! Dictated Brd & Staff Rept by phone & called little
Ann. Long eve., dinner and conf. with Bill Starr.

Thursday, November 16 (Chicago)
Up at 5—good start after poor prayer time at 1A. (Almost no sleep last
n[ight].)

To O'Hare field—flight cancelled—1¼ hr. delay & proceeded via
Baltimore.

Finally arr. Phil 2P, too pooped to do anything. Exhausted beyond
endurance & just about sick. Took a short, "restless" nap at the Sheraton
btwn 3 & 4. Went down & had a sandwich & went to bed somewhere
around 7P.

67 days since the beginning of the long prayer mtg at Frontier—the
entire period vastly "different"—hard to define or explain but God has
done something...

> *Jim's stomach surgery had an unfortunate side-effect which
> plagued him the rest of his life: his stomach (what was left of it)
> would sometimes empty its contents into the small intestine with-
> out performing any digestive function, a process Jim referred to as
> "dumping."*
>
> *In late November, Jim picked up his latest car from the factory
> in Detroit and drove it home in time for Thanksgiving dinner.*

Sunday, November 19 (New York City)
Didn't get good sleep last night. The "dumping" hit me & I was very

uncomfortable until 2A—so I slept late.

> To airport LV N.Y. (Newark) 11:40.
> ARR. Pitts 1:10 p To Hilton.
> Took a nap. Called Harry.[18]
> Have the evening off!!

Wednesday, November 22 (travelling)

Up at 6A. Away @ 6:30. Breakfast sometime** later—Lv Hannibal [Missouri] 8:30 A Lv St Joe [Missouri] 11:30 A.

A most unusual day. For "difference" it rates high. Length of time estimate eng[aged] in prayer itself unusual—unparalleled, perhaps. The degree of concentration was seemingly higher than any I have achieved throughout much of the day. A third amazing fact was the enormous range of subjects & people & then fourth the definitness** [sic] of the subject matter of the prayers including specific requests for individuals—and the amazing number of matters that the Spirit brought to my attention for [Psalm] 32:8,[19] [Psalm] 121:8[20] prayer.

Lunch just across the Kansas border. Got sleepy about 3P so stopped at a very nice place 1 mi west of Bellville [sic, Belleville]. Nap—read—dinner—T.V.

Thursday, November 23 (Thanksgiving Day) (travelling)

Off at 7A. Breakfast an hour later at Smith Center [Kansas]. Would have to write almost the same thing about this day rel[ative] to pr[ayer] that I recorded yesterday—the more** surprising because it was the third day for this unusual activity. There is no way for me to estimate what this apparently special measure of His enabling Grace means.

---

[18] Pittsburgh area director Harry MacDonald.

[19] "I will instruct you and teach you in the way you should go;
    I will counsel you with my eye upon you."

[20] "The LORD will keep
    your going out and your coming in
    from this time forth and forevermore."

Friday, November 24

Worked hard at the office but did not get anywhere near doing the things I had expected to do. After the experiences of the past few days it surprised me & I guess "shook" me in that this was really such a bad day.

———

Monday, December 4

Off to a much better start this morning 6A. & believe it will turn out to be a good day.—

Truly the day was great both from production & real joy & snap in doing it. Completed the "invitation letter" for Pastors' Conference. With a little night work at the dictaphone "stacked" Jo[21] for the time I'll be away & to-morrow.

Very good at home.

———

The year ended with a pleasant Christmas celebration and a trip to Florida with sixteen-year-old Jim III.

Monday, December 25

Sue, Milford & "Trey" over all day. We had a wonderful Christmas. Grand dinner about 3:30 p.

Maxine gave me a beautiful Polaroid Camera & several nice small gifts. I got her a 25 Jewel Waltham—the best they make & the finest watch by far that she ever had.

Sunday, December 31 (Jacksonville, Florida)

A very good day. We went to Riverside Church & heard Al. Kissling[22]—

---

[21] Jo Barnes was Jim's secretary at the time. She married Deane Lees, an Air Force officer, later that month.

[22] Dr. Albert J. Kissling was the pastor of Riverside Presbyterian Church. As chairman of the Southern Presbyterian General Assembly committee investigating non-denominational youth works he went as a guest to Frontier in 1960. He plunged into the camp program with unusual enthusiasm and came away sold on Young Life.

George Sheffer.

then to Charlie Johnston's for brief visit with them, Charlie & Mary Scott, Geo. Sheffer, Bill, "Toddle," "Mike" & Charlie Beaufort with us at church.

[...]

Jim & I had good fellowship—the best—and a fine time this evening. Stayed up for a time of prayer at end of '61 & beginning of '62.

1962

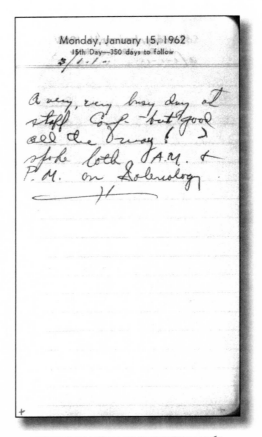

ENTRY FOR MONDAY, JANUARY 15, 1962

Rayburn occasionally added a flourish to his entries, as he did with the glyph at the end of this entry. (The meaning of the "+" in the bottom left corner of this page is unclear; Jim wrote either a "+" or a "o" on each entry for several weeks in 1962.)

More than seven years had passed since Malibu Club had opened for Young Life campers, and Rayburn was excited to have another project in the works. This time it was his idea for an adult guest facility located in Buena Vista near Silver Cliff and Frontier. By the beginning of 1962 the plans were well under way and Jim had asked Oklahoma developer and committee member Jack Johnston to oversee the project. He and Johnston visited the site in early January.

The annual staff conference was held at Star Ranch and Jim used the time to address the staff about Young Life's theology. He had been impressed with the English novelist and playwright Dorothy Sayer's idea that "the dogma is the drama," by which she meant that the Christian message is the most fascinating story ever told. Jim's series of messages was entitled, "Dogma: the Drama and the Dynamic."

Between Jack Johnston's visit and the staff conference Rayburn enjoyed a few days of skiing with Rogers and Loy Ann Carrington.

For Maxine's fiftieth birthday, the Rayburns sailed again to Europe, this time to France and Spain.

Saturday, January 6
Met Jack Johnston at 11:30.

Went directly to Buena Vista. <u>Walked</u> up into the Guest Ranch site—light supper at Flowers'.[1] Home about 8P in storm. I believe the Lord is leading and we will now get the big new Guest Ranch.

Sunday, January 7
Up early for a fairly good start but for interruptions—Got in some good study times** too.

---

[1] Bob and Eva Flowers, who were running Rancho Caballo. Rayburn was fond of Eva's cooking, particularly her chicken and dumplings.

Had a wonderful time teaching Phil 1 this a.m. Lots of favorable comment.

Also a good talk with Jack Johnston about the Adult Guest Ranch. Looks great!

A little work at the office.

Good couple of hours at home—then to DV. Met Rog & Loy at 3:30. To Loveland in a beautiful snowstorm—then back to a little "lodge" or whatnot** about 6 mi.**

Tuesday, January 9 (Winter Park, Colorado)

Couldn't sleep until 2A! Can't think of a reason. Ate lightly but my stomach (or rather bowels) were very uncomfortable**. Up at 6:50A for a very meaningful time of prayer. Good breakfast about 8:15A.

Got on the hill about 10:30—Zero [degrees]—Powder was 15 to 24 inches—very light. I did the best skiing I have ever done in deep powder. Two runs from the top of the Mt.—down the "advanced" hills in the morning—very cold! Then three fast runs from midway on the steep** slope after lunch. Back to lodge—Rog & Loy went on skiing.

Nap—dinner—read—bed.

Sunday, January 14 (Star Ranch)

Big S.S. Class. The teaching on Phil 2 went very well.

Staff Conf. began on a high note of good-will & fellowship with dinner & my first talk on Theology.

Monday, January 15 (Star Ranch)

A very, very busy day at staff conf.—but good all the way! I spoke both A.M. & P.M. on Soteriology.

Thursday, January 18 (Star Ranch)

The staff conference continues to exceed all my expectations. Wonderful spirit of fellowship. I think I did as well as I can do on "Just[ification] by Faith" in 35 min.—to-night. Am very thankful to the Lord for His great help & blessing on me through this series.

Saturday, January 20
Rushed at office & home before & after going to Star Ranch to here [sic] Carl Nelson. He did very well.

Maxine & I left on the "DV Zypher" [sic] for Chicago–N.Y. and Europe.

Restful afternoon. Went to bed early & slept nearly 11 hours.

Tuesday, January 23 (New York City)
Up at 8A Sailed at noon for the Mediterranean on Italian Line "Cristofoa Columbo." Met some pleasant people. Very enjoyable first day at sea. They moved us to a beautiful outside room about 50% more costly than the accommodations we had—no extra charge.

Monday, January 29 (at sea)
Up at 8:30A Thru the Straits of Gibralter [sic] btwn 10:30–11:30. Very interesting. Maxine's [50th] birthday.

Slept & read all afternoon—Maxine slept too for first time (in aft.)

The Kirks[2] ordered Champaine [sic] for Maxine's birthday party and the ship orchestra came in & played "Happy Birthday."

Good day.

——

Sunday, February 11 (Sevilla, Spain)
Wrote letters almost all day.

Walked among the teeming crowds on the street at dusk.

Ate only tea & cakes** & retired early.

The hotel personell [sic] are so friendly. I enjoy it here very much & would like to stay longer—that's a <u>good</u> <u>time</u> to leave.

——

---

[2]   The Kirks were most likely friends they had made aboard ship. This entry is the only time they are mentioned.

Monday, February 26 (at sea)

Began hitting rough weather this morning—by evening it was a terrific storm—by far and away the wildest thing I've ever seen. Mountainous seas—I understand it was "Force 11" gale—(Force 12 is a hurricane) 60–70 mile winds—45′–60′ waves. It is a thrilling experience. This big ship plows right on thru—rolls & pitches but not like one would think. It must have remarkable stability.

———

The Rayburns returned to the States on February 28. Maxine headed for home, but Jim stayed in New York for a few days and then headed back to Europe (this time by air) for several meetings.

His growing interest in foreign outreach is described in a letter he wrote to the staff during his and Maxine's trip.

> Again—as I mentioned in my last letter—the hosts of children and young people all around us, with no hope of ever hearing the truth about the Savior, touched my heart. And again I say, THERE MUST BE A WAY to get the message of the Savior to them. I'm going to the Pastor's [*sic*] Conference convinced that we must take the position that THERE IS A WAY, and the Christian who considers himself in the Apostolic tradition has no right to act like reaching a few here and there discharges our obligation to our Lord. What visionless people we Christians are—nothing *really matters* except "let's keep going about like we are." I don't believe for one second that is the way the Savior feels about it. We could reach all kinds of these poor, desperate people, ANYWHERE,—as soon as we started trying to do it.

In the time since Jim's last visit to Berlin less than a year earlier, the Berlin wall had been built by the communists, splitting the city physically between the free West and the communist East.

Tuesday, March 13 (Geneva, Switzerland)

The greatest day of my trip. Up @ 8, very groggy from the sleeping pills,

BERLIN, 1962
Brad Curl, Hilde Reinartz,
Rayburn, and Mary Ann Wagener
pay a somber visit to the newly-
built Berlin Wall along Bernauer
Strasse.

because I couldn't sleep until 2A. To Conf. with Visser t'Hooft.[3] Then a long conf. with Rod French, W.C.C. [World Council of Churches] Sec. for Youth Work & his staff.

Wednesday, March 14 (Frankfurt, West Germany)
In spite of terrible insomnia again last night—such a wonderful day—3 in a row! Awake** with such a "spirit of prayer" as I have seldom known— and, in spite of interruptions it continued thru the day.

Lv. Frankfurt: 1200 after good conf. w. Johnny [O'Neil].

Arr. Berlin 1320 prayerful & saddened after flying "the corridor" across the 110 miles of "prison land"—Soviet E. Germany, To Kempins-ki**. Got my laundry & cleaning sent off. Note & phone no. from Hilde [Reinartz]. Took a nap. Went down the Ku'damm for dinner ("Cordon Bleu.") then to hotel & bed.

---

[3] Visser t'Hooft was the General Secretary of the World Council of Churches.

Thursday, March 15 (West Berlin)

Slept 'til 8. Good start. Spent most of a.m: writing office (Roy & Jo).

Met Hilde Reinartz for lunch—she talked my arm off but readily agreed to set up all the arrangements I asked.

[...]

Ate a small supper about 5P on way back to hotel—turned in and read—

Friday, March 16 (West Berlin)

Breakfast conference with Brad Curl[+]—then spent the rest of the morning out along "the Wall." A moving experience.

[...]

Saturday, March 17 (West Berlin)

Shopped for "Hummels" at the Ka De We—this a.m and send [sic] Ann & Sue each a gift package.

A long and cordial visit with Bishop Dibelius this p.m. 1) He gave me a "history lesson" on the Russian Orthodox church. 2) Spoke of "New Delhi" as a disappointment[:] "didn't show Asia anything of the vitality of Christianity." 3) Talked about the Evangelical Academies & "Kirchentag."** 4) Churches' resistance to Hitler.

A long talk with Dr. Klicker to-night—rather boring.

Friday, March 23

ARR. HOME! 10:45A.[5]

Maxine and Jo met me.

Sue & "Trey" came over. Met Jim @ school—sure glad to be back.

(Had to go to bed real early again—I suppose because of the big time-zone change.)

+ Curl was on Young Life staff in Europe.

5 Jim had not been home since January 20.

Thursday, March 29 (Buena Vista, Colorado)

Good day at Caballo with Walt Miller.[6] The "Trail West Ranch" plans progressing well & look good.[7]

——~~~——

Thursday, April 12

Up at 6A.

To DV. Breakfast with NAE[8] men & Billy Graham. Good visit with Judge Gilliam.[9] Then a fine talk with Billy.

Good time at lunch with the DV. Committee. Home for an hour of work at the office before dinner.

Sunday, April 15

Studied before S.S. Taught Eph. 5:22ff.[10]

Tried to work on Pastors' Conf. material. Didn't do well.

To brother Bob's Covenant Choir Concert to-nite & Bob home with me for the night.[11]

Tuesday, April 17 (Chicago)

A very good day in spite of some handicaps as to use of time.

[...]

---

[6] Walt Miller had been the architect for the new headquarters building and was being considered for the Trail West project. He officially received the commission in April.

[7] This is the first time in the diaries that he uses the name "Trail West."

[8] National Association of Evangelicals.

[9] Phillip B. Gilliam. Judge Gilliam presided over the Denver Juvenile Court from 1940 through 1964. He and Rayburn had developed a friendship over the years.

[10] "Wives, submit to your own husbands, as to the Lord."

[11] Jim's brother Bob had founded Covenant College in 1955 and served as its president for its first decade.

A grand all-city club with Phil & Lowey.[12] Everything I did went well & the kids gave me tremendous acceptance & listened intently to the Gospel ("Meaning of 'Easter Wk'"). I was so thankful to the Lord!

Long visit with Wes McKinney afterward.

Wednesday, April 18 (Memphis)

[...]

Excellent Men's Luncheon @ the Peabody—A couple of fine hours with dear old Horace Hull—[13]

Fine dinner & long conversation with Chub & Marge [Andrews]— Mac & Margaret.

———

In late April Jim travelled to the East Coast again, this time to speak to a conference of committee members. While there he visited with Emile Cailliet, who was fast becoming one of Jim's dearest friends. Cailliet was beginning to write his book on Young Life.

Saturday, April 28 (Ocean City, New Jersey)

Afternoon with Dr. Cailliett [*sic*, Cailliet] in Cape May [New Jersey].

Spoke this eve on the "Message of the Fellowship." "Gospel of the Grace of God" Eph 2:8,9,[14] Titus 3:5,6[15] [...]

Sunday, April 29 (Ocean City, New Jersey)

Another mig—ergot early—quick relief—afternoon.

---

[12] Phil McDonald and Dick Lowey.

[13] Horace Hull was a Memphis car dealer who, along with his business partner John Dobbs, had built an entrepreneurial empire. Hull was a fairly recent addition to Jim's list of influential friends. He served on the Young Life board from 1961–1964. Hull died on November 2, 1966.

[14] "For by grace you have been saved through faith. And this is not your own doing; it is the gift of God, not a result of works, so that no one may boast."

[15] "He saved us, not because of works done by us in righteousness, but according to his own mercy, by the washing of regeneration and renewal of the Holy Spirit, whom he poured out on us richly through Jesus Christ our Savior."

Closing message of Conf. on Matt 9:35ff.[16] And financial crisis & implications for east & whole work.

This has been a great week-end. I got more than I gave but feel that, for the most part I did my best on the speaking. Learned a lot & somehow believe I took another little step of faith and will be able to walk closer to the Lord. Cailliett [sic] a great help in this too!

Monday, April 30 (Greensboro, North Carolina)
ARR. Greensboro 9:30A.
Conf. with Dan.[17]

> Luncheon speach [sic] to 150 men.
> Conf. with Mal McSwain.
> Rested & read.
> Dinner with Dan & Alice, Mal, Matt Prince.[18]
> Evening mtg with Committee, wives and prospects for Comm.
> Bill Hildebrand introduced me at the luncheon.

———

One of the highlights of Jim's entire life in ministry was the Chicago Fellowship. He had invited leading churchmen from around the country for three days of meetings to discuss matters near and dear to his heart. Jim wrote the staff to explain his lofty goals for the meetings:

The purpose is to explore three areas. 1) What is the God-

---

[16] "And Jesus went throughout all the cities and villages, teaching in their synagogues and proclaiming the gospel of the kingdom and healing every disease and every affliction."

[17] Area director Dan Komarnicki. Komarnicki was originally from Chester, Pennsylvania, and came on the Young Life staff in 1955. After he left Young Life he wrote a book entitled, *Teenagers Are People: A New Concept.*

[18] Matthew Sperry Prince. Prince was Lewis Sperry Chafer's grandnephew. He graduated from DTS in 1954 and had been recently hired by Young Life to help raise money for special projects, including Trail West. He left Young Life in 1964. Prince died in 2002 at the age of seventy-three.

given way to develop the lay leadership of the churches to do a "Young Life type" of mission. 2) Study the relationship of Young Life Campaign to the Institutional Churches and the total cause of Jesus Christ. 3) Give preliminary consideration to the problem of revitalizing the Church's ministry to it's [*sic*] own young people…

For years many of you have heard me say, "There are enough Christians within a mile of most high schools to evangelize the entire student body." Is this or something like it true? If it is, then we must find a way to effectively use these Christians…

[The churches] could call it what they like, "Young Life," or whatever. The job would get done on a grand scale! What a day that will be! Every step in that direction is a move toward vivacious, primitive, New Testament Christianity operating in the Space Age.

The staff who were in attendance could not help but notice that in this summit made up entirely of leaders of leaders, Jim stood out as the leader.

Attendees included the Rev. Robert Cunningham of Vancouver, Dr. Howard Hansen, Jim's pastor in Colorado Springs, Dr. Herbert R. Howard of Park Cities Baptist Church in Dallas, Episcopal Bishop Russell Hubbard of Spokane, Dr. Albert Kissling of Florida, the Rev. John Lancaster of First Presbyterian Church in Houston, Dr. John Mackay, the Rev. Canon Sam Shoemaker, and ten other clergy from around the country.

Like so many other times in Jim's life, his professional success was counterbalanced by troubles at home. The mountaintop experience of intense fellowship with some of the day's leading men of God was immediately followed by mundane meetings, house guests, and an ill wife. Shortly after returning from the Chicago Fellowship, Jim took Maxine to Fairfield, California, for an extended time with Dr. William Nesbitt.

Tuesday, May 8

Bad Mig. this aft—3 Medah. Mid-aft—slow relief

7 Day Interval

This was a most productive day. Got much important business done. The first day I've been pleased with my progress on "Chi Fell." preparation. Good letter about it to the staff and Board.[19] Best start I <u>ever</u> got in Preparation for my opening address. Good progress on schedule and other planning.—

All this in spite of mig sympt. beginning early and the pain getting very tough in the afternoon. Very thankful to God. Better prayer & all.

Maxine very bad again 3rd or 4th day.

Monday, May 14 (Chicago)

Arr. Chig. 9:15A Bill [Starr] met me. To Union League Club for planning, and lunch.

I worked hard much of the day in preparation. Feel more ready for my difficult assignments of the next few days, than I have ever felt about any.

Tuesday, May 15 (Chicago)

The Chicago Fellowship began at 4P with Sam Shoemaker leading a time of Reading & Prayer. The reception at 5:30P went well—about 50 present & stayed for dinner and the entire eve. program. All the "Fellowship" guests spoke—all good—several outstanding & some more just <u>great</u>. Dr. MacKay's address was tremendous. Everyone "captured" by it. The full hour at late time was not a minute too long. Sam S said Dr Mac was the greatest he had ever heard him, "That was prayed into him & prayed out of him." Truly this last few hours ONE of the great periods of my life.

---

[19] The letter just quoted.

Wednesday, May 16 (Chicago)

Thanks be to God. I feel that I did about my best. Then the "Forum" sessions proceeded thru the day with very fine** & enthu[siastic]** participation by most in the group. A spirit of warmth, sympathy, acceptance, love was manifest from the start—Something that only The Spirit could have produced.

MacKay, Shoemaker, Hubbard, Cunningham, Howard, & several others were outstanding. It is impossible to describe the sense of progress & growing love & understanding as the day progressed. The evening program Bade, McDonald, Mitch, Lowey—"The Dealers" [sic, "The Dealer"] was great & contributed![20]

Closed on schedule @ 10P. Unbelievably great day!

Thursday, May 17 (Chicago)

Very severe Mig. Several #3 Emp & 4 Medah. failed to abort until late in eve. This morning they insisted I speak on "The Plan." The way the Lord blessed & helped me, the reception & response—all of it was one of the greatest things the Lord has done for me.

I've just finished three of the greatest, happiest, most rewarding days of my life & I hope—most signifigant [sic].

Friday, May 18 (Chicago)

Great fellowship with Sam after breakfast. Good time with Howard, Cunningham, Lancaster, Kisslings, et. al. A hurried & unsatisfactory "Advisory Comm." mtg. And a boring C Trust[21] mtg which I left about 3:30p.

Dinner & a fine visit with Tim Nuveen.

---

[20] To lighten the mood, Rayburn had chosen an all-star Young Life program team of Tom Bade, Phil McDonald, Bob Mitchell, and Dick Lowey to entertain the conferees. In addition, they screened Young Life's promotional film, "The Dealer," which was a fictional portrayal of a typical high school student's experience with Young Life.

[21] The Crowell Trust.

Lv. O'Hare 7:40 Arr. DV 8P M.S.T. Matt [Prince] met me & drove me home. Arrived utterly exhausted. Maxine ill.

Saturday, May 19

Not much accomplished to-day. Chuck & Ruth Hoffmeister[22] here for eve & I took them to dinner—Maxine ill & couldn't go. (Stan Wick also dropped in.) A serious & disappointing "anti-climax" sort of thing— that seems so unworthy** in light of the Lord's blessing on the GREAT PROJECT.

Wednesday, May 23 (Fairfield, California)

Up at 7A.

Ann & the boys with Maxine & me—drove to Fairfield.

Left Maxine at Dr. Nesbitt's.

Took two units at F. Motor Inn.

Drove like mad to Berkeley. Mitch, Shelton, Pete Girard & Dave Williamson to San F Airport Lv 2P Arr L A 3 P.

Keith K. met—To Statler—To dinner with Paul Jewett & Don Weber of Fuller. To Arcadia for "Trail West" mtg. One fellow said he'd take 2 & there were probably 2 or 3 more sales.[23]

To Hotel late & weary.

A bright spot for Rayburn was his trip to Ft. Worth for a reunion of his old Riverside Young Life club. In a letter to donors, Jim wrote, "I led [the Riverside Young Life Club] back when this whole thing was new and experimental." He continued:

---

[22] E. Charles Hoffmeister and his wife Ruth. Hoffmeister was a seminary classmate of Jim's, serving as vice president of the student body while Rayburn was president. He led Young Life clubs in Seattle in the early 1940s while pastoring a church there. Prior to that, while serving as a minister in Hinckley, Minnesota, he investigated the idea of having pastors lead clubs in rural areas.

[23] In order to finance the adult guest ranch project, Young Life was selling lots to friends of the ministry on which they could build homes. Jim's vision was to have an alpine village centered around a first-class lodge.

Thirty-two adults, whom I knew as teenagers but hadn't seen for sixteen years, met for dinner at the beautiful country club one of them recently opened. The conversation at dinner and afterward kept me close to tears and helped me relive those often frightening and always exciting first days.

One of the original eleven identified himself by, "I was the one without a date." I recalled how the five boys with dates wouldn't get the girls off their laps for my meeting—then the agony of deciding how stern a leader had to be when presenting Christ's love to young pagans.

"Jim, the only serious moments most of us had in high school were in the Young Life Club."

"You didn't try to make us feel like sinners, but I've always remembered that Christ had to come to die for sinners."

"Even though some of us didn't go on with God as much as you wanted us to, we remembered what you said at Club. It made pretty good citizens out of us. Some of my old friends who never came are in the pen."

Included in the group were a minister, 6 church officers, 6 Sunday school teachers, and 2 church youth group sponsors. I had no idea at the time how much some of them were being affected by the Gospel.

Not long after the reunion, the Rayburns moved to Frontier for their annual summer stay.

Wednesday, May 30

This was a red letter day! Tough time leaving. Jim III sick. Discouraging conv. with Maxine. [...]

Jimmy drove me to DV. Lv. DV. 1:10. Only 1½ hrs. to Dallas. Haircut at last. Geo.[24] took me to Ft. Worth. Grand Fellowship. To Orien Browning's beautiful home—a warm reception & then such an evening!

How can I describe my impressions & the surprising blessing & inspiration I received. Orien, Shug [McPherson], Jimmie Eagle, Ed W, M.B. Easter, Jim Shofner (Clev[eland] Browns) is married to beautiful

---

[24] George Sheffer, at the time the regional director for the South, officing in Dallas.

Orien Browning, Jim, and Shug McPherson at the Riverside Young Life reunion.

Nancy Unger**, who had such terrible parental opposition after her conversion. All these yrs I've wondered. The Lord couldn't have brought a
greater answer. Jim (4 yrs in the faith—solid, attractive). Such testimoni-
als, from guys who <u>never</u> give one. Orien about "... sinners ... that's who
Jesus died for ..." Arthur _____[25] Christian preacher, Leo Holliday.

Tuesday, June 5
Hammered out a lot of work to-day.
    Excellent evening meal—Sue & Milford, Maxine and me.

Wednesday, June 6
Advisory Committee Mtg. Very good fellowship and a lot of things
accomplished—altho the placement of personell [*sic*] is a baffling
problem.

Thursday, June 7
Same as yesterday—except that we had to work until 1A ("to-morrow")
    For four straight evenings we had dinner around the table, excellent
menu's [*sic*] & food by Maxine & Sue & swell table conversation. Noth-

---

[25] The blank space is Jim's.

ing like this in years.

Monday, June 11 (Frontier Ranch)

This was one of the worst days & then late to-nite became (thanks to some remarkable change in Maxine) very wonderful—and could be one of the big days of my life.

Camp started off well to-nite with well over 200 for all that we can handle & 19 Foreign students.

Sunday, June 17 (Frontier Ranch)

The past week has been one of the greatest I have had in years. Starting with Monday night I felt better & worked hard—had many great contacts with the kids & gave a series of 6 consecutive messages that clicked & covered the ground I believe is essential. Am certain that the Lord greatly helped & blessed me in the presentation of the truth. Mike from Greece, kids from Norway, Finland, Germany, Switzerland visited with Maxine & me all afternoon. It was a grand experience.

Thursday, July 19 (Frontier Ranch)

A great day! 90 of the Committeemen took the trip up the jeep trail to join in the dedication of the "Mt. Princeton Chalet."

> *This was almost certainly the Committeemen's Conference that Emile Cailliet attended. He was so touched by hearing Rayburn pray one evening that he recorded the prayer in his book,* Young Life.

>> There was Jim, standing at a small desk which at his insistence had been set up at the floor level rather than on a podium high above the delegates. His ruddy, infinitely kind face was lifted up, its features sharply outlined in light and shadow, very much like a Rembrandt portrait. The cares and deep concern of a fully committed life were writ deep in lines and furrows that gave his expression a weather-beaten appearance, like a

Emile Cailliet and Jim visit over breakfast at Frontier Ranch.

man who in any kind of circumstances stood ready to submit to the Lord's will for the sake of the one thing that mattered.

"Good Lord, give us the teen-agers, that we may lead them to Thee. Our hearts ache for the nine million young people who remain untouched by Thy Gospel, and for the tragically large proportion of those who, having once been led to attend Sunday School, have dropped by the wayside and now find themselves without spiritual guidance. Help us give them a chance, O Father, a chance to become aware of Thy Son's beauty and healing power in the might of the Holy Spirit. O Lord Jesus, give us the teen-agers, each one at least long enough for a meaningful confrontation with Thee. We are at best unprofitable servants, but Thy grace is sufficient. O Thou, Holy Spirit, give us the teen-agers, for we love them and know them to be awfully lonely ... Good Lord, give us the teen-agers!"

Jim's whole being was in that prayer. When he had finished, his thin, muscular body was leaning forward in vibrant self-offering. His face, radiant with love, continued to pray long after his lips had closed, as if what he had to say could no longer be put into words. What an ineffable experience his prayer was that evening! I shall always find it inseparable from my thoughts about Young Life.

Monday, August 20 (Seattle)

Talked to D—— this morning. Discouraging—but the Lord is still Lord—that means He <u>rules</u>! I'm not to forget that.

[...]

Friday, August 31

Don't know why I haven't written more about this summer. It was as great as any. I got into speaking & everything more than for years. In some ways I believe it was the greatest.

The new school year was the first since Young Life's very beginning without Add Sewell on the staff. After twenty-one years of service in a variety of places and positions, Add and Loveta moved to Seattle where Add would work under Dr. Robert Boyd Munger at University Presbyterian Church. That left only Jim on staff out of the original five members: George Cowan, Gordon Whitelock, Wally Howard, Add, and Jim.

Once again Rayburn called staff to Frontier for a three-day prayer meeting in September. This time the group was made up of all the men who did not attend the previous year, and all the women with more than three years' experience on staff.

Saturday, September 15 (Frontier Ranch)

Prayer mtg ended to-nite on fine note—a grand experience. About 13 hr. total of prayer to-gether (15, I missed this aft.) and much very imp. explanation.

Sunday, September 30

Lv Okl. C. 10:13A

Arr C.S. 11A

Excellent dinner. Watched some football—took a long nap.

Got wonderful news from John Carter this p.m. $31,000 came in to-day! Under 20,000 needed & there will be more Sept income in next day or two.

Monday, October 1
[...]

$9,000 more income to-day. $10,000 will put us over the top.

Tuesday, October 2
And to-day we were over the top for sure on just Sept. post-marked gifts. Total for month—over $157,000! Unbelievable. How can we ever thank the Lord?!

The fall brought the normal routine of travel and meetings for Rayburn. While on a trip to the East Coast, he experienced still more health trouble. Weariness and insomnia were now becoming his constant companions.

Wednesday, October 31 (Philadelphia)
Jim III's Birthday "17"

Drove down to Cape May [New Jersey] in 1 hr. 45 min from the Phil[adelphia] Sheraton. Spent a wonderful day with Emile & Vera [Cailliet].

Drove back in the rain arriving about 7p. Went to bed & I think to sleep for a few min. then woke up and couldn't [sleep].

Thursday, November 1 (Philadelphia)
Never slept. Terrible feeling that I can't describe in my left arm & legs. Faint & ill whenever I would get out of bed. Finally called Rog [Carrington] at 4A! He came in & helped me get packed & took me to the airport.

Lv Phil 8A Arr Chi 9:10

Still very ill—seems to be some loss of coordination on my left side & apparently some lack of freedom of motion in my left arm & leg. Bill [Starr] met me at O'Hare—got me registered at hotel and Dr. Del Nelson came right away, gave me a check-up & gave me some shots. Went soundly to sleep for 6 hrs & awoke without the discomforting symptoms. A little while with some of the men & then back to bed.

Friday, November 2 (Chicago)

Board Mtg began at 10A.

My report was held up until afternoon—because of the huge build-up of mail & the type of summer results & fall work reported I believe it was the best report I've given the Board in years.

All day was good & important to [the] work. I sure "ran out of gas" to-nite.

Saturday, November 3 (Chicago)

This must go down as one of the greatest days in many yrs. At breakfast mtg w Personell [*sic*] Comm. the Lord enabled me to recount the whole history of my long-standing financial pressures. Members Kiesewetter, Kapple[26] and Yinger listened & enquired with astonishing interest, sympathy and understanding. They took it to Board. Board then called me in and for the first time checked with me and happily did everything I sugg. to be necessary to relieve the financial burden. I can never thank the Lord enough! Feel that a great weight has been lifted & the friendliness of the men greater than ever before (Dave left before this). Bill Yinger & Frank Muncy[27] great additions to the Board. Went with them

---

[26] Frank "Red" Kapple. A Chicago-area businessman and Wheaton professor, Kapple had joined the board in 1960.

[27] Muncy, an accountant who had helped with the purchase of Malibu (he is mentioned in Jim's entry for December 20, 1953), had just joined the board.

to see "The Longest Day" to-nite. Great![28]

Wednesday, November 7 (on the train)

Mild Mig—Medah. early.

Got thru a couple of hours of good work at the office.

Lv. C.S. @ 1:10 Took a 2 hr. nap—had a bite of dinner & to bed early. Extremely weary. Can't remember when I haven't been.

Saturday, November 10 (Chicago)

Med bad, persistent Mig #3s did no good. Medahaler late p.m.

Arr. Chi 8:30A. La Salle [Hotel].

To[o] weary to have any of my apptmnts.

Sunday, November 11 (Chicago)

A good conf. with Bill Starr. Again to[o] "gone" physically to tackle the necessary staff mtgs—D. Stanley conf.—Whitsell etc.

Lv. Chi 5P DV "Zypher" [*sic*].

Ate big dinner right away & went to bed.

Monday, November 12 (on the train)

Up early for best time of prayer in a long time. Feel better than last 10 or 12 days all of which have been rough.

Tuesday, November 13

Took Maxine to her Dr. & then to Penrose for her surgery on throat. Got in some good licks at the office—then back to the hosp. when Maxine got out of recovery room @ 3:30p.

Sunday, November 18 (Philadelphia)

Drove to Cape May [New Jersey] this a.m. to see Emile. Had dinner and a grand afternoon with them. Drove back to hotel after dark. Some dinner & to bed. It rained hard all day.

---

[28] Touting "42 Stars in The Longest Day!" the movie told the story of D-Day. It had been released a month earlier.

1963

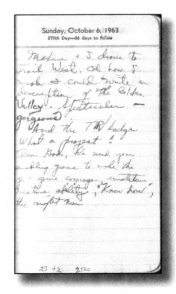

THE FINAL TWO PROPERTIES ACQUIRED DURING RAYBURN'S TENURE
*Jim's entry from October 3, 1963, described a visit to the newly-acquired Castaway
Club in Minnesota, while his entry from three days later showed his enthusiasm for
Trail West in Buena Vista, Colorado, then under construction.*

After fourteen faithful and fruitful years of teaching his Sunday School class at First Presbyterian Church in Colorado Springs, Jim relinquished that position in 1962.

His Sunday School role was not the only thing that was changing in his life. Increasingly, Rayburn's health issues were making it difficult for him to carry out his duties as the head of Young Life.

Following up on the Chicago Fellowship, Jim was speaking to a group of several hundred clergy and lay leaders in Minneapolis when, probably due to a delayed reaction to some of the medicine he was taking, he became incoherent. Roy Riviere and Bill Starr, who were there to assist Rayburn in the presentation, had to help Jim from the stage and take over delivering his message.

Unfortunately, these kinds of occurrences—slurred speech, rambling at the podium, saying indiscreet things—happened with increased frequency as the 1960s wore on. Though Jim does not discuss these events in detail in his diary, that they weighed heavily on him is evident in the lack of confidence with which he records notes about his messages: he seems relieved when things go well. For a man who was a master communicator, this must have been incredibly painful and difficult.

Wednesday, February 13 (Minneapolis)

Grand time with Jerry Kindall[1] @ breakfast. He wants me to come & travel with the Cleveland ball club some this spring or in Sept.

[...]

Ill this aft. Tried to work[2] this evening with Roy & Bill carrying the main speaking. Shouldn't have gone—muffed my part badly. [...]

---

[1] Gerald Donald "Slim" Kindall. Jerry Kindall played baseball for the Cleveland Indians and was a native of the Twin Cities.

[2] Jim often used "work" to mean "speak."

Roy Riviere.

Thursday, February 14 (Minneapolis)
Went to bed after lunch—slept most of time until after the boys finished the evening meeting. Had a bit of late supper and went back to bed.

The boys have very kindly counselled me regarding the "mysterious" signs of cracking up—last night, and the terrible weariness of past weeks. Looking to the Lord to guide as to rest. Know I must.

Friday, February 22 (Chicago)
Very little sleep. Arr Chi 9:30A. Felt bad—stayed in my room @ O'Hare Inn** all day.

Spoke @ Mid W. Committee Conf. to-night. Could tell by crowd reaction that the Lord greatly blessed me. So very THANKFUL to Him—Bill said—no sign of the trouble that hit me in Minn. except the extreme fatigue.

Spoke on "Adventure"—the idea of adventuring for God. We mean to be, need people with that outlook.

Thursday, February 28 (Wichita, Kansas)
Old stuff again—almost no sleep until 3:30 or 4A.

[...]

I've really been ill & most of the time unable to work since Feb 13—

(16 days)—and not over 50% effective, except for a few scattered days, for the past 7 or 8 mos.

⌐⌐⌐

After the Minneapolis incident, both Jim and Maxine spent several weeks in California under the care of Dr. Nesbitt. Jim did keep a few speaking engagements during this time, but they took a toll. In its April 1, 1963 edition, Young Life's Monday Morning *staff newsletter records, "Reports from other sources indicate that Jim made his usual fine contribution at the SE Regional Committee Conference two weekends ago. Bill Starr assisted in the speaking. It took Jim days, though, to get back on his feet after that effort. The present time with the doctor and away from the work needs to be really away."*

All of Young Life was concerned about Rayburn's health—and talking about it. On April 15, Monday Morning *reported,*

Jim's appetite for work is strong, but his capacity for it is still far from strong. Several scattered questions from staff people seem to indicate some explanation here. Jim is suffering from extreme physical exhaustion, which interacts back and forth with some truly formidable stresses. Some of these strains come from the weight of responsibility he carries for Young Life; others from family life. Mrs. Rayburn has for long years endured emotional strains and interacting physical ailments which for her and for Jim have precluded real rest. Now they both share in Ann's pain at the dissolution of her marriage.
… This report has been given not to satisfy curiosity, but to enable us better to bear one another's burdens.

As it had been for months now, the development of Trail West was a priority for Jim, and this unique project required much of his time. Additionally, Emile Cailliet, the eminent scholar, was finishing writing his book, Young Life, *and asked for Jim's input.*

Wednesday, May 1 (Philadelphia)
Mig mild all nite but enough for 2 Migral & a #3 this a.m. Aborted rapidly.

[...]

Drove down to Cape May—Wonderful dinner and evening—Emile had no typed manuscripts so he read me about 4 to 4½ chaps. of the new book "Young Life." I knew it would be good but in [*sic*, it] surpassed my fondest expectations. It is great! Parts of it are positively "inspired."

Thursday, May 2 (Cape May, New Jersey)
Spent all day with Cailliets—again mostly reading excerpts & talking about the work. They took me to the "Lobster House" for dinner— drove back to Philly. Read—hit the sack very late.

Saturday, May 11
Conf. with Roy & Matt re: Chi Fellowship.[3]

Loafed the rest of day but for the most part too nervous or "pent-up" to enjoy or profit by it.

Wednesday, May 15 (Chicago)
Up at 7A

Long day at the [Crowell] Trust meeting. So very thankful to the Lord for the great thing He did—(again, somehow overcoming my resistance to the idea) I asked them to authorize up to $25,000 in case I need it to reach the $150,000 Board subsidy for "Trail West"—and they voted it! As is ALWAYS true I knew HE was in that. To Motel after 6½ hours. Weary but happy!

Jim called and told me Maxine had fallen & broken her leg— Bill came later.

Maxine's broken leg required a multi-week hospital stay, followed by more time in a wheelchair and on crutches.

---

[3] Though it did not have the impact Jim hoped it would, the Chicago Fellowship did improve Young Life's relationship with many churches and pastors.

In the midst of all of the turmoil and pressure in his life, Jim was restored somewhat by a summer of speaking at Frontier. In addition to taking the campers climbing and snow sliding, one of his favorite things to do was take kids on jeep rides up to the new "Chalet" on Mt. Princeton.

Monday, June 3 (Frontier Ranch)

A good day—very busy getting started.

Bill, Phil and I drove the Jeep trip. Wonderful, as always—and the kids get a great kick out of it.

Following last year, again used "What Is the Set-Up"—1) A God, ("What God do you believe in?") 2) A revealed God. 3) He came here—Name! Concl. Don't have to believe it but I have to tell you—for all Christians in all ages that's "the set-up." Marvelous response. As good as I've ever known for 1st night.

Tuesday, June 4 (Frontier Ranch)

Some work on the mail—Drove the Jeep Trip again. The evening meeting went well—I stayed on "What Is the Set-Up?" but used a little more of the John 1:12[4] & Rev 3:20[5] truth & wasn't as satisfied with it—will go back to straight "Christology."

Wednesday, June 5 (Frontier Ranch)

Took the kids to the snow-slides to-day. Found excellent snow at our favorite spot on the Divide above Hancock.[6] A good short slide that most of them did over & over again—and a high cornice at about 13,000′ that I tried out and then let 25 kids come down. It was a long drop and a fast

---

[4] "But to all who did receive him, who believed in his name, he gave the right to become children of God."

[5] "Behold, I stand at the door and knock. If anyone hears my voice and opens the door, I will come in to him and eat with him, and he with me."

[6] Hancock is one of several ghost towns on the way to the area where Jim would lead snow slides and mountain climbs. "The Divide" refers to the Continental Divide.

ride! As always a great experience for the whole camp.

Thursday, June 6 (Frontier Ranch)
Camp proceeding well. I'm not very "well" tho—can't begin to handle all my responsibilities.

Bill took my speaking to-night.

Friday, June 7 (Frontier Ranch)
I spoke on "The Sacrifice of Christ"—did it well but not one of my best efforts. Exc. response.

Sue & family arrived late to-nite!

Saturday, June 8 (Frontier Ranch)
Stayed out of the evening program. Got some work done.

Late to-nite 10P–11:30P—one of the GREAT experiences.[7] Going thru the five big buses, listening to the kids—(Big Guy, Mphs, "How can I know?") So many go a lifetime without this kind of experience.

Sunday, June 9 (Frontier Ranch)
Took Sue & Milford to "Trail West" this a.m. Bill went too. Had a great time. Saw the high mining** claims for first time.

Took Rosie & her mother & Milford to Chalet. Got in a terrific blizzard. It was a grand experience.

Steak dinner & long talk with the Staff men to-nite.

Sue staying.

Monday, June 10 (Frontier Ranch)
Some work on correspondence—a little each day.

Worked with some key men on "C[ailliet] Manuscript" until late to-nite.

---

7 This was as the groups were departing camp at the close of the week.

Tuesday, June 11 (Frontier Ranch)

Opened new camp—Foreign Students didn't get here for start.

Wonderful to have Sue & Tresi & Perri here these past four** nights. Smitty came for them to-nite.

Wednesday, June 12 (Frontier Ranch)

So "pressured" on every** hand to-day. Couldn't get to sleep.

37 "Exchange" students from 19 countries at "Lk Out" this aft.

Spoke to kids to-n. "Incarnation." Got quickly to: Most people don't know the simplest things, there is a Creator God, He is personal! He made you for Himself, He loves you <u>as you are</u>! He CAME HERE! Name was "Jesus"! (Use of name) Got to believe Something about Him!—Best presentation I can make. V. thankful to God!

Thursday, June 13 (Frontier Ranch)

Have been so weary past three days—such pressure—my speaking to the kids, which should always be a kind of "pressure"—the Cailliet manuscript, the L.D. phones,[8] the long hours with key men—the Tr. W. project, et. al. <u>ad. infinitim</u> [sic].

Trip up Chimney R[ock] with all the kids. Reaction Great!

Spoke on "Incarnation & Life of Christ"

Used ("Cross-eyed teacher," "bacteria," "This isn't Heaven.")[9]

Used I J 5:11, 12[10] just ref to "LIFE," Recap to J I, Intro. J 2 (Lk 18 Pharisee & Publican—Jesus always like we want to be—admire—loving—courageous—Wonderful). Closed John 4 ("sign") & 5. with pers. exp. (Aquisition [sic] of Frontier—no answer but "Him.") One of my

---

[8] Long distance phone calls.

[9] Jim often listed the jokes and illustrations he used in his messages. This list is typical, with no details given other than the names of the gags; these three particular jokes appear numerous times over the years.

[10] "And this is the testimony, that God gave us eternal life, and this life is in his Son. Whoever has the Son has life; whoever does not have the Son of God does not have life."

better efforts. Long talk w. kids aft.

Friday, June 14 (Frontier Ranch)

[...]

A "rough" evening that deeply affected me!... —The old problem of having to run the risk of people disliking me in order to be faithful to my calling. Even young counsellors are effected. Hard to take but must just press closer to the Lord & do what I believe to be the best.[11]

Saturday, June 15 (Frontier Ranch)

Got sick after lunch at Hancock. Very sick—Left the snow slide crowd & came home to bed. Had a hard time making the long ride but managed. Too ill to work[12] to-nite? Disappointed until I believed it to be God's will.

Sunday, June 16 (Frontier Ranch)

Didn't do much or feel like it but—to-nite spoke on the Sacrifice of our Saviour & got it RIGHT for me—which is always a spec. blessing.

Thursday, June 20 (Frontier Ranch)

Felt badly to-day & couldn't do much—Maxine has considerable pain and I have given her several shots for it last nite & to-day. All in all this was my worst day of the summer season. Things are piled too high & there is too much respons. in matters that encroach upon my chief interest—time w. the kids!

Friday, June 21 (Frontier Ranch)

Didn't get much work done—but had excellent contact with the new campers on the Chimney Rock climb and afterward. Maxine still hurting a lot.

---

[11] Apparently Jim had found it necessary to correct some of the staff.

[12] Speak at Round-Up.

Saturday, June 22 (Frontier Ranch)

To "Trail West" with Harlan Huff.[13] Great experience. The whole project seems better than ever.

Spoke to-nite on Matt 8 & got it just right. Thank the Lord! Some of the speaking this summer has been hard—but to-nite, I knew the Presence of the Lord with me.

Thursday, June 27 (Frontier Ranch)

Had a great sleep—10 uninterrupted hours—last night.

Staff orientation: With the new staff we went to the T R W Lodge site & held a brief "ground-breaking" service, dedicating the project again to our Lord & His dear cause. Then went up to the upper property. Roy took a group climbing. Bill & I returned to Frontier for a little while.

Good evening around campfire.

Thursday, July 4 (Frontier Ranch)

This was a tough but partly rewarding day. Drove to the Institute[14] with Mitch & Mac, conferring on Brazil.[15]

Spoke at Institute Chapel on "Exposure" as over against "Getting people 'saved.'" All "contact," "club," everything dependent upon this viewpt. Then** manifesting Christ's love for people & making the issues clear & relevant become the major emph[asis].

[...]

Home about 2P. Waited until 7P for Jim III. Then drove back to Frontier. Arr. 11P D.T.

---

[13] Harlan Huff was a supporter of Young Life.

[14] The Young Life Institute, which was being held at the Fountain Valley School in Colorado Springs.

[15] Bob Mitchell had recently visited Brazil to investigate starting Young Life there. Rayburn had approached Harry MacDonald the previous fall about heading up the work in the new country. Harry, Hope, and their family sailed for Brazil five months after this conversation.

Saturday, July 6 (Frontier Ranch)

5th Camp opened to-nite—smaller but again slightly over capacity 200+ -

Tuesday, July 9 (Frontier Ranch)

Another hard morning of work on correspondence. Didn't get as far as I had hoped.

Spoke to-nite on "ALL HAVE SINNED, AND COME SHORT . . ."[16] One proposition. We are unfit for God apart from Christ. One ILL. II Kings 5. Went very well—one of my better efforts.

—⁓—

Saturday, August 31 (Frontier Ranch)

Another wonderful few hours @ Trail West—took several adult guests.

Drove one of the afternoon trips to the Mt. Princeton Chalet. As always great! Downpour of rain all the way down—got drenched.

Camp closed for the summer to-nite—the greatest summer ever! And in many different ways.

Tuesday, September 3 (Frontier Ranch)

As always it was hard to leave Frontier & "the Lookout" this a.m.

Good trip home.

—⁓—

Sadly, it would prove to be Jim's last summer in charge at Frontier Ranch.

Rayburn's heart for high school students in countries outside America continued to grow. For the last several summers he had made a concerted effort to get to know the foreign exchange students who came to Frontier. Now he was desirous to investigate ways to follow-up with them after their Young Life experience in

---

[16] Romans 3:23.

the States. With that in mind, he approached Chicago business-
man John Nuveen.

After their meeting in Chicago, Jim headed to Minnesota to
take possession of Young Life's newest summer camp: the as-yet-un-
named summer home of the Smith family on Pelican Lake (Gor-
don Smith, the son of Jim's old friend Sidney T. Smith of Winni-
peg, had given it to the ministry). It would later become known as
the Castaway Club and provide thousands of campers over many
decades "the best week of their lives."

As always, the end of September proved an exciting time of
watching God's provision for Young Life.

Saturday, September 14 (Chicago)
Arr. Chi 10A. Went to the "Flying Carpet"[17]—

Tim [Nuveen] called.

To Luncheon @ Nuveens' house. John Nuveen gave a most interesting analysis of the proposed trip—and surprise of surprises!—offered
(conditioned upon us taking more time for the trip) to pick up the tab
for the entire expense—around the world.

Very tired—rested in eve.

Tuesday, September 17 (Pelican Lake, Minnesota)
Flew to Fargo[18] with Bill [Starr] & Rollin Wilson.[19] A pleasant few hours
at the beautiful—almost spectacular—place on Pelican Lake.

Tuesday, September 24 (Vancouver)
A great day with the Vancouver staff. The day was characterized by an

---

[17] The Flying Carpet Motor Inn was near O'Hare airport.

[18] Fargo, North Dakota, is only forty-five miles from Pelican Lake and was the
nearest airport to the new property.

[19] Rollin Wilson was a Memphis businessman and volunteer leader who had been on
the board of trustees since 1959. He had accompanied Jim on his November 1960 trip
to Berlin.

evident complete lack of any tensions & very warm fellowship.

Agenda: Each person talked to me of his work (surprisingly fine reports) and I shared the "big projects"—extras with them. e g. proposed World trip, Wichita fellowship[20] et. al. & had them** talk. Never had a better day, with staff.

Wednesday, September 25 (Seattle)
Lv Vanc with Tom Raley[21] @ 9A after breakfast with Bob & Mae Page.[22]

Luncheon w Seattle Staff.

[…]

To-day's rept. from Hdqts. indicates ONLY $48,000 needed of the $180,000 total needed for Sept. It could only be of the Lord.

Friday, September 27 (Wichita, Kansas)
[…]

Lv Wichita @ 12:30P

Deficit about $36,000 with the week-end to go.

Saturday, September 28
Watched Okla U. beat USC 17–13. Great!

Sunday, September 29
Jim III & I went to church—I was surprised & disappointed @ how boring it was—specially for a 17–18 yr old boy.

---

[20] The Wichita Fellowship was a follow-up to the Chicago Fellowship. For many months Jim travelled to Wichita, Kansas, to meet regularly with the pastors there.

[21] Raley was serving as the regional director for the Northwest. At the time, the country was divided into six regions, each overseen by a regional director: Northwest (Tom Raley), Midwest (Bill Starr), West (Bob Mitchell), East (Arnie Jacobs), Southwest (George Sheffer), and Southeast (Roy Riviere). After spending several years in Colorado as Rayburn's right-hand man, Riviere was back in the "field," based in Atlanta.

[22] Bob Page had been heading up the Young Life work in Canada for the last seven years and had just recently left the staff.

Didn't feel very good. Should have gotten some good exercise the past two days.

Deficit down to $22,000. to-day. Amazing!

Monday, September 30

A truly great day! After the morning tally we were about $11,000.00 short. All this came in this aft. [...] Just before 5P I wrote to Committees, Board and Staff stating that we were "over the top." It was possible a day or two earlier than last year! We had an office prayer mtg—trying to express our thanks to Him. What can I say. It was all of Him—just great!

Tuesday, October 1

A good day at the office. I was fast & got a lot done—the accumulated pile of work still bothers me.

Jim III, Maxine & I went down to Perkins'[23] & decided on a '64 convertible.

Wednesday, October 2

Worked at office in a.m. Such a great thing to contemplate the Lord's amazing faithfulness & provision for our needs.

Picked up the new car at noon**.

Lv C.S. 2:15p.

[...]

Arr Fargo 9:15 Phil met me.

Thursday, October 3 (Pelican Lake, Minnesota)

Spent this whole day going over the grounds, buildings, etc., and talking possible plans—It is a great place.

Long session with all of the men to-night re: The financial "crises"— the development @ Wichita—purposed world trip, etc.

---

[23] Will Perkins' car dealership in Colorado Springs. Perkins was one of the businessmen who had accompanied Jim on his trip to Berlin in November 1960.

Castaway Club.

Sunday, October 6 (Trail West)
Maxine & I drove to Trail West. Oh how I wish I could write a description of "The Golden Valley.["] Spectacular—gorgeous.

And the TR W Lodge [—] What a project!

Dear God, We need your enabling grace to make this go—give courage, initiative, creative ability, "Know how," the right men.

———

Sunday, October 20
Went to S.S. Class this a.m.—probably the first time in nearly a year; enjoyed it.

Dr Dilsworth(?) Whitworth spoke—good.

———

The acquisition of Castaway and the construction of Trail West
made the fall an exciting time for Young Life. But the primary

thing occupying Jim's mind and time was his upcoming interna-
tional trip.

For the second time, Jim was going to circumnavigate the
globe. This time, he would be travelling with new staff man Tim
Nuveen and they would have the task of investigating ways to fol-
low-up with the international students who had visited Young
Life camps.

Their trip would take them to Japan, Hong Kong, Singapore,
Pakistan, Turkey, Germany, Finland, and Norway. In each locale
they stayed in the home of one of the foreign exchange students. In
a letter to the staff shortly before his departure he stated his pri-
mary reason for the trip (all emphasis Jim's): "To learn something,
perchance, by God's Grace to learn much! I have no delusions of
grandeur and am certainly aware that Young Life will not solve
the world's problems. But SOMEONE MUST START SOME PLACE to
learn. It is catastrophic that the understanding and treatment of
young people by the Christian missions of the world is even worse
than the churches' failure with young people on this continent."

Rayburn and Nuveen left immediately following the fall
board meeting in Salem, Oregon, in November.

Wednesday, October 30 (Trail West)
Took Bill & Harriet Perry to Trail West. As the building takes shape it
is more & more amazing—the size—the design**, the wonderful, overall
beauty & functional quality of it—just great.

Thursday, October 31
Great Advisory Comm. mtg to-day. Wonderful fellowship.

Friday, November 1
Sam Shoemaker died to-day. I felt such a sadness & loss while all the
time thankful that Sam was thru with suffering and with His Lord. Few
men have meant more to me.

The Adv. Comm mtg. was good—worked until 10:30p.

Sunday, November 3
I taught the S.S. Class for 1st time in about a year. Very large crowd. Taught Acts 3 "Holy One..."

Saturday, November 9 (Salem, Oregon)
Finished Board Mtg @ 11A.

Lv Seattle 10:30p.

Sunday, November 10 (travelling)
Passed the International Dateline a few hours out of Seattle so that washed out this day—it just ceased to be.

Sunday, November 24 (Pakistan)
To Khyber Pass this morning—back for lunch.

Lv Peshawar 5:30p

Arr LA Hore 7:00p

(A very worthwhile side trip)

Late dinner with the "K" family[24] & a daughter & son-in-law. I took some pictures. There was ever** more of the increasing friendliness, goodwill and warmth about the whole thing. Continue to be very thankful to God—and pretty much in the dark about how to capitalize on all this.

Wednesday, December 4 (West Germany)[25]
To Kassel

---

[24] Rayburn and Tim Nuveen were in Lahore, Pakistan, to visit former exchange student and Frontier Ranch camper Shahid K, a Muslim (last name withheld).

[25] This is probably the longest single-day entry in all of Jim's diaries. The writing is very small and fills the entire page.

The day started so poorly except for a warm time of prayer that Tim & I had to begin**. [...] Tim very encouraging! Our relationship becoming warm, close & trustful! Thanks to God.

Lv Fr[ankfurt] (by train 12:15p Arr. 3:15.) (x x x x x x Here the whole day changed dramatically) Gert,[26] Mrs. V[oland] & little sister Brigit** greeted us warmly at station (Brigit a shy, delightful little kid.) Big "coffee". Good visit. My cough bad. They had me nap on the sofa. Mr V came home. A refined, charming man, obviously esteemed by his family. Warm fellowship @ Supper—as tho we were old & cherished friends (Same all over the world. Because of education & culture reached a climax here) Gert had 14 friends in (4 Amer. Exch. students) A long and rewarding evening. Gert asked me "Don't you want to talk to them about Jesus Christ?" Both Tim & I did—even the Amer. Students were obviously surprised and impressed. Gert really got to me. He should be on a 9:38 page![27] He said to Tim "My father sells business machines. Jim sells Jesus Christ" [...]

After the crowd left—the family talked seriously & earnestly with us about our Savior** Y.L. etc., until nearly 1A. A GRAND DAY. The Lord was there. [...]

Sunday, December 8 (West Germany)

This quiet Lord's Day with a family[28] that knows & honors Him a rich experience—specially after the month among people (families) that do not have the Light of the knowledge of His Presence in their homes.

The Morning Worship Service that Pastor Siemens led was truly

---

[26] Rayburn and Nuveen were in Germany to visit former foreign exchange students and Frontier Ranch campers Klaus Wentzel and Gert Voland.

[27] Rayburn always encouraged staff to keep a "9:38 page" of young men and women to pray into ministry. The name came from Jesus' admonition in Matthew 9:38: "Therefore pray earnestly to the Lord of the harvest to send out laborers into his harvest."

[28] Their next stop was to follow-up on former foreign exchange students and Frontier Ranch campers Bernt Rott and Oltmann Siemens. Oltmann's father was a minister.

worship. (Only 35 people—his "parish" numbers 6,000.)

Dinner—coffee—supper all great good fellowship.—

The afternoon at Itzehoe Youth Center very good & important to me.

Oltman[n]'s concern is deep & I believe unquestionably indicative of the Lord's leading.

Wednesday, December 11 (Finland) and Thursday, December 12 (Norway)

Went to "Stockman's" for haircut. Feeling kind of bum. Well, I don't think I should be exactly kicking my heels in the air—after more than a month of this constant exposure to kids in need of help. "Babes" "in Christ" with no shephard [sic] & no fellowship, their hopes (often dim) that we can do something about it—the even more obvious fact that we're NEEDED.

[He has drawn a double line here and titled it "12th."]

Lv Helsinki 10:30A. Arr. Oslo 12:30p

Anne K Rygh[29] phoned us @ airport. We checked in at the "Viking" then took the "slowest train in the world" to Drummen. Dr. Rygh, Anne K., two other Norweg. exchange students—boys from Christiansen & Oslo, met us. To the house for a huge & beautifully served meal of Christmas-time specialties. (Another family** there). The two younger twin girls fine kids. Big, long "discussion" of Christianity with the Oslo boy loaded for us & rudely unfriendly. To the "DRAMMEN SPIRAL"—spectacular! Good talk about Y.L Took 11:05 train Arr Oslo 12:30 Walked!

Rayburn and Tim Nuveen arrived back in the United States on December 13.

---

[29] Anne Katherine Rygh was a former foreign exchange student and Frontier Ranch camper from Norway.

Monday, December 23

I've had some good days in the office since returning—conferring with the men etc., but this is the first day that I have really "hit" the correspondence. Got off a big load and feel much relieved.

A wonderful talk with Ann to-nite—our little girl who has been so sad for so long seems genuinely** happy this Christmas—Oh, dear God......

Tuesday, December 24

Finished up my office work this a.m. and enjoyed the odds & ends of finishing preparation for Christmas.

Some wonderful letters & notes on Christmas cards from my "kids" around the world.

1964

"... PERILOUSLY CLOSE TO THE MARGIN ..."
Jim wrote a note to himself on the January 30–February 1, 1964, spread, expressing his confusion and frustration with his physical condition.

One of Jim's German friends had given him a journal for 1964. It
is appropriate that the diary for this year is unlike any of the oth-
ers, as the year itself was unlike any other in Jim's life. Its black,
somber cover matches the bleak events of that year. The format of
the book was different as well; each week took up two spreads: Sun-
day–Wednesday on one two-page spread and Thursday–Saturday
on the next spread. On the Thursday–Saturday spread there was
a space for Notizen *or notes (all of the diary's pre-printed text was*
in German). Where those notes have been included here they are
placed at the end of the week, although it is not certain what day
Jim actually wrote them.

Some of the entries for the spring show a messy handwriting
uncharacteristic of Jim's normal intelligible script, and some of his
sentences are hard to understand. He was clearly a man in some
sort of physical crisis.

Tuesday, January 14

Couldn't sleep until after 3A. Maxine couldn't either—happens too often, the two of us both awake—wonder why?

Worked hard & fast all morning. Marilyn[1] took me to DV, & we had
an important talk about office & staff con[ference].

Arr Ch. 5:30P—Had a great time with Bill [Starr] & got over some
important stuff prep[aratory] to staff conf. [...]

Thursday, January 16 (Memphis)

The study—specially the constant bombardment from the book[2] recalling how the Lord dealt with me, how Gloriously He led & overruled—
all the part—what I <u>mean</u> <u>to</u> <u>be</u>—what I <u>want</u> <u>to</u> <u>be</u>, and by His Grace

---

[1] Marilyn Horton, Jim's current secretary.

[2] He was studying Emile Cailliet's book, *Young Life*, much of which is devoted
to recounting the early days of the ministry and Jim's own life. The book had been
published only a few weeks earlier.

intend to be—is both a blessing (untold) and a pain & struggle—Since '33 "how to be" "all out" etc. The most He can do IN ME, WITH ME ... MYSTERY.

[...]

───

For years Jim had hoped to meet FBI director J. Edgar Hoover. He had written Hoover numerous times over the years, going back to the early 1940s (his May 1, 1944, diary entry refers to writing "the letter to J. Ed. Hoover") and tried in vain to visit him in Washington. Finally, through board members and political connections, Rayburn was able to present Hoover with a special award from Young Life in early February.

In January the entire staff gathered at Silver Cliff for their staff conference.

Saturday, January 25 (Silver Cliff Ranch)

Perhaps the greatest staff conference in our history ended to-nite. I spoke on Arnie's q. "What do we stand for?" changing to "Where Do I Stand?" (Ten basic points for Y.L.). I believe I handled some sticky ones well—but was VERY DISAPP that I took 25 min over the 45–50 min I had set for myself.

Saturday, February 1 (Chicago)

Slept 13 hours yesterday (incl. last night) Did me a lot of good. Breakfast with Sanny.³ Tim [Nuveen] met me. We had a long talk—very interesting. Went to Dentist (Bob Hansen) who fixed my tooth temporarily so it is comfortable.

A remarkably fine evening 4½ hrs with Nuveens @ their home.

[...]

───────────────────────

³ Lorne Sanny, the head of The Navigators, who was travelling on the same train to Chicago.

Note for January 30–February 1 spread

Since Christmas I have been living perilously close to the margin regarding my health—something MUST be done—so I must wait upon the Lord. He ALONE knows how I can manage timing** and circumstances to achieve the rest that I need for proper restoration. I MUST REMEMBER that—in the light of my gifts & calling—my sense of mission—I bear a responsibility before God to rectify this situation.

Thursday, February 6 (Washington, D. C.)

A tremendous day. Exc. Breakfast Conf. & Fellowship with Ken & Eileen** McNutt. An inspirational time of fellowship with Marv Heaps⁴@ lunch—w Bob Cryer. Prayer & talk with Don Jones.⁵ Then to Mayflower Hotel for planning and prayer and fellowship with Mark [Hatfield], Frank [Morrison] and Don Jones before proceeding to J. Edgar Hoover's office. There we were received with great warmth and courtesy by his staff & by the Director himself. I spoke briefly of the work & Mr. Hoover's influence upon my decision and his career-long impact** upon my life and work.⁶ The warmth and sincerity of his expression of gratitude for the "Young Life" award and his openness to us plus** his unexpected & unqualified commendation of Y.L. went far beyond my fondest expectations**. I remember that our great God made this possible, after 21 years of hoping, praying & seeking to meet him. Then** nearly three hours of amazing fellowship with Jerry Johnson⁷ & Chuck

---

⁴ Marvin Heaps was one of the first southern California Young Lifers. He became a Christian through Young Life's influence in 1949 while a student at Fremont High School in Los Angeles. In 1969 he became the first former club kid to become a member of the board of trustees.

⁵ Donald E. Jones was an FBI agent in Berkeley, California, who served for many years on the board of trustees, beginning in 1958. The first mention of him in Jim's diary is on November 8, 1956: "I liked the luncheon in Berkeley. Particularly fellowship with Don Jones—F.B.I."

⁶ Rayburn often cited Hoover's observations about the relationship between Christianity and good citizenship, as well as the need for a strong moral foundation.

⁷ Jerry Frederic Johnson. Johnson was on staff from 1954–1986. Most of his years

Don Jones, Jim Rayburn, Gov. Mark Hatfield, Gov. Frank Morrison, and William Newell present J. Edgar Hoover with the Young Life Award.

Reinhold before departing for DV.

Monday, February 10
Took Maxine to DV to catch 8:20A train to Fairfield [California].
　　Feel so out-of-it to-day! Tried hard in office but got little done.

Tuesday, February 11
Another bad day—Excellent time with Frayne Gordon[8] @ lunch. The rest of the day was bum—feel ill & mentally "logy"—Didn't begin to get my work done.
　　[...]

Sunday, February 16 (Chicago)
A brief conf. with Bill. Losoge** w. Johnny O'Niel [*sic*]—Booked** train—(Much "Surgical Dumping") I [*sic*] dinner** met** Bud & Louise Anderson of Minn. Very pleasant fellowship thru long dinner hour—to

---

with Young Life were in Baltimore where he was an incredibly effective area director, growing the area to twenty-six clubs, each averaging over 100 students in attendance each week.

[8]　Frayne G. Gordon. He had been hired as the manager of Malibu in 1959 and by 1964 was overseeing all the properties. He was based at Young Life headquarters.

bed & a long long sleep—complete rest. So grateful for this eve & to-morrow completely "off." Must arrange more time for rest. I'm so weary & mentally inefficient.

———

Monday, February 24 (on the train)

Awoke 8A after poor night of sleep. Unusual for me on train. So conscious of my weakened** (tailsend,** physical condition. Maybe emot too. My earnest prayer these days is the rest and "release" I've experienced from extended (two or three mos.) "vacations, or "rest" cure** I've known three times since '40. Two as result of "The Firs"—one, the R the W[9] Ocean voyage. Last 52 or 53. What to do?? Frayne met me. We had a fine time of conferring & fellowship on trip home.

Tuesday, February 25

A very rushed day in the office. Worked hard—several imp conferences—Read mail—much of it handled well by Marilyn & Alec.[10] Enjoyed the day but couldn't get enough done. The Hdqts load is very heavy.

Wednesday, February 26

Our Staff-wide day of prayer went quite well at Hdqts. I worked hard rest of day—finished reading—and studying—the mail—came back to office after dinner & dictated an hour. Worked hard via letter & tele. to Tim [Nuveen] on Brazil, had two (one long) important conferences on Tr. W. All extremely interesting—truly a good day—in spite of nagging headache all day. Good fun @ home with Jim to-nite.

---

[9] Round the world.

[10] Alec R. Mackenzie. After Roy Riviere became regional director for the South, the board hired Mackenzie to serve as Executive Assistant to Rayburn. Prior to joining the staff the previous July, he had been a volunteer leader in Chicago as well as a local committee member. His time with Young Life was short—he resigned in December to become vice president of Wallace Erickson Co. in Chicago. He went on to write several time-management books.

Saturday, March 7 (Memphis)

To Mphs—

Nothing much to-day—did do some reading that was rewarding. Felt so weary. Got some genuine help & inspiration from the Word**, which is unusual** for me at this date. Called Maxie from Mphs after I got settled in. Had much** to do. [...]

Monday, March 9 (Memphis)

Long breakfast conf. with Rollin [Wilson]—great!—didn't sleep well last nite so I fought it until after 3A & finally took pill. (sleeping**) Nasty "hangover" next day, lasting till nearly noon. To Atlanta—then on to Augusta. Good time with Geo. Norris.[11] Fairly good mtg to-nite. Then** a long session with the Vol[unteer] leaders. Wk going great.

Jim's inability to sleep and his various health problems were vexing to everyone, and to no one more than Rayburn himself.

Still, life went on as normally as possible. Jim III was finishing up his senior year in high school. Personnel decisions had to be made and money raised. In April Rayburn spoke to 500 Canadian high school students at Malibu.

Saturday, March 28

Slept late. Didn't do much of anything. Went to the buffet-dinner for the hockey team to-nite.[12]

Note for March 26–28 spread

Sat & Sun. 28–29 were two of my hardest days—the perplexing thing is my inability to articulate the reason for this—even to myself. Leth-

---

[11] Young staff man George Norris. Norris had been a standout college athlete and served on staff for many years before becoming a Presbyterian minister.

[12] Jim III was on the team.

argy—but no apathy to relieve it—anxious to BE more & Do more for Him in the wonderful Calling He has given—can't communicate well (even with M. & Jimbo) can't get down to the interesting & constructive work I have in my mind. Yet (tho sometimes vaguely) conscious of the great blessing that the Lord has poured out.

Sunday, March 29

Slept late. Talked to Maxine a good while—read quite a bit. But it was a bad wk. end with me troubled (about what??) and unable to concentrate & must have been a boor around the house.—Is it spiritual low ebb?— or mostly physical?? Or letting M—— go,[13] plus indecision about route to go for restoring Maxine to health, and happiness?? I can't figure it.

Monday, March 30

"God has not given us a spirit of fear BUT of POWER, LOVE, SOUND MIND."[14] Maxine & I had prayer—so often I sense (?) that He is there— He will take care. The prayer was a struggle (mine) altho I meant every word—words just didn't come easily. Maxie's was better.

Saturday, April 4 (Malibu Club)

Cold, cold day.

The A.M. "Club Mtg." was another good one. ("… The basic historic facts are these …" Emph. on the Person—the Centrality of Christ in everything—closing with the idea "this" is the way God looks (acts) as a MAN. Love, ACCEPTANCE, as we are!, wants Trust. Close (Acts 18 "blind man").

Note for April 2–4 spread

Four Classes (Read each "what kids say and write …")

I "Raised in Ch. home—at college not doubters—found I didn't

---

[13] The board had just fired an employee that Jim liked.

[14] II Timothy 1:7.

have the answers—became doubter."

II "Folks <u>sent</u> me to S.S.—about 13 began to quit, dropped out, don't remember anything—except few Bible stories" ...)

III. "At 17 never had been inside of a church—talked & argued religion with my buddies—we knew we didn't know anything..."

IV "... religious home, don't know if Christian—a Sunday thing, no more that I could tell—never quit** but couldn't say what was important about it ... thing to do ..."

V <u>I know</u>—What, w<small>HO</small>, Why I believe. It has made <u>the difference</u>.

———

Tuesday, April 14 (Memphis)

A terrifically hard day—stayed in this a.m. but "suffered" from the tension build-up for Rotary. It seemed to go well—The World's Kids (my trip) but I wasn't full of zip. From beginning of Rotary Speech 1:05 p.m. until after—adult banquet 10:15—almost constantly talking or conferring with someone, Rollin, Horace, Chub, Scott Oury et. al. Eve. Banquet went well but again I was "loggy" & working was tough. Very little sleep to-nite.

Wednesday, April 15 (Memphis)

Moved to Airport "Benbow"[15] to get out of circulation—extreme fatigue. Don't believe I went out after moving @ noon—meals in room.— Maybe a restful day but didn't seem like it. I'm too tired to rest?? Again, very late getting to sleep.

Saturday, April 18 (Dallas)

Late a.m. & lunch with staff @ Sheffers'. Aft with staff & a few Comm. @ Ralph & Alice Thompson's @ Lake Dallas—difficult time for me.

Maybe the best mtg I ever had to-nite with 60 staff & prospective Vols—mostly young couples—what a** promising group—conf with

---

[15] The Admiral Benbow Inn near the Memphis airport.

Geo S[heffer] after.

Only 3½ hrs sleep to-nite—only God knows what I am going to do about this insomnia, backache, extreme fatigue, etc???

Note for April 16–18 spread
Several very potent mtgs & contacts on this long trip—but all extremely hard work—and takes more out of me than I can afford, I think—??

Sunday, April 19
Up @ 7:15A. Conf w. Geo[rge Sheffer] on way to airport. Lv DL. 9:10A Arr C.S. 11:30

Late & powerful delayed reaction to last nite's sleeping pills, apparently. Had to go to bed during my noon meal. Slept until 6:30 or 7:00— up an hour [then] back to sleep.

Monday, April 20
Believe I slept about 18 or 19 of the first 21 hrs I was at home—am simply exhausted—and see no way out. Some good work @ the office.

Tuesday, April 21
Worked hard & long @ the office. Had the whole crew in for prayer this a.m.

I was amazed at the wonderful comments Marilyn has received regarding my talk at the Wheaton Fellowship.[16] Acc[or]ding to them I was never as effective—and yet it was such a hard day for me???

Reports from the St Charles banquet very encouraging too.

Jim would forever remember May 1964 as the worst month in his life. He faithfully recorded the events in his journal. He knew something was not right when, during a meeting with the Advisory Committee (the regional directors and key personnel of Young

---

[16] Jim had spoken to this group of Wheaton College students on April 12.

*Life) he was summoned to meet two members of the Executive
Committee of the board of trustees in Chicago.*

*It was there, at the Flying Carpet Motor Inn near O'Hare
Airport, that Jim was told he was being removed from his position
and responsibility in Young Life.*

Friday, May 1

Worked @ office but didn't get much done.

Home early.

Saturday, May 2

Stayed in bed all day.

Sunday, May 3

Advis. Comm began late this a.m. Continued until late evening.

Stuck too [*sic*] it—very weary!

Monday, May 4

14 hrs of hard work—exc. fellowship in Advis. Comm. Mtg.

Again I hung in there—so exhausted ...

Tuesday, May 5

Another very full day @ Advis. Comm Mtg.

Call from M—— to meet N—— & him in Chi Sat??? Sounded
grim.

Talked to Advis Comm about this—their unanimous assurance
that they want me in my customary office—will back me, etc.

Wednesday, May 6

Pretty good day @ office.

Thursday, May 7

Worked hard & fast @ office this a.m.

Lv 1:50

Arr Chi 7:30 C.D.T. This was the roughest trip I ever made in a plane.

Thru thunder showers—extreme turbulence—<u>drinks</u> & <u>sandwiches</u>, <u>etc</u> <u>thrown</u> <u>all</u> <u>over</u>. To "Carpet" & to bed——

Friday, May 8 (Chicago)

Slept 'till 10A acct/ couldn't sleep much last night.

Tried to rest and study & meditate—did little good—

This was the night M—— & N—— told me. I left this shocking, late-nite, futile, convers[ation], virtually (possibly ACTUALLY) in a state of shock!

So little to judge me on. So "hearsay" & circumstantial, administration bad, (<u>What</u>?) <u>Poor</u> judgement (about dealing w "separation" dif. than Wheaton??)

ARE THEY QUALIFIED? Vision on Board? (Nil—always) except for an occasional individual.

Saturday, May 9 (Chicago)

How Providential that Gordon Jack & wife were here @ "Carpet" this a.m. Met at breakfast. Gordie & I talked a long time. He advises—"Keep in there"—"Boards are prone to mistakes—and wake up too late.—need you, etc."

Tuesday, May 12 (Denver)

To D.V. Called Advis. Comm. Mtg. M—— & N—— included themselves without communicating with me (???)

Either to-nite or in the morning the Adv. Comm. convened <u>without</u> me, M—— & N—— taking over—(not members, no authorization, "impossible"!

Wednesday, May 13 (Denver)

Exec. Comm of Board (with Advis. Comm. called in from time to time) [he lists four board members] met 1½ hrs <u>without</u> me being able to FIND THEM (Alec said "my guys REALLY TALKED"??) Finally got with them—couldn't believe what was happening; left late aft, "crushed"— <u>no</u> <u>one</u> <u>came</u> <u>to</u> <u>me</u>.

This seems now** to have been the darkest day of my life. I must hang onto the Lord—"I will never leave thee nor forsake the[e].."[17] is for me too.

⎯⎯⎯

On May 20, Jim sent out a letter to the staff and other key supporters explaining what had happened.

Dear friends and companions in the Gospel:

You who know me are aware of the long-standing health problems I have tried to cope with. It now becomes necessary for me to take an extended leave-of-absence because of exhaustion and attendant problems. The Executive Committee[18] has approved such a leave for a year if necessary.

This, of course, necessitates someone taking over my administrative duties. It may be in the best interest of our great and growing mission for this one to continue in the position of Executive Director.

At the June 3–5 National Board Meeting the decision will be made as to who will replace me and whether it will be for the duration of the leave or permanently. You will know that it is a very hard decision for me to face. My whole life is "Young Life." I know you will be praying!

Since REST is one of my principal needs I hope to be around the ranches for the first part of the summer—without responsibilities. I won't know for a week or ten days when the doctor's orders are finalized.

I know you will give yourself wholly and heartily to the one who steps into my place. We'll all keep focused upon Jesus Christ and making Him known!

In His abiding love,
Jim

Rayburn submitted himself to a week of "complete neurological and psychological examination" in late May. At the June meet-

---

[17] Hebrews 13:5.

[18] The Executive Committee of the board of trustees.

ing Jim pleaded his case with the board to restore him to power, but
his arguments fell on deaf ears.

Wednesday, June 3 (Chicago)

Arr. Chi. this A.M. To Ambassador Motor Hotel [*sic*, Embassy Motel]
near O'Hare Field.

Exec. Comm. invited all Board Members then** present to meet
us there this evening. I read my statement—then left. (Again without
questioning from them) N—— left early—apparently very angry, (I
have never seen this facet of his make-up before), and I had no chance to
speak to him. Not in all the last 4 terrible wks. has N——spoken to me
alone—same for [he lists three other board members]. Must correct this
M.O. [*modus operandi*] before I give way.

Thursday, June 4 (Chicago)

Horace Hull fellowshiped with me in such a gracious, wonderful way.
Also Herb Taylor. I was brought into Board Mtg—after all A.M. wait
& told the DV recom. of Exec Comm had been changed & I was voted
<u>Exec</u> <u>Dir</u> (altho on leave, and with no authority) and Bill Starr Assoc.
Exec. Dir. & Gen Mgr. in full charge.

This was ALL I could have expected at this time—very grateful to
God—but it was apparent that they plan to "superanuate" [*sic*, superan-
nuate] me at end of year. That's O.K., as it's IN GOD'S HANDS and a year
can bring many things—HIS THINGS IS WHAT I WANT!!

———

In the middle of all this turmoil, Jim somehow managed to preside
over the May opening of Trail West (an open house for 500 neigh-
bors) and the wedding of Ann to Jim Robertson.

Thursday, June 11 (San Francisco)

This must go down as a very special day. God has wrought something in
my life to bring a marked change in the despondency of the last month—
left Frontier early drove to DV. (Much better prayer en route than I've

had for weeks—still not much.) DV to San Francisco.

Ann & I had some happy laughs recalling pleasant things. Jim Rob[ertson] & I had good talks. With NO "medical reason"—the whole day & specially the evening were much much better. And I'm looking to the dear Savior, my loving Lord & not acting so much like a heathen. Thank God.

Friday, June 12 (San Francisco)

After pleasant but rather sleepless night the experience described above was strongly with me to-day—awoke & BEGAN the day with prayer & REAL blessing as God spoke to me thru His WORD.

Performed the marriage ceremony for Ann & Jim Robertson to-nite. Big, happy reception at their home. Kay Mac and the Bylsma's [*sic*] at the wedding. They drove me to the Hilton Inn.

On June 17 Rayburn wrote another letter to "Staff, key Committee people and special friends of the work" in which he further explained his situation.

Dear Friends:

A brief supplement to my letter of May 20 is long overdue. Forgive me.

The National Board's action was somewhat different than I outlined. I was continued in the office of the Executive Director with the customary votes of confidence and appreciation. (The leave of absence for health reasons was approved—and I am relieved of the responsibilities and duties of the office.)

During my week in the hospital at Wichita I requested and got a most complete neurological and psychological testing and examination, along with some physicals. The verdict is that I have long been suffering from severe fatigue (which I knew) and that now I have an emotional problem officially described as "depression." (That isn't telling you much since there are as many kinds of "depression" as there are people—but it's the best I can do.) Aftereffects of my stomach resection and vagatomy are contributing factors in these last three years of poor health. Soon I'll know more from further examinations.

The doctors are very optimistic about me getting back to complete health and activity with proper rest and treatment! So, be assured that I fully expect to be back in the saddle again.

As you know, Bill Starr has been appointed by the Board to serve as Associate Executive Director and he has, during the coming year or so, the full responsibility and authority of my former office. I know I do not need to urge you to give to him your fullest cooperation. You dear people working under his leadership make the coming year the finest season we have ever had of making Jesus Christ and His glorious things known to the kids.

As for me, I'll give him my loyal support as I have always given him my love and friendship. This, too, I trust goes without saying.

Thank you for your many, many touching and heartwarming letters. Please feel free to write to me—but for "business" and guidance please write to Bill.

More than ever I love this, our mission to the kids, and you people who represent our dear Saviour among them. Please pray for me, for Maxine and our children when you think of it.

Affectionately,
Jim

Thursday, June 25

Slept late. Went out to Sue & Smitty's. Took a nap. Had a good time with dear little Perri & Traci—and a wonderful evening with Sue & Smitty. Sue fixed Italian Spagetti [sic], corn on cob, fried egg plant & cucumbers & onions with a sour cream sauce. Never ate a better meal any place. We had a fine phone visit with Ann & Jim Robertson. Ann seems very happy.

Jim was allowed to begin the summer at Frontier, staying as usual in the Lookout. As if he was cursed, he had a jeep accident that necessitated several days in the hospital.

Friday, July 10 (Frontier Ranch)

Got off the driveway below the "Lookout"—the Jeep rolled—<u>very thankful to the Lord</u> that I got out. Arnie [Jacobs] drove me to the Salida Hospital.

Saturday, July 11 (Salida, Colorado)

Next 6 days in the Salida Hosp.[19] Both Steve Phillips & Robt. Hoover took care of me.

―――

Trail West hosted that year's Committeemen's Conference, and Jim was its honored guest. Unfortunately, during the conference some board members were led to believe Jim had been interfering in the program at Frontier and they ordered that he vacate Frontier Ranch and all other Young Life properties, including the Headquarters building in Colorado Springs. Already in a state of depression, this action plunged him into despair, and Jim would remain depressed until (by his record) late November.

Monday, July 20 (Frontier Ranch)

Natl. Comm. Conf. began at TR W. Good time with a lot of my friends: Ted Johnson,[20] Dewey Cave, et. al. Sale of lots going well. Great interest in the project.

---

[19] Salida was the nearest town to Frontier with a hospital.

[20] Just thirty-five at the time, Ted Johnson was the leader of the National Committeemen's group. He was an executive with the W. R. Grace Company in California. In the 1980s when he retired from W. R. Grace he went to work for Young Life as the head of the Young Life Foundation. He served as interim president of Young Life from 1992–1993, and continued on as senior vice president for many years.

Tuesday, July 21²¹ (Frontier Ranch)

I was told to leave "The Lookout" and all other Y.L. properties "right away."

———

Jim was devastated by this turn of events. He retreated to his daughter Sue's home in Denver for two days and then for several more days with friends in Memphis.

Sunday, August 9

Sent Jim Robertson & Smitty over to look at Hdqts., with my key. That is when I found out they had changed all the locks so that I couldn't even get into the bldg. A low time for me—the ultimate humiliation— just about couldn't stand to think of "my outfit" doing that.

The board had asked Jim to submit himself to a program of psychological therapy. Willing to do almost anything to be restored to his role in Young Life, he agreed, and began a months-long stay in San Francisco to see a doctor there.

One of the reasons the Rayburns chose San Francisco was that it would allow them to be close to Ann and her family. Additionally, Maxine continued to see Dr. Nesbitt in nearby Fairfield. Jim moved into an apartment in the Hamilton Apartments in downtown San Francisco.

Wednesday, August 12 (travelling)

Left home for San F. this a.m. Sure hated to go. Did exactly as I promised the Board—i.e. left in time to make first appt. available with Dr. Sam Nelken.

Monday, August 17 (San Francisco)

To Dr this a.m. Believe I am going to like him.

———

²¹ Jim's fifty-fifth birthday.

Saturday, August 29 (San Francisco)

A bad day. 1) I was quite prayerful & at times "touched" by the Lord and 2) Had some good time in the Word late to-nite. Extreme lonliness [*sic*].

Sunday, August 30 (San Francisco)

This is the first time I have felt like doing any serious writing in this journal since May 8th[22]—Must have arrived here Aug 13. The time with Nelkin [*sic*, Nelken] is still "?" but I am enjoying or at least intensely interested. Last Wed & Thur. were my best days since May 8th. Beginning to do some (a little) meaningful prayer & study of the Word these days. Believe it's coming! "Casting ALL your care …"[23] is a tough one. How little I've known about it.

Monday, August 31 (San Francisco)

A very good day—with the Dr.—like him better every time—and other ways. Had a specially fine evening (dinner at Tadich's[24]) with Bill Nesbitt and Mitch.

    Enjoying Tully's "The Supreme Court"[25]—couldn't sleep last night but it doesn't matter—I enjoyed myself & didn't feel the terrible pressure of lonliness [*sic*], etc.

Tuesday, September 1 (San Francisco)

Good time with the Dr. this a.m. Wrote to Andy (Goldbrick) and also a long letter & enclosures to John C[arter]. Am trying to keep a good record of expenditures and that sort of thing for the first time in years.

---

[22] He had probably gone back and filled in many days in addition to writing this entry.

[23] 1 Peter 5:7: "Casting all your care upon him; for he careth for you" (KJV).

[24] Tadich Grill. Opened in 1849, it is the oldest restaurant in San Francisco.

[25] *The Supreme Court* by Andrew Tully was a best-selling novel of the time.

I think I've gone a wk without even any "Doriden."[26]—One of my major goals is to get completely away from anything that might be a "crutch"—it's coming, even tho I have some bad days & am still frightfully weary.

Jim took his son to Spokane so Jim III could begin his college career at Whitworth. Rayburn's old club kid from Riverside High School in Ft. Worth, Sam Adams, was the school's football coach.

Friday, September 11 (Spokane)
Went to Spokane this a.m. Staying @ Davenport—had a wonderful, inspirational talk with Sam Adams to-nite. Some of his comments (mostly about the "impact" of my life on him & his Riverside buddies) were truly wonderful to hear. Best of all, of course, and again vindicating the "philo[sophy]" or principles we believe God gave us & wants worked out in every ldr's life was his, "I would never have seen Jesus Christ as a wonderful, an attractive person, if I hadn't 1st seen Him in you." (And, as always I wonder, "Dear Lord, what miracle do you work to make this so. What did he see?")

Saturday, September 19 (San Francisco)
Slept late—wrote a letter or two—went to Fairfield in afternoon. Enjoyed a pleasant conversation & dinner with Maxine. We talked a lot—about the Board—etc.—Jimbo—et. al. Went to bed early.

Sunday, September 20 (Fairfield, California)
Maxine & I slept fairly late—had a pleasant morning. Lunch—then I drove back to San F. Traffic fairly heavy on Freeway—1 hr. (exactly 50

---

[26] Introduced in 1954 as a safe substitute for barbiturates, by 1991 Doriden's harmful effects, including addiction, resulted in it being declared illegal. It was used to treat insomnia.

miles to "The Hamilton".) Spent the late aft. & evening in my apt. For some unaccountable reason, I couldn't eat—altho I enjoyed all the day until I got back. Seemed to "experience" more definite "depression" than I ever have had since … ! Went to bed & sleep early.

Friday, September 25 (San Francisco)
Good time with the Dr. and the rest of the day was a mess. Just don't know why I have to feel so lonely & washed up so much of the time when actually things are going well, all things considered.

Went to sleep very late.

Saturday, September 26 (San Francisco)
Felt good this a.m. & did a lot of work. A wonderful letter from Horace Hull.

Then for the "umteenth" [*sic*] time I had a bad afternoon and evening. Just too "worrysome" [*sic*]—what I want to get away from. It sure doesn't seem like "casting <u>all</u> your care upon Him" & I really want to do it.

Sunday, September 27 (San Francisco)
This was just a "nothing" day. Tired—not sufficiently interested in anything to get going on it. The thing seems to me partly compounded of just plain lonliness [*sic*] & not enough to do that I want to do—or perhaps that I know I can do—things I'm used to doing.

Friday, October 2 (San Francisco)
The day of inexplicable "terror". Doc called it an "anxiety attack."

Bkfst with Ross** & Elsie Lane. Haircut then the big trouble. To Dr @ 3P. Still shaking & perspiring so that I could hardly talk to him. The ONLY thing of this kind I have ever experienced. I'm glad I could get to the DR so that he could see me in that state.

[…]

Monday, October 5 (San Francisco)
Slept late.

Only big thing to-day was appt w Dr Nelken. He surprised me by insisting that I should go to the Bd. Mtg. & before that lay plans for getting the reins back in my hands—okayed my proposal that I should then become active head with ONLY Bill reporting to me, until I feel like taking on more. Very encouraged. Am to call Dr R—— C—— […] for consultation re: the dumping syndrome!

———

Wednesday, October 28 (San Francisco)
This was a bad, and "fruitless" day—EXCEPT for some good (tho brief) time in prayer & in the scriptures this a.m.

When, Oh Lord when, will come the end of this and how should I speed the day—while trusting You to do it.

———

It is evident that Jim held out hope that he would be restored to his previous position in Young Life. There was some mention of having him come back in a fundraising role, but Jim would have none of it—he insisted on being more than a figurehead.

He was in Chicago for a meeting with the Crowell Trust when the Young Life board met for its fall meeting in Dallas. He was hoping they were going to summon him to the meeting to discuss his reinstallation. The call never came.

Wednesday, November 11 (Chicago)
Union League Club—C[rowell] Fund Mtg. ALL day—whew! Kept hoping I'd be called to DL.

Thursday, November 12 (Chicago)
Another day—sitting out the forlorn hope—much worse than yesterday…

—᠁—

Monday, November 23 (San Francisco)
This is the best day I've had since that terrible "knock-out blow" (coup?)
by M—— & N—— on May 8 NITE. Exc time with Dr. N. Thinking
clearly—virtually no "depression."

May 8 is my "May Day"

Hungry again for the first time in months!

Wednesday, November 25, 1964 (San Francisco)
                    I am awakened by "dumping" as 25th begins—midnight.
Tired but happy! And ALL MY CONFIDENCE is in the Lord, as much as
is in me! "Put more CAPACITY for Trusting You IN ME, Lord JESUS!"
This a.m: almost a duplicate of yesterday a.m. Feel free, easy, Hungry,
no sign of depression in spite of so many unsolved problems. The prayer
is doing it—but the therapy got me back to prayer & for 2 days actually
feeding upon the Scriptures—devouring passages. M & I went to Ann's
and had such a happy evening, and no strain. It must be "the Joy of the
Lord" again, as so often in "the good old days."

Thursday, November 26, 1964 (Thanksgiving Day) (San Francisco)
A wonderfully happy and relaxed Thanksgiving Day with Ann & Jim[,]
the kids, Robbie & Ruth. I ate all day. Haven't put away so many calories
in a year or more. The kiddies so sweet. Everything went well. For third
day straight I got into the Word for some rich stuff (even tho short time)
and prayer—the same—it is like old times, say 10 or 15 years ago.

Saturday, November 28 (San Francisco)
Enjoyable day watching Army beat Navy for first time in five years.

Good ride in p.m. & good fellowship w Jim Robertson. He took me
to a little winery—first one I've seen.

The children were inside & boisterous—so when I noticed getting
nervous we left. Quiet eve @ "home"—"The Hamilton."

Note for November 26–28 spread

* All this time Nov 23 throu[gh] Dec 5. varies from Fair to Good to Great—with No visible or noticible [*sic*] suffering from the "depression" that orig[inated] May 8 & ran May 8 to Nov 23.

———

Monday, December 7 (San Francisco)

An all round better day but not up to a week ago. I think going completely without medication (except aspirin) may still be a problem—? (That doesn't check out tho in view of the Nov 23 to Dec 4—when being without medication mattered not at all.) Johnny Provin** got me a swell suit to-day.

———

Thursday, December 31 (on the train)

Lv C.S. DV. Zyph. [*sic*] 1:10P. Sue didn't keep her appointment with me in DV. Slept some out of C.S. Then up late. What a very, very difficult year is closing. My constant prayer—"Oh God of lovingkindness & tender mercy—may there not be another so bad—by thy Grace, may 1965 be a wonderful year—made so by REMEMBERING "Lo, I am with you ALWAYS … My times are in His hands & with enabling grace May I find & do the WILL OF God—and truly LOVE the brethren & all men!"

1966

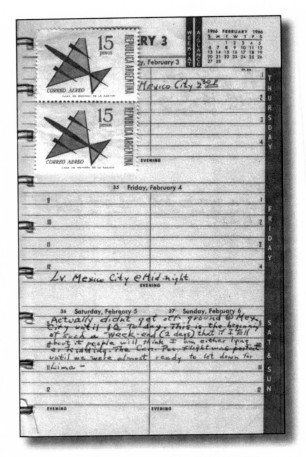

RAYBURN'S FIRST TRIP TO LATIN AMERICA

Jim's first foray to Latin America was in February 1966. The Argentinian stamps have been affixed in his journal since he bought them—over forty years ago.

Unfortunately, the journal for 1965 has been lost. As had been the case for several years, Jim continued to have medical problems, now involving his prostate in addition to his insomnia and other issues.

He agreed to come back to an active role in Young Life when the board issued an invitation for him to do so in May. He was given the title of "Founder and Chairman of Development" and charged with fundraising for special projects, researching foreign fields, as well as some speaking and public relations assignments. Not in the job description were any administrative or executive duties. Instead, the board made Bill Starr's appointment as Executive Director permanent. Rayburn was voted back onto the board of directors.

That summer he spoke for one week at Frontier and lectured for two weeks at the Young Life Institute for new staff. He also spent a few more weeks of the summer observing Young Life camps, and was part of the regional directors' midsummer meeting. He inspected a California Gold Rush town, Woodleaf, on behalf of the ministry to see if it could be used as a camp (Young Life purchased Woodleaf the next year, and it became their sixth high school outreach property).

At the fall board meeting in November Jim began to feel ill and, upon his return to Colorado, was ordered to the hospital for surgery.

Rayburn's journal for 1966 is one of the shortest. In part, that is because it is a "Week-At-A-Glance" diary, and the space allotted to each day is very small. But largely it is because Jim simply didn't write in it very often (he records nothing at all from February 23 through September 7).

On February 1, Jim began his third trip around the world which, for the first time, included stops in Latin America. Once again the purpose of the trip was to follow-up with former exchange students who had been involved in Young Life during their time in the States. All of his entries during the trip are included here. Unfortunately he did not write any record of his time in Brazil, South Africa, Uganda, Ethiopia, India, or the Philippines.

Thursday, February 3 (Dallas)
Lv DL 11:15A—Arr. Mexico City 2:30p

Friday, February 4 (Mexico City)
Lv. Mexico City @ Mid-night.

Saturday, February 5 (travelling)
Actually didn't get off ground @ Mex. City until 1A to-day. This is the beginning of such a week-end (2 days) that if I tell about it people will think I am either lying or kidding. The Can. Pac. flight was perfect until we were almost ready to let down for Lima—

Monday, February 7 (Mendoza, Argentina)
"Mi Amigo" cab driver friend got me at 7A, for a wonder, and arrived Mendosa [sic, Mendoza, Argentina] airport before 8, only to find that plane would go "sometime around 1 pm. or 2p."

Tuesday, February 8 (San Juan, Argentina)
This was my first real good day. The Marcet's [sic] are cordial. Juan is great to be with.[1]

Tuesday, February 22 (São Paulo, Brazil)
Lv. Sao Paulo 10:30A. In Rio taxi to Galleo. Then amazing "LUCK" which was far** above "luck." Stopped to chat w/Swissair agent. Waited hr at Areolenas [sic, Aerolineas] counter—no one showed (strike). My Suisse friend quickly got Pan Am endorsm[ent] & I was on Swissair CV880

---

[1] Juan Marcet had been a camper at Frontier.

non-stop (6 hrs) to Dakar [Senegal, Africa]. At Police in D[akar] met
Chilean to hotel. He shared his room. Ready for bed before 12:30 AM
instead of former "Comet" & 6 hr wait in A[ir] port. All amazing! I
spoke to God, thanking Him every time I awoke. Swissair flight was
perfect every way.

DAKAR interesting, attractive city.

[...]

---

*Two more blows hit Rayburn before his next journal entry. In
May, while in Princeton, New Jersey, he suffered a seizure while
staying at Rogers and Loy Ann Carrington's home and he had to
be hospitalized for several days.*

*The second blow was dealt when the board of directors decided
to officially retire Jim from Young Life. In June a letter was sent to
the Young Life community, which read:*

> Jim Rayburn has won lasting recognition as the founder of
> Young Life, and, for many years, the moving spirit in it. He
> has given unstintingly of his time and energy, even to the det-
> riment of his health, to this unique ministry to the teenage
> young person.
>
> To conserve Jim's health and strength, and to enable him
> to enjoy the rest to which he is entitled, the Board of Direc-
> tors has retired him from active service, effective July 1, 1966.
> He has been elected a life member of the Board of Directors.
>
> We are deeply grateful to Jim for the outstanding services
> he has rendered to Young Life Campaign in its founding and
> its development. It is our hope that, in the relief from admin-
> istrative pressures, he will have many more years of continu-
> ing service for our Lord.

*Yet a third blow would hit in September after he had resumed
journaling.*

Tuesday, September 27

Frank[2] called us from "Travelers** Motel" about 1:30. I, out with [Lorne] Sanny**. Got down there just before Dr. Bruce Pattee** arrived. First Diagnosis Bleeding Ulcer. Ambulance to Memorial. Pattee had me** help force 2 Pints of blood IV fast. Blood pressure came back up o.k.** Pattee & Winternitze** still with him when I left after 4½ hrs. Pattee had me call Dottie[3] to come. He kept telling me there was "something else" they hadn't found.

Wednesday, September 28

Met Dottie @ DV airport at 3A**

Spent most of the day back & forth to Memorial. Frank about the same. Pattee really on the ball.

At night Frank about the same (irrational**.)

Thursday, September 29

My kid brother Frank died suddenly about 8:30A (Heart arrest). Dott[i]e okay post-mortem Found cause of death was (Mallory-Weiss Syndrom[e]—a tear in the asophagus [sic] from vomiting—lets blood & bacteria into the chest cavity—no known remedy!)

Dott[i]e and I flew to K.C. this evening.

Friday, September 30 (Kansas City)

A disagreeable day of funeral, cemetery arrangements & visitors.

Saturday, October 1 (Kansas City)

Frank's funeral @ 11A.

Frank Rayburn was the youngest of the four Rayburn brothers. Young Life magazine featured an article about him in its June

---

[2] Jim's brother, who was travelling through Colorado Springs on business.

[3] Frank's wife Dorothy.

1959 issue (he was a volunteer leader at the time in Kansas City). It described him as "a real man ... having been a frog man during World War II in the U.S. Navy, and one of the daring squad who did the pre-invasion reconnaissance off Iwo Jima and Okinawa. He was awarded the Silver Star and also the Purple Heart. Today he is a commanding officer of the Local Reserve Service division of the U.S. Navy; is president of the Kansas City Athletic Club, where he plays strenuous games of handball three times a week; and he is an elder in the Colonial Presbyterian Church and a teacher of the adult Sunday School Class."

Frank was a lawyer and a judge. He was only forty-seven years old.

Now that he was no longer officially a part of Young Life, Jim decided to exercise his calling to spread the gospel to young people through a new enterprise. He called it Youth Research International and he was determined that his new ministry would be different from his previous one in at least one respect: it would not have a large board of directors.

He sought out old friends to support his new venture, whose purpose was to foster the development of Young Life-type ministries to high school students around the world. He continued to serve on Young Life's board.

Monday, November 7 (Oklahoma City)
With Frog most of the day.

Swell dinner & evening @ Yingers'. Write Bill & Joan [Yinger].

Tuesday, November 8 (Oklahoma City)
Saw Dr. Geo. Priddy—got that _____＋ near my eye taken off in a jiffy.

＋ The blank space is Jim's.

No strain.

Write Clare, Cathy & Ed Headington.[5]

Wednesday, November 9 (Oklahoma City)

Out of 13 men** @ Y.L Committeemen's luncheon and a <u>very soft</u> sell about Youth Research, Inc with Jack J[6] introducing the project—7 men signed up for the Y.R.I. support @ $200.00 each.

[…]

Thursday, November 10 (Oklahoma City)

Over 5 grand days @ Johnstons (Jack & Patty, Jerry and** … all wonderful to me) The most completely satisfactory visit in another's home that I have had—probably since the Sid Smith days.

[…]

Saturday, November 12 (Memphis)[7]

More of the Natl. Bd Mtg. … (Memo: The financial report.) (et. al., et. al.)

"Passed out" when it was over. Intermittent sleep thru the night.

Thursday, November 17 (Chicago)[8]

This was a great day! 6 Hrs. of the usual boreing [sic] time, (except Elnar [sic, Elner] Edman accelarated [sic] the process), of considering req[uest] for grant from Cr[owell] [Trust] & giving most of it to Moody B[ible] I[nstitute] as usual. But—great day! My req[uest] for $5,000 for Y.R.I. Inc. was presented <u>first</u> and okayed in full, at the end of the mtg!! I was

---

[5] Clare Headington had married former staff woman Catherine Klein. Clare and his brother Ed had an oil company, Headington Oil (see January 7, 1957, entry). The couple had three children. Years later, after Clare passed away, Cathy married Ed.

[6] Jack Johnston.

[7] The national board meeting for Young Life, which had begun the previous day.

[8] Jim was there to meet with the directors of the Crowell Trust.

JIM'S SPEAKING STYLE
Rayburn was a captivating speaker, using passion,
humor, and logic to get his point across.

EXHAUSTED and purchased shoes on way to LaSalle,[9] then was asleep in
10′. Off & on sleep. My heart full of praise to God for this great grant &
token of His abiding Love & care!

Thursday, November 24 (Thanksgiving Day)
Smitty insisted on going to get Maxine[10]—Nice!

---

[9] The LaSalle Hotel.

[10] Maxine had been in the hospital.

This was a grand day. We watched Okla U beat (upset) Nebr 10–9 & some pro games. But by far the best part was that we were all here to-gether. The grandchildren Traci & Peri were so sweet. We had a huge, delicious Thanksgiving dinner (by Maxine & Sue). A real family holiday.

Monday, November 28–Tuesday, November 29
[This entry is written across two days.]
These have been two of the toughest days I've had in a long time. Don't feel good. Shades of the old "depression." Couldn't get my work done.

Wednesday, November 30
A very good day.
Worked hard on mail & bills this a.m. Maxine & I went to see the Movie "Dr. Zhavago" [*sic*, Zhivago]—it was one of the greatest ever! Had dinner @ "Pancake House." I worked very hard on the Lilly Endow[ment] presentation—beginning quite late, but felt fit.

Sunday, December 4
Pretty good day.
Had about a 4 hour (!) talk with Bill Taylor,[11] to-nite.

---

[11]   Bill Taylor was brought to the Young Life headquarters from Chicago by Bill Starr to help with the administration of the mission. He worked there from 1964 until 1997. Though he never worked under Rayburn, the two men became close friends, and Taylor was with Rayburn's family at his bedside when Jim died.

1967

DREAMING OF A NEW CAMP

Jim never lost his belief that God could do great things, nor his desire to see young people around the world exposed to the "truths of Christ." Here, in December 1967, on a trip to Argentina with Arnie Jacobs, Jim discovered a spot he believed to be the ideal location for a Young Life camp.

In January, Jim addressed the staff conference at Trail West and Silver Cliff about his "recent thoughts and convictions concerning the outreach to foreign students."

In March he embarked on the first of two international trips he would take in 1967, this one to Latin America and Europe. Both trips were under the auspices of Youth Research International, although he worked closely with the Young Life staff in the countries where Young Life had begun work. Harry and Hope MacDonald had developed the ministry in Brazil and Hal and Judy Merwald[1] had just arrived to take over for them. The Merwalds were in language school in the city of Campinas, near São Paulo. The Young Life program in Brazil was called Alvo da Mocidade *("Target for Youth" in Portuguese) or "Alvo" for short. The Brazilian ministry was in the process of building its own camp in the countryside when Jim visited.*

While in Argentina Rayburn began dreaming of a new camp for that country in the Bariloche area.

Monday, March 6 (Mexico City)

A very busy day & another <u>good</u> one! What a contrast to the way I felt on Sat. I NEED to be "on the road" & doing & promoting things I'm interested in.

Long talk with Bob [Hurlbut]. Lunch with Bob, Bo[2] & another young fellow.

A splendid club mtg of about 60 to-night—I spoke. Good response from the kids.

Late dinner with Rev. Frank Woods & his wife. Bob took me to the airport about midnight.

---

[1]   Hal Merwald had been on staff for several years by this time. After his time in Brazil, he continued on staff in the States, becoming the interim president in 1986. He then served for many years as the head of Young Life in Canada.

[2]   Bo Stalcup, who was on Young Life staff in Mexico City.

Tuesday, March 14 (San Juan, Argentina)

This may have been the most important and significant day I've ever had in my years of travelling among & talking to people in other nations. Juan [Marcet] had about 20 (only 2 girls) over to-nite and showed slides of "Frontier" & I talked to them. The response was far beyond my best expectations ...

(Get names, Mario, Jorge, et. al.)

Must look into the Bariloche project (within the year, if possible). Is this God?!—The sugg. keeps recurring that we should <u>start</u> with the Camp in Argentina—rather than the usual way.

Tuesday, March 21 (Campinas, Brazil)

Another grand day—the high light was spending time out at the "Alvo" camp. It's going to be even finer than I expected. How thankful to God that He Let me conceive the great idea & then enabled me to make it possible! What a project!

Dinner to-nite with the Campinas part of the Board. Good time, but I need MORE evidence that they are ALL out on t/team [the team]. How to get construction at Alvo Camp really "off the ground." Do I have to accept the constant "... this is Brazil," excuse, reason—what have you. Must get into this problem w/Alvo Board—maybe pers. w/Harry Walker.

Monday, March 27 (São Paulo, Brazil)

This was a great day—one of the best. Harry & I had lunch with six U.S. & Brazilian executives. Then I had a long and rewarding conf (chat on <u>vital theological subjects</u>) w/Russell Shedd Ph.D. A remarkable man. Warm heart—balanced—but a true Christian. Surprise: He said "will be glad to transl. into Braz. Portuguise [*sic*], "He That is Spiritual". Now I can go ahead with Harold Van Broekhoven "Outreach" (Gr Rapids, Mich?)

Jim with friends in São Paulo.

Walked these near incredibly crowded streets in downtown Sao Paulo.

Then an <u>excellent</u> <u>hour</u> with 14 Campaigners from U.S. school & Y.L. Club. Response gratifying: spoke on John 13–16 mostly.

Late dinner party for Harry Mac's 41st birthday. Warren S & Grace there. Grand time w/Tommy & Danny McD. Very pleased by their response. Pleasant, prayerful late evening.

Our team Mac, Hope, Grace**, Edgard** are winners.

Wednesday, March 29 (Campinas, Brazil)

A sleepless nite (I've slept quite well—better than since May 8, '64 lately.). Then a Very busy day. Packed & left for Campinas. Noon-day dinner at Hillas [Mariente's] home. Very good contact. Then out to the Alvo camp in the rain. Got muddy & soaked. Progress there slow—but coming. Hillas, Harry Walker, Mac, Hal & I went. Then the Alvo Board Mtg @ John Lane's Clinic. Before that a big talk with Hal Merwald. He and Judy very discouraged. Tried to help!??! Late dinner at the Hotel (Savoy). Very weary! Maxine called. Still strong conviction that I Must learn Spanish—maybe some Braz. Portuguese!??! <u>How</u>? When? Where?

NO headaches while in Sao P & Campinas! Wonder Why? <u>Want</u> <u>to</u> <u>go</u> <u>home</u> <u>instead</u> <u>of</u> <u>Europe</u>!

Thursday, March 30 (Campinas, Brazil)
Harry & I went out to the camp this a.m. Then to lunch with Hal &
Judy Merwald. (I'm quite discouraged with them. Hal not doing well in
the language. Judy showing suspicious signs—probably "cultural shock."
If they don't make it, then what??)[3]

To Varicopas [*sic*, Viracopas][4] with MacDonalds & off for Europe.
(Must have 15 or 16 hrs. to sit on this plane) Somehow I am just not interested in going now, but ... (?) #A huge filet of beef with all the fixings,
then I went to sleep. Had all three seats & four pillows, so a relatively
good rest to Monrovia, about mid-night.

———

*While in Europe, Jim had an opportunity to see Bob Page, his old
club kid from Ft. Worth who had headed up Young Life's work in
Canada for several years and was now doing the same thing in
Bermuda.*

Friday, April 7 (Frankfurt, West Germany)
No sleep until at least 3 A.M. But, thank God I could read & study! Felt
good—when called at 8:30. AM. Felt even better after breakfast and a
long, intimate conf. w/Bob Page. I went all out & very sincerely after
much thot & prayer to simply apologize & seek his forgiveness for what
broke our fellowship years ago in B.C.[5] No equivocation. It was a GOOD
time & I think the thing is over with, and true & warm fellowship will
henceforth be the keynote. This unexpected time w/ Bob & the fellow-

———

[3] It is safe to say that the Merwalds were experiencing culture shock. Their first weeks
in Brazil were a nightmare of bureaucratic red tape, bank closings, long lines, and
unfamiliarity with the language. Their troubles during their first days in Campinas
were capped off by a message written near their house proclaiming, "Americans go
home." Nonetheless, they settled in and stayed for several years and the Lord greatly
blessed their time in Brazil.

[4] The airport for Campinas.

[5] British Columbia. Rayburn gives no other details of their problems besides this
paragraph.

ship with Diether,[6] standing alone, are reason enough & MORE for me to have come by Europe on the way home.

Changed to "Intercontinental Hotel" this noon. Expensive but so much more comfortable it is well worth it. I can tell that I've "roughed it" enough already for this trip. BUT FEEL GOOD.—only tired.

[...]

———

When Rayburn returned home he was faced with the challenge of following up on his trip without the help of a secretary or an office, a problem that often frustrated him in his post-Young Life years.

A far greater challenge for Jim was Maxine's continued dependence on painkillers. He almost never mentions it in his journals, the April 22 entry being one of the only times.

Saturday, April 15

Got home on a couple of close connections. Not time to call Maxine en route. Found out from her after arrival about the big storm last Thursday. Maxine came & got me. Good evening at home.

Total time of trip from Colo Spgs back to Colo Spgs 43 days! Think I should plan the future for that length to be maximum & not many that long.

[...]

Saturday, April 22

I awoke early—managed to get a fair amt. of work done this a.m. but was very enervated this p.m. Took about 1½ hr. nap & then couldn't get anything done.

I believe one of the factors involved is that I have, no secretary & there is an amount of desk work & "nit-picking" that is virtually impos-

———

[6] Diether Koerner. From Germany, Koerner met Jim, Maxine, and Sue during their 1959 trip to Europe. Koerner joined Rayburn on the staff of Youth Research International and began Young Life in Peru in 1968.

sible for me to get done.

Last two evenings Maxine has shown pronounced signs of being back on the "medicine." Don't know what to do so I do <u>nothing</u>.

Thursday, April 27

Bill Yinger returned my call this a.m. Says they are still as enthusiastic as ever about getting out the info & forming a contributing membership for Y.R.I. The lists are up to me! What to do! Good brief talks with Guss [Hill], & with Will Perkins. A lengthy & important conversation with Bill Taylor. How my heart goes out to him. I pray for him. What under the sun has happened in Y.L.—specially at Hdqts. He helped me gain some valuable insights as to my** failures (weak-points). I've simply got to SHOW what my heart FEELS to-ward those who work close to me. No Good the alibis or even the Reasons. They'd NEVER understand. Frayne turned down Jim III's & my plan for beefing up the Jeep program @ TR W FLATLY.

Tuesday, May 2

Not a very productive day except for what was to me a major event: Mitch called, came over, spent 2 hrs, confessed he had been putting it off. I got a chance to explain what I had <u>always</u> thot of his Dad & Uncle John. And asked his forgiveness for anything and everything I've ever done to give them or him any other impression.

Tried again on my trip report—still nothing that suits me—studied & read a lot.

To sleep late—but forgot I'd taken the 2 things [the doctor] ordered, as after reading & going to bed & getting up took 2 (and didn't realize the mistake until this a.m.) Just about "knocked me out"—

Tuesday, May 9 (St. Paul, Minnesota)

At the airport ** to-nite tried to really zero in, both on** thinking thru and praying about the sugg. from Mrs. C—— & SO MANY others that I should get entirely away from Y.L. (at least for a year or two). I have to give heed & wonder if the Holy Spirit is trying to tell me something when these suggestions come to me from so many sources. Mrs. C. says I do not "look good" (couldn't explain) of course I know I'm losing weight again, etc. Seems imperative that I come up [with] some answers. Of course I know some of them.

———

Jim attended the board meeting in May at Trail West. Later that summer he and Maxine spent time there visiting friends who had built homes in the village surrounding the Lodge. The Rayburns were making plans to build their own home there, although the plans never came to fruition.

Jim continued to have terrible trouble sleeping and began to track his sleep in his diary each day the way he had previously tracked his migraines.

Life for Rayburn after May 1964 was heartbreakingly difficult. He tried to be excited about his new work, but never got over his dismissal from the leadership of Young Life. There were some good days, but most days had a rudderless quality to them. For a man who was accustomed to meetings and crowds and exciting challenges on a daily basis, working alone was no tonic and only fed the sense of hopelessness that haunted him.

Friday, July 14 (Trail West)
Maxine and I fooled** around our lot to-day. I put up string around the entire lot so that we could visualize it and plan better.

We had another nice dinner with the Williams[es.][7]

Saturday, July 15
We drove home after breakfast this a.m. Stopped in "Ute Pass" for Maxine to sketch "The Swiss Miss" (Thinking a lot about plans for the chalet

---

[7] Charles Williams and his family. Williams was with the Lilly Endowment and was visiting Trail West.

on our lot ...)

Only fair sleep—beginning very late these last few nights.

—∿∿—

Sunday, August 27 (Trail West)

Had a great talk with Doug Coe and Bob Patton until 2AM last nite—
Good time running around in the jeep—just short hauls—took some of
the families yesterday and the du Bois[es] to-day. It was to me a pleasant
and profitable day.

I spoke to Leaders Seminar @ S.C.[8] to-nite on "Biblical Basis for
Y.L." and felt good about the presentation except that again it was <u>too
long</u>. No evid. of this from the audience but I must carefully check it
out.

Tuesday, August 29 (Trail West)

Not much sleep last few nites so I slept until 10A to-day. Then to Deer
Valley[9] & Silver Cliff—didn't get to talk to Red Kapple. Got very tired
so decided to go back home to-morrow morning.

I've been happy (?) in my work here—i.e. as close to happy as I've
been in many a moon.

Wednesday, August 30

Slept poorly last night but well this a.m. so did not leave for home until
11A. Heavy rains at Tr W., and most of the way to Colo. S.

Then this evening began a succession of <u>real trouble</u>—so "confused,"
"despondent," unable to move out & get my ideas under way sometimes
it's almost like 'strangling.' I must 'get some air' or I'll die. And yet I
don't—and the succession of near-worthless days continues ...

—∿∿—

---

[8]   Silver Cliff is only about ten miles from Trail West.

[9]   Deer Valley is a resort located next to Silver Cliff and run by former Frontier
manager Parker Woolmington.

Thursday, September 21

Sleep: Restless—late—finally took 2 Placydil [*sic*, Placidyl][10] that Maxine gave me—hate to—it's been too long & too hard since June 1st—I hate to interrupt even for 1 nite the struggle to sleep under my own steam—went almost from June 1st—last struggle is close to 30 days.

A hard day—very tired—somewhat depressed & nervous—can't tell WHY. Incomprehensible & near intolerable lonliness [*sic*].

———

Jim rented an office for Youth Research International in October and hired part-time secretarial help.

Sunday, October 1

Apparently 14 days (nites) of good sleep on my own in Sept. That's improvement.

Fair sleep

Didn't do much to-day—restless, unhappy & kind of depressed. Meant to go to church and as it has happened so many times I just didn't.

Watched a lot of AL Baseball and Pro Football on T.V.

Boston won A.L. last game of season.

Monday, October 2

To bed late 12M? To sleep soon & for all nite.

I went out to my new office @ Vrooman Office Bldg 3515 No Chestnut. Bought a desk, table, chair ... for my office. Met Paul Crozier who knows me(?). Good time. Maxine & I went shopping—got most of the rest of office furnishings.

---

[10] Commonly prescribed to treat insomnia in the 1960s, most doctors now avoid treating patients with Placidyl. Its side effects include many that Rayburn suffered from: dizziness, nervousness, restlessness, changes in vision, tingling in the hands, slurred speech, confusion, and trembling.

Wednesday, October 4

Last nite I felt sleepy about 9:30P, went right to bed & to sleep & slept thru till 7:30 with only twice up in 8 hrs. The best sleep I've had since at least June 1st.

Went to the new office this a.m. To-day may turn out to be a great one—I went to Bill & Mitch convicted & intent upo[n] restoring fellowship with no argument about anything. 1½ hrs good conv., Bible reading & prayer.

—⁓—

Friday, October 27

Sleep—good. Even after I got up to take care of the car (no anti-f[reeze]) at 4A

For the fourth straight day I got several important and rather difficult letters done by noon. The itinerary for So A. requires the usual amount of work but Bob Astley[11] has it set now I believe.

The office and Sec. has stepped up my production about 1000%! (Memo to me: These four days I have probably done as much dif[ficult] & tedious dictation & routine office wk. as in most of '63 & early '64—but, possibly, not with the same amt. of enthus[iasm], etc. Is the answer—"to keep plugging"? Am I perhaps "attempting too much"? If so How do I determine God's will for me? Just keep OPEN & ALERT for indications I have lived by from '33–'64. ('40–'64!) (I was always aware of [Psalm] 32:8,[12] 121:8,[13] etc. in these years! Is need then to rest more in these same principals & promises?!)

---

[11] Bob Astley was Jim's travel agent.

[12] "I will instruct you and teach you in the way you should go;
     I will counsel you with my eye upon you."

[13] The LORD will keep
     your going out and your coming in
     from this time forth and forevermore.

Tuesday, November 7 (Chicago)

Fair sleep—intermittent from 12M 'till 7A

This was one of my toughest days—but thanks to the Lord I won! For over 2 hrs (incl. lunch hour**) it looked bad for my request re "Y.L. Forward Fund"[14] at the Trustees mtg (Cr[owell Trust]) but it finally broke & they came thru with 100 g's & 5 for YRI. How can I be THANK-FUL ENOUGH?

Spent a pleasant but exhausted evening alone.

For almost a month, beginning November 21, Jim and Arnie Jacobs travelled to Latin America, visiting Peru, Argentina, and Brazil. While in Argentina, Jim discovered what he hoped would be the next camp the Lord would use him to build.

Monday, December 11 (Argentina)

Slept well—soundly—up once—no aids

This was an exciting day. Saw more beautiful country than I have ever seen in on[e] day. Went First up toward Mt Lanin—10 miles(?) along Lago _____ I said "Stop the car" (Must remember this small thing lest it be "historic"—We all walked out on a penninsula [*sic*] incl. perhaps 200 acres—all had the same reaction—spontaneous. A fabulous spot—even greater than Malibu. The fantastic trees—huge & the flowering "Nostros"—lush vegetation, much of it new to us—a solid carpet of grass—two beautiful sandy beaches ... etc. ad infinitum. The rest of the day through what must be the most beautiful country in the world. Terrible slow dusty road—exhausted when we stopped at V [end of entry]

---

14 The Young Life Forward Fund was a two-year fundraising program to raise money for a camp in the East. Whatever Jim's feelings about the way Young Life had treated him, they did not deter him from raising money for the ministry.

1968

> Monday, August 5, 1968
> 218th Day—148 days to follow
>
> The worst day of my
> life — this morning — in
> TV room — struggling to
> tell Bill Taylor & Martin
> that I wouldn't make it …
> no time left … what to
> do with me etc.

"THE WORST DAY OF MY LIFE."
Jim had horrible health problems in 1968, culminating on this day in August when he thought he was about to die.

At the beginning of the new year, Jim and Maxine sailed to Europe once again. This time their trip included a stay in Rome where Sue Jones Lawrence, a former Colorado Springs Young Lifer, had been living. The Rayburns went from there to Basel, Switzerland, where Sue's husband Fred was studying theology.

Wednesday, January 3

Not much sleep last nite.

A busy & productive hour or two at office—Then Maxine & I drove to Smitty & Sue's & had a visit before going to the Denver Zypher [sic].

Lv DV 4:00 p. for Chicago–New York & Rome.

Saturday, January 6 (at sea)

Sailed at Noon on "Michelangelo" for Naples, enroute to Rome.

A grand lunch & dinner, and pleasant afternoon and evening.

To bed quite early to make up for last night.

Tuesday, January 16 (Rome)

Slept well & late.

[...]

To Pantheon—on the way to a swell little place to eat—then a long way home past some interesting points.

From 3P to 6P another splendid & rewarding discussion with Fred [Lawrence]. He answered key questions that arose in my mind specially yesterday.

[...]

Thursday, January 18 (Rome)

Slept v. well last n. fr. 11:30p on with a boost from chems.

Vacarri's** people called to say he was weathered in in Turin.

Lv Rome on Swissair about 8:30P (From downtown at 7) Peter Drilling** was at the d.t. terminal to see us off. Long wait in Zurich.

Arrived Basel nearly 1A.

Friday, January 19 (Basel, Switzerland)

Maxine had to go to the hospital for treatment & X-Rays to-nite. Fred [Lawrence] & I got in quite a bit of talk.

Maxine was treated for heart trouble and released. After a visit to Germany the Rayburns returned home. Health troubles contin- ued to plague both Maxine and Jim.

Monday, February 5

Pretty good sleep w/o/chems.

Felt strangely weak, short of breath—as I have been repeatedly for past few months—and slightly ill or too enervated to go to the office.

Would describe as a very hard day—without knowing <u>exactly why</u>??

Finally got final word from Chas W[illiams] for Friday & changed meeting Arnie Thur p.m. @ Indianapolis Olympic Club. Looks like Wash & N.Y. contacts imperative for next wk. end . . .

Tuesday, February 6

To sleep w/out chems. Until 2 or 2:30A when "Ping"[1] heard** repeatedly disturbed and Maxine gave me Placydil [*sic*, Placidyl].

A tough morning. In spite of extreme "internal pressure" not to work, I completed the all-imp. letter to Bill Kieswetter and the Report on European Trip to my "mailing list."

A long, lovin' and very satisfactory talk w/Andy (Goldbrick) this p.m.

Friday, February 23

Fair work @ office this a.m. Conference w/Mitch—Dr. Chris gave me a cortisone shot in the back that has been bothering me so much—(it's

---

[1] Ping was the Rayburns' Siamese cat.

been over a year; he said that was good—bad** pain only last 2 or 3 months off & on) Shot made me feel pretty shaky.

Dr Kent had me take Maxine to the hospital this p.m.—don't have diagnosis.

Sunday, February 25
Slept late after almost no sleep last nite—

Jim & I went to get my car which was out of gas—he fixed fried chicken. Called Maxine—she not feeling well—they still think she may have pneumonia—didn't want us to come over.

———

Tuesday, March 19
A bad day—nothing accomplished that mattered.

Wednesday, March 20
One of the worst days I have had in months—just couldn't work, couldn't rest—my mind in a turmoil—the "inner trembling" is back in force.

———

Seeing the need to reach young people in Spanish-speaking countries (and thinking of possibly even moving to South America himself), Jim enrolled in an intensive Spanish language course in Arizona. At age fifty-eight and in failing health, it was not the ideal time to learn a new language. However, Rayburn managed to make it through the course, and the weeks of focused study seemed to help him somewhat.

But there were ominous portents of things to come during this time period. He noted in his journal, for instance, the fact that he had lost almost all memory of his trip from Colorado Springs to Gallup, New Mexico, on his way to Phoenix, even of where he had spent the night.

Wednesday, March 27 (travelling)

Left Colo. Spgs this P.M. and drove to Las Vegas N. Mex. All easy, fast rolling—glad to get on with the next project.

[He has drawn a dashed line.]

Appended later: After arrival Phoenix, could not remember this portion of the trip at all—no memory of landmarks, towns, etc.??) (Later, 5/15, I still don't know where I stayed in Las V., even after looking, on the good trip returning. What does this mean??)

Thursday, March 28 (travelling)

Las Vegas N. Mex to Gallop to-day. I was bored, tired and disconsolate, so I quit early & didn't worry about the short mileage.

[He has drawn a dashed line.]

Appended May 18th.

(After arrival Phoenix—and even on the good return trip I remember NOTHING about this day,—except where I stopped in Gallop. Do not even remember going thru Albuquerque. Very concerned to know what this means!??)

Saturday, April 6 (Phoenix)

The regular 2½ hours of review of the week's 15 dialogues, by two of the conversation teachers proved that I am keeping up and getting it. I certainly didn't know throughout the week. It is a blur. (Of course I speak too slowly. They want me to speak Spanish faster than I have ever spoken English.)[2]

Monday, April 8 (Phoenix)

......Memo: My right arm and hand??....several weeks of it now—intermittent, but most of the time. Ask Charlie [Fisher] or Bill N[esbitt]!

---

[2] Jim's comment will bring a smile to anyone who actually heard him speak. His drawl was quite pronounced, and his speaking tempo was similar to that of actor Jimmy Stewart.

Sunday, April 14 (Easter) (Phoenix)
A bad day—and I was looking forward to it so much ...

Didn't want to go anyplace—couldn't think of anything I wanted to do ... wouldn't call Emile's friends??

Didn't study enough to justify staying in all day. (Face it, Rayburn, these are depression symptoms.)[3]

Jim completed the course on May 11 and the next week he attended the national Young Life board meeting.

Thursday, May 16 (Sacramento, California)
Bd. Mtg All Day!

I seem completely at ease (for the first time since June '64) with this group—and best of all NO APPARENT DEPRESSION SYMPTOMS. Sad and solemn thoughts notwithstanding, my insides don't tremble & hurt!??

Friday, May 17 (Woodleaf)
To Woodleaf this A.M.

Memo: My report for the Board Comm. on International Work, their subsequent reaction—all favorable. (I took 14 min, as against 1½ hrs for some committees ... recommended Board Policy be established on 5 points all voted with a minimum of "hablar."

What a contrast to their reaction (and my performance 65–67.) I felt no stress, "baled my hay,"[4] and got out winning. What does this all mean??

[...]

---

[3] This is a rare third person self-reference, one of only a handful in thousands of entries over the years.

[4] Early Young Life staff were always encouraged to make sure they had "baled their hay" before they spoke, meaning to prepare appropriately and put things in order.

The aspen grove at Trail West was one of Rayburn's favorite spots.

Sunday, June 2 (Trail West)

Just roamed around Tr. W.—didn't do much but I was pleased that the stuff they have goofed up didn't bug me like it has in former years.

Monday, June 3 (Trail West)

I started getting ready to leave about 10A but didn't get away until 1P or 2P. Didn't want to leave.

The Conoco** people in Buena Vista found my oil pump fouled up—tried to fix—finally disconnected the power steering and I got back to C.S. about 7P—rough trip—I often feel that I'd just like to stay over there the rest of my life—which I hope will be a long time. No place I love like F., S.C., Tr. W. et al.⁵

[...]

---

⁵ Frontier, Silver Cliff, and Trail West.

Tuesday, June 4

[...] awoke realizing that there's something wrong & I'd have to go to the Hospital. Hate the idea.

Couldn't get [Dr. Charlie] Fisher, was referred to Stafford—don't remember exactly what went on—got out two imp. letters, told Kay [Baker][6] to take the car (minus power steering) to Perkins [car dealership]—Maxine got Bill Taylor to bring me to Penrose [Hospital]. He was very nice. They started tests right away. The faintness, dizzyness [*sic*], etc persists—never had anything like this.

Wednesday, June 5

They started at 7 or 7:30A & really put me thru the mill on tests—lots of blood tests, head X-Rays from every direction, (that's the ??), chest X-Rays—a breathing test, several in fact—I just about blew the needle off the paper—it's all boring & tiresome but @ 4P still have the same symptoms. So ... ??

Wednesday, June 12

Long confs w/both [Dr.] Charlie [Fisher] & Dr. [Michael] McNally today. Nothing definitive about the tests. At least they both say that I do not have a tumor, blood clot or anything that would require immediate attention.

———

Returning from a trip to Memphis later that month, Jim had yet another frightening episode.

Sunday, June 23

Called home from DV airport—("too sick ... don't know whether I can get home ... meet me & have Dr. @ airport.") Sue paged me—couldn't get to front desk. She found me. I don't remember, but she put me on the plane. Jim III & Dr. Bruce Pattee met the plane—to Penrose. Don't

[6] Kay Baker was Jim's secretary at the time.

remember anything else.

Saturday, July 13
Left Penrose to-day. Couldn't stand it here any longer. [...]
    To home.

---

*Just when it seemed things couldn't get any worse, they did. Jim's
journal entries from July 29 through the end of August are shown
here in their entirety (he wrote nothing from August 7–31).*

Monday, July 29
Strange symptoms with my eyes—shadows, etc.

Tuesday, July 30
Very frightening symptoms with eyes. On TV screen color patches
where there were none, diff[iculty] in focus etc.
    (Siezure [*sic*] about 9P while trying to watch a [Robert] Mitchum
movie about Africa on T.V. Next awareness—ambulance. Penrose ...

Wednesday, July 31 (Penrose Hospital, Colorado Springs)
Penrose

Thursday, August 1 (Penrose Hospital, Colorado Springs)
Penrose.

Friday, August 2
To home but very ill—(worst time with my eyes—no focus possible,
etc. ....)

Saturday, August 3
Still very bad.

Sunday, August 4
Same. No focus.

Bill Taylor has been here almost constantly since Fri.

Monday, August 5

The worst day of my life—this morning—in TV room—struggling to tell Bill Taylor & Maxine that I wouldn't make it ... no time left ... what to do with me etc.

Tuesday, August 6

The dramatic change for the better—like a new world, a new life!— completely free of the frantic & awesome fears of yesterday!

By the end of August things had gotten considerably better. Jim's doctors had pinned down what they believed to be causing the seizures and treated him accordingly. Jim explained in a letter to the Young Life family:

Dear Friends:

This letter is sent for a two-fold purpose. One, to express my heartfelt thanks to the hundreds of people who have prayed for me during my recent serious illness and, two, to give an authoritative account of the illness. Confusing reports have gone out and it is no wonder, for I have lived with this bewildering and harrowing experience all summer; and I did not know what was happening, nor did my wife, who was in constant attendance, nor others who spent endless hours with me.

Dr. Michael McNally, neuro-surgeon, handed me the following statement:

"My patient, Jim Rayburn, has had two seizures with a long interval of over two years in between and feels much better since being on medication for a convulsive disorder. He has also had intermittant [*sic*] signs of speech difficulty, loss of equilibrium and a lapse of memory which is associated with the enlargement of some ventricles in the brain, and felt to be secondary to some degeneration of the nervous system. The outlook for this will only be known after a passage of time, but presently he has greatly improved."

Dr. Matthew Presti, neuro-surgeon, concurs as does Dr. Charles Fisher, who has been my personal physician for fifteen years. All are agreed that no prognosis is possible.

Since I feel better than I have felt for many years, and the doctors have assured me that these conditions often remain static for as long as fifteen or twenty years, I am not concerned. I told them that would be long enough.

I left the hospital four weeks ago. My convalescence has been a fine experience of constant improvement and no recurrence of the many frightening symptoms I experienced throughout the long summer. Maxine has been at my side continually and has ministered to my every need lovingly and with great understanding.

Maxine and our children and I believe that the Lord delivered me, and we shall be eternally grateful to Him and to all of you for your concern and prayers.

Happily and cordially yours,
Jim Rayburn

Interestingly, though not recorded in his journals, Jim spoke to kids for a week of camp in August at Star Ranch. Mal McSwain was the Camp Director for the session and invited Jim to come over and see everyone. When he noticed that Jim sounded better than he assumed he would, he asked him if he felt up to speaking each night at club.

Every night for the week, Jim would be driven from his home to Star Ranch. Sometimes he would arrive in time for dinner, other times he would get there just in time to deliver the message. It was obvious to McSwain and those who knew Jim that it took all the strength Rayburn had to make it through each night. But, McSwain recalled, "I felt like it was some of the best talks I'd ever heard him give."

Friday, September 20
Almost no sleep last nite

Jimbo & I completed the deal for the Pontiac GTO. What a car!

Maxine, Jim & I left for Tr. W. about 4PM. To Yingers' cabin. Late dinner at Tisings**. Jim pleased me by the careful way he drove, and his spontaneous enthusiasm for Tr. W. & us building a cabin over there.

The Aspen[s] are spectacular.

Jim & I took a long walk thru the Aspen [Grove] in the little valley at dusk.

Saturday, September 21 (Trail West)

Only 3 or 4 hrs. of sleep.

Sue & D.T. came about noon. We had a grand day—took a "Scout"[7] up Merc[ury] Creek & to the Mt. Princeton chalet. I Enjoyed the day more than any one day for a long, long time. I wonder if I shouldn't try to make plans to live over there?!

For Christmas, Jim, Maxine, and Jim III joined Ann and her family out in California. Maxine took the train while the men drove.

Wednesday, December 18

Jim & I left Colo. Springs @ 6P and were in Glenwood Springs about 10P in spite of much bad road conditions from Tennessee Pass on to Gl. Sprgs. Jim III drove—with skill & caution—

I started driving at Glenwood. Road & weather conditions variable—arrived in Vernal, Utah about 1 p.m. I drove slightly less than 200 miles.

Thursday, December 19 (San Francisco)

No filling stations open. We wasted $1.00 in a "Self-Service" place that didn't work. Near Roosevelt [Utah] & nearly out of Gas we hit a filling station & nice little restaurant. Ate, fooled around & Jimmy drove.

---

[7] A Scout was a vehicle made by International Harvester similar to a jeep.

While I slept most of the time he had terrible storms & icy roads. I awoke just out of S. Lake City. We gassed up & left @ 6A. Very bad road & blizzard but arrived Wells, Nev. & had good breakfast about 8:30A. Surprisingly I drove to Winnemucca [Nevada] while Jim slept—totaled nearly 300 mi & felt good. Slick roads, some very bad storms. Jim drove. Threw tread out of Reno. Chains at Donner. Fast trip anyway. I drove from Fairfield. Arrived @ Ann & Jim's aprox 26½ hrs elapsed time. Feel tired but relaxed & good!

Friday, December 20 (San Francisco)
Last night—after pleasant time with Ann, Jim & the boys, went to bed @ 10P & for the first time in years slept the clock around w/out chems.

1969

Monday, June 9, 1969
160th Day—205 days to follow

To Bob Beadles office this aft. He beat around the bush + told me I had a prostatic tumor, already spread to the bladder, with urethra et. al. Malignancy of a virulent type. So sorry for him. Told him he didn't need to horse around w/ me just give it to me straight. Bad! Not much else medically speaking It was ~~rather~~ strange + wonderful the measure of peace I had. Am just worse about a broken leg. Bob called Gutierrez @ Penrose Cancer Clinic ...

JIM IS DIAGNOSED WITH PROSTATE CANCER

While looking through the journals several years after Jim's death, Maxine commented to a friend, "Through all of this, there were the happy times and the real fun times because Jim had a tremendous sense of humor. But naturally, you wouldn't put down in a diary things like that, but I don't want to leave that part out because anyone who ever knew him very well, knew that he was always joking and kidding and laughing a lot. And he loved to talk—so naturally, these diaries are mainly the serious aspects of his life, his feelings as well as a sort of a record as to what happened when. But there was always that [humor] with Jim, whenever he was around, even up until he got so sick he could hardly talk."

The period when "he got so sick he could hardly talk" would not be until 1970, but his health steadily declined throughout 1969. Compounding all of this was the fact that Jim felt abandoned by Young Life.

Jim continued his efforts with Youth Research International. As his health deteriorated, an office was set up for him in the Rayburns' home, and in March family friend Millie Carter began to work part-time for Jim as his secretary.

Wednesday, January 1

For the past year (and several before) it has been <u>hard</u> <u>to keep current</u> in the <u>daily work of maintaining this record.</u> <u>Am resolved to DO IT this year.</u>

Fairly good day—sorry I do not feel better physically & mentally. Of course the question ever-present in recent years is prom[inent] in my mind i.e. is this** partly or mostly because I am not <u>in better shape spiritually.</u>

Watched all the "Bowl Games"

Thursday, January 2

Why is it so hard, on this just the second day to keep the resolve of yesterday? I've asked myself that over & over the past few years. Probably partly, at least, because I do not know what to say. (Ex: This day has not been real bad—as some are. Neither has it been any good. Just put off most of the work I'd planned.) Feel achy, melancholy or depressed—very uncertain & probably afraid ... I'm praying but not getting any-place with that either.

Friday, January 3
A difficult day. Nothing very constructive except paying a lot of bills & writing a couple of notes—plus a little reading.

The despondency—shakes—etc., pretty tough.

Long talk to-night with Maxine re. the various symptoms.

Saturday, January 4
Outside of a few good minutes at the office this was sort of a nothing day.

Feel like there is a lump inside of me—two of 'em—one in my chest—one in my head. "... anxiety, boredom, conflicts ..." Oh for a bit of Light on the path. Oh for the guidance & strength of the Holy Spirit that I've always HAD to HAVE. At least I've written currently 4 straight days in this. Very small "victory"—but something.

Sunday, January 5
There is nothing to record—except perhaps the fact that I went ahead and wrote this anyway. A rather dull day. I know that boredom is get-ting to me badly and feel surprised & I suppose guilty that I don't get something done about it.

Monday, January 6
This has been one of the most difficult days in years and that is saying a lot. A good bit of the day I was sick but could not put my finger on any physical reason. Some aches would not account for it. But, as always, trying hard to pin down the reasons, I think they are 1) Indecision as to what to do; job, office, contacts. This is completely bewildering. 2) Fear. 1st that no help arrives on any hand, no guidance from above—that I

can discern, perhaps even "money problems." 3) Am I a permanent in-
valid(?). And the tragedy of it is that all these things can & should be
conquered by a simple childlike trust in the Saviour. I cry to him. I hear
no answer. Bewildered!

———

Monday, February 10
Slept late—rushed to Dr. [Michael] McNally's for 10:30 appt. but he was
nearly an hour late. Seemed to check me over thoroughly—says I'm in
fine condition. In fact acted rather surprised about it. Didn't think my
insomnia, etc. etc had any neurological signif. For the first time since
Aug 1st seems unsure about me having a sclerosis disease but insists that
my trouble is definitely physiological of some mysterious nature.

Bad mig this aft., after a.m. symptoms. Vomited about 8P & slept
about an hour & feel better now. (10:45p)

Tuesday, February 11
Called Bill Culbertson[1] re: the fact that I did not contact the other
[Crowell Fund] Trustees about my request for YRI. He was very cordial, said I had covered the subj. well in my summary—that he had sent
it on with his recommend[ation] (which he had previously told me was
favorable).

Went to headquarters Y.L. Chatted with several. Long, cordial talk
with Mitch.

Monday, February 17
Awoke early after being up several times—no med or drink since 1
Plac[idyl] @ 1A but very groggy this morning.

A fine lunch with Bill Starr @ noon and the first good fellowship

---

[1] William Culbertson (1905–1971). He served as the president of Moody Bible
Institute from 1948–1971 and served on the board of the Crowell Trust for many
years.

I've had with Bill since June '64. Very thankful to the Lord. He proposed that I conduct a "feasibility study" for training of YL key men, (along YLI[2] lines) for Latin America w/the new** Costa Rica converts (I.C.L.)[3] & Br[azi]lian men, "Edgard" et al. in mind = v Board financing** & to draw the YL.C & YRI closer. Sounds like 1st "breakth[rough]"

Rec'd $10[4] grant from Crowell people for Y.R.I.: Things looking up. Don't understand the continued lethargy.

Wednesday, February 26
My new office is nearing completion. It is becoming far more attractive than I visualized. Charlie has done a grand job and so has Jim III, staying right in there.

This must be one of the worst days ever.

Thursday, February 27
The office was carpeted to-day. It is beautiful. I can't believe it. Even tho I feel so bad it is an inspiration.

Friday, February 28
We moved the office from 3515 No Chestnut to-day. Long tough job with good help from Charlie, Terry, _____ _____[5] I did more than I thought I could—for I have seldom felt more—shaky, despondent, etc.

The office is even more attractive & beautiful with the furniture in it!

---

[2] Young Life Institute.

[3] International Christian Leadership, which was the ministry founded by Jim's friend Abraham Vereide and headed by former Young Life staff member Doug Coe.

[4] Almost certainly meant to be $10,000.

[5] The blank spaces are Jim's.

Monday, March 10

I probably felt better to-day than I have any day for several months—physically o.k. in spite of the cold symptoms of yesterday—and a good measure of inner peace.

Late to-nite I put several letters on the dictaphone—some rather hard—(they are all kind of hard for me anymore.)

Tuesday, March 11

Millie [Carter] was here for the second time. We got quite a bit done—i.e., relatively speaking. I'm sure I can work up to a much greater daily output now that I have such a beautiful and comfortable place to work, plus good secretarial help when I need it.

Bothered considerably this aft. & eve. w/despondency(??.)

Wednesday, March 12

This has been a bad day—terrific unrest (maybe boredom). In spite of that there is a note of encouragement; I studied spanish [*sic*] more than I have at any time since my big illness last summer. Even late at night.

Thursday, March 13

Even with 2 Plac[idyl], only slept an hour—about 2 to 3A. Then up quickly with that terrible restlessness in my legs which I haven't had much lately. To sleep some time after 5A 'till 8. Day no good—nervous, tense—can't figure it. Not much done to-day.

Friday, March 14

Turned out some pretty good office work & got some of my desk drawers squared away with Millie's help.

The men from Y.L. Hdqts were over this aft. for coffee & to see my new offices. Good time. Boring evening. Tried to go to bed at 11P but couldn't sleep—as usual (11:15P).

———

The highlight of the year for Rayburn was the trip he took to Latin

America with his son from March 27–April 22. The two travelled to Mexico, Peru, Brazil, Argentina, and Chile, developing contacts for Young Life-style ministry. It was a special experience for father and son to share and would be Jim's last foreign trip.

Jim III had met and fallen in love with a young Brazilian, Lucia. She and her family lived in Campinas where she was working as a travel agent. Prior to that, she had been a language instructor and had been tremendously helpful to the MacDonalds and the Merwalds as they sought to bring Young Life to Brazil. In fact, Young Life, The Navigators, and Overseas Crusade all traced their Brazillian beginnings to meetings in her family's home.

Thursday, April 3 (Campinas, Brazil)

Don & Diether were at the airport at 7:15A. I was tired. With these late nights—even tho agradable[6]—one needs some morning sleep. Left Lima via Braniff, 40′ late @ 8:40. Routine 4½ hr. flight to Viracopas [*sic*, Viracopos].[7] A "despachanti" [*sic*, despachante][8] was with Lucia @ V[iracopos]. Got around immigration but couldn't get Jim's stereo in w/out paying 180% duty. Left it there, altho it has already cost $130.00 excess baggage to get it here. Lucia & her mother, bro. & family, Hal & Judy [Merwald] all very cordial.

At 10PM went to the Alvo camp where I conducted a mid-night communion service, after the N.T. pattern in** with the nite meal. 24 Campaigners attended. A small number but what a far cry from 3 or 4 years ago. So many of them such attractive kids—they can be reached but What to Do? How [to] get leaders? Why doesn't anyone want to go to them?? The camp is beautiful—nothing like it is [*sic*, in] Latin Amer. Still it will be like excruciating pain to get the funds necessary to finish.

---

[6] Spanish for "agreeable."

[7] The airport for Campinas.

[8] Portuguese for someone who cuts through red tape.

Lucia & Jim very happy. Me? I go on abysmally lonely! Why?
[...]

Monday, April 7 (Campinas, Brazil)
[...]

Out for a late dinner w/Merwalds. They look more "right" for this job every day.

Tuesday, April 8 (Buenos Aires, Argentina)
Had to get up early to get to Viracopas [sic, Viracopos Airport] by 8:30A. A lot of people were out there to see us off. [...] Travelled by Sabena,[9] Stopped in Asuncoin [sic, Asuncion]. First time in Paraguay. Arrived Ezeiza[10] O[n] T[ime]. Fast trip to town. Juan [Marcet] was there. Glad. Took a nap. Went to La Estancia (of course) for dinner. Great! Must have gotten to bed by 1A or thereabout.

Wednesday, April 9 (Buenos Aires, Argentina)
We walked over 20 blocks, window shopping, etc. There's nothing like this city. I think Jim III has fallen for it as much as I have. Still—after nearly 5 years—think it's by far and away my favorite city—even tho so HUGE—8,000,000 or so—I'd like to live here.

We had our afternoon wrecked by the clumsiness of ALA people in changing our tickets. A 20 min. job that took them 3 hours.

A late dinner at La Estancia, incl. a great talk w/Juan [Marcet]. Jim was outstanding with him. Left there @ 1:05AM (to-morrow).

Sunday, April 13 (San Juan, Argentina)
Altho I slept well the meal last night was so late, as always, that I didn't get much rest acct. of—awake too early.

From 1P 'till 4P Jimbo & I were guests of honor at a big Fiesta held at

---

[9] The Belgian airline.

[10] The airport for Buenas Aires, Argentina.

[Señora] _____ ['s] home. There were 25 University men there. This was one for the books—bestowing their highest approval, friendship and honor upon us. I'm sure such a thing had never before been done in San J[uan], (and for that matter, for all I know) in Argentina. It got pretty rough for Jim & me because of all the "toasts" to us—seemed interminal [sic]—and, of course, the ultimate guesture [sic] of friendship. <u>I must write more on this "historic" event.</u> It is this sort of thing that keeps pushing my insides—makes me <u>sure that we can do a great</u> job down here <u>and that we must</u>. But how? Where do we find our people? etc, etc. After all those toasts, finally with champaine [sic] we we[re] lucky to get out under our own steam. We both made it. We slept several hours before 11P dinner.

Thursday, April 17 (Mendoza, Argentina)

Jim III & I had to get up at 4A, catch a 5A bus—3 hrs to Mendoza. Taxi to airport. <u>Four hour</u> wait for late plane. Great trip over the big hump to Santiago. Arr. mid-aft. Jim III enjoyed the flight—as I always do.

Nap & late dinner.

Tuesday, April 22

Long day travelling—final leg to C.S.

Lv. early 8 or 9 (?)

Sue met me @ DV Airport. Spent four hours w/her. She took me to airport for 15′ <u>flight</u> to C.S.

Thankful that I made the long, sometimes arduous trip—aprx. 17,000 miles with absolutely no symptoms of the big bad trouble.

Called for Charlie[11] about the Pelvic pain experienced the past couple of day's [sic]. He's been bad sick & [I] can't see him for at least a week. Don't know anything to do but try to wait for him.

---

11 Dr. Charles Fisher.

The final chapter of Jim's life began in late May with a doctor's visit, complaining of pain in his groin. The doctor suspected prostate cancer.

Included here are all of Rayburn's entries for that summer. (It is important to note that many of these entries were written weeks after the events occurred.)

Thursday, June 5

Went to Penrose Hosp this aft. to be preped [*sic*] for the biopsy tomorrow.

Friday, June 6 (Penrose Hospital, Colorado Springs)

They took me to surgery quite early I think and I awoke in the recovery room before noon. Not very bad. Don't remember the remainder of the day ...

Saturday, June 7 (Penrose Hospital, Colorado Springs)

[Dr.] Bob Beadles came by the room this a.m. & said I could leave the Hosp. if I wanted to. Said to come to his office Monday & "by then" he'd have the pathologist's report. Sounds fishy—and ominous. He should know that I know very well that he got the Path. report even before he finished the surgery.

Monday, June 9

To Bob Beadles' office this aft. He beat around the bush & told me I had a prostatic tumor, already spread to the bladder, urethra, et. al. Malignancy of a virulent type. I felt sorry for him. Told him he didn't need to horse around w/me—just give it to me straight. Bad! Not much chance medically speaking. It was strange & wonderful the measure of peace I had. I've felt worse about a broken leg. Bob called Gutierrez @ Penrose Cancer Clinic ...

Wednesday, June 11

I think it was about this date they started examinations, at the Cancer Clinic.

Del Regato in on at least one. For about the next week they really worked me over—at least half a dozen Drs. Pretty grubby sometimes.

Monday, June 16
Began Cobalt 60 radiation to-day. Maximum level of toleration—for max length of time tolerable. They didn't tell me what their computers said that would be.

Tuesday, June 17
To Penrose Cancer Clinic this a.m. & <u>every</u> <u>a m</u> (except Sunday) for 5 weeks.

On June 24, Bill Starr wrote a letter to the Young Life staff and board of directors explaining Jim's medical situation.

> Dear Board and Staff:
> While in California recently, I received news that Jim Rayburn had been to the hospital where a biopsy of the bladder revealed the spread of cancer that evidently had started in the prostate. In talking to Jim, he wrote the doctor giving permission to reveal his diagnosis. His letter is as follows:
> "Mr. Rayburn was examined on the 26th of May, 1969, with a complaint of some pain in his right inguinal area and in the course of his examination, it was found that the prostate felt suspicious for the presence of malignancy. His prostate had been examined by me, in December of 1965, and at that time it was benign to palpation. Because of the suspicious finding, Mr. Rayburn was hospitalized at the Penrose Hospital, Colorado Springs, and studies were done which revealed a carcinoma of the prostate, poorly differentiated, also a biopsy of the bladder revealed spread of the carcinoma of the prostate to the base of the bladder and there was some constriction of the lower most portion of the right ureter and this, presumably, was due to spread of his carcinoma.
> "We were unable to determine any distant spread, however the fact that there was local growth, as far as has been described, and because of the poorly differentiated character of this tumor, it was advised that we have radio therapy in an

attempt to control this growth.

"Mr. Rayburn is now under treatment at the Penrose Cancer Hospital. I do not believe that he will be able to carry on any real activities for a period of a minimum of six months and probably longer."

This letter being interpreted means that Jim's cancer is inoperable and is being treated now by cobalt.

This servant of the Lord, who has been called upon to suffer in more than one manner, has again received a summons to suffer. The doctor has given no time table, but suggests that each case is most unique and the action of this type of malignancy is quite erratic. Conceivably the growth could be controlled to where there is some sense of physical normalcy for several months.

You are the recipient of this information because you care and because your prayers are urgently desired and requested. You can pray intelligently, but I would trust it also would be the prayer of hope, with your faith placed in the Suffering Saviour Who is also the Great Healer.

Those of us who are close are grateful for the ministry of serving that Maxine so faithfully and capably performed last year, and now she is once again called upon to be at his side during this time of mental and physical torment. But Jim stated that in the midst of this new storm God has given a unique sense of His peace and presence. A letter addressed to them indicating your support for them at the Throne of Grace I know would be most appreciated.

Warmly in Christ,
Bill Starr

Monday, July 21[12]

Finished radiation therapy to-day!

The[y] threw a big birthday party (open house sort of thing) for me to-night. 80 plus came, some from D.V., Loveland, et[c]

---

[12] Jim's sixtieth birthday.

Saturday, August 23 (Trail West)
To Trail West—This is (I think) the 5th wk-end I've spent over there this summer. Great! Enjoyed the kids, the crew and some of the guests.

Can't think of much to add to this for 24th.

Monday, September 15
To hospital for "Cystoscopy" (?) etc.

No sweat, except waiting until after 12 NOON to get into surgery.

Was thru surgery, recov. room & eating a good lunch by 3P.

Tuesday, September 16
Hosp.

Wednesday, September 17
Hosp.

Thursday, September 18
Hosp.

Friday, September 19
Dismissed from Hospital this a.m.

---

*Jim III had married Lucia in Brazil in June, and the two of them
moved to Colorado Springs to begin their life together.*

Sunday, September 28
This 1st part is Saturday (September 27).

Not a productive day, but didn't intend it to be. Enjoyed watching Nebr. U clobber Texas A&M. 14–0. Most of day in my office. Up very late.

[He has drawn a line to begin the September 28 entry.]

Nothing much done to-day. (I'm scared, I think—by symptoms similar to the awful stuff I experienced June–Aug '68. [...]

Jim at home, ca. 1969.

Monday, September 29

This day started very early & badly (1AM).

Believe I've got to give some different priority to my prayers—and—O God, to pray more … and more …

9A [—] For years I've been praying that God would grant me great prayer experiences, (as so often before) under the most difficult & unlikely circumstances <u>it happened</u>—not much sleep no more than 10 or 20 min. even the few times I got to sleep—but prayer, earnest, longing, clinging prayer repeatedly,—almost constantly throughout the wakeful times—and, (tho so desperately burdened) the peace—a deep inner peace and repeatedly searching the Word (as just hasn't happened.) Nothing like this since Oct or Nov '64! 5 Years! "Oh God …"

See particularly Col. specially the greatest of all passages on Christology[13]—and just as specially the marked passages in Chap. 3 & 4. Went to Tr. W. later than I expected to** leave.**

---

[13] Probably referring to Colossians 1:15–23.

Tuesday, September 30 (Trail West)
Up early. Fun to have Jim III & Lucia around.

Visited briefly this a.m. w/Ed & Marge Seaberg (and Joe Thieboldt**, my favorite builder.) They will be in their Chalet by next week. Can't help envying them!

Brief visit this eve with B[uena] V[ista] Chief of Police King & the new owners of the "Hi Rocky" store. Walked across "Three Elks Creek" & part of the Powelyn property w/Jim III & Lucia this a.m. Very prayerful. Near exhaustion, a 2 or 3 hr. nap this aft. Feel like a man hop[e]lessly lost. But I keep remembering there is HOPE in God's Word. It's full of it! Too weary to get down my thots to-nite. God forgive the troubled thots—want to—<u>have</u> to—TRUST ... "in nothing be anxious."[14] Anxiety must be sinful in the light of Our Lord's promises—and His Love!

Tuesday, October 7
[...] Didn't get down to writing much about yest. & to-day even tho they were quite interesting and, at least yesterday quite productive. Probably should have taken more care with both days, in case there is medical significance in regard to the reported lethargy, sleepiness, etc throughout both days. Can't understand that at all—unless the obvious reason, i.e., not more than a few minutes of continuous sleep anytime—for weeks— on acct., too much of my insides damaged by the massive level of radiation coming at me from three directions for 5 weeks or 30 times.

—〰—

Wednesday, December 31
Haven't written in this since Oct. 10th. This (nearly the last quarter of the year) has been a time of ups-and-downs—mostly <u>downs</u>. No more of the sleepiness thing after about Oct 10 but for the most part big trouble w/INSOMNIA. The most "scary" symptom has been the inability to do

---

[14] Philippians 4:6 ("Do not be anxious about anything, but in everything by prayer and supplication with thanksgiving let your requests be made known to God.")

constructive work, even on days when "I had to," and gave it my best try. Until Dec 15 much trouble with the bladder. Beadles "dialated [*sic*] it"? & no trouble since. Bowels still bad, most of the time—Also the tremors, etc. that I associate with the '66 & '68 trouble very pronounced at times.

—~~~—

Though he would live another eleven months, Jim would never write another entry in his journal.

1970

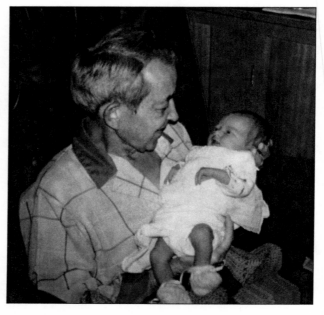

Jim with his granddaughter Shannon, born just a few weeks before he died.

Rayburn continued his cancer treatments, but the disease could not be stopped.

During his last months some of Jim's old Young Life friends would stop by the Rayburn home. Ted Benson watched football games with him. Bill Taylor, though he had joined the staff after Rayburn's tenure, had become a friend and came by regularly. Bob Mitchell visited several times. Two of the occasions when Mitch was there proved very memorable. On one of them, Mitch and Jim were talking about the great tenets of the Christian faith. Bedfast, Rayburn reached over to the bedside table and grabbed an envelope and began writing on it. Mitchell didn't know what Jim was up to. When Rayburn finished he handed his former club kid the envelope. On it he had written "The Finished Work of Christ" and underneath were the words "forgiveness," "redemption," "propitiation," "sanctification," "justification," and a few other theological terms related to salvation that Rayburn had studied under Dr. Chafer at Dallas Seminary over thirty years before. He handed the envelope to Mitchell with a smile and said, "That's what we're all about!"

During Mitch's final conversation with him, Rayburn was even more adamant. "I was there to see Jim," Mitchell recalled. "He was bedridden, he was dying of cancer, but yet his sense of humor was always there. So we were laughing and talking. And he got very serious and he made this statement to me. 'Mitch, don't ever let 'em quit talking about Jesus!' [It was] maybe the most powerful admonition I've ever heard in my life."

Surrounded by loved ones, Jim Rayburn died on Friday, December 11, 1970. He was sixty-one years old.

A few months after Jim's death, Maxine wrote to the Young Life staff to explain some of the details of Jim's final years.

... I want to tell you what the death certificate indicated. For years Jim was a very sick man. I knew this somehow, and I always said I thought it was the cause of some of his behavior problems which many couldn't understand. The death certificate verified my private beliefs. Prior to the cancer problem there was a deterioration of the central nervous system (brain stem) which the certificate said existed for "years." The cancer problem involved the prostate gland, bladder, tubes, etc., spine, bone and bone marrow, and skull, and it said the condition existed for "years." This information (due to autopsy) exonerates him from personal fault. And though it is hard for me to speak of all this, I feel I must inform you. The suffering this caused him and us is all in the dear Lord's will, and we cannot question it. Jim gave his body to science and he was cremated on December 22, 1970. I just wanted you all to have the facts.

My sense of loss is such that there are no words to express it. Jim had knelt by my bed in the middle of the night about a week before he died and told me how much he loved me and what I had meant to him in the call God gave to us to pioneer a new mission. There were tears and the time was privately precious. We made many mistakes in our humanness, but that's just proof that God uses us vessels of clay. And in the words of a popular song, "He never promised us a Rose Garden," but He did promise much, much more. How I thank God for the Young Life Mission, its men and women, and all the young lives who are now Christ's. ...

Eleven months before he died, in January 1970, the entire Young Life staff gathered in California for a staff conference. Jim was to be one of the featured speakers. Including spouses, there were almost five hundred in attendance—a far cry from the little group of five men who gathered for the first staff meeting in a Nacogdoches, Texas, church in the fall of 1941.

Everyone at the conference knew that Rayburn was dying and that this would almost certainly be his last time to speak to a staff gathering.

In From Bondage to Liberty: Dance, Children, Dance, *Jim Rayburn III recounts, "Hours before his message, Jim seemed on the edge of dying. His body wracked by pain, nausea, and radiation sickness, there seemed no way he could speak. We in the family were most concerned with the consequences if he went ahead. But there were things he wanted desperately to say, and at 8:00 a.m. Jim stood before 'his people.' He was greeted with a standing ovation. I'm sure that tears flowed from many faces, as they did from mine."*

Here is Jim's message.

Jim's final message to the Young Life staff, Asilomar, California, January 1970

As all the old timers have heard, I've always felt a little twinge or something when I was introduced as the founder of this outfit. I *am* the founder of this outfit—don't get me wrong! [*Laughter from the crowd*] But the reason for my embarrassment is that I always felt like a fella who founded something should at least know he was founding something. I didn't have the slightest idea I was founding something. [*Laughter*] I know this—I woke up too late in life and it wasn't so late either—most of you are about that far along. But I woke up too late in life, coming out of my fine Christian home, and living in a town where there were churches on every corner—four on some—and YMCA and Boy Scouts, and Camp Fire Girls … I liked that. [*Laughter*] And I woke up with my bride one day in a town where there was a school full of people who didn't have the foggiest chance to know the truth about Jesus Christ. They didn't have a chance; there wasn't anybody there that knew enough about Him to tell them. And, furthermore, they weren't interested in listening to anyone who sounded like someone who might be going to get around to talking about Jesus Christ.

So I had a two-fold job on my hands. The first crack of the bat—right out of engineering school and graduate school in geology—I was suddenly plunked down in northern New Mexico by the Presbyterian Board of National Missions and I was the bishop of all out-of-doors. [*Laughter*] One place where we Presbyterians always had it over the Methodists, Episcopalians, Catholics, and so forth, is you got to work up to bishop there. But with us we're all bishops—it's just automatic. You get to be a bishop right now. [*Laughter*] That's the only way I'd have ever gotten to be one. [*Louder laughter*]

So I had a two-fold job—I hadn't ever thought about it before—but all of a sudden it came slammin' home to me that people were bad off. They were way out in left field; they didn't have a chance—not for a good life, not for God's kind of life, not for the life He meant for 'em—unless they personally knew Jesus Christ. So I'd have to get busy and talk to them about Him. The second thing was I had to get 'em willing to listen.

I imagine that I've set some world records in my time. For example, I suppose I'm the only man extant—and I'm just barely extant—who has been the only football coach in an entire county. Yes, I was it. I coached all the teams in the county. There were sixteen fellas in high school in Chama, New Mexico, when I went there. The only way I could possibly have football for the boys was to divide them into two eight-man teams. And I had to coach them both. [*Laughter*] Some of the hardest parts of my early days was running back and forth across that field ... [*Boisterous laughter*] when the ball changed hands. Well, there you have it—the plan—that's what I was supposed to talk about this morning. It says so right here on your program—The Big Dream. I hadn't dreamed any big dream 'til I got there—and I didn't even know I was dreaming any big dreams then.

I was half smart in engineering and long about two-thirds smart in mineralogy, but I was a dummy when it came to Christianity. I knew one thing, though—I knew that Jesus Christ was important. And I knew that anyone that didn't have a chance to know Him deserved a chance—and that's what Young Life is all about—and don't you forget

it! I believe that we ought to be involved up to our eyebrows in many of
the great social issues of our time, but not for one minute will I ever believe that we ought to be involved in anything that takes away the least
bit from The Big Dream: that everyone has a right to know Jesus Christ,
to know the facts concerning Him, which are a glorious array of facts
concerning the greatest life that was ever lived, which are an unbelievable array of facts concerning God.

This is what God is like. He's like this man that was born in Beth-
lehem, that grew up as a carpenter, that trod the dusty roads of a ...
little country that we call Israel today, but He was God. He was all of
God, the Creator and Sustainer of the universe, that could possibly be
jam-packed into a human being. And He had to work it that way because He'd have scared the bejabbers out of us if He'd have come any
other way. [*Laughter*] We wouldn't have understood Him and we would
have run from Him. But people didn't run from Him. They ran towards
Him. And the lady[1] that—well, she wasn't much of a lady 'til up to that
minute—a woman who had her life fouled up just about every way there
is to foul up a life—spent a few minutes with Him—and went rushing
back to town. She'd have probably made the women's Olympic team if
she'd have lived in our day. And the reason she was in such a hurry was
that, she said, "Come out here and meet this one I met out here at the
well. All I did was to go out there and get some water and I've come back
with a heart bursting with such glorious, marvelous truth that you gotta
come and see for yourselves."

The Big Dream was a pretty little dream in Chama, New Mexico,
and in Tierra Amarilla and in Cebolla and in Payson and Dos Cabezas,
and those places that Maxine and I rambled in the early years. But it got
big because there was such a big idea behind it. One we never thought
of: everyone has a right to know the truth about Jesus Christ. They have
a right to know *who* He is; they have a right to know *what* He's done

---

[1] The woman at the well in John 4.

for them. They have a right to know *how* they relate to that. They have a right to know Him personally. Furthermore, they have a right to make their own choice of Him. And if you got in here accidentally without realizing that that's what Young Life's all about, then you oughta get squared away or you oughta hunt the nearest telephone booth and ask for the bus schedule. That's not just what Young Life's all about; that's *all* that Young Life's all about—Jesus Christ.

Most of you—I don't know if I can say most of you to this crowd or not, I haven't seen you for quite a while; and so, since we grow so fast and you've grown a lot faster since you got rid of me, [*Laughter*] why it might not be most of you—but an awful lot of you know that I've believed that the greatest job in the world today, by far and away the greatest job in the world today, is just to thumb the pages of this New Testament, which was written to make Jesus Christ known, and to do it in the presence of a group of people who are listening, who know you care about them, and no beans about it; people that you've taken the time and the trouble to prove to that you really care that they're people—and that's all you are is people, that you may have one great glorious advantage over them. But you didn't earn it and you don't have any more right to it than they do. And that's a personal relationship with Jesus Christ.

> The very spring of our actions is Jesus Christ. We look at it like this: if one died for all men, then in a sense, they all died, and his purpose in dying for them is that their lives should now be no longer lived for themselves but for him who died and was raised to life for them. This means that our knowledge of men can no longer be based on their outward lives (indeed, even though we knew Christ as a man, we do not know him like that any longer). ... The past is finished and gone, everything has become fresh and new.

Man alive! If there was ever a generation in human history that needed to hear that, it's now.

> Everything's become fresh and new. All this is God's doing—

God's doing, not ours.

> —for he has reconciled us to himself through Christ; and he
> has made us agents of the reconciliation. God was in Christ
> personally reconciling the world to himself—not counting
> their sins against them—and has commissioned us with the
> message of reconciliation. We are now Christ's ambassadors,
> as though God were appealing direct to you through us—

as His personal representatives we say—

> "Make your peace with God." For God caused Christ, who
> Himself knew nothing of sin, actually to *be* sin for our sakes,
> so that in Christ we might be made good with the goodness
> of God.[2]

Young Life's an outfit which was grounded deep down in personal
relationship to Jesus Christ and in the belief that not one of us is any
good, that every bit of goodness that there is in us was given to us as a
gift from God. He made us. If we're good, He made us good. If we're
good, we got good by getting up close and embracing Jesus Christ; there
is no other way to goodness.

The Big Dream we started in the deserts, in the mining camps, in
the out-of-the-way places in our own country. Then we moved on to the
big cities. And we found out another thing that we should've known
before. It was right there to look at. There was no reason why we hadn't
seen it except we hadn't been looking. But the kids uptown and the kids
downtown and the kids out in the country and the kids in the pent-
house and the kids in the ghetto, people growing up every place in the
world were up against it, absolutely up against it because there wasn't
anybody telling them about Jesus Christ.

So The Big Dream stated another way is this: It's a group of peo-

---

[2] This passage of Scripture is 2 Corinthians 5:14–21 from *The New Testament
in Modern English* by J. B. Phillips, translator, © J. B. Phillips, 1958, 1960, 1972
Macmillan Publishing Company, New York, New York, and Collins Publishers,
London, England.

ple—I hope it's all of you people and a lot more—bound together in the single-minded purpose that there's no price too high to pay to see to it that young people have a chance to know the Savior. It's a part of their God-given heritage; but not since apostolic days has it ever been realized.

One of the saddest things to me as I grow older—you notice I said "older." I didn't say "old" 'cause you put a pair of slats on your feet about six feet long and head 'em down hill and I'll beat you down. [*Laughter*] [...] One of the saddest things as I grow older is not the fact that I've got cancer, and one of these days I might keel over and die. That's really not a very sad prospect because you may not have cancer, but one of these days you may keel over and die. [*Laughter*] And I'd be willing to lay odds ... [*Long pause and boisterous laughter*] that some of you will beat me. Well, one of the saddest things is that more people don't care. We're going fast and sometimes I look at the reports in the board meetings and it seems like we're just bustin' out all over, but we're not. We're not even keeping pace with the population explosion. We ought to do at least that well. Not with the explosion, but have a little explosion of our own. We ought to be able to get so many kids wide open to listening to us talk about Jesus Christ that there'd have to be *more* and greater changes than we've already seen in the twenty-five or thirty years of our brief history.

But things'll have to happen in our hearts and in a lot of hearts. A woman gave a pretty fat chunk of money to Young Life a little while back—to Young Life's outreach across the seas. And I happened to have been talking to her about Latin America. I've rambled across the face of this world now, 'round the whole thing, up and down, over and across and around every continent, in fifty-six different countries. I've lived in homes in the African bush. [...] I've lived with Muslim families, Islam families in the interior of Pakistan, and with Hindu families away up in the boondocks of India and with the Chinese in Singapore and Malaysia and the Japanese in ... I've forgotten where. But on this occasion I happened to be talking about the Latin American kids. This woman handed me her check. It had a lot of numbers on it and the decimal point was quite a ways over. It was an impressive check. But as she handed it to me she said, "Jim, I am not the least bit interested in Latin America."

I went one day to visit a multimillionaire fella who got rich selling peanuts. You've all eaten some of his product, Tom's Peanuts. You know on all the counters whenever you're ready to leave the restaurant, there are little sacks of Tom's Peanuts. Well, I was talking to Tom. [*Laughter*] You know what he asked me? One of the more intelligent questions he asked me was, "Where is Peru?" I sent him an atlas the next day with twenty-nine covers off of Tom's Peanuts included. [*Boisterous laughter*]

Why most of you sweet chicks and noble fellas, you think South America's south of here, don't you? You just try going south of here, you'll wind up in the deep, dark, stormy Pacific—several thousand miles from shore, 'cause South America's east. And, if you're heading for there—and I *am* heading for there; I been heading for there for a long time; and now I've got my young son and his nice little ol' Brazilian wife down there; you'll recognize her 'cause she talks kinda funny. [*Laughter*] She's around here. We got a whole bunch of people down there—young folks like we used to have in Chama and later in Dallas and like a lot of you have in San Francisco and on the Peninsula and Chicago and Philadelphia and Dallas and Minneapolis and all. We got a whole bunch of guys who are waiting for us to come and, by the way, since we've talked the idea up so much, they're wondering how come it's taking you so long. [...]

But, anyway, from all across this wide world, from every place in this great country, from the town you work in, and the towns around it, you know the story. There are people saying—not saying, there are people *needing*—to hear about Jesus Christ. And they're not about to hear about Him unless you figure out a way to get to them. They're in every class and every color and every ethnic group and every segment of our society. There's no one part that's worse off than another part. *Everyone* needs Jesus Christ.

I hope a few days from now when this conference is over that you people will get up with new determination and go back to The Big Dream and make it come true in millions of lives. Young people have a right to know Jesus Christ. We're not gonna wait and hope somebody else gets around to taking Him. We're going ourselves. We're going harder and faster and finer than we ever went before. I wish it would be said of us—especially of you young people—what the folks of Thessolonica said when Paul and his cronies headed for their hometown, "What are we going to do? The guys who upset the world are coming here now."

Well, look around you: we Christians aren't exactly upsetting the world. We're not setting things on fire. Nobody's yelling for the fire department because our rapport and our message and our determination is too hot, but that's The Big Dream. Let's help make it come true.

———

Afterword

Maxine Rayburn lived for another twenty-six years after Jim died, passing away at age eighty-five in November 1997. She was miraculously freed from the bondage to drugs that she had suffered for so long, and lived the final seventeen years of her life a transformed person.

Ann Rayburn Robertson and her husband Jim raised Mark, Matt, and Mike in San Rafael, California. Ann and Jim now live in the Seattle area.

Sadly, Sue Rayburn Hayes (she had remarried) was diagnosed with cancer in 1969. Upon hearing the news of his daughter's diagnosis, Jim "looked at me with desperate, unbelieving eyes, put his head down on his desk, and started to sob uncontrollably," remembers his son. "I thought his heart would break into pieces." She fought bravely for several years, but died on July 3, 1973. She was only thirty-three.

Jim III and his wife Lucia had two daughters, Shannon (born shortly before Jim's death) and Michelle. Jim III worked with his father in Youth Research International, and then went on Young Life staff for several years. In 1984 he released his biography of his father, *Dance, Children, Dance*, which was updated in 2000 and re-titled *From Bondage to Liberty: Dance, Children, Dance*. Jim and Lucia live in Colorado, not far from Frontier Ranch, Silver Cliff, and Trail West.

"Oh to WAIT ON HIM—find His will—and then do it with all His might ..."

(from Jim's April 7, 1947, entry)

Index of First Names

Rayburn often used only first names in his journal entries. What follows is a list of many of the first names that appear in the entries included in this book, and to whom they refer.

Index

Page numbers in *italics* refer to illustrations.

Colophon

DESIGN

Book designed by Whitecaps Media

Composed in Garamond Premiere Pro

Cover designed by Michael Patterson (Jim Rayburn's grandson)

ILLUSTRATIONS

Courtesy of the Rayburn family: cover, frontispiece, xii, 28, 52, 164, 169, 177, 187, 198, 201, 248, 266, 295, 296, 309, 323, 337, 345, 399, 409, 411, 444, 473, 479, 517, 522, 532

Courtesy of Mal McSwain: 131, 256, 293, 317, 319, 339, 358, 392, 420

Courtesy of Frontier Ranch: 213, 221, 224, 234, 244, 276, 432

Courtesy of Kit Sublett: 57, 60, 78, 83, 139, 496

Courtesy of Bob Mitchell: 75

Printed in the United States
213158BV00001B/2/P

9 780975 857779